D0984365

HOW TO READ
KARL BARTH

HOW TO READ
KARL BARTH

The Shape of His Theology

GEORGE HUNSINGER

New York   Oxford
OXFORD UNIVERSITY PRESS
1991

Oxford University Press

Oxford   New York   Toronto
Delhi   Bombay   Calcutta   Madras   Karachi
Petaling Jaya   Singapore   Hong Kong   Tokyo
Nairobi   Dar es Salaam   Cape Town
Melbourne   Auckland

and associated companies in
Berlin   Ibadan

Copyright © 1991 by George Hunsinger

Published by Oxford University Press, Inc.,
200 Madison Avenue, New York, NY 10016

Oxford is a registered trademark of Oxford University Press

Library of Congress Cataloging-in-Publication Data
Hunsinger, George.
How to read Karl Barth : the shape of his theology /
by George Hunsinger.
p.   cm.
Includes bibliographical references.
ISBN 0-19-505974-3
1. Barth, Karl, 1886–1968. Kirchliche Dogmatik.   2. Truth
(Christian theology)   3. Theology—Methodology.   I. Title.
BT75.B286H85   19991
230′.044′092—dc20   90-31135 CIP

2 4 6 8 9 7 5 3 1

Printed in the United States of America
on acid-free paper

230.044
B282h

In Memoriam
Hans W. Frei

Preface

This book may be read on at least two levels. On one level, it seeks to help the reader develop a set of skills. By acquiring these skills, the reader will, it is hoped, be in a much better position to understand the argument in any passage of Karl Barth's monumental *Church Dogmatics* than would otherwise be the case. The skills to be promoted are essentially those of pattern recognition. Interlacing the complex argument of the *Church Dogmatics* are a variety of dialectical and often counterintuitive patterns. The elusiveness and strangeness of these patterns, especially as they seem to generate self-contradictory or, at the very least, perplexing modes of thought, have defeated more than one of Barth's sympathetic readers, to say nothing of his determined critics. Yet these patterns need not be experienced merely as frustrating. They are fully capable of clear and distinct formulation, regardless of their fluid, nonlinear, and highly distinctive development in Barth's hands. They might even be regarded as an attempt to translate peculiarly Hebraic modes of thought into the idiom of Western, Aristotelian discourse (or vice versa). In any case, once subjected to clear formulation, the patterns can then be used as felicitous categories of discernment when reading the *Church Dogmatics*.

When the patterns are extracted from Barth's argument, a special danger immediately arises. One might suppose, mistakenly, that merely by understanding the patterns, one had also come to understand Barth. One might even suppose, disastrously, that merely by coming to accept or reject the patterns, one had thereby dealt with Barth. These false assumptions would be like supposing that, because one understands how a lens works, one also understands the nature of an object on which the lens is focused. Just as a lens is merely a device for seeing and not the object perceived, so the patterns are merely instruments of perception and not Barth's argument itself. The difference between a lens and these patterns, however, is that the patterns are embedded in the object of perception rather than external to it. Nonetheless, the patterns are sufficiently formal that they shape but by no means predict the content of Barth's argument at any particular point. Thus Barth constantly speaks of self-transcending events (actualism) in the form of specifiable mysteries (particularism), of historical mediations (objectivism) in the form of personal address (personalism), and of scripturally based analogies (realism) in the form of coherent doctrinal clusters (rationalism). Yet it is always necessary to look through these patterns or motifs (as they are called for the sake of convenience) to the subject matter they serve to shape. It was the subject matter, not the patterns, which Barth was trying to elucidate, and therefore the subject matter by which he wanted his work to be assessed. The patterns were of interest to him only insofar as they were pertinent to illuminating the subject matter. Any pattern might be modified, contradicted, or suppressed in the interest of the subject matter itself. To mistake or confuse the patterns for the substance of the argument would be like discarding the object for the lens.

By offering categories of discernment, this book seeks to redeem a promise issued by its title *(How to Read Karl Barth)*. Yet in the subtitle a further promise is also implicit, corresponding to the second and more ambitious level on which the volume at hand may be read *(The Shape of His Theology)*. By tracing the motifs and their interconnections, this study offers a reading of the *Church Dogmatics* as a whole. It proposes that the motifs exhibit the internal coherence of that immensely long work in a more satisfying way than is found in comparable interpretive efforts. Previous interpretations, such as those examined in the prologue, have all run aground insofar as they have searched for a single unifying conception by which the coherence of Barth's theology could be displayed. On the premise that no single conception is likely to succeed in fulfilling such an interpretive role, a multiplicity of formal conceptions, or motifs, is offered in its stead. The only effective argument for a proposed reading of a complex work is simply to set it forth, not only in relation to other proposals but also in relation to the text of the work itself. The power of the reading depends on the cumulative force of its presentation. The prologue, in which previous interpretations are critically assessed, is thus in an awkward position, for its effectiveness and, to some extent, its intelligibility depend on the rest of the disquisition. It may usefully be skipped by readers whose interests are more nearly at the first level of acquiring some useful skills than at the second level of discerning the shape of the whole. The prologue to this work, if one may make such a comparison, is like that found at the beginning of J. R. R. Tolkien's extraordinary trilogy, *The Lord of the Rings*. It makes much more sense after one has read the whole thing, but there didn't seem to be any place else to put it!

The second level at which this study is written proceeds in relation to the text of Barth's work by taking up his conception of truth. As the motifs themselves make eminently clear, Barth's view of theological truth is multidimensional. Truth is at once miraculously actualized and yet textually stabilized, objectively efficacious and yet existentially authenticated, unique in kind and yet habituated in the midst of the ordinary. It is always entirely subjected to divine validation, and yet its human reception and assertion are open to coherentist modes of justification within a web of communal belief and practice.[1] Above all, it is singular to the point of incomprehensibility. The task of theology is to comprehend this multidimensional truth in the incomprehensibility with which it presents itself, not to make it less incomprehensible than it really is and thereby to turn it into something more familiar and less formidable. Paradoxical and dialectical modes of thought are thereby built into the very heart of Barth's argument. At the point where most other contemporary theologies resort to the language of experience or the language of reason (whether separately or in conjunction, and however conceived), Barth opts instead for the language of mystery. Nothing is more likely to lead the reader of the *Church Dogmatics* astray than a nondialectical imagination. One must never fail to ask about the dialectical conceptual counterparts to the position Barth happens to be developing at any particular moment. Unlike theologies which banish mystery to certain inexpressible fringes beyond the reach of human language (as though everything Christian theology needs to say can be said within the conventional bounds of reason), Barth proceeds from the premise that, with the advent of the truth of God, the structure of language has been ruptured at the very core. In relation to this divine interruption, the interruption of all interruptions, deliberate paradox or conjunction of opposites is the fitting vehicle of expression. The mysteries of truth in Christian theology, as Barth understands them, all have specifiable terms. These terms are the motifs which inform his argument and shape his theology as a whole.

No attempt has been made to move beyond exposition to criticism. In the conviction that we are still in the early stages of even understanding what it was that Barth had to say, this book simply hopes to contribute to the possibility of criticism that is more adequate and fair than most evinced so far. Reading what the critics have to say of Barth's theology is usually like looking at an old map, the kind drafted before the dawn of modern cartography in the eighteenth century. Certain basic aspects of the theology may be present, but the distortion factor is high. Topographic features may be lacking in detail. Whole promontories may be absent or diminished. Monsters, lions, and swash lines may do duty for factual content. The task of responsible criticism presupposes a more reliable depiction of the overall terrain, as well as of the proportional relationships among the various segments, than has usually been the case. A quest for better cartography would seem to be the place to begin.[2]

Bangor, Me.   G.H.
March 1990

Acknowledgments

A work as long in the making as this one has been (I have been reading Barth now for about fifteen years) inevitably accumulates a long list of debts. Many friends, colleagues, family members, and institutions have supported and encouraged me through the trials preceding the outcome. They will know who they are and will forgive me if they cannot all be mentioned here. My friends in the Yale-Washington Theology Group have been a wonderful source of comradeship and stimulation over the years. For detailed and incisive comments I am indebted to colleagues in and outside that group, especially Jim Buckley, Joe DiNoia, Bruce Mc-Cormack, Bruce Marshall, Bill Placher, and above all Mike Root. Although they have saved me from errors and infelicities, those which remain are my own. Deborah van Deusen Hunsinger, my wife and true companion, not only sharpened my ideas in their process of formation but also offered generously of her invaluable editorial skills. The one person to whom my debt is incalculable, who embodied the highest standards as a scholar and as a human being, and who believed in me when I no longer believed in myself is no longer with us to see this book in its final form. In an earlier version it was the last doctoral dissertation which he read. Knowing Hans W. Frei was one of the great privileges of my life. This study is dedicated to his memory.

Contents

Abbreviations

I/1	*Church Dogmatics,* vol. I, part 1 (Edinburgh: T. & T. Clark, 1975, 2nd ed.)
I/2	*Church Dogmatics,* vol. I, part 2 (Edinburgh: T. & T. Clark, 1956)
II/1	*Church Dogmatics,* vol. II, part 1 (Edinburgh: T. & T. Clark, 1957)
II/2	*Church Dogmatics,* vol. II, part 2 (Edinburgh: T. & T. Clark, 1957)
III/1	*Church Dogmatics,* vol. III, part 1 (Edinburgh: T. & T. Clark, 1958)
III/2	*Church Dogmatics,* vol. III, part 2 (Edinburgh: T. & T. Clark, 1960)
III/3	*Church Dogmatics,* vol. III, part 3 (Edinburgh: T. & T. Clark, 1961)
III/4	*Church Dogmatics,* vol. IV, part 1 (Edinburgh: T. & T. Clark, 1961)
IV/1	*Church Dogmatics,* vol. IV, part 1 (Edinburgh: T. & T. Clark, 1956)
IV/2	*Church Dogmatics,* vol. IV, part 2 (Edinburgh: T. & T. Clark, 1958)
IV/3	*Church Dogmatics,* vol. IV, part 3, first half (Edinbrugh: T. & T. Clark, 1961); *Church Dogmatics,* vol. IV, part 3, second half (Edinburgh: T. & T. Clark, 1962)
IV/4	*Church Dogmatics,* vol. IV, part 4 (Edinburgh: T. & T. Clark, 1969)
rev.	revised translation

HOW TO READ
KARL BARTH

Readings Old and New— A Critique

This study offers a new way of reading Karl Barth's *Church Dogmatics*— one not previously developed in detail. A number of attempts have been made in the past to discover a single overriding conception that would serve as a key to reading Barth. Such a conception, if it could be found, would have a number of advantages. Not only would it serve to guide the reader through the nearly ten thousand pages of labyrinthine argument which constitute Barth's masterwork. It would also make it possible to bring Barth more readily into dialogue with other theologies and other fields of discourse than might otherwise be the case. It could even ease the task of developing responsible and penetrating criticisms. The quest for an overriding conception obviously has much to commend it. Barth is so deeply traditional and so strikingly innovative, so rigorous in argument and so daring in conception, so simple in essence and so complex in development, so narrowly focused and so wide-ranging in scope, so passionate in commitment and so relentless in criticism, so exasperating in disagreement and so inspiring in devotion, that nothing would be more welcome than a single conception to unlock the whole.

This essay proceeds on the assumption, however, that such a conception is unlikely to be found. Proposals along these lines have perhaps obscured as much as they have illuminated. An alternative to the quest for a single conception might therefore suggest itself and has sometimes been pursued. Why not just study the doctrines as they come *ad seriatum?* Why not take a *loci* approach, moving disconnectedly from one topic to the next, with no attempt to specify a grand principle that organizes the whole? Why not write an extended table of contents with explanatory notes? Works like this also exist and are not without evident value. Their limitations would seem to be equally evident, however, for they simply go with the genre.

If Barth's theology will not yield its treasures to a single overriding conception, and if inherent limits accompany the *loci* approach, is there perhaps another interpretive possibility? This essay proposes that there is. Several recurrent "motifs" or modes of thought, it is argued, can be seen to run throughout the *Church Dogmatics* and to shape the doctrinal content of Barth's mature theology as a whole. "Actualism," "particularism," "objectivism," "personalism," "realism," and "rationalism" are the names that will be used to designate these motifs. Before moving to a critical survey of particular ways in which Barth has previously been read, some preliminary definitions are in order. Fuller definitions, of course, are the project of the essay as a whole. All that is needed now is just enough to get through the survey. (Readers are reminded that it may be better to skip over this chapter and come back to it at the end.)

"Actualism" is the motif which governs Barth's complex conception of being and time. Being is always an event and often an act (always an act whenever an agent capable of decision is concerned). The relationship between divine being and human being is one of the most vexed topics in Barth interpretation, and one on which the essay at hand hopes to shed some light. For now let it simply be said, however cryptically, that the possibility for the human creature to act faithfully in relation to the divine creator is thought to rest entirely in the divine act, and therefore continually befalls the human creature as a miracle to be sought ever anew.

"Particularism" is a motif which designates both a noetic procedure and an ontic state of affairs. The noetic procedure is the rule that says, "Let every concept used in dogmatic theology be defined on the basis of a particular event called Jesus Christ." No generalities derived from elsewhere are to be applied without further ado to this particular. Instead one must so proceed from this particular event that all general conceptions are carefully and critically redefined on its basis before being used in theology. The reason for this procedure is found in the accompanying state of affairs. This particular event requires special conceptualization, precisely because it is regarded as unique in kind.

"Objectivism" is a motif pertaining to Barth's understanding of revelation and salvation. It describes not only the means by which they respectively occur, but also the status of their occurrence. Revelation and salvation are both thought to occur through the mediation of ordinary creaturely objects, so that the divine self-enactment in our midst lies hidden within them. The status of this self-enactment is also thought in some strong sense to be objective—that is, real, valid, and effective—whether it is acknowledged and received by the creature or not. Revelation and salvation are events objectively mediated by the creaturely sphere and grounded in the sovereignty of God.

"Personalism" is a motif governing the goal of the divine self-manifestation. God's objective self-manifestation in revelation and salvation comes to the creature in the form of personal address. The creature is encountered by this address in such a way that it is affirmed, condemned, and made capable of fellowship with God. Fellowship is the most intimate of engagements and occurs in I–Thou terms. The creature is liberated for a relationship of love and freedom with God and therefore also with its fellow creatures.

"Realism," as used in this essay, is the motif which pertains to Barth's conception of theological language. Theological language is conceived as the vehicle of analogical reference. In itself it is radically unlike the extralinguistic object to which it refers (God), but by grace it is made to transcend itself. Through transcending itself by grace, theological language attains sufficient likeness or adequacy to its object for reference truly and actually to occur. Besides the mode of reference, realism also pertains to the modes of address, certainty, and narration found in scripture as well as in the language of the church based upon it.

"Rationalism," finally, again as used in this essay, is the motif which pertains to the construction and assessment of doctrine. Theological language as such is understood to include an important rational or cognitive component. This component is subject to conceptual elaboration, and that elaboration (along with scriptural exegesis) is what constitutes the theological task. Because of the peculiar nature of the object on which it is based, rationalism takes pains to rule out certain illegitimate criteria and procedures in the work of doctrinal construction and assessment. Within the critical limits open to it, however, doctrines may be derived beyond the surface content of scripture as a way of understanding scripture's deeper conceptual implications and underlying unity.

By specifying the formal patterns which these motifs comprise, and by tracing their interrelations within Barth's theology, this essay offers categories of discernment to the reader of the *Church Dogmatics*. No tightly constructed scheme into which Barth's theology can be seen to fit results from the exercise. Nor does a single overarching conception which unifies Barth's theology as a whole. Yet something more emerges than a set of *loci* strung together like beads on a string: a flexible but unmistakable

repertoire of "thought forms," a repertoire implicitly and explicitly brought
to bear throughout Barth's argumentation in his great dogmatic work.
Pattern recognition is the point of the essay. Readers who learn to recognize the patterns will be able to make their way more fruitfully, it is
hoped, through any portion of the *Church Dogmatics*.

Although no exhaustive survey of previous scholarship will be attempted, five representative works will be examined in the discussion
which follows. Two of them—those by Hans Urs von Balthasar and Thomas
F. Torrance—represent the attempt to find an overarching "formal" principle or thought form which governs the *Church Dogmatics*. Two others—those by G. C. Berkouwer and Robert W. Jenson—represent a similar quest for an overarching principle, but find it to be more nearly
"material" than "formal." It must be admitted that the distinction in
these cases is very rough. Von Balthasar, for example, proposes both a
formal and a material principle, while Torrance's proposal could be read
either way, and Berkouwer and Jenson are not unaware that their respective material principles carry formal implications. In the end the distinction is less important than the lacunae which result, in light of the six
motifs, from a quest for a single conception as the primary interpretive
device. Notice will also be given, finally, to the work by Herbert Hartwell as an example of the kind of *loci* approach which does not look for
overall coherence.

The celebrated work *The Theology of Karl Barth,* by the Roman Catholic theologian Hans Urs von Balthasar, is dominated by a quest for the
Denkform.[1] The author's interest in such a thought form is ecumenical.
He wants to bring Barth into conversation with Roman Catholic theology,
and the proposed way to do that is by clarifying the thought forms which
govern both. "Nothing is more important in ecumenical conversation,"
von Balthasar tells us, "than clarifying the *Denkform*" (201). As it turns
out, Barth is seen to have both a thought form and a material foundation
(Grundlegung) (124–32; 95–102). The thought form is the *analogia fidei,* and the material foundation is christology. Since the foundation of
Roman Catholic theology is considered to be no different, the real issues
can be joined only at the formal or formative level. Von Balthasar, in
agreement with Barth, finds the Roman Catholic counterpart to Barth's
analogia fidei to reside in the *analogia entis* (though whether Barth regarded either of them merely as thought forms is another matter).[2]

On the premise that Barth's dogmatics as a whole display "a strict
formal structure" (46; 29), von Balthasar proves to be a good reader of
the *Church Dogmatics* in general, but not always in detail. Along with

the ecumenical dialogue his book did so much to foster, the great strengths of this work would seem to arise primarily from the immense learning the author brought to it. Barth is positioned not only in relation to a wide variety of Roman Catholic theologians (263–386; 191–266), but also in relation to the relevant philosophical background. Commenting, for example, on the venerable idealist notion that the ground of all reasoning lies in a point of "absolute intensity" beyond the knowledge of reason itself, von Balthasar writes: "It is Kant's transcendental apperception, Fichte's protogrund of the ego, Schleiermacher's primal actuality of religiously toned feeling, Herrmann's personal decision of faith, and Barth's divine gift of faith to the human person" (213; 160). This remark seems exactly right and is typical of the erudition and the level of insight which run throughout the book.

Details, however, are another matter. Some strange misreadings are offered, and they are perhaps not unrelated to the interpretive strategy of appealing to a would-be overarching *Denkform*. For example, concentration on the thought form and the christological ground can become so single-minded that the doctrine of the Trinity is strangely said to play no central role in shaping Barth's theology (272; 197), prompting a later commentator to muse of von Balthasar that "in some respects at least he has not been listening very hard." [3] The suggestion being made here, however, is that the listening has been skewed by the strategy of interpretation. Indeed, more than mere details are at stake. For it is also very strange to read that the doctrine of analogy develops "ever more clearly and victoriously" with each succeeding volume of the *Church Dogmatics* (117; 88), and that, as the series actually unfolds, "Jesus Christ as divine and human" replaces "God's Word" as the "central concept" (124; 95). From the standpoint of motif research these things would not be said.

All six motifs were in place by the initial volume of *Church Dogmatics,* and it might be argued that clarity on all six was what allowed Barth to proceed in unfolding the distinctiveness of his mature theology. From the beginning of the series to the end, his rejection of the *analogia entis* did not waver. Certainly as the series goes on, a greater use is made of analogical constructs in nonpolemical contexts, but this use would seem to be more a development *in* his thought than a development *of* his thought. That is, his outlook has not changed, as von Balthasar seems to imply, in any fundamental way; Barth simply finds occasion to use analogical constructs (*not* a single "doctrine" of analogy) whenever they help to explicate the doctrinal matter at hand. The quest for a single *Denkform* would seem to have skewed the reading at this point.

The same is true of the "central concept." From start to finish the centrality of Jesus Christ is never in question. As new topics arise from one volume to the next, this centrality is spoken of in different ways. The "changes" within the christology are not fundamental. They simply pertain, or so it might be argued, to the method of explication, being merely a function of what seems appropriate from one doctrinal setting to the next. A close reading would perhaps disclose a shift in emphasis from the name to the narrative of Jesus Christ. If so, the name would nonetheless always be understood to be embedded in the narrative, and the narrative would always be the narrative of a concrete individual who bears a particular name. No doubt can exist that an extraordinary "christological concentration" marks the *Church Dogmatics*. But perhaps it is not a monolithic *Denkform* but a variety of motifs in concert which will make it possible better to appreciate just what that "concentration" is.

The one motif to which von Balthasar devotes sustained attention in his own way is "actualism." It is rightly noted that the "concrete Word of God" as incarnate in Jesus Christ is regarded by Barth as "a surpassing miracle," as "a pure happening," and as an event so "unique" that no law can be invoked to explain it (94; 70). It is also rightly seen that the *analogia fidei* is conceived along the same lines. The analogy in question is essentially between divine and human actions. The divine activity of grace finds its proper analogue in the human activity of faith. God, who is "pure act," makes the crucial decision to which all creaturely decisions and actions finally correspond, most especially those of faith (117; 89). That the same motif (actualism) governs both conceptions (the Incarnation and the *analogia fidei*) already suggests, however, that it is actualism, and not a doctrine of analogy, which is functioning as the relevant mode of thought. Moreover, von Balthasar might have seen more clearly that in strict correspondence to the Incarnation, the *analogia fidei* is presented as a surpassing miracle, unique in kind. Had he done so, his interpretation might have been spared the strange oscillation which seems to mark it in the end.

Von Balthasar seems unable to decide whether Barth finally succumbs to "monism" or ends up making his peace with the once dread *analogia entis* (and with Emil Brunner at the same time!). Surely the two claims are incompatible. "Actualistic monism" or "monistic reduction" would mean that the creature must finally be seen as overpowered by divine agency, having no real independence of its own (99, 105, 108, 140; 74, 79, 81, 109). This problem from Barth's early theology is regarded as still residual at the end (255, 380; 185, 254). On the other hand, we are told that the *analogia entis* was at last embraced. In Barth's theology "there seems to be room for the *analogia entis* after all" (177; 137). Did Barth really have no choice but to accept the *analogia entis*, since it is "an unavoidable problem" which is "imbedded in the ontic-noetic nature of creation itself" (175; 135)? Certainly Barth always resisted the forced option which von Balthasar and so many others have urged upon him: either a monism which obliterates the creature or else some *independent* capacity in the creature, whether prior or subsequent to the actualization of grace. Careful attention to the motifs (especially actualism, particularism, personalism, and rationalism) will make it possible for the problem of monism to be examined at the end of this book. For now one can only suggest that perhaps the quest for a single *Denkform* makes it difficult if not impossible for a way beyond that forced option—the way Barth actually took—to come into view.

In turning from von Balthasar to the Reformed theologian Thomas F. Torrance, one enters into an entirely different theological atmosphere.[4] Whereas Von Balthasar never ceases to wrestle with an intractable subject matter, Torrance leaves no other impression than always feeling right at home. Indeed, the central difficulty by which von Balthasar is so thoroughly exercised can receive smooth-as-velvet formulation by Torrance, as though nothing could be more obvious: "When we hear the Word, it is the Word confronting us, impinging upon us from beyond, from moment to moment in actual address and concrete communication, in ever new event or unexpected happening which is itself the creative source of every possible response on [our] part, and which conveys to [us] the rational forms for [our] understanding of it" (98). Von Balthasar would wonder along with many others what role we human beings can really be thought to play in this event, if "every possible response on our part" finds its "creative source" *entirely* in the Word which impinges upon us from beyond. It is characteristic of Torrance's book *Karl Barth: An Introduction to His Early Theology, 1910–1931* that questions like this are never directly tackled.

Although not offered as an interpretation of the *Church Dogmatics* itself, the Torrance volume obviously wants to provide the background by which Barth's later theology can be read. The heart of Barth's theology is not found in a formal doctrine of analogy, nor in a shifting christological foundation. It is found in "the theology of the Word" (95). It was this element in Barth's theology which became "more and more deeply characteristic throughout the years" (95). Barth's monumental break with liberalism, his transition "from dialectical to dogmatic theology," was essentially his turn "to a theology of the Word, to a positive Christian dogmatics centered in Jesus Christ" (131). No transition is envisaged, as with von Balthasar, from God's Word to Jesus Christ. On the contrary, "God's Word is identical with Jesus Christ, and therefore it is in the power of Christ that the Word is heard as well as spoken" (104, italics deleted). After the break with liberalism, the primary thing to be said is simply that Barth's theology becomes more and more "unambiguously *Theology of the Word*" (132).

The doctrine of the Word of God, it would seem, is being proposed not only as the essential content but also as the essential structure of Barth's theology in its later development. It is at once a formal and a material principle around which everything can apparently be organized. All the main themes in Barth's theology, one supposes, can be presented in its light. With great skill, as a matter of fact, Torrance demonstrates something truly essential of all six motifs by means of this interpretive device.

The motif of greatest interest to Torrance, and the one by which the others are usually subsumed, is objectivism. More precisely, his interest gravitates toward objectivism in its revelational mode. Soteriological objectivism receives virtually no mention, the one real lacuna in his account. At one point he even speaks (quite traditionally) of justification and sanctification as "objective and subjective grace" (103). Whatever its merits for Barth's earlier theology, this formulation would not fit the *Church Dogmatics,* in which it is a peculiarity that sanctification is considered to be no less "objective" than justification. In any case, more than anything else the Word of God at the heart of Barth's theology is emphasized as objective. "From first to last his theology is a plunge into the absolute objectivity and actuality of divine Revelation. . . . It is all-important to realize that for Barth the Word of God refers to the most completely objective reality there is, for it is the Word of *God* backed by God's own ultimate Being" (96).

Revelational objectivism so dominates Torrance's reading of Barth that the other motifs have difficulty emerging in their own right. There is indeed something valid about this way of reading. Revelational objectivism is undoubtedly pivotal in Barth's theology, and no one has seen this more clearly and more appreciatively than Torrance. Both the positive implications and the polemical background of the motif are exceptionally well set forth. Of the positive implications Torrance writes:

> Behind all this questioning on Barth's part lies a deep humility before the face of the Truth: in his recognition that the Truth will not and cannot be mastered by our distinctions and formulations, that we cannot give shape or

form to the Truth, but that we can only follow after it, inquire of it, listen to it, and seek to be obedient to it; and in his recognition that all our expressions and expositions of the Truth are human attempts that fall far short of the Truth itself, so that far from resting content with what we have already done, we are driven on by respect for the Truth and in unceasing obedience to it to continue our inquiry and to say again and again in ever new ways what we learn of the living and inexhaustible Truth of God. (21)

The polemical background is stated with equal cogency and force. In antithesis to liberal Protestantism, Barth insisted that "theology is not concerned with determinations of the consciousness or the analysis of religion or experience—there may well be a place for that sort of thing, but that is not theology. Theological thinking is not thinking from a center in ourselves, in our own faith or piety, but a thinking from a center beyond ourselves, in God" (97). No doubt is left about the centrality and objectivity of the Word.

Nevertheless, it is difficult to shake a nagging feeling about the way Torrance reads Barth. Barth's early theology has been called "revolutionary theology in the making" and the "theology of crisis." From Torrance, however, one cannot help but feel that one is somehow getting revolutionary theology without the revolution, and the theology of crisis without the crisis. The energy, dynamism, and sense of collision which enter Barth's theology by way of the actualistic and particularistic motifs never quite come through in Torrance's account. Instead of actualism and particularism enlivening the objectivism, the objectivism is allowed to mute and soften the actualism and particularism. Torrance's favorite analogy may have something to do with this imbalance.

Barth's theology, Torrance urges, bears close comparison with "an *exact science,* such as physics" (179). Like physics, theology is said to restrict its activities "to the limits laid down by the nature of its concrete object" and to develop "a method in accordance with the nature of its object" (179). Theology is said to be a form of "scientific activity" in which reason is "unconditionally bound to its object and determined by it." The mode of rational activity is strictly prescribed by "the nature of the object" (192). Torrance is not wrong to say these things of Barth, yet perhaps entirely too much of the atmosphere of the physics lab hangs subtly over the account. Revelational objectivism in Barth's later theology is more powerfully informed by an audacious "exceptionalism," if you will, actualistically and particularistically rooted, than Torrance's analogy seems to allow. The continuities which interest Torrance between theology and physics are illuminating, but the discontinuities—the sense of rupture which was always so important to Barth—ought not to be suppressed in the process. A somewhat clinical emphasis on the theology of the objective Word, as an overall interpretive device, allows more of the content than the spirit of Barth's theology to come through.

Be that as it may, Torrance has the merit of conveying a sense of Barth's greatness. "Karl Barth has attempted," he writes, "to give fresh articulation to the Christian faith as a theology of the Word of God which breaks through the frame of every form of human thinking while employing all that ancient and modern thought can offer by way of tools and instruments of thought and speech" (179). This appreciation for the depth and significance of Barth's achievement leads Torrance, who brings a certain cultural, philosophical, and scientific breadth to his reading, to a definite reticence when it comes to critical evaluation. "It would be impossible to claim for his achievement a *theologia perennis,* but it is certainly true that it will take many generations, if not centuries, to evaluate his service adequately" (179). Even were one inclined to be less adulatory, it would be hard to deny all truth to this remark.

No such reticence born of appreciation intrudes itself upon *The Triumph of Grace in the Theology of Karl Barth* by the prolific Dutch Reformed theologian G. C. Berkouwer.[5] Berkouwer knows a departure from received tradition when he sees one. Where Torrance finds fresh articulation, Berkouwer perceives hopeless innovation. He seems as untroubled by the received tradition as Barth is ready to rethink it christocentrically from the ground up. It would be difficult to produce a single instance in which Barth senses an intolerable problem demanding fresh consideration, where Berkouwer does not opt instead to stay hard by well-worn paths. The most appreciative comment Berkouwer has for Barth, and the main reason he gives for turning his considerable theological acumen to a thorough study of Barth's theology, is simply the phlegmatic remark that "Barth has dominated the theological debate of our century now for about thirty years" (9). Nonetheless, as a reliable guide to the basic content of Barth's theology, there is probably no better combination of comprehensiveness and detail than can be found in *The Triumph of Grace.*

Berkouwer, whose knowledge of the Reformed tradition would be difficult to match, devotes a well-aimed section of his work to refuting von Balthasar's claim that Barth eventually embraced the *analogia entis* (186–95). "We are of the opinion," Berkouwer writes, "that von Balthasar's interpretation that Barth has undergone a 'change' is in error at a decisive point and that therein the fundamental fallacy of his masterful and in certain respects irenic book is to be found" (186). A strong case is made for what should have in any event been fairly obvious: "Barth continues to reject the *analogia entis* radically" (190). Of special interest, however, is the reason Berkouwer cites for the perceived rejection. "The triumph of *free* grace is *the* counter-pole to the *analogia entis*" (190). Barth opposes the *analogia entis,* as Berkouwer rightly argues, in part because it posits an independent human capacity for receiving and cooperating with grace in revelation and salvation (194).

"The triumph of grace," of course, is Berkouwer's candidate for an overarching single conception suited for interpreting Barth's *Church Dogmatics.* Exposing "the central thought" of Barth's theology is, Berkouwer admits, no easy task. "An added complication," he continues, "in crystallizing its basic thrust arises from the new and strange elements upon which one comes again and again, and which are far removed from 'traditional' theological thought patterns" (12). The "strange elements" are treated as barriers to be gotten around rather than as invitations to sustained attention. The best way to bypass them is to locate "the central motif." What is sought is also found. "Barth wishes to emphasize above all the triumph of God's grace. . . . It appears that this theme has become the dominant motif in the theology of Barth. In one way or another all the discussion centering around Barth is related to this emphasis on the triumph of grace" (19).

Although disagreeing with von Balthasar on the question of the *analogia entis,* the Dutch Reformed theologian eventually comes to conclusions very similar to those of the Roman Catholic. Barth is unable to avoid the danger of "a *monistic* conception of the works of God" (253). However, whereas von Balthasar analyzes the problem of monism in terms of actualism, Berkouwer analyzes it in terms of objectivism (to the extent that one can speak of any sensitivity to the motifs in his work at all). The problem, as Berkouwer sees it, lies in Barth's "wholly *objective* conception of the triumph of grace" (279), and the roots of this conception are undoubtedly to be found in "the decisive place which election occupies in Barth's dogmatics" (52). Because the divine decree of election is presented by Barth as a priori and eternal, and because it elects all humanity to salvation, "monism" is the inevitable result. The act of election—eternal, a priori, and sovereign—overpowers all. The triumph of grace is secured, but only at the expense of genuine human decision and the deeccisive significance of history. Humanity and history are effectively and monistically absorbed into the triumphant eternity of God and thereby virtually evacuated of all but illustrative significance (253, 256–57, 279, 381). The triumph of grace is "*eternal* in God" but merely "*revealed* in history" (260).

Barth replied to Berkouwer, but not exactly on this point. Berkouwer had also charged, along the same lines, that no place was left in Barth's theology for genuine evil. Evil, too, was robbed of reality and significance by the a priori triumph of grace (215–43). It was on the relationship between God and evil that Barth chose to reply: "I am not trying unilaterally to think through the principle of grace to the point at which I reach 'the triumph of grace' in this relationship. I should regard such a procedure as quite illegitimate. My desire is that from the very first, at every point, and therefore in answering this question too, we should take with unconditional seriousness the fact that 'Jesus is Victor.' "[6] Elsewhere the distinction between "abstract principle" and "concrete, living person" could be even more programmatically expressed: "I have no christological principle and no christological method. Rather in each individual theological question I seek to orientate myself afresh—to some extent from the very beginning—not on a christological dogma but on Jesus Christ himself *(vivit! regnat! triumphat!)*."[7]

More was at stake, however, in Berkouwer's criticisms than Barth confronted with such remarks. Monism, as a recurrent criticism of Barth's theology, can arise from at least two relatively distinct lines of reflection. The one, represented by von Balthasar, arises from the actualism; the other, represented by Berkouwer, from an aspect of the objectivism. The one concentrates on the event of divine–human encounter; the other on what is said to have taken place "prior" to that encounter in election. The actualistic line of criticism will be analyzed at length at the end of this study. The objectivist line, unfortunately, is very complex and falls outside the scope of what can appropriately be discussed here. A few remarks of general orientation, however, can be made within the limits of our theme.

What critics like Berkouwer do not see, and what Barth only partially expresses in attempted reply, is the extent to which Barth departs from commonsensical conceptions of "time" and "eternity." Even Barth's more sustained discussions of these conceptions are not always as helpful as certain incidental comments which fall along the way as the *Church Dogmatics* unfolds. No topic in Barth interpretation is more in need of clarification, and none more requires working with the *Church Dogmatics* as a whole, than this one. Veiled behind Barth's appeal to the particularity of Jesus (veiled perhaps even partially to himself) is the extent to which all dimensions of "temporality" are subjected to radical reinterpretation according to christological and trinitarian modes of thought. Barth knew what he meant when he appealed to the particularity of Jesus, but what he meant remained at least partially intuitive and therefore did not become fully explicit in statement. The procedure of particularism and its basis in the uniqueness of Jesus Christ was being brought into play in a way which only served to perplex Berkouwer and many others readers as well.

Although the charge of monism as Berkouwer states it is not implausible, it is not easily resolved. More attention would need to be devoted to those "strange elements" and "untraditional patterns of thought," before what Torrance calls Barth's "service" on this matter could be adequately evaluated. The essay at hand hopes to be a preliminary step toward such an evaluation. Clarification of the motifs and their interrelations may be one way to bring the strange patterns into focus. It may then become more possible to determine whether Barth's conception of time and eternity is finally sustainable theologically. Occasional remarks on this matter will be made elsewhere along the way.[8] For now the point is simply to suggest that Berkouwer's "central motif" puts him in a good position to pose an excellent question which interpretation by such an isolated motif also blocks him from adequately answering.

Whereas we are left by von Balthasar and Berkouwer with mere misreadings, and by Torrance with an all-too-cautions "non-misreading" (except for the benign "scientism"), Robert Jenson greatly advances the discussion by fully rising to the level of a "strong misreading."[9] In his unjustly neglected work *God after God, The God of the Past and the Future as Seen in the Work of Karl Barth*—perhaps the most provocative, incisive and wrong-headed reading of Barth available in English—Jenson reempowers the Barthian text by cutting through the usual tradition-bound mystifications and capturing the real pulse of what Barth actually had to say. In contrast to the others, Jenson puts his finger on the true significance of Barth's particularism and yet finally misses the full import of what he himself has seen. Rather than asking the flat-footed question of the single dominating thought form or material concept, Jenson is agile enough to ask instead about "the basic move" (68). Since it is a "move" and not a "constructive principle" which Jenson rightly sees at the heart of Barth's theology, it is a shame that Jenson wants to turn the move into a metaphysical principle for his own constructive work in the end. Be that as it may, the metaphysical turn in Jenson's own thought is readily separable from the compelling reading that he offers of Barth's theology.

The basic move which Jenson sees is "the absolute priority of Jesus' existence" (72). This particularist priority is what Barth was driving at in his reply to Berkouwer. In reading Barth, Berkouwer imagines an orig-

inal separation of eternity from time such that time never really has a
chance. Time is thought to be so overpowered by an a priori eternity that
it is effectively "eternalized," being monistically absorbed, as it were,
into God. Hence absolute separation leads, paradoxically, to monism. By
contrast, Jenson rightly and refreshingly sees that for Barth the human
existence of Jesus is accorded not only epistemological but ontological
priority, and that in both cases the priority is absolute. For reasons of his
own, however, Jenson proceeds to advance the ontological priority in
such a way that eternity becomes so fully "historicized" that it is virtually drawn into dialectical identity with history. It is just this full "his-
toricization" of eternity which Jenson finds wanting in Barth, and so
undertakes to supply it for him.

The key to Barth's theology is impressively stated as follows:

> It is this absolute priority of Jesus' existence, of the life of our brother-man,
> which is the key to the otherwise puzzling convolutions of the great dog-
> matic theology which Barth has developed through his years at Gottingen,
> Bonn and Basel, and recorded in the twelve huge volumes of the *Church
> Dogmatics*. That one starts with the story of this man, is the key to a think-
> ing which hammers on the sole and absolute majesty of God and the irrel-
> evance of all our works and thoughts to reach him, yet finds anything human
> an appropriate object of dogmatic reflection. It is the key to a theology
> which is really one vast doctrine of God, yet involved its creator in the most
> direct sort of political action. If we forget the priority of Christ in consid-
> ering any Barthian doctrine we will infallibly turn it into its direct opposite,
> the kind of isolation of God which people have mislabelled "Barthianism."
> (72)

Even if one were inclined to doubt the possibility of a single "key" to
Barth, it would be difficult to deny the power of this observation, especially considering what Jenson proceeds to make of it.

Especially good use is made of this insight in explaining that aspect of
Barth's thought which falls under the category of objectivism. Consider,
for example, what Jenson says about the "eternal decree" in contrast to
what we heard from Berkouwer: "The 'decree of predestination' made in
God about us is in fact identical with the decision in which God chooses
to be God. What God chooses is to be God *as* Jesus Christ" (131).
Although the word *identical* in this statement is not unproblematic and
will need to be discussed, a central insight has been laid bare. What
Jenson sees in contrast to all the Berkouwers is that Jesus Christ in Barth's
theology *is* the unity of time and eternity. Eternity is not to be understood
in abstraction from Jesus of Nazareth. However difficult the resulting

conceptuality might turn out to be (or however illuminating and deep), eternity is *defined* as inseparable from the particular temporality of Jesus, as ontologically filled and shaped by it. There is neither a general divine nor a general human temporality which takes ontological precedence over the particular temporality of Jesus. No general divine or human temporality has ever occurred in abstraction from his. "There *is* no human life in itself, and surely no meaning of such a life. Rather, the event of Jesus Christ's life, because it is the central event in the life of the eternal God, is the eternal presupposition of all else that happens" (69). This insight is the gateway to the great themes of revelational and soteriological objectivism as they will be explored later in this study. Both God to humanity and humanity to God (and therefore, in a way this study cannot fully probe, eternity to time and time to eternity) are mediated in and through Jesus Christ (cf. II/2, 97).

Two closely related problems need to be noted about the point where Jenson's reading becomes strangely idiosyncratic. The one pertains to the doctrine of analogy, and the other to the christological "is." Von Balthasar has, but for Jenson, been univerally acclaimed for pointing out the transition in Barth's theology from "dialectic" to "analogy" as the benchmark separating the earlier from the later Barth. Jenson demurs.[10] According to him (with express contradiction of von Balthasar), "no change whatever" took place on this score "after 1920" (202, 77). Dialectic and analogy are merely two sides of the same coin—where you have one you have the other—and Barth had both from the early period onward. From the standpoint of motif research, this observation is a half-truth which misses the change that took place in Barth's understanding of theological language. After 1931, dialectic was thoroughly subjected on principle to analogy (though not expunged, as von Balthasar also made clear), because Barth found a way he had not seen before to conceive of theological language as the vehicle of positive analogical reference to God. Prior to that, only negative, self-canceling analogies had been thought to be fully suitable as vehicles of linguistic reference.

The interesting thing about Jenson's version of analogy, however, is not a quibble about interpretation, but the way it connects to larger and more important themes. Analogy, in Jenson's reading, is not connected to the discovery of a "realist" conception of theological language, but to Barth's conception of time and eternity. No great change in Barth is thought to have taken place on this score either, and for Jenson the more's the pity. Time and eternity were allegedly conceived by Barth, early and late, as contraries, as time and timelessnness, and also as distinct realities—rather than as merely two different aspects, dialectically related, of the same essential process. Actually, it is not entirely clear whether Jenson thinks Barth kept them as contraries (although his reading seems at times to imply it), for he surely knows that Barth carefully denied any such thing. Jenson fails to reckon, unfortunately, with the later Barth's nontimeless, thoroughly trinitarian conception of eternity as a reality ontologically other than and transcendent (though inclusive) of time. Jenson has no interest in any such conception, however, since by his lights (or so it seems), everything but a merely analytical distinction between "time" and "eternity" (i.e., two names, one process) has to go.

Analogy and an ontologically other eternity, as Jenson perceptively insists, go hand in hand. Accordingly, a distaste for analogy accompanies his revisionist conception of eternity. Analogy is a notion shrouded in ambiguity. "After all," we are told, "'analogous' is in a way just another word for 'ambiguous'" (92). Analogy is theologically unnecessary. It can be dropped and God's transcendence can be defined in temporal rather than strictly ontological terms. "We will define God's deity as his futurity to himself and so to us" (155). The interesting question here is not so much the merit of this proposal per se as the way Jenson sees himself extracting it from Barth, and the reasons why Barth undoubtedly would have resisted it.

"Barth can insist on the otherness of God," writes Jenson, "because his God is from the beginning one person with the man Jesus; God's otherness is therefore the otherness of one man from another, which is the very condition of mutual involvement" (72). It is not always clear from this and similar remarks just where Barth is thought to end and Jenson to begin. Seeing the ontological unity of God with the particularity of Jesus, is, it has been suggested, the great strength of Jenson's reading. The further suggestion may now be ventured that it is also the point of great weakness. Insight passes over into misreading, it would seem, under the hidden influence of a Lutheran doctrine of the *communicatio idiomatum*. When the Lutheran Jenson encounters the christological "is" (as in "God 'is' Jesus"), different bells go off than they would for the Reformed Barth. Identifying the divine otherness in so unqualified a way with the otherness of one human being from another, as occurs in the passage cited, would have been quite unthinkable for Barth. The Reformed theologian would want that christological "is" to denote an ontological difference in the midst of real though inconceivable unity. "Dialectical identity," as perhaps rooted in some conceptions of the *communicatio idiomatum*, would be all too intelligible and would be thought to generate grave problems of its own—like the danger of seeing God more nearly as a "happening" than as a personal agent, or the danger of identifying the Creator with the creature. Analogical reference would be proposed—not with "pervasive ambiguity" and not requiring "a timeless deepest reality of God"—precisely as a device to prevent just such problems (92, 154).

Particularism is the methodological point which underlies the material difference now emerging. Jenson does not pursue the implications of Barth's particularism to the end. Barth wants to keep everything under the control of a single particular. That control is fatally lost, he believed, when the mystery of the particular is allowed to disappear into a mere metaphysic of the particular. Deliberately collapsing the distinction between time and eternity would have been regarded as an option for metaphisics (73). If "religion is the mixing of time and eternity" (9), and is therefore (Jenson agrees with Barth) earnestly to be avoided, what will be the result of conceiving them in dialectical identity? Particularism for Barth meant that the Incarnation was conceivable only in its inconceivability; that eternity had to be radically reconceived in incarnational and trinitarian terms, but without losing the ontological difference between Creator and creature; and that analogical reference by the miracle of grace provided a conception of theological language which allowed for both the necessary clarity and the necessary mystery, for revealedness as well as hiddenness, in the doctrine of God. These are at least matters Jenson might have pursued. Because his interest in the use of Barth finally takes precedence over his interest in interpreting Barth, the full potential of his interpretation is not exploited. Barth's own positions eventually get short shrift, and Barth's predictable worries about where Jenson himself ends up are not explicitly entertained. Nonetheless, the power and vitality of his work are more than enough to compensate for these shortcomings, which after all are not so serious as to undo the exceptional radiance of the reading.

Finally, it is good to acknowledge a debt and to make brief comment on the humble but sturdy volume *The Theology of Karl Barth: An Introduction* by Herbert Hartwell.[11] Of the books of its kind in English, Hartwell's is still perhaps the best. The prose is not scintillating, no interpretive device is offered, and no ambitious goals are set, yet the book is accurate, fair, and judicious. Barth has been read closely and summarized intelligently. Some attempt is made, always to good effect, to place Barth in relation to other contemporary and historic theologians. Although not rising or pretending to rise above the *loci* approach, Hartwell compiles and explicates a little list which many years ago was the original inspiration for the project which became this study. Particularism is not named as such, nor is personalism, but their content is clearly identified and set forth in an introductory way. Actualism is the motif Hartwell understood the best, and a good running account is kept of it through the book. Objectivism entails much more than he saw; his unfortunate term "historicism" became the "realism" of this study; and the rudiments of rationalism are noted but not named or pursued. Hartwell's book has the advantage over those by von Balthasar, Torrance, and Berkouwer of having been written at a time when the *Church Dogmatics* as a whole could be taken into account, and the copious footnotes indicate how industriously the task was undertaken. No interested reader just starting out with Barth will be harmed by anything Hartwell has to say, and those who persist with him will not fail to receive the rewards his book has to offer.

To sum up, none of the proposals examined can be said, really, to catch the complexity-in-unity and unity-in-complexity of Karl Barth's *Church Dogmatics*. By contrast, the promise of motif research as presented here is not only that it can move closer to that daunting goal, but also that it can help to pinpoint some important ways in which the older readings fall short. That is to say, defining the motifs accurately and charting their complex interrelations promises to offer a more compelling taxonomy of the *Church Dogmatics* and its inner logic or coherence than otherwise currently available.

The strengths of von Balthasar's reading seem to be largely independent of his attempt to account for the unity of the *Church Dogmatics* as a whole. The weaknesses, on the other hand, would seem to be twofold. His account of the unity is neither complex enough to be satisfying nor accurate enough to be convincing in detail. In itself the *analogia fidei* is not a *Denkform* (although the actualism which informs it is), and even if it were, it would not be sufficient to describe what unifies Barth's *magnum opus*. Not even the *analogia fidei* in combination with Barth's christological concentration as a material principle would provide an adequate description of the unity. (They would not do so even if von Balthasar were not mistaken, as he is, in his analysis of how each of them supposedly develops within the course of the *Church Dogmatics*.) In the end, von Balthasar misses the full significance even of what he accurately perceives. For although he rightly concentrates on the actualism, he misses the radicality with which Barth applies it in his conception of the *analogia fidei*. Yet it is that very radicality which allows Barth to avoid lapsing into the *analogia entis* that von Balthasar would sometimes ascribe to him. Attention to the other motifs also helps to explain just how this way of reading falls short. Insofar as he underplays the concrete and indivisible uniqueness of the subject matter as associated with particularism, the unity of objectivism and personalism in Barth's conception of the one Word of God, and the complementarity of realism and rationalism in Barth's theological method, von Balthasar leaves something to be desired.

On the whole Torrance perhaps displays a better sense of the overall complexity of Barth's theology than does von Balthasar. Yet the unity of that complexity does not really emerge, and there is a certain distortion factor at work in Torrance's account. A prominence is assigned to revelational objectivism which is not really there in Barth. At the same time there is a corresponding underestimation of the radicality of Barth's actualism and particularism (even though these do not go unexamined). The result is not only a stultifying effect which tends to drain away some of the vitality of Barth's thought, but also an unfortunate if implicit nomination of revelational objectivism as the motif which unifies Barth's theology as a whole. That unity, however, depends on a much richer and more supple way of interrelating the motifs than the nomination of a single candidate will allow.

In his own workmanlike if ultimately plodding way, Berkouwer reads Barth's work much more for content than for method. It is therefore perhaps not surprising that he ends up isolating a material rather than a formal principle of unity. The overarching principle which supposedly unifies the *Church Dogmatics* is the triumph of grace as grounded in the doctrine of election and then as applied systematically from there. The triumph of grace is presented almost as a theorem from which the major moves in Barth's theology can be shown to follow as though by way of a mathematical deduction. It is no wonder that Barth resisted this caricature. Berkouwer was obviously stymied by those "new and strange" patterns of thought which he apparently believed he could simply read past, perhaps just because they seemed so far from being traditional. If he had opted to pay more attention to them, however, perhaps he would have found not only more room for appreciation and caution, but also more precision in working out the kind of critique that seemed so important to him. As it is, by bypassing the complexity of Barth's thought forms, Berkouwer ends up by distorting the content and missing the unity of Barth's theology as well.

Robert Jenson, who sets out not only to explicate Barth, but also at the same time to develop an alternative theological proposal, discerns the concreteness but not fully the uniqueness invested in Barth's motif of particularism. Insofar as Jenson attends to the concreteness, he avoids the mistakes of others and gives us a Barth who really sounds like Barth. However, insofar as Jenson underestimates the uniqueness, he generates mistakes of his own and misses a chance to define the real disagreements between himself and Barth in a more precise and helpful way. Although there are motifs in Barth which Jenson does not explore, for the most part their absence does not damage his presentation, given the primary interest he has in pursuing his own dogmatic proposals. Yet he is simply mistaken in his account of Barth's conception of eternity,[12] and it is this mistaken view which he sets up as a foil against which to develop an alternative. The deficit is twofold: materially, we are deprived of the real contrast between Barth and Jenson (whose alternative is worth considering against Barth's); methodologically, their differences are obscured. The radical uniqueness Barth ascribes to the relevant particulars not only informs his actual view of eternity, but also requires a more chastened mode of coherence and consistency in dogmatic theology than Jenson's metaphysical proclivities will permit. In Barth's theology the place and function of rationalism are circumscribed by just that aspect of his particularism which Jenson fails to take into account. Despite the considerable merits of Jenson's way of reading, neither the complexity nor the unity of Barth's theology in the *Church Dogmatics* as a whole is brought adequately into view.

The limitations of Herbert Hartwell's study are found partly in its conception and partly in its execution. In its conception the study exemplifies the *loci* approach which simply moves from topic to topic without raising the question of complexity-in-unity and unity-in-complexity. It would obviously be unfair to criticize such a study for failing to accomplish a task it did not attempt to take up. In its execution, on the other hand, the study is at once flawed and yet full of promise. Although it attempts in a rudimentary way to delineate the shape of Barth's theology by means of an imperfectly realized set of categories, those categories are not without promise. If refined and refashioned, they might well be developed in ways far beyond anything Hartwell himself ever seems to have imagined.

In short, none of the works surveyed offers a satisfying account of the coherence and internal logic of Barth's theology in the *Church Dogmatics*. What they have in common is a failure to show how that work combines genuine unity with irreducible complexity. The various proposals tend to explain either the unity at the expense of the complexity, or the complexity at the expense of the unity. Various distortions and errors thereby creep in along the way. Once these inadequacies have been seen, the way is cleared for a different approach to the question. Rather than on a single formal or material principle, perhaps the internal logic of Barth's theology depends on a variety of hierarchical though shifting arrangements that obtain among an interrelated set of motifs. The thesis to be argued here is that these motifs and their interrelations can help to disclose the shape of Barth's theology as a whole.

PART I

The Motifs in Survey: The Shaping of Doctrine in the *Church Dogmatics*

CHAPTER 1

Four Motifs:
A Preliminary Survey

Often referred to as the greatest theologian of the twentieth century, Karl Barth has achieved the dubious distinction of being habitually honored but not much read. Although many reasons might be found to explain this, surely one of them is that reading Karl Barth can be a discouraging experience. What reader of the *Church Dogmatics* has not gotten bogged down in one of those long, complicated, and seemingly interminable sentences? At such times Barth's writing may seem reminiscent of a famous quip by Mark Twain. The German sentence, Twain declared, is like a dog that jumps into the Atlantic Ocean, swims all the way across to the other side, and climbs out at the end with a verb in his mouth! Yet long sentences are not the only problem. Not only can it be difficult to keep track of the antecedents to pronouns, but Barth apparently keeps repeating himself as he unfolds his thought. Furthermore, the content seems to present as many problems as the style. It can seem to be too familiar to be interesting, or paradoxically, too strange to be relevant. As though all this were not enough, his dialectic can be very bewildering, seeming to take away with one hand what he has just established with the other. Why then should anyone bother to make the effort?

Perhaps the best answer is that those readers who have managed to get past the initial difficulties find that they are in the midst of something truly magnificent. Barth's theology in the *Church Dogmatics* could be compared to the cathedral at Chartres. Once one's eyes get used to the light, one discovers that one is inside an awesome and many-splendored structure, soaring with vaulted arches, arrayed with intricate passageways, adorned with exquisite statuary, and crowned above all by rose windows dancing with fire. The problem, then, is for one's eyes to get used to the light. But once they do, no other architecture, no other theology, is likely to be quite the same. Back in the light of day, some contemporary theologies will begin to look more like lecture halls than cathedrals, others will stand out as respectable but limited sanctuaries, still others perhaps as monuments to suburban kitsch. There will of course be other cathedrals to visit, but they will have been constructed long ago. One effect of getting to know the cathedral of Barth's theology is that it can help one appreciate the older cathedrals and make one want to spend time in them, too. But none of this will happen if one leaves the cathedral before one's eyes get used to the light.

It might help the beginning reader who feels bogged down in Barth's syntax to remember that one is reading a translation. The translation, which of course we are fortunate to have, is certainly workmanlike; but it is also stolid, uneven, and generally uninspired. Frustrated beginners are sometimes surprised to learn that Barth was awarded the prestigious Sigmund Freud Prize for the eloquence of his academic prose. Even with our English translation (such as it is), attentive readers can still perceive that in the style of composition there is a certain music to the argument. What first appears as mere repetition turns out on closer inspection to function rather like repetition in sonata form. It is the author's method of alluding to themes previously developed while constantly enriching the score with new ideas. Here it can be helpful to remember Barth's great love of Mozart, whose music he listened to every morning. Like Mozart, Barth preferred to work with sharply contrasting themes resolved into higher unities and marked by regular recapitulations. Themes or fragments of themes, once dominant, are constantly carried forward into new settings where other themes take the ascendancy. Materials are constantly being combined, broken up, recombined, and otherwise brought into contrapuntal relationship. Part of what Barth seems to share with Mozart, in other words, is a certain taste for thematic interplay, a taste which includes the custom of complex recapitulation, modification, and allusion. The more deeply one reads Barth, the more one senses that his use of repetition is never pointless. Rather, it serves as a principle of organization and development within an ever forward spiraling theological whole.[1]

An intimate connection exists between this style of composition and Barth's understanding of the subject matter. No one ever seems to have had a stronger sense that in Christian theology every theme is connected to every other theme. It is as if he envisioned the whole subject of Christian theology as forming one great and many-faceted crystal. He would, as it were, take the great crystal in his hands and say, "Now we are going to look at the basic structure of the crystal through this facet, this particular doctrine, of the Christian faith. Notice how it connects not only with those facets which adjoin it, but also with those more remote and those on the opposite side. Above all, notice that the light which infuses the whole is the very light which refracts through this facet as well." Having conducted this examination, Barth then turns the great crystal in his hands and directs our attention in a similar way to yet another facet of the whole. The technique of allusion and recapitulation thus expresses his profound sense of the interrelatedness of all Christian doctrines. The task of theology, in this view, is to describe as carefully as possible, from many different angles, the network of interconnections which constitute the great crystal in its totality.

However, the image of theology as being concerned with a crystalline subject matter could easily become misleading. It could suggest that theology is a more "systematic" enterprise than Barth actually conceived it to be. In this sense the image of musical composition is probably a more reliable indication of Barth's theology than imagery of stability and order, complete in itself, like a cathedral or a crystal. Barth thought systematically about the subject matter of theology but he did not think in terms of a system. The subject matter of theology, as he understood it, is richly dynamic, endlessly surprising, and deeply mysterious. Even the most refined theological conceptualities are too crude to capture it. Because it is more nearly musical than architectural, more nearly verbal than substantive, it cannot be imprisoned in a system. Theological construction must therefore in principle be more like musical invention than like architectural formation. It must try to correspond to the subject matter without containing it.

Wending one's way through the *Church Dogmatics* can be made easier if one learns to recognize the presence of several constantly recurring motifs. Although I will designate each of them as an "ism," they will be entirely subject to the strictures just mentioned. Despite their appearance as "isms," they are not meant to imply that Barth's theology is governed by certain systematic or philosophic principles. The motifs are adjectival in force, not substantive. Being qualifications of the subject matter (never the subject matter itself), they are simply meant to call attention to certain distinctive traits, patterns, or thought forms by which Barth's theology is shaped. Barth works with these motifs, not because he thinks they have interest or validity on their own, but because he thinks they help to illuminate certain peculiar modes of thought implicit in the witness of scripture. Learning to recognize these motifs, of which I shall specify six, can greatly aid any reader of the *Church Dogmatics* who starts to feel lost in the argument, or who wants more deeply to appreciate the distinctiveness of Barth's theology. To gain one's bearings, the reader can always ask whether one (or more) of the motifs is being deployed—as is almost always the case.

The Motif of Actualism

The first of these will be called "actualism." Actualism is the most distinctive and perhaps the most difficult of the motifs. It is present whenever Barth speaks, as he constantly does, in the language of occurrence, happening, event, history, decisions, and act. At the most general level it means that he thinks primarily in terms of events and relationships rather than monadic or self-contained substances. So pervasive is this motif that Barth's whole theology might well be described as a theology of active relations. God and humanity are both defined in fundamentally actualistic terms.

For example, when Barth wants to describe the living God in a technical way, he says that God's being is always a being in act. Negatively, this means that God's being cannot be described apart from the basic act in which God lives. Any attempt to define God in static or inactive terms, as is customary in certain theologies and philosophies, is therefore to be rejected. Positively, the description means that God lives in a set of active relations. The being of God in act is a being in love and freedom. God, who does not need us to be the living God, is perfectly complete without us. For God is alive in the active relations of love and freedom which constitute God's being in and for itself. These are the active relations of God's trinitarian self-differentiation. From all eternity the Father loves the Son, and the Son loves the Father, in the unity of the Holy Spirit. God is free to be God, to constitute the divine being, in this distinctively trinitarian way. God is the Lord, the acting subject, of this self-constituting, mysterious event. Although there is much more to it than this, the basic point of the actualism can already be suggested, as far as the doctrine of God is concerned. Actualism emphasizes the sovereign activity of God in patterns of love and freedom—not only in God's self-relationship, but also in relationship to others (II/1, 257–321).

As far as human beings are concerned, the basic point is to understand them strictly with regard to the patterns of God's sovereign activity. Negatively, this means that we human beings have no ahistorical relationship to God, and that we also have no capacity in and of ourselves to enter into fellowship with God. An ahistorical relationship would be a denial of God's activity, and an innate capacity for fellowship would be a denial of God's sovereignty. Positively, therefore, our relationship to God must be understood in active, historical terms, and it must be a relationship given to us strictly from the outside. Our active relationship to God is a history of love and freedom; we are capable of it not because it stands at our disposal, but because we who stand at God's disposal are given it. Our relationship to God is therefore an event. It is not possessed once and for all, but is continually established anew by the ongoing activity of grace. Paradoxically, however, although befalling us from the outside and exceeding our creaturely capacities, the event of grace deeply enhances rather than diminishes us. It draws us beyond ourselves into a relationship of communion, of love and freedom, with God. The sovereignty of grace is thus not the negation, but the condition for the possibility, of human spontaneity and fulfillment. God's sovereignty in our lives is enacted as God establishes with us a history of love and freedom.

Barth's theology of active relations is therefore a theology which stresses the sovereignty of grace, the incapacity of the creature, and the miraculous history whereby grace grants what the creature lacks for the sake of love and freedom. This pattern appears again and again in the *Church Dogmatics*. The church, the inspiration of scripture, faith, and all other creaturely realities in their relationship to God are always understood as events. They are not self-initiating and self-sustaining. They are not grounded in a neutral, ahistorical, or ontological relationship to God independent of the event of grace. Nor are they actualizations of certain ontologically given creaturely capacities. Rather, they have not only their being but also their possibility only as they are continually established anew according to the divine good pleasure. They have their being only in act—in the act of God which elicits from the creature the otherwise impossible act of free response. God is thus the Lord—not only of the mysterious event which constitutes the divine being, but also of the mysterious event which constitutes our being in relation to God.

This point may be drawn to a close with a simple but telling example. Barth's actualistic mode of thought enables him to explain why it is a mistake to reverse the biblical dictum that "God is love" (1 John 4:8, 16) so that instead it would say "Love is God"—as though God could be equated with an abstract concept of love in general. As Barth carefully shows on exegetical grounds, "God is love" is a concise way of describing God's activity. It means that "God acts in a loving way." The statement cannot be reversed, because "God" refers to an acting subject, and "love" to the quality of God's activity. (Or more precisely, it could be reversed only if one were to take this sense into account.) This example illustrates how Barth wants his actualistic sensibility to arise from and point back to scripture. The actualism is considered valid only insofar as it can illuminate scriptural patterns of thought (I/2, 374; II/1, 275; IV/2, 756).

It is worth noting in passing that the actualistic motif is bound up with Barth's important use of the terms "abstract" and "concrete." To charge that a theological proposal is "abstract" is one of the chief lines of criticism in the *Church Dogmatics*. A proposal is abstract not merely if it mistakes the part for the whole or the quality for the object, but more precisely if it is formulated without reference to the nexus of active relations in which God and humanity have their respective modes of being. Conversely, a proposal is "concrete" only if it is formulated with careful attention to the patterns of God's sovereign activity. No proposal can be concrete, according to Barth's theology, if it does not somehow articulate the fundamental events of grace.[2]

The Motif of Particularism

A second and closely related motif will be called "particularism." Barth's theology makes a concerted attempt always to move from the particular to the general rather than from the general to the particular. Barth writes programmatically: "It is not the general which comes first but the particular. The general does not exist without this particular and cannot therefore be prior to the particular. It cannot, then, be recognized and understood as the general prior to it, as if it were itself a particular. Thus we cannot move from the general to the particular, but only in the opposite direction—from this particular to the general" (II/1, 602).

Negatively, this procedure means that Barth does not first ask about what might be true or meaningful on general grounds and then move to fit theological statements into that framework. He does not first ask, for example, what we might mean by the word "love" and then go on to apply this general concept to God. Nor does he amplify this procedure. He does not first decide on general, systematic or nontheological grounds what sorts of things are real and what sorts are possible. He does not attempt to apply neutral or generally applicable standards of reality and possibility to our language about God. Such procedures, Barth felt, were a procrustean bed. Procrustes, it will be recalled, was the mythical giant who made his captives fit one of two beds of unequal length, either by stretching their bodies or cutting off their legs. In this light Barth's hesitation about espousing philosophical systems can be understood. When placed at the heart of theological reflection, he argued, such systems force one either to stretch certain categories to the breaking point or else to lop off too many vital portions of the Christian faith.

Positively, the motif of particularism means that Barth strove to take his bearings stricdy from the particularities of the biblical witness, especially its narrative portions. The particulars from which he wanted to move toward general theological constructions were the events of grace as attested in scripture and centered on Jesus Christ. These were the particulars from which theology would determine what sorts of things were real and what sorts possible within its special realm of competence. These were the particulars from which all relevant standards of reality and possibility had to be derived, if human beings would speak meaningfully about God. Only through a single-minded devotion to these particulars could theology avoid the disasters of the procrustean bed.

Barth's particularism therefore committed him to a strongly revisionist use of language and to a respect for the presence of mystery. The particularities of the biblical witness, Barth was convinced, are utterly singular in their content. Ordinary words as they are generally used are profoundly inadequate when it comes to speaking of God. Consequently it would be fatal, were we to assume that we know in advance what words like "love," "person," "father," and "lord" mean in a theological setting. We must rather let ourselves be told what these words mean by attending to the particularity of their scriptural usage. Only by meditating on the deeper patterns of the biblical witness, and in particular on patterns of divine activity to which it attests, can we begin to understand the theological semantics of these terms. Only then will we see, for example, that God's "loving" is uniquely concerned with seeking and creating fellowship for its own sake, that God's "personhood" involves a perfect coincidence, or coincidence without discrepancy, between being and act, that God's "fatherhood" is a relationship of creative self-giving, and that God's "lordship" comes to its fullest expression in servanthood. Only by fixing our gaze strictly on God's unique activity, not allowing ourselves to be influenced unduly by ideas derived from elsewhere, will these matters come clearly into view. Only by breaking up and reforming our ordinary conceptions will we be able to do justice to these particularities. Only by conforming our ideas to the subject matter (rather than the other way around), regardless of how strange that subject matter might be, will we truly learn to think theologically.

There comes a point, however, where human language can no longer be revised. There comes a point where the particularities of the biblical witness drive human language to its inherent limits and therefore to the edge of mystery. A high tolerance for mystery is a hallmark of Barth's theology—a tolerance which at once separates him from standard modern theologies and unites him with the historic faith of the ecumenical church. His loyalty to the particularities of the biblical witness led him not to shrink from various anomalies as they arose from the subject matter. These anomalies might take the form of unresolved conceptual antitheses, as for example in the doctrine of the Trinity or in the doctrine of the Incarnation. Or they might take the form of discrepancies between eye and ear, as for example in the doctrine of reconciliation, which announces that the world has been reconciled to God, whereas the world as ordinarily observed would seem to be far from being so reconciled. Governed by the particularities of the biblical witness, Barth was inclined to approach such anomalies not by explaining them away, but simply by letting them stand. He was more concerned to avoid premature closure, when the biblical witness did not warrant closure, than to achieve orderly conceptual outcomes. In this sense, the motif of particularism entailed a deep respect for mystery. It was an expression of Barth's conviction that we walk by faith and not by sight.[3]

The particularist motif was also an expression of Barth's extraordinary sensitivity to the divine complexity and fecundity. Perhaps no better initial illustration of particularism could be offered than Barth's remarkable description of God's freedom (from which only a part can be quoted), for it was above all a revitalized sense of God's freedom which the motif of particularism was meant to reflect. Of God's high and majestic freedom to be present with the creature, Barth writes:

> It is not, then, the rigid presence of a being whose nature we can, so to speak, formulate in this or that principle. God is free to be present with the creature by giving himself and revealing himself to it or by concealing himself and withdrawing from it. God is free to be and operate in the created world either as unconditioned or as conditioned. God is free to perform his work either within the framework of what we call the laws of nature or outside it in the shape of miracle. . . . God is free to conceal his divinity from the creature, even to become a creature himself, and free to assume again his Godhead. . . . God is free to clothe himself with the life of the

world in all its glory as with a garment; but free likewise himself to die the death which symbolizes the end of all things earthly, in utter abandonment and darkness. . . . God is free to be wholly inward to the creature and at the same time as himself wholly outward: *totus intra et totus extra* and both, of course, as forms of his immanence, of his presence, of the relationship and communion chosen, willed and created by himself between himself and his creation. This is how he meets us in Jesus Christ. His revelation in Jesus Christ embraces all these apparently so diverse and contradictory possibilities. They are all his possibilities. If we deny him any one of them, we are denying Jesus Christ and God himself. (II/1, 314–5)

The Motif of Objectivism

Objectivism, the next motif, has two important aspects. The one concerns knowledge of God, the other, salvation in Christ. On the first, Barth was convinced that the knowledge of God as confessed by faith is objective in the sense that its basis lies not in human subjectivity but in God. Negatively, this conviction required Barth to make a decisive technical move. In light of modern liberal theology (as associated with Schleiermacher), he had to show why what faith says about God could not be collapsed, as Feuerbach had powerfully argued, into nothing but statements about human nature. He had to show why such anthropological reduction was not warranted by the internal logic of the church's knowledge of God.

Feuerbach, Barth believed, had accurately diagnosed the logical dilemma of modern liberal theology. He had shown, as Barth read him, that in liberal theology there was no avoiding a forced option between method and content. Either liberalism's method could be retained at the expense of its theological content, or its content could be retained (and expanded) at the expense of its theological method. There was no alternative, because no theological method (such as that of liberalism) which wanted to maintain the existence of God strictly on the basis of certain anthropological phenomena would, logically speaking, ever get beyond mere assertions about anthropological phenomena—regardless of their theological form. The anthropocentric method of liberal theology not only failed to prevent but logically even invited Feuerbach's reversal and reduction of theological into merely anthropological assertions. Only if theological assertions could be shown to display a different logic—one not grounded in anthropological premises—could the force of Feuerbach's objection be met.[4]

Positively, therefore, Barth set out to counter Feuerbach by showing a way beyond the liberal dilemma. His decisive move was simply to restate a conviction which had long been implicit in the Christian tradition, namely, that God's being in relation to the human creature was no different from God's being in relation to itself. God's identity in history was essentially the same as God's identity in eternity, for otherwise God would not have engaged in an act of self-revelation, that is, God's essential identity would not have been disclosed. Given this analysis, Barth could argue that God's eternal being in and for itself could be inferred from God's being as enacted for and among us in history. If, for example, God is loving and free in relation to us, we can infer that God's being is loving and free in and for itself. If God's being is disclosed as trinitarian in history, we can infer that it is also trinitarian in eternity. These conclusions, once drawn, could then be turned into premises. God's being as it is in itself thereby became the ground for the assertions of faith about God. For example, the ground of God's love and freedom in relation to us could be conceived only as God's love and freedom in and for themselves. Or again, the ground of God's trinitarian self-disclosure in history could be conceived only as God's trinitarian identity in eternity. The logical basis for these assertions had thus been shown to lie in God and not in anthropological phenomena. The knowledge of God as confessed by faith had been shown to be irreducible and objective, logically speaking, on the grounds that God's self-revelation in history gives faith a share in God's own self-knowledge as it is in eternity.

Barth was well aware of the circularity of this argument. He had in no way tried to prove that God has engaged in an act of self-revelation. Rather, in essentially coherentist fashion, he had simply made candid the logic of believing in such an act of divine self-revelation.[5] Therefore he had not directly tried to counter Feuerbach's other famous charge that the objectivity of God is not real but merely an illusion. Barth was convinced that God could be known by God alone, that proofs of God were neither necessary nor possible, and that the self-revelation of the living God could take care of itself. What Barth had successfully countered, however, was the logic of Feuerbach's anthropological reduction. He had shown that the concept of God's self-revelation, as affirmed by faith, logically entailed the concept that faith's statements about God are objectively grounded. Although faith could not coherently find within itself the condition for its own possibility and all attempts to do so were logically self-defeating, faith could coherently believe that its basis lay not in itself but in God.

An important corollary to this objectivist construal of God's self-revelation was that God is revealed in God's unity and entirety (II/1, 51–53). Nothing essential of God's identity ever needs to be sought elsewhere, Barth argued, than in Jesus Christ, God's definitive, final, and binding act of self-revelation. There is no God apart from, beyond, or behind God as God is in Jesus Christ. In Jesus Christ, God's being is present in its unity and entirety. There is no hidden God beyond the revealed God. The hidden God and the revealed God are essentially one and the same. The hiddenness of God is given in and with God's self-revelation, and God's self-revelation does not exclude but includes God's hiddenness. As revealed in trinitarian self-disclosure, God's identity in and with Jesus Christ is ineffaceably mysterious—concealed in the midst of disclosure and disclosed in the midst of concealment. The terms of God's identity are made clear—they are the terms of the doctrine of the Trinity and of the Incarnation—but exactly so they are the terms of an impenetrable mystery. God's self-disclosure is thus at the same time God's self-concealment. God's essential identity as disclosed in Jesus Christ is the mysterious identity of the triune God.

What Barth says about God's objective self-involvement in Jesus Christ finds a remarkable parallel in what Barth says with respect to humanity. For humanity, too, is conceived as objectively self-involved in Jesus Christ in a manner at once hidden and revealed. Just as God is ontologically present in Jesus Christ, so too is the human race ontologically present in him in the sense that in and only in him is its own true reality to be found. Christian theology has traditionally emphasized that God comes to the human race in Jesus Christ. Barth shares that emphasis, but goes on to develop an extraordinary anthropological correlate. When God comes to humanity in the history of Jesus Christ, humanity at the same time is brought to God in that history objectively. It is not faith which incorporates humanity into Jesus Christ. Faith is rather the acknowledgment of a mysterious incorporation already objectively accomplished on humanity's behalf. "One has died for all; therefore all have died" (2 Cor. 5:14). That all have died in Christ (and been raised with him) is the hidden truth of humanity as revealed to faith. Our true humanity is to be found not in ourselves but objectively in him. God's real presence to humanity in Jesus Christ (revelational objectivism) is paralleled by humanity's real presence in Jesus Christ to God (soteriological objectivism). Barth writes:

> In Christian doctrine . . . we have always to take in blind seriousness the basic Pauline perception of Colossians 3:3 which is that of all Scripture—that our life is hid with Christ in God. With Christ: never at all apart from him, never at all independently of him, never at all in and for itself. We as

human beings never at all exist in ourselves. And Christians are the very last to try to cling to existing in themselves. We exist as human beings in Jesus Christ and in him alone; as we also find God in Jesus Christ and in him alone. The being and nature of human beings in and for themselves as independent bearers of an independent predicate, have, by the revelation of Jesus Christ, become an abstraction which can be destined only to disappear. (II/1, 149 rev.)

Note the implicit connection here between the objectivist and actualist motifs. Our existence apart from our (objective) existence in Jesus Christ is an "abstraction" in Barth's special (actualist) sense of the term. Our existence apart from Christ, in whatever aspect, can be taken as the basic truth about us only by disregarding God's sovereign activity on our behalf. Concretely, we are who we are before God (and therefore objectively) only who we are in Jesus Christ (and therefore actually). Everything else about us is regarded as an abstraction destined to disappear. The counterintuitive nature of this claim is bound up with its eschatological character. For it is a claim about matters real, hidden, and yet to come, matters which for the time being are visible only to faith. In the following passage Barth nicely brings out the counterintuitive, eschatological nature of this objective soteriological claim:

The actual alteration of our existence, of all things, of the whole being of the world, is hidden from us in the sense that it cannot be observed or experienced except in this event, in the living Jesus Christ himself. The alteration of our situation effected in him is concealed as it were by a veil which our eyes cannot penetrate. Do we not walk by faith and not by sight (II Cor. 5:7)? Is not our life hid with Christ in God (Col. 3:3)? Yet its concealment, and the fact that we cannot "see" in this concealment, does not alter in the very least the fact that in this concealment (with Christ in God), in which we can know it only by faith, it is really our own life fully and radically renewed on the basis of and in correspondence with true reconciliation accomplished in Him. (IV/3, 317–18)

The idea of humanity's real presence in Christ can be further elucidated by noting that Barth characteristically did not think in terms of the "real" and the "ideal," but rather in terms of the "real" and the "unreal." Perhaps this point can best be made by drawing a contrast between Barth and Reinhold Niebuhr. Niebuhr exemplifies the kind of theology which thinks in terms of the real and the ideal. Niebuhr thought of love, for example, as representing an unattainable ideal. Although impossible to attain, the love ideal had at least two important functions. It served constantly to remind us of human sinfulness, and it stood as a warning against identifying any human achievements or institutions with the absolute. It was a critical standard which (without ever losing its status as an imperative) disclosed that human beings, no matter how hard they might try, would always fall short. Love, for Niebuhr, thus had to be described as an "impossible possibility," for human nature as such determined what could be called "real." Niebuhr's concept of the real was grounded in his anthropology of sin so that love, being unattainable in its essential fullness, could only be conceived as a critical but elusive ideality.[6]

Barth, by contrast, thought in terms of the real and the unreal. Whereas Niebuhr's thinking about "reality" was anthropocentric, Barth's was theocentric. It was God who set the terms for what was real. Anything opposed, hostile, or contrary to the reality of God was "unreal" by definition. Therefore for Barth the "impossible possibility" was not love but sin. Sin (and sinful human beings) existed in a netherworld of unreality. Sin's origin was inexplicable, its status was deeply conflicted, and its destiny was to vanish. Meanwhile, it was actually there and had somehow to be taken into account, but (being essentially absurd) it could only be described in paradoxical terms. It was an impossible possibility and an unreal reality. Since God's love in Jesus Christ established Barth's concept of the real, his anthropology of sin had to be articulated in terms of the shadowy, the conflicted, the unreal (IV/1, 408–10). Thus Barth and Niebuhr both used the term "impossible possibility," but in diametrically opposite ways. What for Barth was the touchstone of reality (love) was for Niebuhr the "impossible possibility," whereas what for Barth was the "impossible possibility" (sin) was for Niebuhr the touchstone of reality.

In this light we may return to Barth's idea of humanity's real presence in Jesus Christ. Humanity's presence in Christ as an objective, eschatological reality was conceived as the soteriological counterpart to humanity's unstable existence in sin as an objective, eschatological "unreality." Left to itself, humanity's existence in sin could be resolved only by a dissolution into chaos. But the human race had not been left to itself. Its inclusion in Jesus Christ, now hidden though revealed to faith, was the ultimate truth of its destiny. For by virtue of God's sovereign activity, the human entanglement in sin and its conflicts was destined to disappear. Barth's ethics thus constantly took the form of saying: "Become who and what you are! Become who you truly are in Jesus Christ!" For that was one's true humanity—real, hid with Christ in God, yet to come. Everything else about one was destined to disappear.

The Motif of Personalism

The motif of personalism may be dealt with initially in this context. If objectivism were to be too strongly or too one-sidedly emphasized, the conclusion might easily be drawn that Barth propounded a scholastic, disengaged, or soulless form of theology. Yet the objectivist motifs in his theology, whether revelational or soteriological, were there in no small measure for the sake of the personalistic side. They were there to make it possible to speak irrevocably and responsibly about the personalism of our human encounter with God as confessed by faith. The objective side was meant not to deny but to establish the framework of God's personal encounter with us, and of our encounter with God. In Jesus Christ the innermost reality of God's life had bound itself to the innermost reality of our own. Therefore it was all the more imperative that this most intimate of personal encounters be secured against misunderstanding.

The great misunderstanding, especially in modern times, Barth believed, was to suppose that a personal encounter with God was somehow given with the structure of human nature itself. It was to suppose that in the depths of human self-consciousness or human moral experience, God was somehow waiting to be discovered and encountered. The condition for the possibility of encountering God was thus found in the depths of human subjectivity or in some other privileged aspect of human nature itself. Yet when our personal encounter with God was understood in these terms—the terms set by human nature—it was inevitable, Barth argued, that two things would and did eventually happen. First, Jesus Christ would cease to be understood unequivocally as the Lord; and second, we ourselves would consequently come to usurp the center which rightfully belongs to him. Rather than understanding ourselves from him, we would come to understand him from ourselves. Rather than take him on his own terms as the Lord—as God's unique, final, and binding revelation—we would take him on our own terms as a postulate of our experience—"as an ideal case or an idea of our possibility and our reality" (II/1, 150).

To prevent this misunderstanding, Barth sought to retain the personalism of humanity's encounter with God by radically reconceptualizing it. This encounter with God, he argued, was mediated, not immmediate, and was given by grace, not by nature. The encounter was objectively mediated by Jesus Christ, and given only by the free decision of God. The condition for its possibility was thus extrinsic, not intrinsic, to human nature. Humanity's personal encounter with God, Barth proposed, could not be understood, if one failed to see that it takes place in and with

Jesus Christ. The encounter so bound Christ to human beings subjectively that it marked him off against them objectively, and it so subjectively bound them to him that he stood unsurpassably above them as the Lord, while they stood appropriately and honorably beneath as his servants (II/1, 150). Except in this irreversible order, Jesus Christ did not encounter them as the one he is, nor did they otherwise come to be who they are in him. In this ordering it was clear that a personal encounter with God was not given to humanity by nature (as, for example, in the depths of human self-consciousness) but only by God's free decision of grace (as, for example, in the event of pretemporal election, in which God graciously determined to be our God, and to make us be God's people, in Jesus Christ). Above all, in this ordering no anthropological structure or experience would swallow up the mystery of Jesus Christ's identity; he would be acknowledged unequivocally for who he is as the one Mediator of God to us and of us to God. He could not be misunderstood as a mere postulate of human experience, for he was instead its living and objective presupposition. He was to be understood neither as an idea nor as an ideal case of what might be humanly possible or real, but instead as both the acting subject and the event of something far transcending all human possibility and reality, namely, the personalism of our salvation.

The personalist motif shows up most obviously whenever Barth speaks in terms of I–Thou relations. In Jesus Christ (objectivism), God establishes an active, historical relationship with us (actualism), a relationship of love and freedom, and thus a relationship of deepest intimacy (personalism). It is the event of an I–Thou relationship. "God comes before us," writes Barth, "as the one who addresses us and who is to be addressed in return"—as an "I" who addresses us as "thou" and to whom we may freely say "Thou" in response (II/1, 58). The Word by which God comes to us, by which God addresses and encounters us, is Jesus Christ. We have our true being only as we are addressed and encountered, only as we come before God, in him. Objectivism is the external basis of personalism, and personalism is the internal basis of objectivism. Objectivism is the condition which makes personalism possible, and personalism is the goal which objectivism establishes and entails. Being incorporated into Jesus Christ is the necessary and sufficient condition of our encounter with God, and personal encounter with God is the necessary and sufficient goal of our incorporation into him. Through Jesus Christ, through his mediatorial person and work, we are drawn (individually and communally) into the mysterious dynamics of God's own inner life. We come to be partakers of the eternal love and freedom which constitute God's innermost trinitarian being. We are made capable in Jesus Christ of what for us (as mere creatures and especially as sinners) would otherwise be impossible—an I–Thou relationship (or pattern of relationships) in the eternal life of the triune God. The transitory and sinful creature is lifted up in Jesus Christ to an eternal life of love and freedom in and with the Trinity. This encounter, as initiated here and now, and culminated in the life to come, is the core of the personalistic motif.

Two More Motifs:
A Detailed Survey

The Motif of Realism

"Realism," the fifth motif, designates the way Barth interprets theological language. Theological language, as represented by scripture (or based on it), is understood to refer to its subject matter by way of analogy, to address its subject matter to the whole person, to convey its subject matter with certainty, and to narrate its subject matter in the form of legendary witness. The realism of this interpretation can be indicated in each case by contrasting it with two alternative views, which for the sake of convenience will be called "literalism" and "expressivism." Barth's realism, which transcends these views while incorporating elements of each, differs from them primarily in its construal of the subject matter.[1]

Theological language, as Barth understands it, refers to its subject matter by way of analogy. Analogy, as a category for the mode of reference, has several advantages. It admits the incapacity of human language to refer to God, it respects the essential mystery of the subject matter, and yet it also allows for the occurrence of genuine and proper reference. The incapacity of human language in itself and as such is what separates Barth's view from literalism. Literalism, as I am here using the term, tends to assume that human language is intrinsically capable of referring to God, and that the mode of linguistic reference is "univocal." No discrepancy is thought to exist between the signifier (human words) and the signified (God). On this assumption the linguistic form as such (scripture) tends to become an independent source of revelation, thereby (as Barth sees it) displacing the sovereign activity of God; furthermore, God's essential otherness tends to be underestimated, thereby blurring the basic distinction between Creator and creature. For both these reasons Barth rejects the idea of literal or univocal reference (I/1, 321; II/1, 310).

The occurrence of genuine and proper reference, on the other hand, is largely what separates Barth's view from expressivism. Expressivism, as I am using the term, tends to assume that theological language is symbolic of certain emotive or noncognitive experiences, and that as such its mode of referring to God is basically "equivocal." A fundamental discrepancy is thought to exist between the signifier (emotive symbols) and the signified (the divine source from which such symbols derive). The emotive symbols of theological language, it is stressed, are not to be taken literally, for in themselves they are essentially incapable of conveying any cognitive information about God or of supplying any definite predicates of God. They are far more symbolic of emotive experience than of its divine source. Their linguistic form may vary greatly while their content remains (or is thought to remain) the same. From Barth's standpoint expressivism has a better appreciation of God's linguistic transcendence than does literalism, but literalism has a better appreciation of God's readiness to be known. Whereas literalism underestimates the mystery of God's otherness, expressivism underestimates the miracle of God's self-revelation. We may indeed speak in an authentically informative way about God, Barth believes, but only because the miracle of divine grace has designed to overcome our intrinsic linguistic incapacity. Although intrinsically incapable by nature, theological language has been made to correspond to its subject matter by grace. Its mode of reference is thus conceived as being neither univocal nor equivocal, but analogical. It is at once like and unlike its subject matter. Yet what is most distinctive is not simply the conception of analogical reference, but its being viewed as an event dependent on the miracle of grace (II/1, 210; III/1, 379; IV/3, 118).

Barth's realism differed from literalism and expressivism with respect not only to the "mode of reference," but also to the "mode of address." Theological language, as Barth understood it, addressed its subject matter to the whole person. By contrast, literalism and expressivism each tended, whether implicitly or explicitly, to single out some special aspect of human nature as having privileged access to divine revelation (as variously conceived). Literalism, for which the linguistic form of revelation was essentially propositional, tended to grant privileged status to modes of apprehension and address that were cognitive. Expressivism, on the other hand, for which the linguistic form was essentially symbolic, tended to grant privileged status to modes of apprehension and address that were emotive. Perhaps without great exaggeration it may be said that literalism saw revelation as addressed to the head without the heart, whereas expressivism saw it as addressed to the heart without the head. From Barth's standpoint, both failed to see that revelation was primarily a form of personal address from God to the whole person as mediated through the witness (in word and deed) of the church. Both underestimated the primacy of God as the acting and addressing subject—the one by focusing abstractly on the neutral proposition, and the other by focusing on the vacuous symbol. Either way, revelation was overlooked as an essentially "kerygmatic" event (with a linguistic form, or set of forms, to match)— an event of personal encounter that was as wholly self-involving for the initiator (God) as for the recipient (the human being). No special aspect of human nature could be singled out as gaining privileged access to this event, nor could any aspect be excluded on principle. The cognitive, the affective, the practical, even the conative or instinctual life of the recipient were all implicated, and *any* one of these aspects might take the ascendency, depending on the contingencies of the situation. A life-transforming response was to be enacted by the recipient at every level, in gratitude for the life of total self-giving enacted in grace on our behalf by the self-revealing God.

Not only the mode of reference and the mode of address, but also the "mode of certainty" distinguished Barth's realism from the other two views of theological language. Literalism—with its emphasis on univocal reference, propositional revelation, and cognitive address—assumed a mode of certainty which tended to be "absolute" with a neutrality that was virtually mathematical. Theological truth was thought to be true in much the same sense that numerical calculations were true. Theological propositions were either true or false, and when they were true we could be certain of them. Expressivism, on the other hand—with its emphasis on equivocal reference, emotive revelation, and noncognitive address—assumed a mode of certainty which tended to be "relative" with a discretion that was virtually aesthetic. Theological truth was thought to be true in much the same sense that poetry was true. Theological symbols were not so much true or false as functional or dysfunctional with regard to evoking emotive experience; when they were thought to be functional, we could be certain only of their "truth" for us.

By contrast, Barth's realism—with its emphasis on analogical reference, kerygmatic revelation, and self-involving address—assumed a mode of certainty which might best be described as merely "sufficient," though with a complexity that was virtually eschatological. Theological truth was thought to be in a category by itself. Although not neutral it was objective, and although not discretionary it was provisional. It was not neutral, because it was always self-involving. Yet it was objective, because its validity did not depend on our experience of it or on our right use of it in our lives. It was not discretionary, because its normative modes of thought had been given by God in the event of self-revelation. Yet it was provisional, because no human assertion of it could ever adequately or exhaustively reflect it, though by grace such an assertion could be appropriate in and for a given situation. Theological certainty in this life thus had what might be called a twofold mode: one intrinsic to the subject matter ("the view from above") and one intrinsic to the situation ("the view from below"). Barth often spoke of certainty in the strongest possible terms when taking the view from above. Yet elsewhere he would also speak of it from below, throwing out, as it were, a dialectical counterweight meant to qualify but not to weaken the view from above. Between the clarity intrinsic to the subject matter and the ambiguities intrinsic to our fallen and creaturely situation, it was considered possible to wrest sufficient certainty, whether cognitive or existential, for us to hear and repeat the Word of God, that we and others might come to trust and obey it in life and in death (II/1, 7, 24, 249, 251, 439).

Finally, Barth understood the "mode of narration" in scripture differently from the other two views. Whereas the biblical narratives were construed by literalism as "factual reports," and by expressivism as "mythological pictures," Barth construed them as "legendary witnesses." By regarding the biblical narratives as factual reports, literalism viewed the mode of narration in essentially "precritical" terms. Even when modern historical–critical tools were employed (as literalists found it increasingly difficult to avoid doing), they were pressed in the service of arguments that no discrepancy (or serious discrepancy) existed between narrative "report" and historical "fact." A similar lack of discrepancy was argued to exist among the various narrative "reports" themselves. The perfect or univocal fit between word and object assumed in matters of reference to God was reiterated in matters of history. (Thus literalists typically held that the Bible, in both its narrative and nonnarrative portions, was factually "inerrant" or "infallible.")

By regarding the biblical narratives as mythological pictures, on the other hand, expressivism viewed the mode of narration in essentially modern or "critical" terms. Modern historical–critical tools were pressed in the service of arguments that vast discrepancies existed between the narratives and the events they depicted. Similar discrepancies were discovered among the various narratives themselves. The imperfect or equivocal fit between word and object assumed in matters of reference to God was, not unlike the previous case, reiterated in matters of history. When the divorce between narrative and history was not thought to evacuate the texts of theological significance (and quite often it was not), then that significance was typically found in the following way. First the narrative depiction was construed as "mythological" (or "symbolic" or "metaphorical," etc.); then the mythic element (putatively of universal significance) was interpreted for its contemporary relevance. Not surprisingly, that significance and relevance typically turned out to be essentially noncognitive and emotive.

By regarding the biblical narratives as legendary witnesses, Barth, in contrast to the previous views, construed the mode of narration in essentially "postcritical" terms. The results of modern historical criticism were neither simply accepted nor simply rejected. Rather, even at their most compelling, they were conceived as essentially external to the theological task, for the subject matter of theology was, by definition, categorically beyond their reach. For example, traditional dogmas such as the creation of the world *ex nihilo,* the incarnation of the eternal Word of God, and the resurrection of Jesus from the dead were, in the nature of the case, beyond the competence of historical–critical method. Narratives about the world's creation, the virgin birth, and the empty tomb were, as historical criticism had helped us to see, presented unmistakably in the form of imaginative and legendary depictions. But if such narratives were not to be taken as "factual reports," neither were they to be construed as "mythological pictures." "Myth" was an appropriate category only for narratives in which the subject matter purports to be universally and conceptually accessible. The biblical narratives, however, as Barth (and the historic creeds of the church) read them, were not about ideas or universals (not even the idea of an experiential–emotive universal), but about unique and unrepeatable events. "Legend" (or, to use the more obscure term preferred by Barth, "saga") was thus the more generically appropriate term. Unlike other proposals, it allowed for two things at once: a narrative form that was truly imaginative and a narrative content that, while unprecedented, was truly eventful (I/1, 326–29; III/1, 80–94; IV/2, 478–79).

The biblical narratives, as Barth understood them, functioned as "witnesses." Their imaginative, legendary form—far from being damaging (as literalists feared and historical critics readily assumed)—was actually intrinsic to their theological content. The form was appropriate to the subject matter, because the subject matter was beyond ordinary depiction. Events like the creation, the incarnation, and the resurrection were, by virtue of their legendary narration, aptly and profoundly depicted for what they actually were claimed to be: events real though inconceivable and inconceivable though real. The work of divine inspiration in the formation of the narratives was not precluded by the work of human imagination, nor did the inventiveness involved in the work of human imagination necessarily preclude divine inspiration. Human imagination, disciplined by the mystery of the subject matter (in and with the history of the transmission of the traditions), was construed as the source from which the narratives were proximately produced. The narratives did not refer to historical "facts" as conceived by modernity, nor did they merely express emotive "experiences." They bore "good enough" witness to the living divine subject, by whom revelatory events had been enacted, for whom their scriptural depictions functioned as identifying descriptions, through whom the depictions themselves had been shaped, and by whose grace they served as a means of personal address to those who received them in the present. The narratives were thus understood to have been created for kerygmatic purposes, the divine self-witness taking place through the medium of a disciplined and imaginative human narrational response. The authoritative and referential aspect of the narratives was not so much the literal details as the underlying patterns and structures (although the details were the carriers of the patterns and thus could not be dispensed with). The mode of reference, furthermore, was once again conceived to be analogical. The narrative patterns stood, both historically and theologically, in analogical relation to their subject matter, regardless of the results or the limits of modern critical methods. At once historically grounded, humanly imagined, and divinely inspired, the narratives bore appropriate analogical witness to the kerygmatic presence of the risen Christ and the living God.[2]

Barth's realist understanding of theological language may thus be summed up as follows: the mode of reference was conceived as analogical (rather than univocal or equivocal), the mode of address as self-involving (rather than merely cognitive or emotive), the mode of certainty as sufficient (rather than absolute or relative), and the mode of narration as one of legendary witness (rather than one of factual report or mythological expression). In each case Barth differed from literalist and expressivist understandings of theological language by regarding the subject matter strictly as the presence of the living divine subject—the God who engages in personal address by acting mysteriously in history, and who acts mysteriously in history by engaging in personal address.[3]

The Motif of Rationalism

The final motif to be considered will, with some hesitation, be called "rationalism." Here again it must be emphasized that—as is also true for each of the previous motifs—the term is meant to be defined by Barth's theology, not Barth's theology by the term. Rationalism as conventionally understood in philosophy has almost nothing to do with what is intended here. It has nothing to do, for example, with the idea that theological truth is somehow to be established by relying on reason alone, or with the idea that reason in itself is a source of knowledge superior to and independent of revelation, or that reason establishes the fundamental criteria in the solution of theological problems. On the contrary, the rationalism peculiar to Barth's theology, being internal and not external to faith, might instead be described as "reason within the limits of revelation alone." Faith in revelation is understood as the inviolable presupposition on whose basis rational reflection in theology is to occur. "Faith seeking understanding," as Barth appropriated the phrase from Anselm, meant seeking to understand the content of faith strictly within the limits of faith. The nature of the *intellectus fidei*—faith's critical understanding of itself through rational reflection—can be presented, in the sense Barth conceived of it, under two organizing rubrics: "no knowledge without faith" and "no faith without knowledge."

No Knowledge Without Faith

"No knowledge without faith" is meant to suggest the critical limits that Barth constantly described as essential to the knowledge of faith. Faith seeking understanding meant, in no small measure, faith seeking the limits of understanding, faith seeking to understand the extent to which we actually *can* understand, and thus faith seeking to understand precisely what it is that we *cannot* understand. Critical limits to the *intellectus fidei* can be brought to light by noticing the extent to which Barth's theological rationalism was circumscribed by some of the other motifs. "No knowledge without faith" can then be explained to mean that in the *intellectus fidei* there is no neutrality, no speculation, no apologetics, and no system.

No Neutrality

"No neutrality" in the *intellectus fidei* followed from the way that rationalism in Barth's theology was strictly circumscribed by the motif of *personalism*. The rejection of neutrality was a way not only of doing justice to the subject matter, but also of avoiding the pitfalls of rational orthodoxy (which was typically unable to explain how to integrate the personalist and rationalist dimensions; it was unable to account adequately for the context of personal encounter within which rational reflection in theology was to occur). Neutral understanding was impossible for faith, precisely because faith by definition was self-involving—a living response to personal encounter with the living God. Neutrality (though not knowledge) was thus precluded by the holistic nature of faith—a point that could be made with reference to either the concept of faith or the concept of knowledge. As a committed stance with objective content, faith might be presented in a variety of ways. Barth typically preferred to diversify the idiom in order to suggest that the subject matter always transcends any formulations we might devise for it.

Consider two formulations of the relationship between faith and knowledge. The one goes like this: *"Pistis* says more than *gnosis,* but in all circumstances it says *gnosis* too" (I/1, 229). Yet in another formulation the two terms are so related that knowledge is described as "the determination of faith as a whole" (II/1, 17). The first formulation is more straightforward; the second, more dialectical. The first suggests a relation which is perhaps more quantitative; the second, one more qualitative. The first starts by describing faith as trust and then goes on to state that, as trust, faith always includes the aspect of knowledge while yet being more than knowledge. The second, by contrast, starts with the concept of faith as a whole and then goes on to state that, taken as a whole, faith has several qualitative determinants, knowledge being irreducibly among them (the others are love, trust, and obedience). Either way, however—whether as a single aspect or as a determination of the whole—knowledge as the knowledge of faith always meant fundamentally the *union* of the knower with God and only secondarily (yet still inalienably) the *rational content* of that knowledge. "Knowledge," as Barth used it, was thus an ambiguous term, embracing both personal and cognitive elements. This ambiguity, as he was capable of explaining at length, he found embedded in biblical usage itself (IV/3, 183–85). It was the primacy of the personal over the rational, however, in our knowledge of God which ruled out mere neutrality and required theology to proceed from a stance of self-involvement. "Theological work is surely inconceivable and impossible at any time," he thus wrote, "without prayer" (IV/3, 882).

No Speculation

"No speculation" was a maxim which followed from the way that rationalism in the *intellectus fidei* was circumscribed by the motif of *particularism*. Indeed, particularism was a mode of thought expressly designed to forestall speculation. Speculation designates, in the Barthian lexicon, just that procedure which seeks to move from the general to the particular, from an a priori understanding of what sorts of things are generally possible and actual (as established by reason apart from faith) to an understanding of what sorts of things are possible and actual in theology. Thus, for example, in interpreting biblical texts, speculation would be the assumption that we already have a basic knowledge of what can or cannot have happened, and that the statements of the text are thereby to be interpreted accordingly (I/2, 724–25). The events which are presupposed or depicted by the text would be assessed on that prior basis as real, potentially real, doubtful, or illusory. By contrast, an interpretation not so circumscribed could allow the text to speak on its own terms of what is possible. It could allow our general sense of possibility to be challenged and broadened, perhaps eventually to be shattered and recast. In certain circumstances it might even, for the sake of faith seeking understanding, admit "possibilities which hitherto and in other circumstances we regarded as impossibilities" (I/2, 724–25). In short, speculation would subject the text to our sense of possibility, whereas particularism would subject our sense of possibility to the text.

More broadly, speculation is a term used to designate the deriving of doctrine from anything other than the biblical witness to Jesus Christ as the center and norm of God's self-revelation. For example, when developing his doctrine of election, Barth rejects certain older Reformed versions of the doctrine on the grounds that they removed the original decree of election to a divine sphere that was somehow beyond the reach of christology. But, Barth objected, such a sphere "could not in fact be known as Christian truth," and thus no sure knowledge of election would be possible, for election had been set "in the light of a purely speculative axiom." The alternative was to understand the decision of election to have taken place not above and behind, but in Christ, who was actually definitive of that sphere where the original decree took place (II/2, 69). In short, the rejection of "speculation" was the rejection of any rational reflection—whether in biblical interpretation or in doctrinal construction—which proceeded as though valid inferences could be drawn on some other basis than assertions about Jesus Christ as attested in scripture (cf. I/2, 720).

No Apologetics

"No apologetics" was a maxim which followed largely from the way that rationalism in the *intellectus fidei* was circumscribed by the motifs of *personalism* and *particularism*. Whereas personalism meant that theological truth could never be understood as other than self-involving, and particularism meant that theological truth could never be grounded in anything other than itself, apologetics (of the kind Barth rejected) defended theological truth as if it were something netural, and capable of being grounded in general possibilities otherwise known to us. Apologetics in this sense was the attempt to validate the truth claims of Christian theology by means of rational reflection. Such validation would show that these truth claims are either not precluded or else, more strongly, are actually required (or are at least confirmed) by certain philosophical principles, or by the results of certain historical or scientific research. Apologetics might also attempt to show that Christian beliefs are commendable, because they enable us to obtain certain ends which we know on other grounds to be valuable or beneficial. The validity of Christian theology—its possibility, its necessity, or its instrumentality—is thus to be demonstrated on external grounds. The problem with apologetics, as Barth saw it, was that apologetics so conceived amounts to a denial of revelation. Revelation is denied whenever its necessity and sufficiency to impart itself are circumscribed or whenever its content is subjected to alien standards. Apologetics attempts to validate revelation by subjecting it to standards acquired from elsewhere. Revelation, however, cannot be confirmed, commended, or even adequately construed by such standards, because they are simply inapplicable to a subject matter whose content by definition is as radically singular and unique as Barth conceived it to be. Revelation so conceived is received by faith or not at all. *"Credere* is to believe," writes Barth. "But we cannot believe and yet at the same time not believe but want to know [on independent grounds]. This is not to believe at all" (III/3, 403). Revelation is "its own basis," and the Holy Spirit is "the only conclusive argument" (IV/3, 109). "Faith dares to trust the Holy Spirit" (III/3, 403).

No System

"No system," finally, was a maxim which followed from the way that rationalism in the *intellectus fidei* was circumscribed by the motifs of *particularism* and *actualism*. Whereas particularism meant that revelation could not be understood as other than mysterious, and actualism that it could not be understood as other than miraculous, systematization in theology was the attempt to explicate revelation by means of regular and formal patterns accessible to sheer or autonomous reason. The quest for a "system" would be the quest for a general conceptual scheme capable of encompassing the totality of relevant terms and of explaining more or less exhaustively their underlying formal unity. The whole and its parts (the unity of the totality) would thus be subject to rational apperception, explanation, and formalization. But (if anything) only concepts and principles, not persons and histories, could be systematized in this way, to say nothing of a mysterious person available to us only by way of a miraculous history, as Jesus Christ is affirmed to be by faith. The name of Jesus Christ, wrote Barth, "is not a system representing a unified experience or a unified thought; it is the Word of God itself" (I/1, 181). "There must not be any systematization, or setting up of a principle. . . . For the Gospel is what it is in the divine–human person of Jesus Christ himself. And this person does not permit himself to be translated into a proposition" (II/2, 73). The explication of revelation will thus always be "less a system than the report of an event" (I/1, 280), and the event concerned will have to be understood under a diversified variety of concepts rather than a unified conceptual scheme.

Everything depends, Barth argued, on whether our rational reflection remains bound to the subject matter of revelation. But this subject matter as such is mysterious and elusive. Our rational reflection does not really have of itself the power to keep true to this subject matter, "or even in the first instance to grasp it" (II/1, 588). In relation to this subject matter, therefore, our rationality itself is so far from being able to construct a system, that it too can finally be understood not as a neutral capacity but only as an event. In this case "our rationality is conferred on us solely by the fact that we really hear what God has to say to us, so that if we failed to do so we would cease to be a rational being" (III/2, 130). The mystery and miracle of the subject matter find their parallel not only in the conceptual diversity and nonsystematizability of its explication, but also in the miracle and mystery of its mode of rational apperception.

Summary

"No knowledge without faith," therefore, means that faith itself establishes the peculiar kind of knowledge that is possible within the web of Christian belief. This knowledge is not neutral, because engagement is inseparable from its conent. It is not speculative, because its content is not grounded in possibilities external to its christocentric subject matter. It is not apologetic, because it does not commend itself on external grounds. And it is not systematic, because it cannot be explicated within the scope of a formally unified conceptual scheme. The knowledge of faith might thus be said to be, in various ways, self-involving, self-grounded, self-commending, and self-interpreting.

No Faith Without Knowledge

"No faith without knowledge," on the other hand, is meant to suggest that faith was never conceived (in the *Church Dogmatics*) as anything other than intrinsically rational. Faith was impelled to seek understanding, precisely because cognitive content was one of its direct and essential constituents. The rational explication of this content was a way not only of doing justice to the subject matter, but also of avoiding the pitfalls of theological liberalism. Like rational orthodoxy, liberalism was typically unable to integrate the personalist and rationalist dimensions of faith, but for nearly opposite reasons. For liberalism, any cognitive content implicit in faith could not be directly explicated. It could not be grasped in terms of the idiom native to faith, but (typically) only in terms of some other conceptual language. Only when the essentially emotive symbols of faith were correlated with this other, properly denotive language—whether philosophical, historical, sociological, psychological, or whatever—could the objective references implicit in faith be identified and understood. The cognitive deficit of the emotive symbol was thus to be remedied by means of correlation. Faith had no cognitive content which its own ordinary, emotive language could possibly denote. That content could be denoted (and explicated) only by other domains of discourse.

Barth, by contrast, refused to step outside the discourse of faith in order to explicate the content of faith. He refused to surrender its content to the necessity of external identification and description. He did not construe this discourse as merely (or essentially) emotive. Reflective discourse was thus not to be distinguished from ordinary discourse by divorcing the cognitive from the emotive, the denotative from the connotative, and the rational from the personal (or "experiential"). Regardless of whether or how the content of faith might or might not show up in other domains of discourse, nowhere else did it (or could it) show up in all its proper uniqueness and singularity than in the discourse of faith. The ordinary language of faith, as displayed normatively in scripture, was thus the direct and fitting object of theological reflection. Although never to be confused with divine truth itself, and therefore always in need of the miracle of grace in order to be true, this language was (among other things) still denotative and thus included within itself a significant cognitive dimension. Because the rationality of faith was intrinsic to the language of faith, reflective discourse differed from ordinary discourse more nearly by function than by kind. Reflective discourse (theology) functioned to elucidate the conceptual implications of the ordinary language of faith. The alternative Barth posed to the liberal project of correlating noncognitive religious symbols with denotative concepts can thus be described as a form of coherentism.

"Anselmian coherentism" might serve as a fitting overall designation to characterize the positive implications of "no faith without knowledge." "Faith seeking understanding," the famous Anselmian phrase, meant in Barth's theology "faith seeking to understand the implications of the cognitive content intrinsic to faith." The *intellectus fidei* was a matter of faith coming to display its own peculiar and intrinsic rationality. Theology, as the reflective discourse by which the *intellectus fidei* was worked out, can thus be described, formally, as a set of internal logical relations and, materially, as a set of internal cognitive relations (where "cognitive" stands for a range of epistemic and ontic considerations). Theology so conceived is a form of coherentism in the sense that no theological assertions and beliefs can be justified independently of other theological assertions and beliefs—all of which are rooted directly or indirectly in faith. Theology as a set of internal logical and cognitive relations can thus be explained by noting several "rationalist" procedures: deriving, grounding, ordering, testing, and assimilating.

The Procedure of Deriving

"Deriving" is meant to indicate that aspect of the *intellectus fidei* which engages in the construction of doctrines. Doctrines, as Barth understood them, are derived in a coherentist fashion (that is, from within the circle of faith); once constructed, they are regarded as constitutive, not merely as regulative, in status. Although they can and do function as rules, they are also (and perhaps primarily) legitimate extensions and clarifications of the knowledge of faith. Constructing a doctrine is a logically complex process which resists the possibility of exhaustive formal description. Nonetheless, some recurring general features may be noted in Barth's practice of construction. Perhaps the most important feature is that doctrines are understood to be hermeneutically based (I/1, 308–11). Doctrines arise from and point back to the interpretation of scripture. Scripture as a whole is interpreted to bring out its essential underlying conceptual patterns as they converge upon and are clarified by the name and narrative of Jesus Christ.

The status of warranted assertions is ascribed to certain complex beliefs which are themselves derived from scriptural interpretation. That God has engaged in an act of self-revelation, that the Bible is the Word of God, that Jesus Christ is the center and norm of the scriptural witness, that Jesus Christ is at once fully God and fully human, are all examples of beliefs to which warranted assertability is ascribed. Their epistemic justification is understood to be confessional and hermeneutical (and thus, formally speaking, coherentist). Once a belief achieves the status of warranted assertability, however, it can then become the basis for further doctrinal construction. Examples of the constructive process have already been presented earlier in this discussion. The doctrine of the Trinity, as Barth understands it, was said to be derived not only from exegetical considerations, but (more conceptually) from the belief that God's being is no different in itself than it is in relation to us, which is itself an inference from the hermeneutically warranted assertion that God has engaged in an act of self-revelation. (That God's being in itself is a being of love and freedom was also said to be derived by a similar process of inference.) Once established, a doctrine like the doctrine of the Trinity can then itself sometimes become the basis for further doctrinal construction—as, for example, when God's own mode of temporality (i.e., eternity) is construed not (as is common) as mere "timelessness," but according to trinitarian patterns as a mysterious and fluid conjunction of simultaneity and sequence (II/1, 615, 639–40).

The point is that, for Barth, the doctrine of God's internal trinitarian relations, though derived by a chain of inference, is taken as a matter of real knowledge which can itself be the basis for the development of further theological knowledge. The doctrine is thus not regarded as a mere postulate whose function would be exclusively (or primarily) regulative, and whose status would be merely hypothetical. On the other hand, the constitutive and cognitive status of the doctrine does not rule out a regulative hermeneutical function. Through a kind of doctrinal–hermeneutical feedback loop, the results of doctrinal construction, having arisen (however complexly) from scripture, can then be brought to bear on the interpretation of scripture. The result, in the hands of a master like Barth, can be a hermeneutic of close textual readings richly informed by doctrinal considerations not immediately suggested by the text itself but rather by a deepened appreciation for the larger dogmatic or hermeneutical context. Derived from a complex of exegetically based doctrines and doctrinally based exegesis, it is the sort of reading which can be the despair of literalists and technicians while yet enhancing the faith and preaching of the church.[4]

The Procedure of Grounding

"Grounding" is meant to indicate that aspect of the *intellectus fidei* which thinks about relations of necessity, possibility, and actuality. Revelation itself is thought to put the question of these relations to us, and the act of theological understanding is precisely the act of taking up that question and attempting to answer it. "What is the necessary and sufficient condition for the possibility of the occurrence of a given actuality?" This question often dominates the pattern of argumentation in the *Church Dogmatics*. A certain actuality is taken as a given (usually on the basis of Holy Scripture). The question is then posed about what makes this actuality possible. What condition or set of conditions had to be met in order for this actuality to have occurred? What conditions, had they not been met, would have made the occurrence of this actuality impossible? Given that this actuality did occur, what conditions were necessarily met?[5]

Such questions, for example, dominate much of Barth's discussion of our knowledge of God. The knowledge of God in the church is taken as a given event from which we can think, but for which we cannot argue (in any external or independent sense). Given the event of this knowledge, what conditions are presupposed within it as making it possible? The general outlines of Barth's answer can be stated rather simply. God is known, first, because God is ready to be known, and second, because we are ready to know God. God could not be known if either of these conditions were to remain unmet. God's readiness to be known (which is explained as a matter of God's freedom) and our readiness to know God (which is explained as a matter of our utter incapacity overcome in Christ by the freedom of God) are the conditions presupposed in the occurrence of the event. The event is thus grounded—and this is typical of Barth's theology—in the freedom of God, for not only the divine readiness but also ultimately the human readiness are seen to depend on it (II/1, 63–178). The unique possibilities which ground the unique actualities of God's revelation, and which cannot be known on any other basis than those actualities, are always expressions of God's freedom. Since no necessity precedes the freedom of God's will, all actualities ultimately find their possibility (however variously) as grounded in that freedom.

The Procedure of Ordering

"Ordering" is meant to indicate that aspect of the *intellectus fidei* which asks how the part is related to the whole and the whole to the part in Christian theology. Barth's sense of the interrelatedness of all Christian doctrine sometimes leads him to work with patterns of "dialectical inclusion," in which the part is included in the whole, and the whole in the part. Each part is thought to contain, from a certain vantage point, the entire structure. The part includes within itself the entire pattern and way of functioning of the whole. The part is not just a division of the whole but a reiteration of it. This mode of ordering shows up in the *Church Dogmatics* in large ways and in small. A small way is exemplified when Barth writes: "Everything that God is, is implied and included in the statement that he is patient" (a statement which is then worked out in some detail) (II/1, 408).

A much larger way, which can barely be touched on here, is exemplified by one of the most vexing matters in Barth's theology—namely, the question of how the modes of divine temporality are related to those of our human temporality. Each of the divine modes (whether "pretemporality," "supratemporality," or "posttemporality") is thought to include within itself the entire content of God's whole dealing with the creation. Where we might by common sense expect to find straightforward temporal distinctions, we instead find patterns of dialectical inclusion. Thus it sounds at some points as if everything of importance has already happened, at other points as if everything of importance is yet to come, and at still other points as if everything of importance occurs now in the present. Only a limited remark can be made here about this difficult material. Each temporal mode is understood to include and reiterate, from a particular standpoint, the content and pattern of God's whole relation to the world. Each mode distinctively embraces the entire structure within itself, yet without making the other two superfluous. The inclusion is "dialectical" in the sense that the content of the whole not only shows up simultaneously under mutually exclusive modes, but is also understood to proceed and develop sequentially from one mode to the next.[6]

Another aspect of ordering the relation between part and whole which ought not to go unmentioned has to do with what might be called the root metaphor in the *Church Dogmatics*. It is the metaphor of the circle comprising center and periphery—a metaphor which is constantly employed to bring out the centrality of Jesus Christ. The task of theology is to make clear at every point that Christ stands at the center of the gospel: "To explain the Gospel is to expound, unfold and articulate its content, with no effacement of its unity and simplicity, but rather in enhancement of its unity and simplicity. It is to assert and honor it synoptically in all its richness, displaying the place and manner of each individual part. It is also to make known the periphery in each section as that of the true center, and the center as in every respect that of the distinctive periphery" (IV/3, 850). Jesus Christ is understood as the central content of its witness, for Jesus Christ is the name of the God who deals graciously with sinful humanity. "To hear this is to hear the Bible—both as a whole and in each one of its separate parts. Not to hear this means *eo ipso* not to hear the Bible, neither as a whole, nor therefore in its parts." The one thing said in the midst of everything, the center which organizes the whole, is "just this: the name of Jesus Christ" (I/2, 720).

The Procedure of Testing

"Testing" or "substantiating" is meant to indicate that aspect of the *intellectus fidei* which justifies doctrinal beliefs not by direct appeals to scripture (although a scriptural foundation is, of course, presupposed), but by appeals to the relation of the part to the whole, and of the periphery to the center. This mode of doctrinal justification is at once Anselmian and coherentist in a strong sense. The Anselmian nature of the procedure is openly acknowledged by Barth. Describing the procedure as he finds it to be at work in Anselm, Barth writes: "Under the presupposition that this article of faith is true, Anselm examines and shows how far it is true. In so doing, he does not make use for the time being of the validity and authority of this article . . . , but demonstrates its basis and to that extent its rationality in the context of all the other articles of faith which are presupposed as valid and authoritative" (II/1, 92).

Faith, in standard coherentist fashion, is understood to be rational and intelligible only within a network of doctrines and beliefs. The validity of any particular doctrine or article of faith can be tested or substantiated by hypothetically suspending its validity and checking its coherence with the remaining network. Any particular doctrine must therefore be coherent not only with scripture but also with the whole network of scripturally derived doctrinal beliefs in which that doctrine has its place.

Coherence is to be tested not only in terms of relations between part and whole, but also at times in terms of relations between periphery and center. It is by virtue of relating the periphery to the center, for example, that Barth claims to "prove" or substantiate the dogma of creation. Jesus Christ is taken to be the known quantity, and creation to be the unknown quantity. The question is whether creation is a mere hypothesis or postulate, or whether it is actually a true and necessary article in the web of beliefs which constitute the knowledge of faith. The "unknown quantity" is shown to be true and necessary on the basis of the "known quantity" at the center of Christian doctrine. Just because Jesus Christ, the known quantity at the center, is "the Word by which God has fulfilled creation and continually maintains and rules it" (III/1, 28), we know that the Creator does not exist without the distinct reality of the creature, and that the creature does not exist without the distinct reality of the Creator, but that both exist in the differentiated unity of reconciliation accomplished in Christ by the omnipotent and incomprehensible love of God. It follows that the article here being tested as an unknown quantity can only be accorded the status of true and necessary knowledge. For it could not be denied this status at the periphery without that status also being denied at the center, where it is integral to the definition of Jesus Christ.

Barth can thus assert that it is in light of the known quantity (Jesus Christ) that the truth and necessity of the unknown quantity (creation) are to be perceived and understood. This justification of a "peripheral" belief by virtue of its relation to the "central" belief finally leads to the following extraordinary and otherwise counterintuitive summation:

> I believe in Jesus Christ, God's Son our Lord, in order to perceive and to understand that God the Almighty, the Father, is the Creator of heaven and earth. If I did not believe the former, I could not perceive and understand the latter. If I perceive and understand the latter, my perception and understanding are completely established, sustained and impelled by my believing the former. Thus the confession of God the Creator belongs integrally to the rest of the confession. (III/1, 29)

Note that it is not belief in creation which has thus been established, but rather the perception of its essential truth and the understanding of its "intrasystemic" necessity. It is integral to the confession, because the center cannot be understood without it. It is integral as an object of true knowledge, because presupposed as such at the center. Coherence or consistency in the *Church Dogmatics* is always understood primarily in this intrasystemic or coherentist way. Doctrinal beliefs are tested and substantiated by virtue of their material coherence with the whole and especially by their coherence with the center of the whole.

The Procedure of Assimilating

"Assimilating," finally, is meant to indicate that aspect of the *intellectus fidei* which explicates the content of faith by critically appropriating concepts first used and developed outside the circle of Christian theology. Whereas the derivation of doctrines might be thought of as "analytic," the assimilation of concepts might be thought of as "synthetic." That is, whereas derivation proceeds by way of inference from beliefs (or statements of belief) established as doctrinally warranted, assimilation proceeds by way of critically rethinking or reconstructing concepts first devised elsewhere in order to make them compatible with Christian theology. Assimilation, it is important to note, exists in the service of derivation and therefore in the service of biblical interpretation. Concepts are critically reconstructed for the sake of illuminating the content of Christian doctrines and thus the content of the biblical witness. At the same time, the reconstruction of any given concept serves to highlight the critical distance between Christian theology and the body of thought from which the concept was taken (cf. II/2, 522–42).

For example, when the metaphysical idea of "being" (as that which neither comes to be nor perishes) is critically appropriated, then, in Barth's theology, it is thoroughly shattered and recast in terms of the idea of an "acting subject." To equate God with "being itself," a lifeless and inert entity, would be tantamount, Barth asserts, to equating God with death (II/1, 494). The idea of "being" can be made serviceable to the doctrine of God only if it is seen that the God of the biblical witness is always and everywhere indicated as "the living God." The idea of "being" can thus be made serviceable, Barth proposes, only by subordinating it to "God" and connecting it with "act" so that it can then be said that God's being is a "being in act" (II/1, 257–72). This critical assimilation of the concept of "being" is meant at once to explicate the doctrine of God, illuminate the biblical witness, and distance theology from all philosophies and philosophical theologies operating with the purely metaphysical concept.

Or to take another example, when the modern existentialist idea of "nothingness" (as the object of human anxiety and the essence of ulti-mate reality) is critically appropriated, then, in Barth's theology, it is thoroughly broken and recast in terms of the biblical idea of "chaos." Nothingness is thereby denied the status of ultimate reality, while at the same time its intrinsically evil character is intensified as that which ter-ribly but incomprehensibly disrupts and threatens the good creation. Barth can thus assert that, from a theological standpoint, existentialist philoso-phers like Heidegger and Sartre do not know what "real nothingness" is, even though they may well in some sense have encountered it. While "we may certainly learn from them, if we have not learned it already, a more intense and acute awareness," we cannot credit them with having adequately depicted the reality. Existentialist philosophy provides a use-ful and suggestive category of discernment, but little more (III/3, 345). For the category of "nothingness' takes on a very different meaning when assimilated into the network of Christian beliefs. It thus seems fair to say that in this case the line between critical assimilation and doctrinal deri-vation is kept tolerably clear. For even if there were no extrabiblical concept of nothingness to criticize and assimilate, sufficiently strong bib-lical warrants could be found for a theologian to explicate chaos as an opaque but nonultimate force which threatens to undo creation. The de-marcation between assimilation and derivation, however, is not always easy to discern, and the question arises whether at times they might not get confused.

A case in point, where an assimilated extrabiblical concept might seem to be presented as if it were biblically derived, would be Barth's inter-pretation of human nature in terms of "I–Thou relationships." Barth does say explicitly that he means to proceed by way of derivation: "The man Jesus is one nature with us, and we unreservedly with him. But this means that we are invited to infer from his human nature the character of our own, to know ourselves in him, but in him to know ourselves" (III/2, 54). As an inference, however, the interpretation could be dis-missed as forced. It would arguably be more consistent with Barth's ac-tual practice (and thus less perplexing) to suppose that what he really carries out is simply an act of appropriation from the writings of Confu-cius, Feuerbach, and Buber. Yet as Barth himself points out, his own concept of I–Thou relationships is, despite all similarities, rather different from theirs (III/2, 277). Any appropriation has obviously not been un-critical. A close reading of the argument, furthermore, indicates that the concept of I–Thou relationships is meant to interpret the idea of "cohu-manity" as "the basic form of humanity," and that that idea, in turn, is derived doctrinally from the idea of Jesus' humanity as a humanity of "self-giving" with us and for us, as well as hermeneutically from the idea of the *imago dei* as found in the Genesis creation narratives. Cohumanity is thus the derived doctrine, and I–Thou relationships is the assimilated concept. Although Barth might have done more to help his readers keep the distinction clear (especially because the assimilated concept is used greatly to amplify the derived doctrine well beyond anything tightly entailed by the material from which the doctrine was derived), it again does not seem unfair to assert that the distinction is tolerably maintained. Whereas the test for derived doctrines is, as shown earlier, strictly coherentist and hermeneutical, the test for assimilated concepts would seem simply to be usefulness and suggestiveness in explication.[7]

Summary

To sum up: "No faith without knowledge," as Barth understood it, can be explained to mean that, because faith is never less than cognitive, it is always impelled to understand itself in various ways. Faith cannot understand itself without *deriving* doctrines by which its content is clarified and by which the church's reading of scripture is enhanced. It cannot understand itself without *grounding* the events to which scripture testifies in the conditions that had to be met in order for those events to be possible. Again, faith cannot understand itself without *ordering* its content not only so that the whole is seen in relation to every part and every part in relation to the whole, but also so that the center is made known in relation to every aspect of the periphery and every aspect of the periphery is made known in relation to the center. Nor can faith understand itself without *testing* each particular doctrine for its material coherence with the web of belief centered in Christ as well as for its hermeneutical or scriptural adequacy. Nor, finally, can faith understand itself without *assimilating* extrabiblical concepts by critically reconstructing them in order to explicate doctrine, interpret scripture, and position theology polemically relative to other bodies of thought. Deriving, grounding, ordering, testing, and assimilating all presuppose that faith does not exist without possessing a cognitive content that it seeks to understand. And because they are all practices internal to faith as a self-involving personal commitment, they are the alternatives in Barth's theological rationalism to modes of understanding that are neutral, speculative, apologetic, and systematic.

When the motif of rationalism is considered in relation to that of realism, it becomes clear that Barth's theology attempts to combine aspects

of two different notions of truth—namely, those of coherence and correspondence—while going beyond each if taken by itself. Yet Barth's rationalist view of the *intellectus fidei* might at first seem to be incompatible
with his realist view of theological language. For the notions of truth,
knowledge, and language would seem to be different in each case. The
one views truth as coherence; the other, as correspondence. The one views
knowledge as warranted inference; the other, as accurate representation.
The one views language as the vehicle of inference; the other, as the
vehicle of representation.

It seems clear, however, that the rationalist view presupposes the realist view, rather than conflicting with it. Truth as coherence in the *intellectus fidei* presupposes truth as correspondence in the discourse of faith.
Likewise, knowledge as warranted inference presupposes knowledge as
accurate representation, and language as the vehicle of inference presupposes language as the vehicle of representation. Coherence would be
meaningless without presupposing correspondence, as would warranted
inference with accurate representation. Coherence gives the criterion of
truth; correspondence, (in part) the nature of truth. Coherence governs
internal relations of sense; correspondence, external relations of reference. Coherence, that is, governs internal relations of deriving, grounding, explicating, and testing; correspondence, external relations of analogical predication. Coherence of one judgment with another would be
meaningless, if the central theological judgments were not accepted as
independently true. Barth would not write (as he typically did) that "we
have taken a circular course" (i.e., a coherentist course), nor would he
regard that course as veracious, if he could not also appeal "to God's
revelation and grace as the necessity and basis of the right to move in
this particular circle" (i.e., as the actual necessity and basis of truth as
correspondence) (II/1, 244, 245).[8]

The mention of God's revelation and grace, however, not only because
they are revelation and grace, but especially because they are God's,
suggests that there is much more to truth in Barth's theology than simply
coherence and correspondence. Truth is a category governed by all the
motifs we have considered, not merely those of rationalism and realism.
A study of how the remaining motifs come to bear on the category of
truth will serve not only to deepen the previous discussion, but also to
explain in greater detail the significance of the motifs themselves.

The Motifs Applied: The Conception of Truth in the *Church Dogmatics*

PART II

The Maxims Applied:
The Conception of Truth
in the Christian Dogmatic

Truth as Event and as Unique in Kind

Actualism: Truth as Event

As the motif of actualism signifies, in Barth's theology truth is always conceived as an event. Truth is not a static datum, nor is it a fixed and deposited state of affairs. It is essentially a predicate of God's own living reality as the Lord. Truth is always therefore in essence identical with God's being itself—a divinely living truth, unified, yet rich and varied in its unity, a truth that continually assumes surprising and ever new forms in constancy with itself. This living truth is also a supremely sovereign truth. It is a truth that can and does speak for itself (and which can be known and received only as a truth that speaks for itself). It is a truth that, at God's own prerogative (and only at this prerogative), makes itself known with power. It is thus a truth that cannot be had without the consent and decision of the sovereign God, and therefore a truth that cannot be had in abstraction from an encounter with the person of the living God.

Because truth is a predicate of the living God, our human perception and reception of this truth can only be an ongoing event. They can only be understood as an event continually created and given by the living God as such. It is only by the continual bestowal of grace that God is knowable at all. God is not knowable as a given and passive entity that can be rationally apprehended and thereby controlled. On the contrary, the truth of God is a truth that is never behind us. It is a living truth that must always become truth anew. Even as a truth once given, it is something that goes continually before us, a truth that is always future. "The truth," writes Barth, "is in no sense assumed to be at hand. The truth comes, i.e., in the faith in which we begin to know, and cease, and begin again." It always involves a "fresh human effort," a fresh human start. "It always takes place on the narrow way which leads from the revelation once enacted to the revelation yet promised" (I/1, 15 rev.). The truth as received by faith is always an event that transcends and renews itself, because it is never less than an engagement with the vitality of God.

Moreover, because truth is a predicate of the God who is not only living but sovereign, our human perception and reception of this truth cannot be grounded in ourselves. In ourselves as mere creatures and indeed as complete sinners, we are simply incapable of perceiving and receiving this truth. It is something whose content transcends our human capacities. In the ongoing event in which just this truth is given and received, it is never given and received as anything other than that of which we are inherently incapable. This truth thus never comes in any other form than as a miracle. Its giving and receiving are an ongoing miraculous event whose possibility is to be found not in any creaturely or natural capacity, but strictly in the freedom of God. The faith by which we receive this truth is thus a faith whose being is purely in act. Faith has its being in the act of God by which it is evoked as a free human response. Faith does not occur in abstraction from the event in which God gives it, nor in abstraction from the event (the very same event) in which we receive it. Faith is the event of a free human decision that is continually to be renewed by the grace of God, in order that the freely given truth of God might be received. Faith is thus a miracle grounded in grace, enacted in freedom, and receptive of living divine truth.

This free giving and receiving of truth constitutes an ongoing history. In this history the words of faith become true with a truth which cannot be humanly controlled, bestowed, or proven. The words of faith become true only as witnesses to the truth which they cannot master, but which continually masters them. Yet as mastered by this truth, they are so drawn beyond themselves, by the sovereignty of grace, that they enter into analogical correspondence with the truth of God. It is a correspondence for which faith in itself has no capacity, over which it has no control, and on whose behalf it can offer no conclusive argument either for others or for itself. Here too one walks by faith and not by sight. Faith can only believe in the event of analogical correspondence. Despite all that might seem to count against it, faith can only renew its free decision for God again and again at this point (as at all others) in the face of ongoing temptation. Faith can only wait—in fear and trembling, in the confidence appropriate to itself, and above all in prayer—for the event of correspondence that can only be proven, confirmed, and guaranteed by grace alone. (Faith as the reception of truth is in this sense thoroughly eschatological.) Here and now faith can only submit to the truth of God by entering into the self-effacing action of obedience and witness. Faith can only point away from itself to the truth that speaks for itself or not at all. Barth never tires of insisting that divine truth cannot be received unless it is received by faith as self-confirming.

The living nature of theological truth, however, does not mean that theology must restrict itself to devising assertions that constantly point away from themselves by virtue of their self-canceling, dialectical form. Although Barth once adopted this strategy during his earlier "dialectical" period, by the period of the *Church Dogmatics* he had ceased to regard it as a matter of absolute conceptual necessity. Dialectic was retained in the *Church Dogmatics,* but only in the demoted sense of being one tactic among others, not in the previous sense of being necessarily the domineering or controlling strategy of theological explication. For when dialectic itself was exalted systematically so as everywhere to become the controlling form of thought and expression, it actually served to undermine and obscure what Barth later came to regard as the decisive point— the event of correspondence between human word and divine truth, the analogy of truth (II/1, 230). In this sense the motif of actualism came to be checked or qualified by that of realism, and once this qualification was in place, the way was clear for the motif of rationalism to do its work. In other words, it was Barth's acceptance of the concept of analogical predication (even as this concept was integrated with the actualistic concept of event) which then made it possible for him to undertake a rational explication of the content of faith in the form of positive or nondialectical statements. Whereas dialectical statements could yield no more than "negative analogies," positive statements were now understood to be required of theology by its subject matter.[1]

At the same time such statements were still subject to the strictures of actualism. Positive statements in theology were not to be regarded as "propositions given and sealed once for all with divine authority in both wording and meaning," for the insights of actualism had rendered any such notion to be "theologically impossible" (I/1, 15). The solution to the dilemma of how to combine the positive statements required by the realist concept of analogical predication with the at least tentative (if not necessarily dialectical) statements required by the actualist concept of self-transcending and self-renewing events was found by placing all positive statements, however necessary in principle, under the qualification of an "eschatological reservation." The statements of theology could and often had to be nondialectical, yet without ever being conclusive or definitive once and for all. The statements of dogmatic theology (like those of dogma itself) had to be conceived as eschatological in status (I/1, 269). Insofar as they were conclusive and definitive (and by virtue of realism and rationalism they strove to be so as much as possible), they could be so only in a decidedly provisional and amendable sense. In principle nothing was incorrigible, so that everything had to be reconsidered again and again in new situations by each new generation. The positive results of previous theological work were to be received with respect and at times with veneration, yet not by repristinating those results, but by rethinking them in light of the subject matter as it bore on the needs of the present. The positive statements of theological formulation could only aim toward revelation and strive after it while never capturing it. For the subject matter had an independent life of its own against all conceptual pinning down.

This combination of the provisional (as required by the insights of actualism) with the normative (as required by the insights of realism and rationalism) represented Barth's attempt to avoid two perennial problems in assessing the status of theological formulations. A kind of intellectual works-righteousness (as represented perhaps by the "inerrant" propositions of rational orthodoxy) was to be avoided on the one hand, while a kind of conceptual antinomianism (as represented perhaps by the linguistic permissiveness of emotive liberalism) was to be avoided on the other. The alternative was to tread a narrow conceptual path reminiscent of "justification by faith alone" in which all valid theological assertions, whether positive or dialectical, stood under the sign of *simul justus et peccator*. Formulated by faith for the sake of faith, and inherent inadequacy of all such assertions could finally be judged and overcome only by a truth whose fullness might now at best be glimpsed through such assertions but not known more directly until the life to come.

Particularism: Truth as Unique in Kind

The motif of particularism signifies that in Barth's theology God's reality, God's truth, and therefore God's revelation are all conceived as *sui generis* or unique in kind. They are grounded only in themselves, and therefore cannot be explained in terms of anything other than themselves. They represent, rather, the *prima veritas,* the truth that is original and basic— "the kind of truth on which not even the tiniest shadow of contingency or inferiority can be cast by any higher truth'' (IV/2, 36). God's being, in essence, shares in no truth and no reality other than itself, and by nature nothing other than God shares in the truth and reality of God's essential being. Ordinary categories of being or of thought (e.g., quantity, quality, causality, space, time) cannot in themselves be used to define or limit God. Nor is God subordinate to certain general laws of being which might then be used to define and measure God apart from God's self-revelation. "God is subordinate," writes Barth, "to no idea in which he can be conceived as rooted by which he can be properly measured" (II/1, 334).

Whatever characteristics God exemplifies are exemplified uniquely. They are exemplified originally, supremely, and perfectly, and thus in a way that transcends all analogies conceivable to us. God's being (as disclosed by revelation) is uniquely particular and particularly unique. It is the being of the triune God, which cojoins what we must otherwise distinguish and distinguishes what we must otherwise conjoin. It is just this mysterious conjunction of what for us is otherwise disjoined that makes the characteristics exemplified by God to be perfect, original, and supreme. This conception of the unique particularity of God has significant implications not only for how we think of God in relation to other realities, but also for how we think of other realities in relation to God.

God's Unique Relation to Other Realities

The unique particularity of God has implications for how we think of God in relation to other realities. Most especially, we cannot think of God on the basis of what we may know about other realities. What God is is not borrowed from anything other than or outside of God. God's unique particularity, being beyond conceivable analogy, is what makes it impossible to proceed from the general to the particular in the formulation of theological judgments. "There are not," writes Barth, "first of all power, goodness, knowledge, will, etc. in general, and then in particular God also as one of the subjects to whom all these things accrue as a predicate" (II/1, 334). Or again: "It is not that we recognize and acknowledge the infinity, justice, wisdom, etc. of God because we already know from other sources what all this means and we apply it to God in an eminent sense, thus fashioning for ourselves an image of God after the pattern of our image of the world, i.e., in the last analysis after our own image" (II/1, 333–34).

God and other realities are separated by an ontological divide. Any generalizations we may perceive as governing other realities offer us no basis at all for crossing over to God. The divide cannot be crossed by either the *via negativa* or the *via eminentiae,* because both remain fatally grounded in that side of the divide which is not God. It cannot even be crossed by a concept of the "inconceivable," for in itself this concept can tell us nothing about God's unique and particular inconceivability. It is as though we are confronted by a ditch deeper, wider, and uglier than anything Lessing may ever have dreamed.

If God cannot be conceived on the basis of what we may know about other realities, then only one possibility remains open. Although we cannot cross over conceptually to God, God can cross over to us. Although it is not possible for us to make God manifest to ourselves as we can other objects by the power of our own cognition "—because God is the *prius* of all cognition and of everything known—yet it is possible for God to make himself manifest to his creation. And it is this possibility which is reality" (II/1, 197). But it is a reality only by virtue of the miracle of God's love and grace, not by virtue of anything immanent to the creation and therefore conceivable to us. What is said of God's love could also be said of God's truth. It "always throws a bridge over a crevasse. It is always the light shining out of darkness" (II/1, 278). The truth of God not only eludes all our efforts to cross the divide, but subverts them by itself crossing over to us.

If, by crossing over the divide, God reveals to us the truth of God's unique particularity, then the truth of this revelation can be grounded only through itself. "Revelation is not made real and true by anything else, whether in itself or for us" (I/1, 305).

> According to Holy Scripture God's revelation is a ground which has no higher or deeper ground above or below it but is an absolute ground in itself, and therefore for us a court from which there can be no possible appeal to a higher court. Its reality and truth do not rest on a superior reality and truth. They do not have to be actualized or validated as reality from this or any other point. They are not measured by the reality and truth found at this other point. They are not to be compared with any such nor judged and understood as reality and truth by reference to such. On the contrary, God's revelation has its reality and truth wholly and in every respect—both ontically and noetically—within itself. (I/1, 305)

The God who as such is known only to God, and who can be viewed and conceived only by God, is therefore also as such the God who alone is "capable of speaking of himself aright, i.e., in truth" (II/1, 197). (The truth of God's unique particularity is then disclosed as the unique and particular inconceivability of the triune God.) Our knowledge of revelation cannot be grounded elsewhere, because revelation as such is grounded only in itself.

The unique particularity and particular uniqueness of God's being, which can be known only by virtue of God's self-revelation as grounded in itself, is thus the ontic basis for the noetic procedure that has been designated as particularism. Ordinary categories of being and of thought reach an absolute limit at the point of God's uniqueness and therefore cannot be used to limit and define God of themselves. Again, it is general laws of being that are subordinate to God (not God to them); therefore they, too, cannot be used to define and measure God independently. Again, it is precisely because we do not already know what concepts like "infinity," "justice," or "wisdom" mean when applied to God that we must allow ourselves to be told what they mean by God's revelation. We must attempt, in this case, to allow the uniqueness of God to limit the categories rather than allowing the categories to limit (or distort) the uniqueness of God. We must attempt to allow God's uniqueness to measure the general laws of being rather than allowing them to measure (or eliminate) God's uniqueness. We must attempt to allow our concepts to be interested by the particularity of God, not God by the particularity of our concepts. In practice this means that we must allow our ordinary concepts to be conscripted, broken, and reformed, if they are to be made serviceable for the depiction of God's unique particularity. (As illustrated earlier when discussing the assimilation of extrabiblical concepts, Barth seems to think of this procedure as a kind of Hegelian *Aufhebung.*[2] Concepts external to theology, whether ordinary or sophisticated, can only be appropriated, shattered, and then reconstituted on a higher plane—"raised from the dead," Barth says at one point—if they are to be brought into conformity with this unique and particular subject matter.) The peculiarity of the object thus grounds the rule that in this case we move from the particular to the general.

The Unique Relation of Other Realities to God

The unique particularity of God, moreover, has implications not only for how God is conceived in relation to other realities, but also for how other realities are conceived in relation to God. Most especially, we cannot think of other realities except as originating from, and therefore oriented toward, God. As the absolute goal and origin of all other realities, God does not act inappropriately in making our words do what they cannot do, namely, truly correspond and conform to God's innermost and proper being; nor do we act inappropriately in receiving this determination of our words from God. God can be the limit and boundary of all other realities and truths without being limited and bound by them. God is free to be their limit and boundary in such a way that God can encounter them on *their* side of the ontological divide. God is alive and free not only as their transcendent limit but also as their immanent ground—as "the being of all beings, the law of all laws," and therefore, as the truth of every truth (II/1, 334). Nothing has truth and reality except as imparted to it by God, and nothing is imparted to it by God that does not have reality and truth. Reality and truth find their source and goal in God.

Therefore, when God makes our words do what they cannot do by making them genuinely correspond to the divine being, God "does not perform a violent miracle" (II/1, 229). Nor does God "alienate" our words from their proper and original sense or usage. Nor does God endow them with "a purely fictional capacity," as if they did not enter into genuine correspondence but were surrounded by a haze of equivocation. On the contrary, when God gives our words this correspondence in the act of self-revelation, God does no more than claim what already belongs to God by rights as their Creator. God restores them to their proper and original sense and usage, and endows them with true and genuine reference (II/1, 229).

> With our views, concepts and words we have no claim on him, that he should be their object. He himself, however, has every—the best founded and most valid—claim on us and on all our views, concepts and words, that he should be their first and last and proper subject. Therefore, he does not annul his truth or deny it, nor does he establish a double truth, nor does he place us in the doubtful position of an "as if" cognition, when he allows and commands us in his revelation to make use of our views, concepts and thoughts to describe himself, his Word and his deeds. On the contrary, he establishes the one truth, his own, as the truth of our views, concepts and words. (II/1, 229)

Through the miracle of a divine *Aufhebung,* our views, concepts, and words are brought into genuine conformity with their original and proper object, the unique particularity and particular uniqueness of God.

The same event may also be described from the human side or "from below," for just as God does not act inappropriately in giving our words this determination, so we do not act inappropriately in receiving it. Everything depends, Barth argued, on seeing that God's act of revelation is performed with pure grace. "That is, it is a bestowal which utterly transcends all our capacity, being and existence as such, but does not destroy us, does not consume and break our being and existence'' (II/1, 197–98). Or perhaps it might be said more dialectically that the bestowal of grace in the knowledge of God utterly annuls our capacity, being, and existence by utterly transforming them, destroys us by renewing us, consumes and breaks our being and existence only to reestablish them at a higher level of wholeness. In any case, ''from our point of view this is a miracle, an inexhaustible reality that cannot be established, deduced or explained—it is present to us to our salvation, and it can be affirmed and grasped by us in faith, to become a determination of our being and existence'' (II/1, 198). The grace of this miracle and the miracle of this grace are therefore to be met with gratitude. ''It . . . lies in the nature of this revelation that we can meet it only with the praise of thanksgiving'' (II/1, 198).

Therefore the truth in which we know God in all the particularity of the divine uniqueness and all the uniqueness of the divine particularity is not our creation but God's creation, not our truth but God's truth. ''It is his truth in a very different way from what it is ours—with all the distinction of the Creator from the creature. It is obviously his truth originally, primarily, independently and properly, because creatively. It is our truth only subsequently, secondarily, dependently and improperly, because creaturely'' (II/1, 228). It is our truth only as it is first God's, but as originally and strictly God's it is made to be ours as well. The relationship is irreversible. Any control of God's truth on our part is excluded as impossible. We follow and cannot possibly precede. Nonetheless, what is impossible by nature is granted by grace. Although our truth is not God's, God's truth becomes ours. ''This is the unity of truth in him who is the truth'' (II/1, 228). As the object of our miraculous cognition and grateful acknowledgment, there is established among us the truth of God's unique particularity.

CHAPTER 4

Truth as Mediated: Revelation

As the motif of objectivism signifies, in Barth's theology truth is always conceived as "mediated." Truth is not immediately apprehensible in matters of revelation and salvation; it is not directly accessible to us on the basis of general considerations or by our own innate powers of cognition and perception. Whether it is a question of God's identity in relation to us ("revelational objectivism") or of our identity in relation to God ("soteriological objectivism") the truth is never something that is accessible to us except as mediated by Jesus Christ. In matters of revelation and salvation, Jesus Christ must be regarded as the sole Mediator of truth. For he alone is the very being of God in human nature and the very being of human nature in God.

Revelational Objectivism: The General Aspect

Revelational objectivism, as Barth understands it, has both a general and a particular aspect. The general aspect is that the God who is otherwise hidden from us absolutely, takes form for us objectively without dissolving the divine hiddenness. By nature, as we have seen, God is hidden from us absolutely. There is no way from us to God. We are separated from God by an ontological divide. Yet, as we have also seen, God is not separated from us in precisely the same way. It belongs to the sovereign freedom of God that God can cross over the divide in an act of self-revelation. This self-revelation can only mean, however, that God takes form for us in terms of the creaturely sphere—the only kind of terms we can apprehend. By taking form in this apprehensible way, God becomes a genuine object of our knowledge; yet by doing so in terms of the creaturely sphere—the sphere of that which is not God—God becomes a unique object of knowledge and remains hidden in the midst of revelation.

God becomes an object of our knowledge by taking form in the creaturely sphere. God could not take form in this way without in some sense becoming one object among others. "Biblical faith lives upon the objectivity of God," writes Barth. "In one way or another, God comes into the picture, the sphere, the field of our consideration and conception in exactly the same way that objects do" (II/1, 13). Nonetheless, God is not merely one object among others, but "the utterly unique object of a unique human knowledge" (II/1, 14). No other object in the field of our knowledge remains "indissolubly subject" at the same time (III/2, 176). No other object so completely retains the power of its own self-disclosure.

> Even in the form he assumes when he reveals himself God is free to reveal himself or not to reveal himself. In other words, we can regard his self-unveiling in every instance only as his act. . . . Revelation always means revealing even in the form or means of revelation. The form as such, the means, does not take God's place. It is not the form, but God in the form, that reveals, speaks, comforts, works and aids. . . . The fact that God takes form means that God himself controls not only us but also the form in which he encounters us. God's presence is always God's decision to be present. (I/1, 321)

God's objectivity is determined, so to speak, by an absolute subjectivity. It is established and maintained in the sovereign freedom of God. God's objectivity is therefore particular and unique.

Special emphasis is laid on the reverse point, however, that God's particularity and uniqueness are objective. The quest for a nonobjective or immediate experience of God would be the quest for a knowledge that was "without concepts, without an image, without a word, without a sign—God himself speaking, not through something else, but through himself" (II/1, 11). It would be the quest for an apprehension of God that, in effect, removed us from the confines of the creaturely sphere. Regardless of the historic pedigree attaching to such a quest, ranging from at least certain statements in Augustine to certain statements in Schleiermacher, it is the special insistence of Barth's theology that this quest amounts to an avoidance of the objective form assumed by revelation. "Instead of finding [God] where he himself has sought us—namely, in his objectivity—we seek him where he is not to be found" (II/1, 11).

Therefore, God's particularity and uniqueness are not to be sought or conceived as nonobjective. "It is not the case that in the non-objective we are dealing with the real and true knowledge of God but in the objective with a deceptive appearance. Just the reverse" (II/1, 11).

God's objectivity in relation to us, Barth argues, is grounded in the objectivity of God's own self-knowledge. "God is first and foremost objective to himself" (II/1, 16). Barth's entire argument follows from the idea that God is the object of God's own self-knowledge. The objectivity of this divine self-knowledge occurs in the sense that from all eternity the Father knows the Son, and the Son knows the Father, in the unity of the Holy Spirit. Objectivity and knowledge are thus not alien to God, but are intrinsic to God's innermost being. God's self-knowledge is trinitarian self-knowledge, and its trinitarian content is known by God in immediate and primary objectivity. This same content is also disclosed to us by divine revelation, and with a corresponding objectivity, but in our case the objectivity is not immediate but mediate, and not primary but secondary. The difference between God's primary and secondary objectivity, in other words, concerns the form but not the content of truth. The secondary objectivity that God assumes in revelation "is distinguished from the primary objectivity, not by a lesser degree of truth, but by its particular form suitable for us, the creature" (II/1, 16). The objectivity by which God confronts us in this secondary form does not prevent its content from being "fully true." For it is in God's primary objectivity that our form of this knowledge finds its "correspondence and basis." The objectivity our knowledge thus reflects is "the inner truth" of God's triune identity, for our cognition "acquires truth as the external expression of that inner truth." Our knowledge of God in secondary objectivity is finally nothing less than a participation in the truth of God's own self-knowledge as it is in eternity. "It is here that the door is shut against any 'non-objective' knowledge of God" (II/1, 16).

The idea that we receive only a mediated and secondary share in God's own original self-knowledge does not mean, however, that God is revealed to us only in part. It does not mean that "we have to do with a limited quantity of his being and not, or not yet, with some other quantity" (II/1, 51). Nor does it mean that "we still have to await the revelation of another God in another and higher order, or the revelation of the same God in a different form" (II,1, 51). On the contrary, revelation is not something partial or quantitative. No higher or different or more complete truth exists above and beyond it. Regardless of the secondary form, God's revelation is categorically given as self-revelation. "God is who he is, the Father, Son and Holy Spirit, Creator, Reconciler and Redeemer, supreme, the one true Lord; and he is known in this entirety or he is not known at all. There is no existence of God behind or beyond this entirety of his being" (II/1, 52). The truth of God's identity is not partially but wholly disclosed to us. "If our knowledge of God is under a quantitative limitation it is obviously under a limitation of its truth. But this is excluded by the self-demonstration of God in his Word." The truth of God's identity is mediated to us in the name of Jesus Christ, who is the being of God in human nature. "When this name is rightly given, it is not given to a part but to the being of God in his unity and entirety. We either know God himself and therefore entirely, or we do not know him at all" (II/1, 52). No truth of God's identity is higher, different, or more complete than the truth of God's identity in the humanity of Jesus Christ.

Mediation Means Hiddenness in the Midst of Revelation

Several important implications may be noted about this mediation of the divine truth by the human nature of Jesus Christ. First, this mediation means that the truth of God's identity remains hidden in the midst of revelation and revealed in the midst of hiddenness. The human nature of Jesus Christ is the form taken by the being of God when God, in sovereign freedom, becomes fully manifest in the creaturely sphere. The human nature of Jesus Christ is thus at once the means and the limitation of God's self-revelation. It is the means of this self-revelation, because it is the creaturely medium by which the otherwise inapprehensible God comes to be apprehensible for us. It is the object and event within the sphere of that which is not God by which God has chosen to make manifest the truth of God's own inherent objectivity and eventfulness. It is the creaturely reality which, without for one moment ceasing to be creaturely, discloses the truth of God's identity in the form of secondary objectivity. It is the creaturely reality which reveals, in its unity and entirety, the trinitarian identity of God.

The human nature of Jesus Christ is thus the means of divine self-revelation in the sense of being its creaturely mediation or form. Because of God's freely chosen self-involvement with it, this form does not detract from its being definitive and unsurpassable. In this form, after all, it is not merely a matter of revelation but of self-revelation. On the other hand, neither does the divine involvement with it detract from its remaining a form that is strictly creaturely. Divine self-revelation is precisely the event by which the form, without ceasing to be creaturely, becomes, by grace, the means to an end that it could not possibly serve by nature or in itself. It becomes the means to the end of revealing the truth of God's inmost identity.

As a form that does not cease to be creaturely, however, the human nature of Jesus Christ is not only the means but also the limitation of God's self-revelation. By being imparted in a creaturely form, God's self-revelation is imparted "in an objectively different from his own, in a creaturely objectivity. He unveils himself as the One he is by veiling himself in a form which he himself is not" (II/1, 52). By coming to be clothed and veiled in the human nature of Jesus Christ, God makes that human nature to be the sacrament of revelation and hence the sacrament of truth. "He uses this form distinct from himself, he uses its work and sign, in order to be objective in, with and under this form, and therefore to give himself to us to be known." The truth of revelation is imparted by the giving of sacramental signs. "Revelation means the giving of signs. We can say quite simply that revelation means sacrament." It means "the self-witness of God, the representation of his truth, and therefore of the truth in which he knows himself, in the form of creaturely objectivity and therefore in a form which is adapted to our creaturely knowledge" (II/1, 52). What confronts us directly, therefore, is not the reality but the sacramental sign, not the divine but the creaturely form of objectivity, not the deity but the humanity of Jesus Christ. The distinction of the Creator from the creature has not been renounced ontically, but it has been surrendered, in any direct sense, noetically. That is, the distinction of the Creator from the creature is not visible but concealed by the very form of its revelation. "When the creature in its objectivity becomes the representative of the objectivity of God himself, it hides it. When God makes himself visible through it, he accepts the fact that he will remain invisible as the One he is in himself and as he knows himself" (II/1, 55). God accepts the fact that God's objectivity will be concealed by the very different objectivity of the creature.

As the Mediator to us of the truth of God's identity, Jesus Christ in his human nature thus exemplifies at one and the same time the revelation, the hiddenness, and the freedom of God. Each of these themes is well brought out in Barth's exposition of Philippians 2:5ff., a text which speaks of Jesus Christ "emptying himself" by taking "the form of a servant."

Positively his self-emptying refers to the fact that, without detracting from his being in the form of God, he was able and willing to assume the form of a servant and go about in the likeness of a human being, so that the creature could know him only as a creature, and he alone could know himself as God. In other words, he was ready to accept a position in which he could not be known in the world as God, but his divine glory was concealed from the world. This was his self-emptying. . . . His deity becomes completely invisible to all other eyes but his own. What distinguishes him from the creature disappears from everyone's sight but his own with his assumption of the human form of a servant, with its natural end in death, and above all with his death as that of a criminal on the cross. . . . He can so empty himself that, without detracting from his form as God, he can take the form of a servant, concealing his form of life as God, and going about in the likeness of a human being. . . . It all takes place in his freedom and therefore not in self-contradiction or with any alteration or diminution of his divine being. . . . This means that so far from being contrary to the nature of God, it is of his essence to possess the freedom to be capable of this self-offering and self-concealment, and beyond this to make use of this freedom, and therefore really to effect this self-offering and to give himself up to this self-humiliation. In this above all he is concealed as God. Yet it is here above all that he is really and truly God. Thus it is above all that he must and will also be revealed in his deity by the power of God. (II/1, 516–17 rev.)

The truth of God's identity, as mediated in Jesus Christ, remains hidden in the midst of revelation, not only (as we have seen) by virtue of its form, but also by virtue of its content. It remains hidden by virtue of its form, because its form is the form of that which is not God, the creaturely form of Jesus Christ's humanity. It remains hidden by virtue of its content, on the other hand, because its content is the truth of the inconceivable content that God's inmost identity is trinitarian. Each aspect of this twofold hiddenness may be understood as a function of the divine freedom. For it corresponds to the greatness of God's freedom "not to be tied down and limited by his own nature" (I/2, 31), but to be able to assume creaturely form for our sake. It also corresponds to the divine freedom not to be tied down and limited by the constitutive forms of creaturely being, but rather to live independently of them in another, different, and truly perfect mode of being—a trinitarian mode of being that conjoins what we must otherwise distinguish, and distinguishes what we must otherwise conjoin. By virtue of both form and content, therefore, God as revealed in Jesus Christ remains revealed in the midst of hiddenness and hidden in the midst of revelation.

God's Incomprehensibility:
A Theological, Not a Philosophical, Conception

It is worth noting that this twofold hiddenness or twofold incomprehensibility—as grounded in the freedom of God and derived from the content of revelation (in its particular uniqueness and unique particularity)—distinguishes Barth's view, as he himself repeatedly emphasizes, from any more general or philosophical views of divine incomprehensibility. "We do not," writes Barth, "teach this distinction between the knowledge of God and its object on the ground of a preconceived idea about the transcendence and supramundanity of God; nor do we teach it in the form of an affirmation of our experience of faith. On the contrary, we teach it because of what we find proclaimed and described as faith in Holy Scripture" (II/1, 15).

> For example, nothing can be more misleading than the opinion that the theological statement of the hiddenness of God says roughly the same thing as the Platonic or Kantian statement, according to which the supreme being is understood as a rational idea withdrawn from all perception and understanding. If we have to say that God is in fact withdrawn in this way, this does not mean that the rational idea, surpassing all cognitive experience and all cognitive categories, is identical with God. For on this view God is understood as a rational idea, which, however transcendent, is general, "pure" and non-objective (i.e., objective only in intention). This shows us at once that it has no identity with God, and any such identity must be denied. The God who encounters us in his revelation is never a non-objective entity, or one which is objective only in intention. He is the substance of all objectivity. (II/1, 183)

In this statement about the transcendent divine hiddenness, it might be said that the motifs of objectivism and particularism are both in evidence. It is an aspect of God's mediated *objectivity* that God is revealed to us in unique particularity, and it is an aspect of God's unique *particularity* that God is revealed in mediated objectivity. God's *objectivity* is uniquely mediated, and God's *particularity* is uniquely objective. God's mediated *objectivity* displays the particular uniqueness of God's freedom, and God's *particularity* displays the unique objectivity of God's identity. The particular uniqueness of God's freedom is (among other things) the freedom to assume creaturely form. The unique objectivity of God's identity is the unique content of the Trinity. The freedom to assume creaturely form and the unique content of the Trinity are the two main aspects of God's unique incomprehensibility. The uniqueness of God's incomprehensibility, therefore, is not the uniqueness of a nonobjective rational idea. For God's incomprehensibility surpasses all cognitive experience only as it makes itself available to our cognitive experience, and it transends all cognitive categories only as it takes form in our cognitive categories. The uniqueness of God's incomprehensibility is the uniqueness of God's freedom. It is the uniqueness of the living God. It is the uniqueness of the God who incomprehensibly assumes creaturely form in the humanity of Jesus Christ (objectivism) in order to disclose to us the incomprehensibility of a triune identity (particularism).

This point is further developed in terms of the motif of actualism. It is this motif especially which serves to distinguish Barth's concept from philosophical concepts of divine incomprehensibility. For it is this motif which serves to underscore that divine incomprehensibility, as Barth understands it, is strictly a matter of revelation and faith.

> And when [God] encounters us as the hidden One, his hiddenness not only concerns human perception and understanding, i.e., our capacity for it. It concerns the act of human knowledge and its intentions; it concerns ourselves. And it concerns ourselves even as God's revelation concerns us. God's hiddenness is not the content of a last word of human self-knowledge; it is not the object of a last performance of human capacity; it is the first word of the knowledge of God instituted by God himself, which as such cannot be transposed into self-knowledge, or into the statement of a general theory of knowledge. When we say that God is hidden, we are not speaking of ourselves, but, taught by God's revelation alone, of God. (II/1, 183).

The truth of God's hiddenness cannot be given by rational reflection as such. It cannot be given by a general theory of knowledge or by reflecting on the outer limts of human self-knowledge. It cannot be incorporated into theology as an element in a rationally comprehensible system established independently of revelation.

> There can never be any question of a system in the sense of Platonic, Aristotelian or Hegelian philosophy. For the basic thought essential to such a system is not only, as even the philosophers say, the thought of an ultimate, inconceivable reality, but as such—and it is here that the inconceivability of the theologian differs from that of the philosopher—it is not at our disposal. We cannot attain to it as the thought of a true, i.e., a present reality, or we can do so only improperly, i.e., in the form of recollection and expectation. Even the biblical witnesses themselves cannot and do not try to introduce revelation of themselves. They show themselves to be genuine witnesses of it by the fact that they only speak of it by looking forward to it and by looking back at it. (I/2, 483)

The truth of God's hiddenness or incomprehensibility or inconceivability is not a truth at our disposal. It is not at our disposal either in derivation or in reception. It is not derived and received through reflection on the limits of our rational capacities. Therefore it cannot be incorporated as the capstone in a philosophical system. On the contrary, as a truth derived from revelation and received by faith, it cannot be incorporated in theology as the content of a system, but only as the content of a witness. The truth of God's inconceivable freedom is a truth that can only be received by the grace of this same inconceivable freedom, and it is a truth which can be attested in all its proper objectivity only by pointing forward or by pointing back to a unique and particular event. The "inconceivability" of the theologian is, in both derivation and reception, the inconceivability of a miraculous and gracious, self-transcending and self-renewing, self-grounded and self-commending event. It is an inconceivability whose truth cannot be derived and received by pure reason, but only from revelation by faith. In short, it is an inconceivability grounded primarily, properly, and exclusively in our cognizance of God. "Only in secondary and derived sense is it also a confession of our own incapacity" (II/1, 192).

Mediation Means Vulnerability to Rejection

The vulnerability and the protectiveness of God may also be noted, along with hiddenness in the midst of revelation, as implications of the assertion that the truth of God's identity is mediated through the humanity of Jesus Christ. By virtue of being mediated through the creaturely form of a human being, God asssumes a certain vulnerability. "Vulnerability" means that God becomes susceptible, because of the creaturely form, to nonrecognition, misapprehension, and rejection. Nonrecognition is a possibility, because the creaturely form may be all that is visible. In that case there would be hiddenness, but without the corresponding revelation. "God exposes himself, so to speak, to the danger that we will know the work and sign but not himself through the medium of the work and sign. A complete non-recognition of the Lord who has instituted and used this medium is possible" (II/1, 55). Misapprehension or misunderstanding is the reverse possibility that God will actually be confused with the creaturely form, thereby resulting in idolatry. The sacrament of revelation is then perverted into something like the revelation of sacrament, as if the sacramental sign were identical with the reality it was meant to convey. Because revelation takes place through the sacramental sign, the sign in itself and as such can be misconstrued as "identical either with revelation or with the real knowledge of God" (II/1, 55). Rejection, finally, is also a possibility to which revelation is vulnerable because of its creaturely form. "The demand that the objectivity of God must be known in the objectivity of the creature can be rejected because of the too great humiliation and alienation in which the glory of God has to be believed and known. God himself can be rejected in the grace of his condescension to the creature" (II/1 56). In these ways, then, the objective mediation of revelation means that God becomes vulnerable to human nonreception.

Excursus: Three Larger Formal Patterns in the *Church Dogmatics* (the Chalcedonian, the Trinitarian, and the Hegelian)

Parenthetically, it might be observed as a point of theological method that the moves we have just seen are a typical reflection of how throughout the *Church Dogmatics* Barth continually makes use of what might be called the "Chalcedonian pattern."[1] Indeed, it is probably safe to say that no one in the history of theology ever possessed a more deeply imbued Chalcedonian imagination. The Chalcedonian pattern, formally speaking, is a pattern of unity ("without separation or division"), differentiation ("without confusion or change"), and asymmetry (the unqualified conceptual precedence of the divine over the human nature of Jesus Christ). Nonrecognition, misapprehension, and rejection, as indications of the divine vulnerability, can be viewed as an application of the pattern's logic. Each has to do with the relationship between divine reality and revelatory sign. Nonrecognition is thus a case of separation or division; the sign is divorced from the reality. Misapprehension is a case of confusion or change; the sign is identified with the reality. Rejection is a case of inverting the asymmetrical order—a complex or imperfect case; the sign is given precedence over the reality in such a way as to exclude the reality on principle. In large ways and in small (and here, of course, it is small), this pattern is regularly, if often implicitly, brought to bear in Barth's argumentation, both critically and constructively.

The Chalcedonian pattern, it might be added, would seem to be one of at least three such formal patterns that are at work throughout the *Church Dogmatics*. The other two are the Hegelian pattern of *Aufhebung* and the trinitarian pattern of dialectical inclusion. *Aufhebung* is the Hegelian pattern of affirming, canceling, and then reconstituting something on a higher plane (a pattern whose underlying metaphor would seem to be "incarnation, crucifixion, and resurrection''). It has emerged previously in our discussion of the motifs of particularism and rationalism, for it is not only the pattern by which ordinary terms are brought into conformity with theological subject matter (an aspect of particularism), but also that by which extrabiblical concepts are to be assimilated (an aspect of rationalism). Dialectical inclusion, on the other hand, is the trinitarian pattern by which the whole is understood to be included in the part without rendering the other parts superfluous. It made a brief appearance previously in our consideration of rationalism in its ordering mode, for it is a principle by which the *Church Dogmatics* itself is structured, as well as being a structural principle for various doctrines such as that of eternity as the divine temporality.

None of these three formal patterns (each of which is in some sense dialectical) would seem to have an exclusive connection with any of the six motifs or modes of thought which are the special object of this essay. *Aufhebung,* however, as suggested, would seem to have a special affinity with particularism, as would dialectical inclusion with actualism (insofar as actualism pertains to the occurrence of complex, self-transcending events, whereby each moment of occurrence somehow includes the whole connected series of events within itself). Nonetheless, these cases would seem to be merely affinities and no more than that. The Hegelian pattern, for example, is a structural principle in Barth's soteriology (in a way that has nothing to do with particularism) insofar as it is understood that in salvation human beings (and all else with them) are and are to be somehow affirmed, negated, and reconstituted on a higher plane in Christ. Likewise the trinitarian pattern, as the very name suggests, is a structural principle in Barth's doctrine of God in a way that has no direct connection with actualism (regardless of the way in which the doctrine and that motif may in some ways be integrated). The Chalcedonian, the Hegelian, and the trinitarian patterns are thus noteworthy as significant structural principles that are, in any number of different ways, woven into the fabric of Barth's theological argumentation. (Some of these ways will be indicated as our exposition proceeds.)

Mediation Means Divine Vulnerability: Conclusion

In any case, to resume where we left off, the subject–object relationship to which God submits by condescending to be revealed through the mediation of creaturely objectivity is a relationship fraught with ambiguity and danger. Not even the supreme and definitive instance of this crea-

turely mediation, the humanity of Jesus, is free from the indicated vulnerability (indeed, it is its central exemplification). Thus Barth writes that
"even the man Jesus as such is always enigma as well" (II/1, 56). The
humanity of Jesus as such is (especially at the point of the cross) a creaturely form which in itself can only hide the divine revelation. It is thus
God in and through the creaturely form who does the revealing, not the
form in itself and as such. If the human Jesus is not only enigma, "if as
enigma he is also illumination, disclosure and communication, then it is
thanks to his unity with the Son of God and of the faith in him effected
by the Holy Spirit" (II/1, 56). Once again it is made clear from this angle
that faith never knows God immediately. "Our knowledge of faith itself
is knowledge of God in his hiddenness. It is indirect and mediate, not
immediate knowledge" (II/1, 57).

Mediation Means Protectiveness
and Solicitude Toward Humanity

Protectiveness, on the other hand, might be thought of as the positive
reverse side to the divine vulnerability. Although God becomes vulnerable to nonrecognition, misapprehension, and rejection, we are protected
by the creaturely mediation of God's reality from what for us could only
be the total catastrophe of a more immediate encounter with God. Direct
and immediate knowledge of God would not only *not* be more than the
mediated variety, nor would it merely be less, it would actually be "nothing
at all—indeed, something negative" (II/1, 19). We cannot see God's
face, "God's naked objectivity," without exposing ourselves to the an-
nihilating wrath of God. "It would have to be a second God who could
see God directly" or who could know God immediately (II/1, 19).

> It is good for us that God acts as he does; and it could be fatal for us if he
> did not—if he were manifest to us in the way we think right, directly and
> without veil, without secularity or only in the innocuous secularity that can
> be pierced by the *analogia entis*. It would not be love and mercy but the
> end of us and all things if the Word were spoken to us thus. The fact that
> it is spoken as it is, revealing in its concealment, is a decisive indication of
> the truth that it has really come to us instead of our having to go to it, an
> attempt in which we could only fail. In its very secularity it is thus in every
> respect a Word of grace. (I/1, 169 rev.)

As creatures we cannot stand directly before God, but only before other
objects. Faith, therefore, is always a matter of knowing God indirectly.

It is always a matter of knowing God in the works of God, in the particular works within the creaturely sphere by which God has chosen to make
known who God is. It is always a matter of knowing God in the particular
creaturely realities that God has singled out and chosen to bear witness
to God's own objectivity. "What distinguishes faith from unbelief, erro-
neous faith and superstition is that it is content with this indirect knowledge of God. It does not think that the knowledge of God in his works is
insufficient" (II/1, 17). What distinguishes God from various idols and
human projections, moreover, is that God does not hold out the false
promise of an immediate human encounter with the divine reality. God
instead protects us from the annihilation of such an encounter by disclosing the divine reality through the mediation of creaturely realities. The
objective mediation of revelation is thus a sign of divine solicitude and
protectiveness. The very mediation that makes God vulnerable is the mediation without which our encounter with God would not be possible.[2]

The objective mediation of revelation, therefore, represents not only
the limit, but also "the positive possibility of our cognition" (II/1, 209).
Even the transition from faith to sight, from knowing God in this life to
knowing God in the life to come, will not mean the abolition of all mediation. The mode of knowledge will change, but the terms and the truth
of this knowledge will remain the same. The mode will change from faith
to sight. "God will then be no more hidden from us in faith. But God as
God, in himself, will still be hidden from us even then." Even then we
will be protected from a confrontation with the naked objectivity of God.
It is as though within the inmost life of God there is a glory whose
splendor is too intense, a love whose holiness is too demanding, a freedom whose potency is too highly charged, for the poor creature to with-
stand, if not protected by some sort of mediation. "Even this knowing of
God face to face will still be a miraculous bestowal of his grace, an
incomprehensible descent of God into the sphere of objectivity of our
cognition. . . . The point is that the authenticity of our knowledge . . .
will still be an authenticity which is adapted to us as human beings and
as creatures." The divine accommodation will still be a kind of limit
even as it functions in self-disclosure. Yet neither here and now nor there
and then is this limit a limit on the truth. "The truth of God can and
should be known by us in the darkness of faith no less than in the light
of sight." Either way, the limit is qualitative, not quantitative. It is thus
a limit that, in the life to come, will continually recede even though it
will not be abolished. "The blessedness of our perfect knowing of God
will consist in a being on the way." It will consist in an ever deeper and

richer consecration into the knowledge of God's trinitarian being. "There can be no knowledge of God," writes Barth, "in time or even in eternity which will lead us beyond this entirety of his being. On the contrary, a further knowledge of God will only lead us deeper into just this entirety of his being." It will lead us ever qualitatively deeper into the knowledge of just this God within the limits appropriate to us as creatures (II/1, 209).

To sum up: revelational objectivism means the mediation of divine truth to us through the human nature of Jesus Christ as the central and determinative instance of this mediation.[3] Nonobjective knowledge of God is ruled out, because even God's own self-knowledge, being thoroughly trinitarian, is not nonobjective. Immediate knowledge of God is likewise ruled out, because this mode of knowledge is appropriate only to God and would be catastrophic for the mere creature. Mediated knowledge of God thus describes the mode of knowledge that is appropriate to us, because it corresponds not only to the objective mode of God's own self-knowledge, but also to our inherent creaturely limitations. Form and content both ensure that God remains hidden in the midst of revelation, because the form is not divine but creaturely, and the content (being trinitarian) is inconceivable. Freedom is the characteristic that allows God to be God in both these inconceivable ways (i.e., revealed in truth through creaturely form, and trinitarian in essential content), and it is this characteristic that distinguishes the inconceivability of revelation from any inconceivability posited philosophically by pure reason. Finally, vulnerability for God but grace for us (for us not only in this life but in the life to come) are both a consequence of revelation's christological mediation.

Revelational Objectivism: The Particular Aspect

Revelational objectivism, however, is viewed not only under this general but also under a more particular aspect. Commenting on Colossians 2:3 ("In him are hid all the treasures of wisdom and knowledge of God"), Barth writes: "This does not have only the general meaning that we must know him in order to know God. It has the particular meaning that we must know him as the first and proper Subject of the knowledge of God" (II/1, 252). Jesus Christ in his humanity is not only the objective mediation of the truth of God (the general aspect), but also at the same time for our sakes the ground of its subjective apprehension (the particular aspect). Previously, in considering the motif of particularism, the point emerged that in Barth's theology God is not only the transcendent limit but also the source and ground of all that is. It was noted, for example, that God is described as "the *prius* of all cognition and of everything known" (II/1, 197) as well as "the being of all beings, the law of all laws" and therefore the truth of every truth (II/1, 334). Ideas like these, which emphasize God as source and ground, are finally subjected to a christological concentration. That is exactly what happens in the material at hand. Jesus Christ is presented as the Mediator, as the objective ground, not only of God's self-presentation to us in creaturely form, but also of our subjective apprehension of God. He himself is said, as noted, to be "the first and proper Subject of the knowledge of God" (II/1, 252).

The mediatorial work of Jesus Christ is thus conceived to be subjective as well as objective. Our subjective apprehension of God is not direct but indirect. It is mediated by and grounded in Jesus' own subjective apprehension of God. Our subjective apprehension cannot be understood as something grounded in ourselves. "We have to seek the subjective possibility of revelation," writes Barth, "our freedom for the Word of God, only in the Word itself, in Jesus Christ" (I/2, 265). The condition that makes possible our subjective apprehension is to be found in "this objective factor" and not in any "effects" it may have on us or in us. "Therefore, in so far as it now becomes our freedom, we have to understand it as a miracle, and not in any sense a natural freedom and capacity" (I/2, 265). In ourselves we have no "capacity" for subjectively apprehending God. "All capacity in this respect is his capacity. . . . In relation to revelation all capacity is concretely the capacity of the Word, the capacity of Jesus Christ" (I/2, 247).

The christological grounding of our subjective capacity in that of the human Jesus is what guarantees the truth of our apprehension, for it is through his subjective apprehension that we ourselves come subjectively to share in the truth of God's own trinitarian self-knowledge.

> God himself is the truth. The truth—not simply a truth. For the origin and source of all truth lies in the fact that God is not hidden from himself but open to himself. Truth means unhiddenness, openness. Because God is open to himself—the Father to the Son and the Son to the Father, by the Holy Spirit, himself, the Lord of all things—all things are open to him, all openness which exists elsewhere is originally and properly his openness. (II/1, 68).

Our openness to God, our capacity for subjectively apprehending God, is originally and properly the openness of the Son to the Father in the unity of the Holy Spirit. It is this openness of the Son, in and through the Holy Spirit, in which our own openness comes to be grounded and through which we gain subjective access to God. "God himself," writes Barth, is "the real and primarily acting Subject of all real knowledge of God" (II/1, 10). God is therefore said to be "objectively present" to us in a double sense that reiterates (with appropriate modifications) the pattern of God's inner trinitarian life. "In His Word He comes as an object before the human subject. And by the Holy Spirit He makes the human subject accessible to Himself, capable of considering and conceiving Himself as object." God in Jesus Christ by the Holy Spirit is thus "the real and primarily acting Subject" of our own subjective apprehension; that is, our subjectivity is here grounded in that of Jesus, whose subjectivity in turn (by the mystery of the Incarnation) is grounded in that of God the Son, as the Son knows the Father in the unity of the Holy Spirit to all eternity (II/1, 10). As will be discussed later in detail, this participation of our subjectivity in that of Jesus Christ is conceived as the true and proper grounding of our own subjectivity, not as its violation or obliteration. Although it has nothing to do with a "magical invasion" of our life "by supernatural factors and forces," it does represent "a limitation and interruption of our existence. Our existence is confronted by something outside and over against it, by which it is determined, and indeed totally determined. But it is determined as the act of our self-determination in the totality of its possibilities" (I/2, 266).

For now, however, the point to be emphasized is that our subjective apprehension of God is grounded in and mediated by the subjectivity of Jesus Christ in his humanity. This point—which (as we have seen) Barth makes in terms of "the first and proper Subject," the "subjective possibility of revelation," "capacity," and "openness"—is a point that can also be made simply in terms of "faith." To say that Jesus Christ is the "pioneer of faith" (Heb. 12:2), Barth suggests, is not to say that his faith is merely the exemplar of ours, but that it is the vicarious ground and source of our faith. "There is vicarious faith," writes Barth, ". . . only in the form of the faith which Jesus Christ established for us all as the *archegos tes pisteos* (Heb. 12:2), who empowers us for our own faith, and summons us to it, even as he stands there in our stead with his faith. Through his faith we are not only moved but liberated to believe for ourselves" (IV/4, 186). Our faith may be said to exist "as a predicate" of his in the sense that whatever is real and true "in this Subject" is the foundation for whatever is correspondingly real and true in us (cf. II/2,

539). In short, our subjective apprehension of God does not exist independently, but only insofar as its source, mediation, and ground are found in the humanity of Jesus Christ.

Mediated subjectivity in our apprehension of divine truth is a concept, it might be said, that arises from an integration of the motifs of objectivism and actualism. That is, it arises by integrating the idea of the mediatorial work of the humanity of Jesus Christ (objectivism) with the idea of our human incapacity for knowing God as something that can only be overcome miraculously by a sovereign act of divine grace (actualism). More simply, it might be said that Jesus Christ is at once the Mediator and the miracle through whom we come to the reality of subjective apprehension. As the Mediator of our subjectivity, the human Jesus stands before us in his unique and irreducible singularity; as the miracle in whom our incapacity is overcome, he stands before us as the sole and exclusive ground of our access to God. It might thus be said that the actualist side of this relationship is a presupposition of the objectivist side, and yet that the objectivist side leads to the culmination of the actualist side. That is, the problem of our radical incapacity (an aspect of the actualist motif) is presupposed by Jesus Christ's miraculous and mediatorial work, while the gracious freedom of this work, apart from us and on our behalf (an aspect of the objectivist motif), is a condition by which the problem of our incapacity is finally overcome.

Human Incapacity for Revelation
and the Need for Mediated Subjectivity

Our human incapacity is a concept that Barth develops at length before introducing the idea of mediated subjectivity as its solution. In and of ourselves, Barth argues, we have no readiness at all to know God. Openness for grace is the concept by which the idea of human readiness is explicated. This openness would involve at least three things on our part: neediness, knowledge, and willingness. Neediness indicates our objective condition. It means that we cannot know God under any circumstances apart from the miracle of grace—the miracle that God is open not only for the reality of God's own inner trinitarian life but also for us as well, that God is open for sharing this inner life with us who are mere creatures. Neediness also means that we are "dependent on God's grace as grace," that we "cannot just as well exist without knowing God," and that we "cannot know him just as well without his grace" (II/1, 129). Knowledge indicates what would have to be our related noetic situation.

We would have to know that we really need grace and that we cannot get along just as well without it. We would also have to know that God is really gracious and open to us. The reality of God's graciousness and openness would not be evident to us if we ceased to be aware of our need (II/1, 129). Willingness, finally, indicates what would have to be our corresponding volitional situation. We would have to be willing to accept God's grace for our need. We would have to be ready to allow this grace to encroach upon us, overcoming our deprivation and inaptitude. The miracle of grace would not be evaded, but gratefully accepted (II/1, 130). In short, if we were really open to grace, these three—neediness, knowledge, and willingness—would all "cohere and mutually condition one another." None would be present without the others (II/1, 130).

Having developed this idea of readiness for God as openness for grace, Barth then employs a procedure whose outlines were observed in our consideration of the motif of rationalism. He subjects the idea of openness for grace to a kind of testing. He asks about its possible validity by checking its coherence with the remaining network of doctrines or articles of faith which are presupposed as valid and authoritative. Can the idea that we are open for grace be said to correspond to anything real about us either in general or else more particularly as we may exist within the life of the church? Assuming the validity of the proposed description of what it would mean for us indeed to be open for grace, can this description be said to apply to us, given everything else we know about ourselves by faith? Can it really be said that we are open for grace in ourselves or at least as we live within the church?

It cannot be said that we are open for grace in ourselves. On this level "absolutely nothing" has been said about our real human readiness to know God. It is true that we are needy in just the way described. We are in need of knowing God and on no other terms than by grace. In actual fact, however, our "complete closedness" always accompanies this neediness. Our "deepest and most real need" for the miracle of grace is not really objective but subjective. For our need is nowhere deeper than in our ability to "cover up and hide" our true neediness. It is nowhere deeper than in the illusion that we are not really needy, that we are already sufficiently rich, that we can live without God's grace or even allot it to ourselves. Our objective neediness does not prevent us from supposing to be rich in this way. But in just this delusion we are "necessarily closed against God" (II/1, 130).

It follows that we are also lacking in the requisite knowledge. This lack can be a subtle affair. Our knowledge can assume the proper external

form, yet be without the real inner content. We can become "sensible of
the truth of grace" and thus even of our own neediness. But considered
in itself, our human knowledge is "not strong but weak, not to salvation
but to condemnation" (II/1, 130). Insofar as we remain centered on ourselves, our knowledge of our neediness will remain hopelessly "abstract," as will our knowledge of God's grace. Our neediness will be
known only in the form of an "abstract misery" which can easily be held
in tension with the delusion of our self-sufficiency, and God's grace will
be known only in the form of an "abstract law" which casts us down
"by its sublimity and severity" while still allowing us to "dream again"
that we can perhaps fulfill it. Therefore, this sort of knowledge will leave
us just as closed to being ready for God as we were without it (II/1, 131).

It also follows, furthermore, that under these circumstances we will
not be able to break through our self-enclosure. Not even our greatest
willingness will get us beyond "the dialectic of need and grace," which
is all we can know when centered on ourselves. No willingness under
these circumstances can "burst the fatal cycle of this dialectic," for we
will still be trapped within our abstract knowledge of need and grace.
Even though we may accept that we are needy, we will still harbor within
ourselves the unsurrendered fantasy that at bottom we know how to cope
with our neediness and have the resources to surmount it. Moreover, even
though we may try to live by grace, we will still do so inappropriately
and without real willingness. We will still be occupied with grace in the
form of the law. We will thus think of grace either as something to which
we must conform (thereby verging on despair), or else as something to
which we can conform (thereby verging on presumption). Either way, we
will remain just as closed to being ready for God afterward as we were
before (II/1, 131).

The idea that we are open to grace, therefore, does not correspond to
anything real about us in general. For at all three points (neediness,
knowledge, willingness), our actual situation is determined by our sin.
The condition of sin is not accidental and transitory, therefore not something we can overcome of ourselves. It is permanent and pervasive (II/1,
130). We are determined by it (or determine ourselves by it) at all points.
Therefore, when subjected to doctrinal testing, the idea that we might be
open to grace fails to conform with what we otherwise know about ourselves by virtue of the doctrine of sin.

The testing, however, can be conducted from a different angle. What
would be the result if we were to look at our possible openness to grace

not simply from the standpoint of our sinfulness, but more concretely from the standpoint of human existence in the church as determined by the Word of God? Is it not in the church that human existence is opened to grace by grace? Is it not here that human beings can at least be described as ready for God? It is one of the most striking features of Barth's objectivism, with its insistence on the centrality of christological mediation, that it consistently leads to an unsparing analysis of existence in the church. Even in the church, human existence in itself and as such is still existence as determined by sin. Even in the church, as long as human existence holds the center of attention as the object of an independent interest, it is still an existence closed to grace. Even in the church—indeed, perhaps there most of all—the self-enclosure of our existence in resisting God's grace will emerge "in all its clarity and necessity" (II/1, 134).

For in and of ourselves, Barth argues, we can and do tolerate what the Word of God has to say about our existence. We can bear it when we are told about our existence in sin—that we are "really entangled in guilt," that we are "sunk in death," that we are "filled with fear and despair" (II/1, 133). Through it all we continue to uphold and assert ourselves. Even in all our poverty we cling to the dream of a life rich and sufficient unto ourselves. We are perhaps not as radically shattered, says Barth, as we sometimes make ourselves out to be by the awareness of our entanglement in guilt and death. We endure this reality "far rather and far more easily" than the grace of God, which would relieve us of the need to sustain and control our own lives. We can also bear it, moreover, that God's grace meets us "as really as possible in the word and sacrament, even in God's own revelation" (II/1, 134). We can have no deeper reality than in being addressed by God's Word and thereby awakened to real existence. "But even our deepest reality is still separated by an abyss from our openness for God's grace and therefore from the knowability of God for us" (II/1, 134). At all points the reality confronted by God's Word is the reality of an existence that in itself and as such is "not at peace but at war with grace" (II/1, 133). When centered on our own reality. on "the light of the divine truth in the prism of our own existence," the only thing manifest at all will be our war against grace, not our peace with it, and therefore simply our wretchedness (II/1, 134). It would seem, then, that even when conducted from a second angle, the results of this testing are no different from those of the first.

Natural Theology in the Church as a Sign
of Human Unreadiness for Grace

It is this conception of human existence as in itself hostile to grace, even and especially when confronted by God's Word, that underlies Barth's analysis of the persistence of natural theology in the church. Natural theology, it might be said, is presented as a theology that violates the essential precepts of objectivism, actualism, and particularism. Not mediated, not miraculous, and not unique in kind is the way our access to God appears, from the standpoint of natural theology. According to natural theology, as Barth understands it, our access to God is not something mediated exclusively in and through Jesus Christ; rather it is, at least in part, immediately open to us (and we to it). Again, it is not something miraculously enacted and bestowed (in and by Jesus Christ) by virtue of a special and self-renewing event, but is rather, at least in part, at the disposal of our own innate capacities. Again, it is not something uniquely grounded in itself both ontically and noetically, but is rather, at least in part, independently and generally given to us apart from the particular history of divine self-revelation as centered in Christ. Natural theology is thus conceived as a theology according to which our access to God is not mediated but immediate, not miraculous but natural, and not unique in kind but generally given.

This idea of an immediate, natural, and general access to God is understood, when it persists in the church (and in the theology of the church), as a symptom of our sorry attempt to preserve and affirm ourselves in self-sufficiency, even when really confronted by the Word of God. It shows the extent to which we would rather bear our own lives, even through the wretchedness of guilt and death, than be carried solely by divine grace. It shows the extent to which we can endure the offer of God's Word without being thrown off course. It shows the extent to which natural theology is something that has already been lived out before it has been thought and developed as such. Above all, it shows the extent to which we are prepared to affirm in self-sufficiency and self-justification that we ourselves already stand in the truth. "The core of this theology is that for us the truth can be had without the truth itself, because we ourselves are the truth itself, or at any rate, we are also the truth itself, in independence of the truth of God. This theology of life only needs to be made explicit as such and the whole of natural theology is in force in its basic idea" (II/1, 135–36 rev.).

In the section of Barth we have been following, the critique of natural theology is developed especially in terms of actualism, but the constructive alternative especially in terms of objectivism. That is, the critique argues primarily that by affirming our natural capacities this theology ends by denying the miracle of grace, whereas the constructive alternative argues that our capacity for grace is mediated in an exclusively christological fashion. For the question of truth, the argument means that we do not have the kind of independent access to the truth that we would ordinarily like to ascribe to ourselves, but that even subjectively this access is rooted and grounded externally in "Someone" quite other than ourselves—"so rooted and grounded that it lives entirely by him, and derives its whole reality from him" (II/1, 133).

Natural theology is criticized as an expression of illusory self-sufficiency in matters of theological truth. It is a rampart in our defense against the miracle of grace. Because the content of this miracle is grace, it means that God comes (and will continue to come) to help us in our deepest need. But because the form of this grace is miracle, it means that God comes (and will continue to come) only with a grace that is sovereign and free. The miracle of grace thus means that God comes (and will continue to come) in the midst of our deepest need to carry us through guilt and death, but only in a way that involves the surrender of human self-sufficiency (and thus of the concealment of human neediness).

This surrender, however, is precisely what natural theology would disallow. Natural theology assumes that we have some sort of independent and autonomous leverage with respect to grace. It is thus a theology that allows us to parry the threat to our sense of adequacy. It allows us to absorb and domesticate grace rather than be dethroned by it. It allows us to transform revelation from an unnerving if liberating question into an answer that we ourselves can control. Without sacrificing our own "capacity" and even in line with it, we suppose that we can turn revelation into a possibility to be chosen by ourselves. We take hold of grace as though it stood at our disposal. Human capacity, "very far from being sacrificed, has at once undergone an immense inner enrichment, an addition, so to speak, to its furniture" (II/1, 139 rev.). Revelation (without mediation) and grace (without miracle) become possibilities (without uniqueness) that we can choose with equanimity.

Natural theology thereby presupposes what Barth takes to be an impossible understanding of nature and grace. It presupposes that grace exists *alongside* nature, in the sense that nature is understood to have its own independent, autonomous, and self-grounded capacity for grace (at least in part or ostensibly in part). It presupposes (and Barth finds this to be completely inadmissible) that nature in itself and as such establishes certain external conditions to which even grace is bound to conform and which thereby pose a limit to grace in its sovereignty and freedom. It presupposes that nature has its own quotient of sovereignty and freedom apart from that established and sustained by grace itself.

> If grace is alongside nature, however high above it it may be put, it is obviously no longer the grace of God, but the grace which we ascribe to ourselves. If God's revelation is alongside a knowledge of God proper to us as human beings as such, even though it may never be advanced except as a prolegomenon, it is obviously no longer the revelation of God, but a new expression (borrowed or even stolen) for the revelation which encounters us in our own reflection. If the miracle acknowledged by us—perhaps an inspired Scripture or an infallible Church—is included in our own reckoning, if it is placed by us alongside the other phenomena of our world, it is obviously no longer the miracle of God, but an astounding element in our view of the world and of ourselves. No supranaturalism which we can choose on this higher rung can hold its own against the fact that in the last resort, as chosen by us, it is only a higher, though masked, naturalism. (II/1, 139 rev.)

The relationship between nature and grace, it might be noted, is, in Barth's very different understanding, one that falls within the purview of the Hegelian pattern. That is, nature has no autonomous or independent freedom alongside or over against the freedom of grace. Instead, nature is subjected by grace to a kind of *Aufhebung,* in the sense that nature is affirmed, negated, and then reconstituted on a higher plane. In its distinction as a reality other than and over against grace, nature is affirmed. In its corruption as a reality that supposes itself to be autonomously grounded apart from grace, nature is negated. In its destiny as a reality to be drawn beyond itself into genuine fellowship with grace, the negation is negated, and nature is miraculously reconstituted on a higher plane. Two points here are especially to be noted. First, nature has no capacity for grace apart from that miraculously granted and sustained *in actu*—in and by the act of grace itself. Second, unlike the Hegelian pattern as it may be found or used outside Barth's theology, within this theology it is never used to assert or imply that nature is drawn into a kind of synthesis with grace, as if the end result of the miraculous transformation were a kind of monism. As will be explored later in more detail, the end result, far from being understood as a monistic synthesis in which nature is swallowed up by grace, is rather understood to be the establishment of a genuine and free relatedness or fellowship between them.

When subjected to an actualistic critique, therefore, it becomes clear that human nature in itself has no *autonomous* capacity apart from grace by which it becomes possible to choose revelation.

> God's real revelation simply cannot be chosen by us and, as our own possibility, put beside another, and integrated with it into a system. God's real revelation is the possibility which we do not have to choose, but by which we must regard ourselves as chosen without having space or time to come to an arrangement with it within the sphere and according to the method of other possibilities. By treating it as if it does not do the choosing but is something to be chosen, not the unique but just one possibility, Christian natural theology very respectfully and in all humility re-casts revelation into a new form of its own devising. But for all that its behavior is so respectful and forbearing, for all that it subordinates itself so consciously and consistently, natural theology has already conquered it at the very outset, making revelation into non-revelation. (II/1, 139–40 rev.)

The heart of the actualistic critique, therefore, is that natural theology (for all its good or bad intentions) not only reinforces human nature at its most unfortunate point, but also in the process fails to allow grace to be grace, revelation to be revelation, and God to be God.

Mediated Subjectivity as the Solution to Human Incapacity

The constructive proposal that corresponds to this critique is objectivist in orientation. If in ourselves we are not at all ready for God and open to grace, and if all our efforts to prove that things are otherwise only end (like natural theology) by making matters worse and by confirming us in the futility and falsehood of our existence, then the contours of the proposed alternative are already clear. Our readiness for God and openness to grace must be found not in but apart from ourselves, and the futility and falsehood of our existence must thereby be overcome from without, but in such a way as also to be efficacious for us from within. The efficaciousness from within is a theme to be taken up when we return to a consideration of personalism. It is the readiness for God and openness to grace established apart from us for our sake in Jesus Christ that will be taken up and investigated here.

In and of ourselves we are not ready for God and we are not open to grace. We are rather opposed to God and hostile to grace. We are not subjectively open but closed to divine revelation, and we stand not in truth but in falsehood. If there is anyone who is ready for God, it is not we ourselves. Is there, in fact, anyone who is actually ready for God? Is there anyone who is not hostile but open to grace, who stands not in falsehood but in truth? There is someone, Barth believes, who fits the description. There is someone who is not opposed to but ready for God and who is not hostile but open to grace. There is someone who is not subjectively closed but open to divine revelation and who thus stands not in falsehood but in truth. The human being ready for God is not someone identical with us in ourselves, but a person who confronts us "in infinite promise" (II/1, 148). "How can it be Christian theology and proclamation if in all this—even in its illusions, even when it identifies the human being ready for God with ourselves as such—it does not mean Jesus Christ?" (II/1, 148 rev.).

Jesus Christ is the missing center which has so far been absent from the discussion. He is the center which remains displaced and invisible as long as the focus falls directly on our existence in itself and as such. Yet when he is restored to the center that is rightfully his, everything else falls into place. Human existence in general, and more particularly in the church, becomes properly ordered in relation to its true center. Human existence as it is in itself is not abolished (i.e., not yet), but is nonetheless (i.e., already) superseded by human existence as it is in Christ. Therefore it can be viewed in its fullest and deepest reality only in light of its true center. "Anthropological and ecclesiological assertions arise," writes Barth, "only as they are borrowed from Christology. That is to say, no anthropological or ecclesiological assertion is true in itself and as such. Its truth subsists in the assertions of Christology, or rather in the reality of Jesus Christ" (II/1, 138–39). Truth in Barth's theology is always christocentric, even and especially the truth of human existence. As "independent bearers of an independent predicate," human beings are "abstractions" destined to disappear (II/1, 139). Although Jesus Christ is external to us, we are not external to him. Our existence in itself and as such does not include his, but his existence includes ours in itself. Grace is external to nature, but nature is not external to grace. Nature is rather taken up, purged, and transformed by grace and is therefore really established by it. It is in this sense that our readiness for God and openness to grace have no *independent* status in themselves, but are included and established apart from us by the mediation of the human nature of Jesus Christ. It is in this sense that our subjective capacity for God is included, established, and grounded in his.

> Our truth is not the being which we find in ourselves as our own. The being which we find in ourselves as our own will always be the being in enmity against God. But this very being is a lie. It is the lie that is seen to be a lie in faith. Our truth is our being in the Son of God, in whom we are not

enemies but friends of God, in whom we do not hate grace but cling to grace alone, in whom therefore God is knowable to us. This is our truth as believed by faith. . . . To believe means to believe in Jesus Christ. But this means to keep wholly and utterly to the fact that our temporal existence receives and has and again receives its truth, not from itself, but exclusively from its relationship to what Jesus Christ is and does as our Advocate and Mediator in God himself. (II/1, 158–59 rev.)

The "basic rule of all sound doctrine," writes Barth, is that the truth about ourselves should be sought "in Jesus Christ and nowhere else" (II/1, 162). When this rule is applied to determining the truth about our subjective apprehension of God, then the result is that Jesus Christ emerges as its "first and proper Subject" (II/1, 252). It is because our knowing of God is so grounded, established, and mediated by his knowing that we may be confident about the truth of our knowledge. Realism is thereby connected with revelational objectivism in its subjective aspect: "In him who is true God and true humanity it is true that in his true revelation God gives to us a part in the truth of his knowing, and therefore gives to our human knowing similarity with his own and therefore truth" (II/1, 252 rev.). Actualism is also connected with this aspect of revelational objectivism insofar as our inclusion in the knowing of Jesus Christ occurs as a miraculous event: "On the basis of the grace of the Incarnation, on the basis of the acceptance and assumption of our humanity into unity of being with God as it has taken place in Jesus Christ, all this has become truth in this human being, in the humanity of Jesus Christ" (II/1, 252 rev.).

Particularism, furthermore, is also connected with revelational objectivism at this point insofar as our subjective apprehension is uniquely, originally, and properly grounded not in what may be generally accessible, but exclusively in the wholly self-grounded knowledge of God as it occurs within the Trinity and is mediated to us through Jesus: "The eternal Father knows the eternal Son, and the eternal Son knows the eternal Father. But the eternal Son is not only the eternal God. . . . When we appeal to God's grace, we appeal to the grace of the Incarnation and to this human being as the One in whom, because he is the eternal Son of God, knowledge of God was, is and will be present originally and properly" (II/1, 252 rev.). Personalism, finally, is also connected with this theme insofar as the knowing mediated to us by Jesus entails the promise of our fellowship with God: "When we appeal to God's grace, we appeal to the grace of the Incarnation and to this human being as the One . . . through whom, because he is the eternal Son of God, there is promised to us our own divine sonship, and therefore our fellowship in his knowledge of God" (II/1, 252 rev.). At each of these points, therefore—whether as the One whose knowing of God guarantees the analogical truth of our knowing (realism), or as the One through whose knowing God's truth miraculously becomes ours as well (actualism), or as the One through whom our knowing partakes of the mysterious, unique, and self-grounded inner-trinitarian divine knowing (particularism), or finally, as the One whose knowing entails the promise that our knowing will share through his in the inner-trinitarian life and fellowship of God (personalism)— Jesus Christ in his humanity is the Mediator of our subjective access to God. "It is not our knowledge of God, but the knowledge which is and will be present in this man Jesus, that we have described in our description of its reality, its possibility, and . . . its limits" (II/1, 252). In him the truth of our own knowing of God is really, actually, particularly, and personally true. "In him are hid all the treasures of wisdom and knowledge" (Col. 2:3).

Mediated objectivity and mediated subjectivity are thus the two main aspects of revelational objectivism. In Jesus Christ the being of God and our human being meet in the event of revelation. In his humanity he not only mediates God to us, but also mediates us to God. He mediates God to us by bringing to us the objectivity of the divine knowing, and he mediates us to God by bringing to God the subjectivity of our human knowing. He brings the objectivity of the divine knowing to us by disclosing God's trinitarian identity, and he brings the subjectivity of our knowing to God by opening us to God's inner-trinitarian life. The triune identity and triune life of God are both understood as mediated to us in and through the humanity of Jesus Christ. In him the truth of God becomes ours, and our truth is established through his.

CHAPTER 5

Truth as Mediated: Salvation

Soteriological objectivism, the other major category pertaining to christological mediation in Barth's theology, signifies that Jesus Christ is regarded as the sole Mediator not only of revealed truth, but also of saving
truth. Truth in Barth's theology is a category that governs not only our
knowing of God's identity, but also God's knowing of our identities in
Jesus Christ. Soteriological objectivism, briefly stated, means that there
is finally no other truth about us than the truth of who we are before God
in Jesus Christ. We have no existence before God that stands in independence of Jesus Christ. "The truth of our existence is simply this—Jesus
Christ has died and risen again for us. It is this and this alone which is
to be proclaimed to us as our truth" (II/1, 167 rev.).

Soteriological objectivism is a motif which Barth develops with un-
common and perhaps unprecedented consistency. Even when not neglected, the objectivist moment in the event of salvation is not usually
understood, within any given Christian theology, as taking unqualified
conceptual priority at all points over the more subjectivist or existential
moments. Indeed, the more usual procedure, at least in Western theology, would seem to be that the objectivist moment is ordered, whether
loosely or tightly, implicitly or explicitly, so as to exist (at least at some
point) in the service of the subjectivist or existential moments, and to that
extent in subordination to them. Even when objectivist moments like predestination or the atoning work of Christ on the cross are strongly emphasized, as they are for example in theologies like those of Augustine
or Calvin, the more existential moment still is not thoroughly subordinated to them insofar as the event of faith itself may in some sense be

regarded as decisive for the occurrence of salvation. Coming to faith or failing to do so is, in such theologies, ultimately decisive for whether salvation actually obtains or not in the case of any particular individual.

The broad differences between Augustine and Calvin on this question are instructive. Calvin's understanding of how the objectivist and existential moments of salvation are related is developed with a consistency which at times approximates that later achieved by Barth. Especially insofar as Calvin's theology approaches a doctrine of limited atonement, a doctrine which would make his theology of the cross consistent with the argument for double predestination in Book III of the *Institutes,* the objectivist moments would seem to be decisive and determinative in some thoroughgoing sense for whatever may occur existentially in someone's coming (or not coming) to faith. However, not even Calvin, it would seem, could entirely disregard those aspects of the New Testament witness in which the objectivist moments of salvation are associated in some sense with the idea that salvation is not limited but universal in scope, especially as accomplished by Christ on the cross. In any case, the approach to a doctrine of limited atonement remained ambiguous in Calvin's theology as a tendency that was not fully brought to conceptual realization. What did not remain ambiguous was the idea that one's coming to faith is constitutive in any given case to the actual occurrence of salvation. Those without faith are not saved.

By contrast to Calvin, Augustine did not always deal so self-consciously or comprehensively with the question of how the objectivist and the existential moments in the occurrence of salvation are to be seen as related. His approach, being more nearly local or ad hoc than Calvin's, not only led to a kind of overall looseness on the question of how these moments might be related, but also allowed him (apart from certain polemical situations) to gravitate most naturally toward a view in which the existential moment was of preponderant interest. Despite instances in which he could emphasize just as strongly as Calvin would later that God's action in predestination or in the cross was decisive and determinative, Augustine typically wrote elsewhere as though human existence itself were the decisive locus of salvation. Ideas like infused grace, or Christ working in us through love, could become so predominant in the discussion that, as Adolf von Harnack remarked, "what is called 'objective redemption' is left pretty much in the background."[1] Overall, therefore, Augustine's theology, when taken as a whole, may be read not only as being fairly ambiguous on the question of how objective and existential moments in salvation were finally related, but also as containing within itself more than one possible direction in which the question might be resolved.

One of those directions clearly pointed toward an understanding in which human decision played a final and deciding role in the occurrence of salvation for any particular individual. Even when human decision is conceived as coinciding mysteriously with the inner workings of divine grace, as it is when conversion is discussed in the *Confessions* or the two loves are presented in the *City of God,* the possible role of any objective christological mediation is often typically neglected and at any rate remains far from clear. When human decision (however assisted by divine grace) and personal growth in the spiritual life are conceived as decisive for the occurrence of salvation, then a split vision of human destiny readily follows in which the human race diverges finally into two cities, the one under way to eternal life, the other to eternal perdition. Destiny somehow depends on existential decision, even if the ground for that decision is traced back to the mystery of predestination. Whether finally understood more in terms of love (with Augustine and much of later Catholicism) or in terms of faith (with the Reformers and the ensuing Protestantism), human decision here and now plays a decisive and constitutive role in the occurrence of salvation. Regardless of how the existential and objectivist moments are understood to be related, and regardless of all residual ambiguities, human existence is the decisive locus of salvation insofar as the right decision leads to one kind of eternal destiny, whereas the wrong one leads to quite another.

The Central Question: How Is What Occurs in Christ Related to What Occurs in Us?

Another way of approaching this matter would be to ask how what happens in us with respect to salvation is related to what has happened in Christ. Soteriological objectivism, as the term will be used here, is not meant to refer to any position which emphasizes what took place in Christ to the exclusion of what takes place in us. Rather, it refers to that position which so relates them that anything taking place in us is thoroughly and radically subordinated to what has taken place in Christ. Soteriological existentialism, on the other hand, will be used to refer to the reverse position in which what has taken place in Christ is somehow at some point subordinated to (or perhaps conflated with) what needs to take place in us. The term existentialism is adopted for lack of a better alternative and is meant in a strictly formal sense (having nothing to do with the modern philosophical movement of the same name). Regardless of how the existential moment may be defined (whether it be more individualistically or socially or sacramentally), soteriological existentialism is characterized by the view that salvation in itself and as such is not constituted or complete until something decisive takes place in one's human existence. To that extent, what took place in Christ does not acquire validity and efficacy until something decisive also comes to take place in us.

A certain artificiality has admittedly been hard to avoid in the exposition which follows. By virtue of discussing soteriological objectivism and personalism in two separate chapters respectively, the inner unity between them, which Barth always presupposed, may be obscured. Compounding the problem, furthermore, is the fact that Barth's conception of this unity is highly innovative, complex, and counterintuitive. He often presupposed more about this unity than he made explicit, and when he did become explicit he was not easily understood. The concrete unity he saw between the objective and existential aspects of salvation cannot really be grasped apart from a fuller definition of these aspects themselves. Perhaps a preliminary description of this unity, however, will help to prevent the initial and lengthy discussion of objectivism from throwing the deferred discussion of personalism entirely into eclipse.

Two points above all seemed essential to Barth about salvation. First, what took place in Jesus Christ for our salvation avails for all. Second, no one actively participates in him and therefore in his righteousness apart from faith. The first point constitutes the objective aspect, the second the existential aspect, of salvation. The objective aspect is determinative and creative, the existential aspect responsive and receptive, in status. These differences in status are not to be confused. The human act of faith is in no way determinative or creative of salvation, and the divine act of grace is in no way responsive or receptive to some condition external to itself as necessarily imposed upon it by the human creature. The divine act of grace is conditioned, in its response to and reception of the human creature, only by its own inner movement. Grace therefore confronts the creature as a sheer gift. The human act of faith, moreover, in no way conditions, contributes to, or constitutes the event of salvation. Faith therefore confronts the Savior in sheer gratitude and sheer receptivity (which is not the same as mere passivity), and is itself inexplicable except as a miracle of grace.

The real efficacy of the saving work of Christ for all, the absolutely unconditioned and therefore gratuitous character of divine grace in him, the impossibility of actively participating in Christ and his righteousness apart from faith, the absolutely receptive and therefore nonconstitutive character of human faith with respect to salvation—all these were axiomatic and nonnegotiable for Barth, because he took them to be the assured results of exegesis when the Bible was read christocentrically as a unified and differentiated whole. The field of tension established by these assertions when taken together was something to be respected and worked within, not something to be explained away or resolved for the sake of achieving a tidier conceptual outcome. No possible tidier outcome could be achieved except at the expense of hermeneutical adequacy. Any gains in technical consistency at the conceptual or doctrinal level could be had only by suffering unacceptable losses of coherence with the subject matter of scripture. In such cases adequacy was to be regarded as a higher virtue than consistency. The sheer mystery and incomprehensibility of the subject matter (particularism), as attested in and through the biblical text (realism plus actualism), not only imposed important limits on the possibility of achieving technical consistency, but also established the very conditions for the possibility of any intelligibility in theological discourse worthy of the name (rationalism). All doctrinal construction, ordering, and testing, and all assimilation of extrabiblical conceptions, had to be done with a sure and uncompromising sense of the limits to conceptualization imposed by the subject matter. Otherwise the subject matter, whose mysteries as such fell into specifiable patterns, would no longer be comprehended in terms of its own intrinsic and indissoluble incomprehensibility.

The patterns within which the mysterious unity of soteriological objectivism and personalism seemed to Barth to fall were largely those of actualism and dialectical inclusion. The motif of actualism made it possible to speak of the unity of a single, once-for-all event which yet occurred uniquely and mysteriously in a variety of differentiated and self-transcending forms. At the same time the formal "trinitarian" pattern of dialectical inclusion made it possible to speak of each form of this occurrence in such a way that the whole was always somehow present in each one of the forms without making any of them (whether subsequent or prior) superfluous. Each distinctive form of this occurrence made its own contribution to the unified whole, and yet nothing less than the whole was present as such in each distinctive and irreplaceable form. This dialectical inclusion or reciprocal coinherence of each differentiated form in the unified whole, and of the unified whole in each differentiated form, was itself an internally ordered or structured occurrence. For the occurrence as such had a "center" and a "periphery," and never the one without the other. All the differentiated, living, and actualistic forms constituting the whole were unified by the unique and once-for-all form of the event alive at their center—Jesus Christ himself. These complex conceptual patterns, it is important to see, are developed precisely in order to respect (and not to compromise) those assertions mentioned as constituting the assured results of exegesis. They are designed to work within (and not to resolve) the conceptual field of tension—of patterned and therefore specifiable mystery—which these assertions, taken together, serve to establish.

When these conceptual patterns are applied to the unity of soteriological objectivism and personalism, the results are as follows. First of all, they are applied to the objectivism in itself. What takes place in Jesus Christ is seen as governed by actualist and dialectically inclusivist patterns of mystery. These patterns are especially meant to respect and incorporate the biblical testimony that what took place in Jesus Christ took place for all. Perhaps no theologian of the church since Athanasius, in whom the same strong association of "in Christ" with "for all" is constantly present (though of course in a more spontaneous and less thematized way), has so consistently tried to do direct justice to the universalistic aspects of the New Testament witness to Jesus Christ as has Barth. He simply refuses to qualify this aspect for the sake of a tidier conceptual outcome, as he seems to think has all too habitually taken place (and not without severe doctrinal distortions), especially in the Christian tradition of the West, and especially since the idea of "two cities" flowed almost indelibly into that tradition through the powerful pen of Augustine. Instead, Barth resolutely incorporates this universality as it stands (in an undeniably prominent strand of scripture) into his doctrinal scheme. The pattern of dialectical inclusion thus describes how the history of every human being is included in that of Jesus, and the pattern of actualism describes how the history of Jesus is included in that of every human being.

The history of every human being is seen as included in that of Jesus. The history of Jesus is taken as the center which establishes, unifies, and incorporates a differentiated whole in which the history of each human being as such is included. This act of universal inclusion is his accomplishment and achievement. He enacts our salvation as a gift which is valid and efficacious for all. The validity and efficacy of this gift cannot be denied without compromising (among other things) the absolutely unconditioned and therefore gratuitous character of divine grace in him.

This denial would therefore be unjustifiable within the web of Christian (or biblically derived) beliefs. The inclusion of every human being's history in that of Jesus is therefore described according to the pattern of dialectical inclusion. No one is excluded from the validity and efficacy of what took place for our salvation in Jesus Christ. In his history is objectively included the history of each and of all.

Conversely, the history of Jesus is viewed as included in that of every human being. Although his history and what it accomplishes occur in a definite sequence of time and a definite location of place, they are not encapsulated in that time and place in an unqualified way. On the contrary, they are present, in a mysterious and differentiated way, and in ways known and as yet unknown, to the history of each and every human being as such. Just as their history is enclosed in his, so is his enclosed in theirs, with all its efficacy and validity. The continual, miraculous, and mysterious presence of his history (and therefore he himself) to theirs (and therefore to themselves) cannot be denied without denying (among other things) his resurrection from the dead. Therefore this denial, too, would be unjustifiable within the web of Christian beliefs. The inclusion of Jesus' history in that of everyone else's is therefore described according to the pattern of actualism. The once-for-all event of Jesus' history, without ceasing to be such, reiterates itself so as to be present to the history of each and every human being. In the history of each and of all, his history is objectively included.

Second, these same conceptual patterns are applied to personalism as the existential moment of salvation. Personalism is so structured by these patterns that they not only serve to inform the existential moment in itself but also its inner unity with the objective moment of salvation. Thus the patterns of actualism and dialectical inclusion are not only employed to incorporate the biblical testimony that what took place in Jesus Christ avails for all. They are also employed to incorporate the testimony that it is impossible for anyone actively to participate in Jesus Christ and the salvation he has accomplished apart from the decision of faith. The objective validity and efficacy of salvation in Christ by no means eliminates the necessity of actively receiving it by faith, nor does the necessity of actively receiving it by faith eliminate the objective validity and efficacy of salvation. The necessity at stake is, so to speak, a necessity of freedom rather than of compulsion. Faith is necessary as the only apt response to the objective validity and efficacy of salvation. It is the response of gratitude, joy, trust, love, and obedience. Its status is, so to speak, internal and analytic rather than external and synthetic. It does not in any sense constitute, contribute to, or bring about the occurrence of salvation. It simply undertakes to enact the appropriate consequences in response to an occurrence of salvation which in itself and as such already avails in validity, efficacy, and completeness for each one and therefore for all.

The need to partake actively of salvation by faith could not be denied without at once incurring obvious hermeneutical inadequacy with respect to scripture and also serious incoherence within the web of doctrinal belief. Salvation could not be merely objective in its validity and efficacy (as Barth realizes as clearly as anyone else), without its turning the human being into a less than responsible acting subject. At the same time, however, the human recipient's active participation in salvation by faith must not be conceived as in any way effecting the occurrence of salvation for that person. The nonconstitutive character of one's faith with respect to one's salvation could not be denied without denying (among other things) not only the absolutely unconditional and gratuitous character of divine grace, but also the saving work of Christ as something finished, complete, and unrepeatable in itself. The resulting situation is obviously deeply paradoxical. If grace is unconditional, how can faith be necessary? If faith is necessary, how can grace be unconditional? Any resolution of the paradox would obviously result in a tidier conceptual outcome. Yet technical consistency could be achieved in this way, Barth contends, only at the twofold cost of hermeneutical inadequacy and doctrinal incoherence within the larger web of belief. The tension between grace as unconditional and faith as indispensable is therefore simply allowed to stand. The paradox which results at this point is taken as the conceptual emblem of an underlying mystery. It seems to be the unavoidable outcome when the events of grace and faith as attested by scripture are conceptually redescribed in their mysterious ordering, differentiation, and unity.

These events in their ordered and differentiated unity can indeed be conceptually redescribed, Barth believes, but only in such a way that the mystery of their interrelation is respected. Although the larger pattern which informs this mystery will be specified later in detail (see chapter 7), it can at least be seen for now that Barth characteristically makes a fundamental distinction between description and explanation.[2] The events of grace and faith can be conceptually redescribed in their complex interrelation, but not at all conceptually explained. The only relevant explanation is why there can be no explanation. Why isn't it possible to explain conceptually *how* the events occur in an ordered and differentiated unity except by means of antithetical formulations which subvert the very project of explanation itself? In and with the hermeneutical derivation and coherentist testing of the paradoxically related statements, another consideration seems never to be far from Barth's mind. If an explanation of how the events of grace and faith can and do occur in just this mode of relation were possible, if the condition for the possibility of this mode of relation could be specified without paradox, then it could only be by means of some generally accessible analogy, system, or scheme. The occurrence of these events and their mode of relation would therefore no longer be depicted in as miraculous, mysterious, and unique a form as they seem to possess in their scriptural attestation. The explanation of why there can be no explanation thus involves the perception that by definition these events manifest themselves in, but do not ultimately arise from, the order of created reality. They are rather to be seen as irruptions in the created order of another and divine order by which the created order itself is relativized, limited, and contained. This new and alien order is something which the created order cannot control, whether conceptually or otherwise. The events of its manifestation are always somehow radically disjunctive of the created order in which they occur (even though they lead this order to its ultimate fulfillment). The paradoxicality of the statements by which these events are described is thus taken as a sign that mystery precludes mastery, just as the inexplicability of the mode by which the events are related is taken as a sign that in and of itself the created order has no access to ultimate reality.

For reasons such as these, theology must content itself with description and resist the temptation to explanation. In the case of such events it must content itself with describing the mysterious facticity of the *that*, which facticity intrinsically excludes the possibility of explaining the corresponding *how*. It is in just such terms that Barth disavows the possibility of explaining the mode by which the events of grace and faith are related. The pattern of this relation—its ordered and differentiated unity—can be described, but its mode defies explanation. The pattern is a conjunction of opposites and therefore of irreconcilably antithetical assertions. The unity of grace and faith occurs in such a way that grace is always universal and unconditional in its objective efficacy and validity, yet at the same time faith is always necessary and indispensable in its existential receptivity and freedom. A theology which could explain *how* this unity occurs as it does or how it occurs as a unity would be explaining the *modus operandi* of the Holy Spirit.

> How gladly we would hear and know and say something more, something more precise, something more palpable concerning *the way* in which the work of the Holy Spirit is done! *How* does it really happen *that* the history

of Jesus Christ, in which the history of all human beings is virtually enclosed and accomplished, is actualized, in the first instance only in the history of a few, of a small minority within the many of whom this cannot so
far be said, but even in the history of the few typically for the history of
the many? *How* can it really be—the question of the Virgin in Luke 1:34—
that there is an actualizing of this history in other human histories? *By what
ways* does God bring it about that in the perverted hearts, in the darkened
knowledge and understanding, in the rebellious desires and strivings of sinful human beings—for that is what even the few are—there takes place this
awakening, in which they can know Jesus Christ as theirs and themselves
as his? *How* is there really born *in them* the new human being who knows
and recognizes and confesses Jesus Christ? *How* can there be in history such
a thing as Christianity, and human beings who seriously want to be Christians? (IV/1, 648–49 rev., emphasis added)

It is as important and unavoidable to formulate such questions, Barth
contends, as it is to leave them unanswered, except for the obviously
indispensable appeal to the miraculous and mysterious mode which informs the work of the Holy Spirit as confessed by faith. "The confession
credo in Spiritum Sanctum does not tell us anything concerning this How.
It merely indicates the fact all this does take place, did take place and
continually will take place" (IV/1, 649). Moreover, the evident reticence
of the creed at this point is simply a reflection of the reticence of the
New Testament itself. "Even the New Testament . . . does not really
tell us anything about the How, the mode of his working" (IV/1, 649).
Beyond simply describing and asserting the facticity of the Holy Spirit's
working, all questions as to its explanation are consistently repelled. To
try to go beyond the New Testament at this point would obviously, Barth
believes, be futile.

Barth therefore resolves to work within the terms of this inexplicability. The pattern of dialectical inclusion is used, as indicated, to describe
(but not explain) how the history of each and every human being is objectively enclosed in that of Jesus. That same pattern is then used in
conjunction with the pattern of actualism to describe (but not explain)
how the history of Jesus is in turn objectively included in that of each
and every human being. The objective moment of salvation is thereby
understood as being at once fully actualized once and for all and yet not
encapsulated or imprisoned within its central and definitive form of temporal occurrence. Without compromising this central and definitive form,
the objective moment as such assumes secondary and derivative form by
actualizing itself in relation to the history of each and every human ex-

istence. The actualization of the objective moment of salvation in this twofold form (central and derivative) is (descriptively speaking) a condition for the possibility of its subjective actualization by faith. The existential moment of salvation is thereby understood as occurring entirely within the context established by the objective moment.

The existential moment may therefore not be spoken of as making the the objective moment real or concrete, as though the objective moment were somehow unreal or abstract as such until the moment of its existential appropriation (a commonplace but ultimately blasphemous way of speaking). Nor may the existential moment be spoken of as effecting a transition from being outside to being inside the objective moment, as though the objective moment did not already include each and every human existence within itself, or as though the existential moment could somehow contribute itself to the objective moment in such a way that the objective would otherwise be deficient. Nor, finally, may the existential moment be spoken of as effecting a transition from being potentially to being actually saved, as though the objective moment were not already in itself the real, valid, and efficacious actualization of salvation for the sake of all. Each of these mistaken ways of speaking makes the event of existential appropriation less incomprehensible and mysterious, Barth believes, than it actually is in its scriptural attestation.

The transition effected by the existential moment of salvation is seen as a transition from the opaque mystery of sin to the luminous mystery of faith. It is therefore a transition from nonacknowledgment (whether in the form of ignorance or indifference or hostility) to acknowledgment, from a mode of participating in salvation which is virtual and unresponsive to a mode which is active and alive. Faith as such does not create or contribute anything new. It consists solely in the existential actualization of a salvation which cannot be conceived except as already objectively actualized. From the point of view of eternity, so to speak, the transition is one in which an already actualized salvation is manifested, attested, and confirmed. Yet from the point of view of the active historical recipient, the transition is clearly one in which all things have become new. As something real, valid, and complete in itself, the objective moment of salvation is existentially manifested, acknowledged, attested, and received with gratitude and self-surrender. The inner unity of the two moments is so conceived that the objective does not occur without this free existential reception and response, nor does the existential occur without this sovereign objective precedence and actualization.

The ordering, differentiation, and unity of these two moments of salvation clearly involve a complex conceptuality wherein mystery is textured within mystery. There is the mystery of dialectical inclusion whereby all are enclosed in Christ. There is the mystery of actualism whereby the central form of this occurrence assumes secondary form in the history of each and every human being. There is the mystery of the whole self-contained yet all-inclusive actualization of salvation in its objective aspect. There is the mystery of the need to participate in this actualization existentially through the free response of faith. There is the mystery that sinful human beings are enabled to make this response by a faith that is evoked and sustained entirely from without. There is the mystery that not all make this response even though salvation avails efficaciously for all, and the mystery that those who do make this response make it so imperfectly and inadequately. There is the mystery of the unity of the objective and existential aspects of salvation such that neither occurs without the other while yet each retains its own peculiar (and apparently antithetical) status. And there is the mystery of the destiny of those who never seem to make the appropriate response of faith at all despite salvation's universal efficacy. In various ways and from various angles, the discussion which follows will attempt to elucidate Barth's understanding of this complex texture of mystery in more detail. (For material pertinent to this preliminary discussion, see IV/1, 608–50, 740–79.)

"In Christ" as the Decisive Locus of Salvation

Perhaps no single observation can be of more assistance to the careful reader of the *Church Dogmatics* than to note that Barth always uses the ubiquitous but inconspicuous term "in Christ" (and its cognates) in what is virtually a technical sense. Phrases, sentences, paragraphs, sometimes even entire sections (such as "The Verdict of the Father" in IV/1) cannot fully be understood, unless it is seen that the argument turns on the objectivist soteriology conveyed by that little phrase. "In Christ" is the key indicator of Barth's soteriological objectivism. It indicates that salvation is understood to be entirely constituted, complete, and effective apart from and prior to any reception of it that may or may not occur here and now in our existence. It indicates that Jesus Christ is the decisive locus of salvation in the sense that his existence is so inclusive of ours that we can recognize our true selves only in him. It indicates that whatever may or may not take place in us, it cannot add to or subtract from the actuality of our salvation as it avails for us apart from ourselves in him. Above all, it indicates that Barth is much more dialectical in relating what took place in Christ to what takes place in us than is customary in the history of theology.

In what is perhaps the definitive summary of this theme in the *Church Dogmatics,* Barth writes:

> "In Christ" means that in him we are reconciled to God, in him we are elect from eternity, in him we are called, in him we are justified and sanctified, in him our sin is carried to the grave, in his resurrection our death is overcome, with him our life is hid in God, in him everything that has to be done for us, to us, and by us, has already been done, has previously been removed and put in its place, in him we are children in the Father's house, just as he is by nature. All that has to be said about us can be said only by describing and explaining it as an existence in him; not by describing and explaining it as an existence which we might have in and for itself. That is why the subjective reality of revelation as such can never be made an independent theme. It is enclosed in its objective reality. . . . For by Christ we will never be anything else than just what we are in Christ. And when the Holy Spirit draws and takes us right into the reality of revelation by doing what we cannot do, by opening our eyes and ears and hearts, he does not tell us anything except that we are in Christ by Christ. . . . We are invited and challenged to understand ourselves from this and not from any other standpoint. (I/2, 240; cf. II/2, 117)

Because Jesus Christ is himself the decisive locus of human salvation—because this salvation is fully actualized, complete, and vital in him—the existential moment of salvation here and now consists solely in recognizing that regardless of what one may find in oneself, the reality of salvation is to be found not in oneself but in him. One's eyes and ears and heart are to be opened simply to this fact. One's existence is to be described and explained on this (and only on this) basis. By nature one's human existence (as created and fallen) does not include but excludes his existence, but by grace his existence (as the saving Mediator of God to the world and of the world to God) does not exclude but includes one's own. He is external to one's human existence but one's existence is internal to him.

Men and women are therefore summoned to understand themselves as being incorporated "in Christ by Christ." It is his action, and not in any sense theirs, by which they are incorporated into his reality before God and therefore into salvation. The actuality of salvation, which comes to them as a gift complete in itself, depends solely on the mediatorial work of Jesus Christ apart from them, against them, and for them. This mediatorial work (which in its full complexity includes pretemporal election as well as eschatological judgment) can be explicated in its essence by a brief glance at the cross as the event of salvation.

The cross, as Barth understands it, occurred as the event of salvation by virtue of the true humanity and true deity of Jesus Christ. In his true humanity Jesus Christ was at once the embodiment of grace and the victim of human enmity toward grace. He embodied grace as the true human covenant partner which God had always intended and sought, but which human beings in their sin had failed miserably to become. In his role as the true covenant partner, Jesus Christ took the place of humankind before God in a positive sense, enacting obedience and service to God on humankind's behalf. Yet in the course of fulfilling this role, Jesus Christ was at the same time rejected and slain, becoming the victim of humankind's enmity toward the very grace which he embodied. In his true deity, furthermore, Jesus Christ made himself to be the embodiment of the very sin by which he was victimized, and of God's righteous enmity toward sin. Although sinless in himself, he bore the consequences of sin in humankind's place and on its behalf. By his suffering and death he thereby also took humankind's place before God in a negative sense, assuming to himself the accusation, judgment, and punishment that were rightfully humankind's. As the Son of God he could do this. "As the Son of God he could enter into our place, into the place of every individual human being, of the whole human race. And as the Son of God he has actually done it" (II/1, 152). The cross is therefore the event in which the depth of humankind's enmity toward grace is at once disclosed and yet fully overcome. At the same time it is also the event in which the depth of God's enmity toward sin is at once disclosed and yet expiated and abolished. "This is the victory of grace over human enmity against grace" (II/1, 152). It is the victory in which human enmity is confronted and obliterated. "And if it is obliterated before God, it is obliterated in truth. What happens in the truth, what is indeed truth, is what happens before God, by God, in our place. And it has happened before God, by God, in our place, that our enmity against his grace has been expiated and abandoned" (II/1, 152).

The Reality of Salvation in Christ

From this understanding of Jesus Christ's mediatorial work, it follows that in him the salvation of humankind is already accomplished. By virtue of his accomplishment, we human beings are no longer outside but inside the grace of God. Whether we see and acknowledge it or not, salvation comes to us as a gift that is already actual and complete. It needs no further actualization or completion by us or even in us, for by Christ we already have our being in Christ. "There can be no question," writes Barth, about "the being of Jesus Christ" for us, "and therefore about our being in him. There can be no question as to the love with which God has loved us from all eternity and once for all in time. This does not need our assistance or completion or co-operation or even repetition. It does not even need to be seen by us" (IV/2, 296 rev.). It obtains, whether we have come to acknowledge it yet or not. For the great alteration of the human situation—our being reconciled to God—has already taken place. "This being is self-contained. It does not have to be reached or created. It has already come and cannot be removed. It is indestructible, it can never be superseded, it is in force, it is directly present" (IV/1, 90). Our being in Christ is understood in the strongest possible terms: as an "ontological connection." It is a connection that is grounded and established not by our action but solely by his action, not in our experience (whatever it might be) but solely in his experience (i.e., his death and resurrection), and therefore, most simply and comprehensively, not in ourselves but solely in himself (IV/2, 275).

It follows, by virtue of this ontological connection, that the gospel "does not indicate possibilities but declares actualities" (IV/2, 275). The gospel declares that we human beings are actually in Christ by Christ. Our being in Christ by Christ confronts us "not merely as an offer and possibility, but as a reality, an event, which in its scope is actually determinative of all human existence. The significance of the existence of this man for ours is not just potential but actual; a significance to which we and all persons are to be referred at once and without reserve" (IV/2, 267 rev.). The gospel does not proclaim that if only we will fulfill certain conditions, salvation will then be effective for us. It does not proclaim that if only we will make the necessary decision, or undergo the stipulated religious experience, or right the appointed social wrong, or receive the properly validated sacrament—if only we will meet some particular requirement or actualize some particular possibility—then and only then will salvation be ours. The gospel does not turn itself at the last moment back into the law from which it was meant to deliver us. It does not abandon the realm of freedom by sending us back into the throes of necessity.

Our salvation in Christ, as Barth understands it, is already effective. We need only to receive and acknowledge it in freedom, not to make it effective ourselves. "Is Jesus Christ only the possibility and not rather the full actuality of the grace of God? Is his intervention for us sinners anything other or less than the divine forgiveness itself? And what does this forgiveness lack in order to be effective if it has taken place in him" (IV/1, 487)? Salvation is not an open possibility but an effective reality, precisely because it is an event—an event that is "comprehensive, total and definitive" (IV/1, 547). It takes place apart from us, but not without including us. It takes place just by including us in the history of Jesus Christ. "His history is as such our history" (IV/1, 548). His history is our history, because in his life, death, and resurrection he has made our situation his own. "We are the participants in this great drama. That history is, in fact, our history. We have to say indeed that it is our true history, in an incomparably more direct and intimate way than anything which might present itself as our history in our own subjective experience" (IV/1, 547).

Therefore, if we sinful human beings are to find the truth of our existence, the reality of our salvation, and the ground of our selfhood before God, the basic rule is that we should look away from ourselves to Jesus Christ. "The greater the concentration with which we look at him, the better will be the knowledge that we have of ourselves" (IV/2, 269). We are not to seek knowledge of our salvation by means of introspection or self-examination. We are to look away from ourselves as consistently as possible. "It is a matter of knowing ourselves . . . in Christ," writes Barth, "and therefore not here in ourselves, but there outside ourselves in this Other who is not identical with me, and with whom I am not, and do not become, identical, but in whose humanity God himself becomes and is and always will be another, a concrete antithesis" (IV/2, 283). Our self-knowledge as the knowledge of who we are in Christ (who stands over against us even in uniting with us) can only occur as we learn to recognize ourselves in him, since "in truth" we are not outside but are so within him that he is our "truest life" (IV/3, 545).

Seeking to know our true being as our being in Christ is an idea that Barth applies not only to the doctrine of justification, but more surprisingly to the doctrine of sanctification as well. In other words, it is not as though justification is understood as the objective moment of salvation, which then finds its subjective counterpart in sanctification. Sanctification, in Barth's theology, no more describes an immanent and discernible process of personal transformation than does justification. They are to be found, in both cases, solely in Christ according to the pattern of thought just outlined. In both cases christological mediation is understood to require christological location as well. The humanity of Jesus Christ is regarded as an inclusive humanity. It includes within itself the truth and reality of our humanity as well. It includes within itself, objectively, our existential transformation. The transformation of our existence before God, whether in justification or sanctification, is not an immanent process within us, but a christological event. Jesus Christ *is* our justification, and he himself *is* also our sanctification. "Our existence is enclosed by his. . . . It is only because this is the case, because we are what we are in Jesus Christ before God and therefore in truth, that it can be said of us that we are righteous before God and that we are also holy before God" (IV/2, 273–74). We have no justification and sanctification (and therefore no salvation) that is not mediated and located in him and therefore that is not continually given and received *in actu*—given, that is, by him and received by those who live in fellowship with him as the one who constitutes the ongoing depth and center of their lives.

If we ask how our inclusion in the humanity of the Mediator comes to pass, how our humanity comes to partake of the justification and sanctification that are real and true for us only in him, then the first and primary answer is simply that he himself sees to it. Faith in Jesus Christ is precisely the faith that we do not have to do anything to ensure our inclusion, because the freedom and grace of his love are such that he himself sees to it. "Jesus Christ himself sees to it," writes Barth, "that in him and by him we are not outside but inside. He himself sees to it that . . . what is true in him in the height is and remains in our depth. It is not another work that begins at this point, a work that will have to become ours" (II/1, 156). From beginning to end the actuality of our justification and sanctification, the truth of our salvation in the presence of God, is to be found (ontically) nowhere else but in him, to be accomplished (volitionally) by no one else but him, and to be disclosed to us (noetically) by no other source than his Holy Spirit, who has nothing else to tell us (materially) but that we are in him by him to all eternity.

The Hiddenness of Salvation in Christ

Real and actual as our salvation in Christ is conceived to be, it is nonetheless at the same time conceived as something completely hidden as well. Once again, and perhaps here most of all, Barth contends, we walk by faith and not by sight. It is necessary to walk by faith and not by sight, precisely because faith itself does not directly transform us. Nor does faith initiate within us any immanent process of transformation that we might identity with our salvation. On the contrary, the truth and actuality of salvation do not prevent, but in fact actually entail, that our being in Christ remains hidden from us in a strong and twofold sense. It is neither perceptible nor comprehensible in any terms other than its own. At the heart of Barth's soteriological objectivism stands the conviction that the actuality of our salvation does not detract from either its imperceptibility or its incomprehensibility, and that its imperceptibility and its incomprehensibility do not detract from its actuality. We are actually in Christ, but our being in Christ is not something we can perceive by looking within ourselves, nor is it something we can possibly comprehend by comparing it to anything else.

We are said, it will be recalled, to be participants in the great drama of Jesus Christ's life, death, and resurrection. His history is understood to be, in fact, our history. It is understood to be our history "in an incomparably more direct and intimate way than anything that might present itself as our history in our own subjective experience" (IV/1, 547). Yet to these affirmations it must now be added that our participation in this drama is "not in any sense perceptible" to ourselves (IV/1, 546). We have "no self-experience of this drama." The truth and actuality of our participation in it are not to be perceived "in some depth of our own self." They cannot be recognized "in the contemplation of one of the phenomena which meet us in these depths" (IV/1, 546). They are grasped by faith or not at all, and when grasped by faith, they are grasped as a truth and actuality which are otherwise quite inaccessible. "That this history is my history, that I am the one who is so forcefully divided by the righteousness and grace of God, that I am caught up in this transition, that I am the person who participates in this drama, that that which is said of the prodigal is said of me—this is something which I do not see and therefore do not understand (IV/1, 547, rev.).

Our being in Jesus Christ is therefore "a hidden being" (IV/2, 285). It cannot be known to us directly, but only indirectly as we look to him. "In him we are hidden from ourselves. Only in him can we be revealed. We cannot, therefore, be revealed to ourselves or know ourselves directly, but only indirectly, in relation to the One who for us too is the Mediator between God and human beings" (IV/2, 271 rev.). The hiddenness of our being in the humanity of Jesus Christ is precisely why we must look away from ourselves to him, if we are to know the truth of our existence. For the truth of our existence is hidden in him apart from us. "A true knowledge of ourselves as such, and therefore of our Christian actuality, stands or falls for all of us with the knowledge of Jesus

Christ. . . . We can boast of ourselves only as we do not boast of ourselves, but of the Lord'' (IV/2, 271).

If, by faith, we come to perceive our true being as it is hidden in Christ, then this perception can only be understood as an actualization of the miracle of grace. It is a perception that transcends our ordinary capacities. "If he is seen, and we in him, it is not the kind of seeing of which we ourselves are or ever will be capable. We have no organ or ability for it, nor the corresponding will and resolution to use it" (IV/2, 285). The objective truth of our salvation can be seen only by virtue of an event that conforms to the pattern of the actualist motif. "This seeing is not a possibility of our own. It can be a reality, not in the actualization of a potentiality that we ourselves possess, but only as it is given in pure actuality" (IV/2, 285). The event by which we come to see ourselves in Christ therefore does nothing to remove the hiddenness of our being. It is an event that occurs with all the incomprehensibility of a miracle. "It can only take place, in a way which is quite incomprehensible to ourselves, that we do actually know him, and in him ourselves. And when it does take place it is always a confirmation of the fact that he is hidden from us, and that in him we too are hidden from ourselves" (IV/2, 285–86). The truth of our being in Christ is a thoroughly hidden truth disclosed only to faith by the miracle of grace.

The Ambiguity of Experience as a Sign of the Hiddenness of Salvation

The hiddenness of our being in Christ, its imperceptibility and its incomprehensibility, means, when taken together with the truth and actuality of this being, that any attempt to understand our salvation by looking directly to ourselves can only bring results that are frustrating. Considered in itself, our experience of salvation will always be abstract, ambiguous, and unreliable. Experience is therefore a category which Barth typically treated with suspicion, especially since it had been made into the object and norm of theological reflection ever since the days of Schleiermacher. Experience, Barth acknowledged, can scarcely be presented as absent from the life of faith, but neither can it be regarded as central to the life of faith. We believe in Christ, he insisted, not in our experience of Christ; in the gospel, not in our experience of the gospel; in salvation, not in our experience of salvation. Jesus Christ is not an experience but an event, the gospel is not an experience but the news of an event, and the presence of salvation is "not an experience, precisely because and as it is the divine decision concerning us" (I/2, 532). That is to say, none of these realities is to be perceived, postulated, conceived, or defined directly on the basis of whatever may happen to be its subjective or experiential content in the life of faith. Jesus Christ, the gospel, and the presence of salvation are rather to be perceived and defined as events that transcend (while including) our experiences, precisely because their apprehension is gracious and miraculous (actualism), their content is hidden, self-grounded, unique, and mysterious (particularism), and (as has yet to be developed) their experiential accompaniments are, at best, provisional and filled with promise (objectivism).

Considered in itself, the experience of salvation in the life of faith will always be ambiguous. "We are not asked about the faith-incidents as such, which can certainly be seen in our lives, but obviously only in the greatest ambiguity. We are not asked about any sort of humanly demonstrable actuality as such" (I/2, 707). We are not asked about such things, because they have no central bearing on salvation and therefore on the Christian life. Being inherently relative and ambiguous, they "cannot be the object of our faith and witness" (I/2, 709). The object of Christian witness is not the experience of the Christian, but something conceptually prior to and independent of that experience, and which in itself is neither relative nor ambiguous. "Thus, while I can and must say that I know from my own experience the help which I have to attest, this experience of mine must not be put in the center, it must not be the autonomous theme of what I say, if my word is not to lose the character of true witness" (I/2, 442). For the center lies hidden, beyond my experience, in the person of Jesus Christ. "I am not really concerned to speak at all about myself and my sin and my experiences as an independent theme, but only about . . . the name of Jesus Christ as the essence and existence of the loving kindness in which God has taken to himself sinful humanity, in order that we should not be lost but saved by him" (I/2, 443 rev.). It is precisely this name, and only this name, that transcends all relativity and ambiguity in the life of faith.

The ambiguity of experience also prevents it from becoming what it is sometimes urged to be, namely, the proper object of assurance and trust in matters of salvation. Contrary to certain forms of both pietistic and modern liberal theology, there can be no real "assurance of salvation," no "genuinely peaceful and happy awareness of our good and glorious existence," so long as we regard it as being "grounded in some way in ourselves," so long as we do not see that our personal Christian existence

. . . is a second thing which results from something else which is really first, being secured in this and not in our own experience" (IV/3, 566). Indeed, when one's experience is made into the object of assurance and the basis of trust, the results will be anything but genuinely peaceful and happy. For what does one really see in one's own life if not "all kinds of attempts and fragments, all kinds of unfulfilled and therefore very doubtful beginnings, all kinds of half-lights which may equally well be those of sunset or sunrise" (II/2, 775)? How, then, can one find assurance or put trust in these things?

> Those who trust in these things, in their conversion and new birth as such, in their walk before God as an element of biography, ascribing credibility and the force of witness to a supposed 'pneumatic actuality' in the sphere of experience, and thus trying to live in faith in themselves, building their house upon the sand, are only involved in a feat of juggling in which they may achieve a sensational but very dangerous interchange of supreme rapture and the most profound disillusionment, but will know nothing of the death of the old human being and the life of the new, and therefore nothing of our direction, preparation and exercise for eternal life. (II/2, 775–76 rev.)

Indeed, one might go so far as to say that in such cases disillusionment is devoutly to be wished. For without it those trusting in their own experiences will never come to see that, regardless of such experiences, their own being as such, far from corresponding to their being in Christ, actually "contradicts" it (IV/1, 97). For when confronted with "the clear light of that being," with our life as truly "hid with Christ in God" (Col. 3:3), what do we actually see? What do we find when we look directly to ourselves, if not that the old human being "is not yet dead or the new created"? What do we find again and again if not that we are "a covenant-breaker, a sinner, a transgressor" (IV/1, 97)?

In our own being—contrary to who we are in Christ by Christ—we will "never find the faithful servant and friend and dear child of God." In our own being we will never with our own eyes see ourselves as "in any respect" justified, sanctified, or saved, but always "in supreme need" of justification, sanctification, and salvation by God (IV/1, 97). Our being in Christ is hidden in such a way that it can never be perceived by looking to our experience in the life of faith, for what we see by looking at such experience is the opposite of our being in Christ. It is his history that coincides with our history, not our history that coincides with his. "There is no sense in imagining that my history coincides with that of Jesus Christ. That triumphant restoration has not really taken place in my heart, in my activities and attitudes. Nothing has taken place or can be perceived in me of the glory of that right and life" (IV/1, 773). Salvation is not a process immanent within us in any sense that we can observe or perceive directly from our own experience.

The hiddenness of being in Christ, its imperceptibility and incomprehensibility, and its contrast with what can actually be perceived in us directly (in light of our true being in him) may all be summed up by citing the following remarkable passage from Barth, a passage made possible by his soteriological objectivism with its strong emphasis on christological mediation:

> Let us be honest. If we relate to ourselves, to you and me, to this or that Christian (even the best), that which is said about the conversion of the human being in the New Testament, and which we have to say with the New Testament, it will have the inevitable smack of hyperbole and even illusion—and the more so the more we try to introduce it, either by way of analysis or assertion, in the form of statements about the psychico-physical conditions or impulses or experiences of individual Christians or Christians generally, or in the form of general or specialized pictures of the Christian life. What are we with our little ending and new beginning, our changed lives, whether we experience them in the wilderness, or the cloister, or at the very least at Caux? How feeble is the relationship, even in the best of cases, between the great categories in which the conversion of the human being is described in the New Testament and the corresponding event in our own outer and inner life! (IV/2, 582–83 rev.)

What we do not find in ourselves, Barth characteristically goes on to add, we do find in Christ: "But everything is simple, true and clear when these statements are referred directly to Jesus Christ, and only indirectly, as fulfilled and effectively realized in him for us, to ourselves" (IV/2, 583). Our being is hidden though real, and real though hidden, in him.

The Promised Future of Salvation in Christ

The truth of our being in Christ, as Barth understands it, is not only real and hidden; it is also yet to come. It defines and determines the future promised to us, and actualized for us, in him. Jesus Christ is not the inclusive human being without also being the eschatological human being. We are not only included in his being, in his humanity, in his history, in his transition from shameful death to glorious resurrection, in his transformation of the old creation into the new. We are also confronted by his being, here and now, as the real but hidden future of our own being, as the pledge that our resurrection in him and with him to the glorious lib-

erty of the children of God is already ours today. We are confronted by
his being as the promise that our transformation as he has accomplished
it from old creation to new will not always remain hidden but will one
day be manifest fully in the light of his resurrection and in the glory of
his eternal life. We are confronted by his being here and now as the new
being of our common future.

What has already happened in his existence for us "has not actually
happened in our existence as such" (IV/1, 552). But our existence as
such is not the same as our being in him. Our existence as such is the
old humanity which has died with him, whereas our being in him is the
new humanity which is raised with him. He himself is the form and
content of our new being, and he attests himself here and now as the
truth of the promised future. Jesus Christ attests himself as the truth of
precisely that future which is based on the actuality of atonement. "The
One who bears this name is himself this truth in that he is himself this
actuality. He attests what he is. He alone is the pledge of it because he
alone is the Mediator of it. He alone is the truth of it. But he is that truth,
and therefore it speaks for itself in him" (IV/1, 137). The truth that is in
him is not yet in us; the actuality which is ours in him is not yet actualized in us. Nor can it be produced or actualized by us. "But it encounters
us majestically in him—the promise of the truth which avails for us as
the atonement—of which it is the truth—took place for us and as ours,
the truth which for that reason can and should be heard and accepted and
appropriated by us, which we can and should accept as the truth which
applies to us" (IV/1, 137). It therefore encounters us as the eschatological truth that is, and is yet to be, ours. "It encounters us in him as the
promise of our own future" (IV/1, 137). It encounters human beings as
the present truth of their future salvation.

We human beings do not yet exist in this future. "We do not exist
(yet) in such a way that space and time, nature and history and the human
situation are one continuous demonstration of the being of Jesus Christ
and our being in him and therefore of his love" (IV/2, 286). Our perception of his being is not yet "complete and unbroken." Our response to
his love is not yet "full and perennial." For now we merely wander
about "from one small and provisional response, from one small and
provisional perception and love, to another." Our perception of his being
and our response to his love are "not yet a state, a steady and perfect
clarity, but an event; an infrequent, weak, uncertain and flickering glow
which stands in sorry relationship to the perfection of even the smallest
beam of light." But one day the event, as it takes place provisionally in

us and among us here and now, will be disclosed as a perfected state of being in him. One day our experiences, which are never more than provisional and which always point away from themselves, will shed their ambiguity. One day our perception, response, and experience will stand in "a steady, all-embracing and all-pervasive light by which we are surrounded on all sides in accordance with the being of Jesus Christ, and our being in him, and therefore his love" (IV/2, 286). One day we will perceive him as he perceives us, love him as he loves us, and find our being in him fully manifest as his being in us, to all eternity.

As the human being who is at once inclusive and eschatological, and who confronts us in the miracle of grace by Word and Spirit here and now, Jesus Christ places our human existence under the sign of a great but mysterious simultaneity. Our human existence, by virtue of its relation to him (a relation grounded solely in him), is an eschatological existence. Grounded in him, who died in our place and who was raised to establish us in his place before God, our present existence is determined simultaneously by his death and resurrection. As determined by his death, our existence as sinners, as those who are at war with grace and who are consequently abandoned by God, is completely past. It is the past that is truly past, because (though it would otherwise have been our future) it came to be the past by his death. As determined by his resurrection, on the other hand, our existence as those who are saved, as those who are bestowed with grace and accepted into fellowship with God, is an existence that is completely future. It is the future that is truly future, because (though it would not otherwise be ours) it came to be ours by his resurrection. Here and now, therefore, we are at once sinners whose existence is completely past and the saved whose existence is completely future. We are both these things at once, not partially but totally, by virtue of our being in Christ, who is present to us as the one who died and rose again.

In Christ we human beings are both these things at once, Barth argues, but we are not both these things in the same way. Our past and our future do not coexist in a state of mere equilibrium. They are not "equal and equally serious" determinations of our existence (II/1, 627). Although we are placed between them in the present, we are not thereby placed "in an endless dialectic" (II/1, 628). We are placed, rather, in a moment of existential turning—a turning from the past that is really past, to the future that is really future, because the former has really been abolished and the latter really established apart from us in Jesus Christ. We are certainly placed, says Barth, between this past and this future. "But first of all and above all Jesus Christ stands between them. It is in this way and in him that we are in this position. But in him the equilibrium between them has been upset and ended. He is the way from the one to the other and the way is irreversible. He is the turning'' (II/1, 628). Our turning from the past and to the future must both be referred to him.

This turning of human existence, therefore, is again understood in objectivist soteriological terms. The turning is not a state within us, but an event that befalls us; not a process we undertake, but a gift we acknowledge by faith. ''For not we and our present, but Jesus Christ and his present are the turning from one to the other. The past is that from which we are set free by him, and the future that for which we are set free by him'' (II/1, 628). Our human existence in him, for all its hiddenness apart from faith, is therefore to be understood as an existence that is moving out of the past he has abolished and into the future he has established. Although we are ''still here in this life,'' we are ''already in the life beyond,'' living here and now, by virtue of our hope itself, ''in the fulfillment'' that lies before us (IV/2, 276). Our being in Christ is in this way a being in hope. ''But . . . it is still a *being:* not just an experience that we have, nor a disposition, nor an attitude of the will or of the emotions, nor a possibility that is available but has still to be realized; but our truest reality, in which we are to see and understand ourselves in truth'' (IV/2, 276). The truth of our being as hidden in Christ is an eschatological truth. Contrary to all appearances as they may either assail us (because we fall so short) or inflate us (because we acquit ourselves too readily), it is the truth that our future as human beings is none other than our future in him.

To those who would acquit themselves too readily, or who would see salvation as a process in some sense grounded (and manifest) in themselves, Barth says, as we have seen, ''Let us be honest.'' To those who would assail themselves, however, or who would take the eschatological and christological hiddenness of salvation as an indication that, for them at least, it is not a reality, Barth offers a correspondingly vivid passage. It consists of an imaginary dialogue between a person filled with such doubts and the Word of grace. The doubter admits to not being able to find the truth and reality of the promised future—''this new, peaceful, joyful human being living in fellowship''—in the doubter's own personal experience. The doubter asks leave honestly to admit that the doubter does not know this person, or at least himself or herself as this person (IV/3, 250 rev.).

The Word of grace replies: All honor to your honesty, but my truth transcends it. Allow yourself, therefore, to be told in all truth and on the most
solid grounds what you do not know, namely, that you are this person in
spite of what you think.''

Doubter: "You think that I can and should become this person in the
course of time? But I do not have sufficient confidence in myself to believe
this. Knowing myself, I shall never become this person.''

The Word of grace: "You do well not to have confidence in yourself.
But the point is not that you can and should become this person. What I am
telling you is that, as I know you, you already are.''

Doubter: "I understand that you mean this eschatologically. You are referring to the person I perhaps will be one day in some not very clearly
known transfiguration in a distant eternity. If only I had attained to this!
And if only I could be certain that even then I should be this new person!''

The Word of grace: "You need to understand both yourself and me better
than you do. I am not inviting you to speculate about your being in eternity,
but to receive and ponder the news that here and now you begin to be the
new person, and are already that which you will be eternally.''

Doubter: "How can I accept this news? On what guarantee can I make
bold to take it seriously?''

The Word of grace: "I, Jesus Christ, am the One who speaks to you.
You are what you are in me, as I will to be in you. Hold fast to me. I am
your guarantee. My boldness is yours. With this boldness dare to be what
you are'' (IV/3, 250 rev.)

Note that from Barth's objectivist standpoint salvation involves not something that we need to become, but something that we need to acknowledge; not something grounded in ourselves or in our knowledge of ourselves, but something grounded in Jesus Christ and in his knowledge of
us; not something, finally, that perhaps awaits us in a distant eternity, but
something that confronts us here and now as what we already are and
will be eternally. Even now, Barth states, we can dare to be what we are
in Christ. But none of this is guaranteed in any other way than by the
Word of grace as received by faith.

The Universality of Salvation in Christ

The full implications of Barth's position become clear when it is realized
that he understands salvation in Christ not only to be real, hidden, and
yet to come, but also to be universal in scope. Jesus Christ is the inclusive human being in a sense that is universal and universally valid. Not
just some but all human beings are "included in this One'' (IV/2, 271).

Not the cause of just some but the cause of all "is advocated and conducted by this One." No one is excluded. "There is no one who does
not participate in him in this turning to God. There is no one who is not
. . . engaged in this turning. There is no one who is not raised and
exalted with him to true humanity. 'Jesus Christ lives, and I with him' "
(IV/2, 271). The decision that has been taken for us in Jesus Christ does
not apply only to those who come to have faith in him. It is a decision
that "has been taken objectively for the world as well, and for all those
who live in it" (IV/2, 275). The "ontological connection" that establishes our being in Christ pertains not just to believers, but to all other
human beings and to every human being as such (IV/2, 275).

No one is righteous and holy before God except "in the truth and
power" of Jesus Christ's righteousness and holiness, but in this very truth
and power all are included. His truth and power are not restricted in their
extent. They are, objectively, "effective and authoritative for all, and
therefore for each and every human being, and not merely for the people
of God" (IV/2, 518). His accomplishment of our salvation concerns "all
the human beings of every time and place" (IV/2, 519 rev.). With reference to the text that "He is . . . the firstborn of every creature" (Col.
1:15), Barth comments that we are to understand every human creature
as exalted in Jesus Christ. "What took place in him—the exaltation of
the human race, and therefore its sanctification for God—took place as
the new impression of humanity as such" (IV/2, 519 rev.). His life,
death, and resurrection took place for the salvation of all. "It was accomplished in the place of all others . . . with all the mercy of the love
which seeks all; with all the seriousness of the will which extends to all;
with all the power of the act which is done for all; with all the authori-
tativeness of the decision which has been taken for all" (IV/2, 519). In
this uniqueness of his being and work, Jesus Christ is singular, but he is
not isolated. "In his singularity Jesus Christ never was or is or will be
isolated. For in this singularity he was and is and will be, and worked
and will work, from and to all eternity, for all" (IV/2, 519). We overlook
him completely if we do not see him in the place of all (and therefore
also in our place), and in our own place (and therefore also in the place
of all).

It is this universal scope of salvation that exposes the full implications
of Barth's soteriological objectivism. Salvation, as we have seen, is
understood to be "effective and authoritative for all" regardless of whether
one has come to believe in Christ yet or not (IV/2, 518). Barth thus
thoroughly dispels any residual ambiguity that may traditionally surround

the idea of "justification by faith," to say nothing of other Christian ideas of salvation. Faith as such, as Barth understands it, is not to be regarded as saving for either of the two main (but very different) reasons that have traditionally been given in Western theology. Faith as such cannot be said to be saving either for the traditional Roman Catholic reason that faith is animated by love, nor for the traditional Protestant reason that it clings to its object. Faith is indeed animated by love, Barth would say, but only because it is so animated by its object. And it is solely the object clung to—not the faith that clings to it, nor the love animated by it—that can properly be said to be saving. Salvation is in no sense unequivocally manifest as an immanent process of transformation. Its truth simply cannot be seen directly in us, by attending either to our faith or to our love. For salvation is not essentially manifest but hidden, not essentially a process but an event, not essentially a transformation in us but a transformation in Christ, not essentially something we undertake but something we undergo. Salvation is miraculous in form and mysterious in content. It is an eschatological miracle and a christocentric mystery. It has already occurred decisively for our sakes in Jesus Christ. It does not first acquire significance or effectiveness at the moment someone comes to believe or in the animation of faith by love.

Jesus Christ is understood as objectively effective and significant in himself. He is the decisive locus of salvation prior to and independent of our faith (or lack of faith) as well as prior to and apart from our love (or lack of love). From this standpoint Barth is able to eliminate the last vestiges of an idea that lingers even within the theology of the Reformers (to say nothing of other theologies)—the idea that God's grace is somehow conditional. For despite the denials of official doctrine that grace is conditional, and despite some very important moves in the opposite direction, in actual practice the Reformation proclamation of the gospel could still commonly take the following form: "If you repent and believe, you will be saved; if you do not repent and believe, you will not be saved." Barth's theology, by contrast, makes the following form of proclamation to be categorically normative: "This is what God in Jesus Christ has done for your sake; therefore, repent and believe." The second form (which, of course, was also strongly validated by the Reformation) is obviously distinguished from the first by being unmistakably unconditional.[3] It proclaims the gospel as an invitation to respond accordingly, and not in any sense as a summons (or an implicit threat) to do something (however defined) so as to include oneself within salvation's reality and truth. Since, in Barth's understanding. God has already freely included us, it falls to us henceforth freely to receive our inclusion as the gift it is proclaimed to be.

Three things are to be noted about the universalist direction evident in Barth's objectivist soteriology. First, the salient difference between Barth's position and more traditional views has primarily to do with the locus of mystery. The great puzzle for more traditional views like those of Augustine or Calvin is why God should decide to save some but not others. Regardless of where the decision is thought to be taken—whether in predestination, in the cross, in the convergence of grace and faith in the individual's spiritual life, in the last judgment, or in some combination of these and similar factors—it is still understood to be primarily a mystery about the inscrutable good pleasure of a deity who loves but does not save all (or who condemns all yet still saves a few). By contrast, the great puzzle for the Barthian view is more nearly anthropological than theological in location. The divine disposition, decision, and work for our salvation are presented in unequivocal terms. No disposition, decision, and work of God are to be found elsewhere than in Jesus Christ, who died to cancel our past, rose again to establish our future, and pleads for us to all eternity.

The mystery pertaining to God as such is not the puzzle of an inscrutable decision to save some, but not all. It is the mystery of an unfathomable mercy that (at great cost) saves all, not just some. But there is still a puzzle of what might be called the "dark mystery," and it corresponds to the puzzle embedded in the more traditional views. The dark mystery for the traditional view is, as noted, that God does not will to save all. For the Barthian view, however, it is rather that not all human beings will to accept God's salvation. The dark mystery is that human beings inexplicably (i.e., "inexplicably" within the terms of Barth's theology) are by all appearances actually capable of rejecting the divine disposition, decision, and work in their favor. It is the puzzle of our rejection of grace, the mystery of sin, but here raised to a very high pitch, since salvation is somehow effectively rejected even though it fully avails for those who reject it. This is not the place to explore the intricacies of Barth's conception of sin as a dark mystery.[4] The point is simply that the problem of an inexplicable puzzle has been shifted but not eliminated. The puzzle for the more traditional view is that God's will seems to be truly inconsistent. For the Barthian view it is that the human will to reject the divine grace, while actual, would appear to be truly impossible. It is Barth's contention that the gospel finally leaves us with just this mystery, and not with some other "very different mystery" (IV/2, 520).

Second, despite his objectivist soteriology, Barth stops short, as widely noted, of unequivocally proclaiming universal salvation. The reason why Barth finds it necessary to stop short, however, is not always well understood. Criticisms of Barth for being inconsistent at this point are criticisms that he could fairly regard as irrelevant or at the very least as inconclusive. For what Barth would want to see would be a fully articulated theological alternative that did not result in an even worse inconsistency or puzzle than the one he thinks the gospel leaves us with. What is in the background here is the coherentism of Barth's theological rationalism. No other proposal about what to do with the irresolvable puzzle of a dark mystery, Barth seems to argue, can be seriously advanced without infringing in some intolerable way on the remaining body of Christian beliefs. Logically, the puzzle could be either shifted or eliminated; but either way, the cost would be too high. Again, this is not the place to explore the intricacies of Barth's position. It can at least be suggested, however, that from his point of view no conceivable alternative could avoid some intolerable doctrinal loss, such as infringing upon the fullness of divine sovereignty, the fullness of divine love, the radical human neediness for the miracle of grace, the actuality of human freedom as grounded in grace, or the evilness of evil and the sinfulness of sin. The material or coherentist inconsistencies that would result in either shifting or eliminating the puzzle would all be worse, Barth seems to propose, than placing the puzzle just where he leaves it.

Third, Barth therefore makes a very strong move in the direction of universal salvation while leaving the question open. His objectivist soteriology points, as we have seen, in a universalist direction. At the same time, as we have also seen, the puzzle of our human rejection of grace is regarded as something that can be neither overlooked nor resolved by theological thought, and therefore as something that must simply be allowed to stand as an absurd or inexplicable fact which manifests the absurdity of sin. The universal efficacy of grace is therefore understood to mean that we may not give up hope for any human being regardless of his or her decisions in this life. Not even Judas—who is understood typologically as the culminating instance of those in the biblical narratives who are rejected by God, in that they have rejected their election—can be regarded as finally beyond the pale of hope (II/2, 458–506, esp. 501–5). This aspect of Barth's thought is summed up in the following remark: "But it is only where there is no hope—and the Rejected on Golgotha, and the rejected in ourselves and in all others, has no hope—that there is real hope, for it is only there that the work of the Holy Spirit can intervene and proclamation can become comprehensible and faith really alive" (II/2, 458).

The puzzle of our human rejection of grace, on the other hand, is regarded as something that can in no way be minimized. The proper—one might almost say the normal—response to grace, and the only one that is theologically intelligible, is faith. Along with hope and love (and all that they entail), faith is the only possible event that corresponds properly to the event of grace (where "event" is understood in Barth's special actualist and particularist sense). But we know not only that the event and decision of faith do not always occur, but also that they actually occur only in the case of a relatively few persons (when the human race is considered as a whole), and even more that even in those cases the occurrence is broken, intermittent, and far from perfect. This aspect of Barth's thought may be summed up as follows: sin simply cannot be understood or explained. "There is no reason for it. It derives directly from that which is not, and it consists in a moment toward it. It is simply a fact, *factum brutum*. . . . To try to find a reason for it is simply to show that we do not realize that we are talking of the evil that is really evil" (IV/2, 415–16).

Therefore Barth sees no choice but to leave the question of universal salvation open. The actuality of the divine decision of grace in Jesus Christ undoubtedly avails for all. Yet over against this actuality stands the *factum brutum* of human sin, even and especially in the face of the divine decision of grace. To resolve the tension between these conflicting actualities cannot be the project of theological thought. Any attempt to resolve the tension conceptually would only result in an abstraction. The final extent of the circle of those who are saved is not our concern but God's. How to resolve the tension between the mystery of a universally effective grace and the puzzle of a universally (in one way or another) persistent sin (even, that is, in the lives of the faithful) is a matter for the free decision of God. "If we are to respect the freedom of divine grace, we cannot venture the statement that it must and will finally be coincident with the world of the human race as such (as in the doctrine of the so-called *apokatastasis*)" (II/2, 417 rev.). Nor, on the other hand, can the statement be ventured that not all will be included in the circle. "But, again, in grateful recognition of the grace of the divine freedom we cannot venture the opposite statement that there cannot and will not be this final opening up and enlargement of the circle of election and calling" (II/2, 418).

In itself the actuality of grace would lead to the statement, "All will be saved." Yet in itself the actuality of persistent sin would lead to the opposite statement, "Not all will be saved." Neither statement, however, is concrete in the sense Barth uses the term, for neither takes all the relevant actualities into account. "We avoid both these statements, for they are both abstract and therefore cannot be any part of the message of Christ, but only formal conclusions without any actual substance" (II/2, 418). The alternative is not merely a neutral agnosticism but rather a reverent agnosticism. It is not simply to leave the two statements balanced in dialectical equilibrium, but rather to see a definite pattern of priority and subordination. The alternative is to take both sin and grace with the full seriousness appropriate to each, and therefore finally to take grace more seriously than sin. "The sign," writes Barth, "points unambiguously in one direction, that the gracious God is in the right and the human being who denies him is in the wrong. The free decision of God alone can lead further, but this step is one which gives us every reason and confidence to believe and hope that there will be further steps of the same kind, further confirmations and repetitions of the same truth, further signs pointing in the same direction" (II/2, 418 rev.). The pattern of grace, in other words, leaves every reason to hope that no one will finally be excluded, because the truth of salvation in Jesus Christ is such that there is always more grace in God than there is sin in us.

Therefore, according to Barth's objectivist soteriology, the difference between believers and unbelievers is not that believers are saved while unbelievers are not. Nor, even more emphatically, is it that believers have acquired in themselves some spiritual or moral merit before God that unbelievers lack. On the contrary, believers and unbelievers are bound together not only by a solidarity in sin, but also and all the more by a solidarity in grace. What distinguishes Christians from non-Christians is not their ontic but their noetic situation. Christians will know, that is, in a way that non-Christians will not, of their own perilous situation in sin and of their all the more protected situation in Christ. They will know of the persistence of non-Christianity in their own lives as Christians.

> Yet, however that may be, to the extent that we may be Christians in spite of our non-Christianity, our real distinction from non-Christians will consist in the fact that we know that Jesus Christ himself, and he alone, is our hope as well as theirs, that he died and rose again for those who are wholly or partially non-Christians, that his overruling work precedes and follows all being and occurrence in our sphere, that he alone is the perfect Christian, but that he really is this, and is it in our place. (IV/3, 342)

The rest of humanity "does not yet participate in the knowledge of Jesus Christ and what has taken place in him" (IV/3, 715). For those who do so participate, however, this participation is not just something but everything; not just neutral or intellectual knowledge, but liberating and life-renewing knowledge. This participation is not a small thing but a great thing—indeed, the only thing. It is a participation in knowledge whose content can be known only as it is continually proclaimed and shared—not only among those who already take part in it, but also among those who do not.

Those who take part in this knowledge by faith are understood as those who belong de facto to Christ here and now. Those who do not yet take part in this knowledge by faith, however, are not to be regarded apart from their relationship to him, or rather from his relationship to them. "Virtually, prospectively and *de jure* all human beings are his own" (IV/ 3, 278 rev.). They can only be addressed as those they already are "in virtue of the work and Word of God" (IV/3, 810). They can only be addressed according to the truth of their being in Christ, and therefore, if not as "anonymous" Christians (for their names in Christ are surely known to God), then most certainly as "virtual" or "potential" Christians—as *christiana designata* or *christianus designatus, as christiani in spe* (IV/3, 810). For their being is understood "as already established and secured *de jure* in Jesus Christ" (IV/3, 811). The christological sphere is seriously misunderstood, if it is not seen to be "universal in its particularity" (IV/3, 279). As a universality that is real, hidden, and yet to come, it can only be seen as we look away from ourselves to Christ.

> Hence all the required and necessary looking away from the world and all human beings, even from the Church and faith, in short from ourselves to him, can only be with a view to seeing in him the real world, the real human being, the real Church and real faith, our real selves. To be sure, we see them in all their differentiation and distinction. But we also see them in the communion which he himself has established, in the communication which he himself has actualized, with this very different Other, and therefore in their reality as promised, given, maintained and controlled by God in him. (IV/3, 279 rev.)

Salvation in Christ: Summary

Salvation, then, is understood in Barth's objectivist soteriology to be real, hidden, yet to come, and universal in scope. "Real" or "actual" describes the truth of our status in Christ. It describes the state of affairs or objective situation brought about in Jesus Christ by the divine intervention on our behalf. Our salvation is defined by the ontological connection that Jesus Christ has established with us, so that our being before God can only be understood as our being in him. "Hidden," however, describes the noetic situation of our status in Christ. The ontological connection that runs from him to us does not run noetically from us to him. We cannot perceive it by looking at ourselves, but only by looking to him by faith. Faith alone can perceive the connection, and it does so solely by trusting in the truth and promise of the revelation which discloses that the connection is indeed actual.

"Yet to come," moreover, describes the future and ultimate convergence of the ontic and noetic situations. The ontological connection that is valid even now will not always remain hidden, but will one day be made manifest to sight in just the same actuality that it was always already visible to faith. This future manifestation of the ontological connection will not be the disclosure of an immanent process of transformation that had gotten under way within us here and now. It will, rather, be the disclosure of the inexpressible divine gift that we were mysteriously drawn into, partaking in the drastic and miraculous transformation that took place on our behalf in the death and resurrection of Jesus Christ. It will, that is, be the disclosure of his history as our history.

"Universal in scope," finally, describes the global and historical reach of salvation as it is valid and effective in Christ. The universality of salvation means that, by definition, salvation is valid and effective for us regardless of our faith (or lack of faith), of our love (or lack of love), and of our hope (or lack of hope). Salvation is valid and effective for all, because it has been actualized in Jesus Christ on behalf of all and in the place of all. The puzzle that not all receive this gift by faith, and that those who do, do so only very imperfectly, does not infringe on salvation's objective validity and effectiveness for all. It only means that it behooves us all the more to cling in faith, hope, and love to the object of our salvation (Jesus Christ), not only for our own sakes, but for the sake of the entire world.

Saving truth, according to Barth's soteriological objectivism, is therefore understood simply to be identical with Jesus Christ. He is, "whether we realize it or not," this saving truth: "the truth of the grace in which God has turned to the world in him and which has come to the world in him; the truth of the living brackets which bring and hold together heaven and earth, God and all human beings, in him; the truth that God has bound himself to humanity and that humanity is bound to God" (IV/1, 137 rev.). Saving truth is therefore not merely an idea, but a personally embodied actuality. "The One who bears this name is himself this truth in that he himself is this actuality" (IV/1, 137). The one who embodies this saving truth is also the one who attests it. "He attests what he is. He alone is the pledge of it because he alone is the Mediator of it. He alone is the truth of it. But he is this truth, and therefore it speaks for itself in him" (IV/1, 137). We are not this truth, it is not in us, "we cannot produce it of ourselves" (IV/1, 137), and yet it is indeed our truth.

"Our truth is not the being which we find in ourselves as our own. The being which we find in ourselves as our own will always be the being in enmity against God. But this very truth is a lie. It is the lie which is seen to be a lie in faith" (II/1, 158). Our truth, as grasped by faith, is the truth of our being in Christ. "Our truth is our being in the Son of God, in whom we are not enemies but friends of God, in whom we do not hate grace but cling to grace alone, in whom therefore God is knowable to us. This is our truth as human beings as believed by faith" (II/1, 158–59 rev.).

The "question of truth" in matters of salvation has been answered by "God's act fulfilled in him for us" (IV/1, 252). Jesus Christ is therefore the answer to the truth question, both ontically and noetically, and through him this saving truth is made to be ours as well. "He is the truth. He is the disclosure and knowledge of that which is. For he is. To be of the truth means to hear his voice. . . . To be of the truth means . . . to believe in him. And to proclaim the truth means to proclaim him" (IV/1, 252). The divine answer to the question of truth is the divine act in Jesus Christ which establishes the truth as truth for us and therefore as saving truth. To be of this truth one needs only to acknowledge and receive it by faith, not to actualize it or to validate it in oneself.

Objectivist Soteriology Differentiated from Existentialist Soteriology

The difference between soteriological objectivism and soteriological existentialism, as both are conceived by Barth, can now be brought into focus.[5] How to relate the objective and the existential moments of salvation is the formal question to which each conception provides a different answer. The existential answer is one in which the objective moment depends decisively at some point on what occurs existentially. For until the existential moment occurs, the objective moment is understood, in some essential sense, as not being effective or valid or significant. To that extent the objective moment depends for its actuality on the moment of existential realization, and the two moments are conceived as necessarily and essentially interdependent. The objectivist answer as given by Barth, on the other hand, is one in which the objective moment retains conceptual priority and independence at all points over the moment that is existential. The objective moment is understood to be effective, valid, and significant, in some strong and necessary sense, regardless of the occurrence or nonoccurrence of the existential moment, even though the puzzle of nonoccurrence will require some kind of teleological resolution whose dimensions are not revealed to us but whose direction gives us every reason for hope. The objective is not in any sense understood to be conceptually dependent upon or necessarily conditioned by the existential moment of salvation.

Soteriological existentialism, Barth seems to propose, falls into the pattern just described, regardless of how existence may be defined. Whether the decisive locus of salvation is understood to be more nearly individualistic or social or sacramental, existential soteriologies are all species of the same genus insofar as the objective moment of salvation is in some sense understood to depend for its effectiveness, validity, or significance on the occurrence of the existential moment. Whether the objective moment is to be actualized in the individual, in the society, or in the sacrament (or in some combination of these), it still requires some such actualization if it is not to remain a mere potentiality or an empty ideal. For it is the existential, it would seem, that is finally the locus of the actual, and the objective that is significant only (or primarily, or ultimately), insofar as it enables the actual to occur.

Against Existential Soteriology: The Individualistic Type

Against the individualistic type of existential soteriology, Barth argues that the decisive locus of salvation is not to be shifted from Christ to the individual. In Roman Catholic theology this shift is seen when a greater interest is devoted to *gratia interna* than to *gratia externa,* to *gratia cooperans* than to *gratia operans,* to habitual grace than to actual grace— in other words, when a greater interest is devoted to the existential than to the objective moment of salvation. Greater interest is devoted to "the state and life and activity of grace in us" than to "Christ as the One who

accomplishes the sovereign act of God and what we are in and by him"
(IV/1, 87 rev.). Barth sees this as a "system of fatal preferences" in the
theology of Rome (IV/1, 87).

Protestant theologies, however, are by no means exempt from this sort
of problem. The theologies of the younger Luther and of Barth's contemporary Rudolf Bultmann are singled out, for example, as illustrating a
similar defect. What takes place when we ourselves come to recognize
"the *pro me* of Christian faith," writes Barth against such theologies,
"is not the redemptive act of God itself, not the death and resurrection
of Jesus Christ, not the repetition of his obedience and sacrifice and victory" (IV/1, 767). The redemptive act took place "once for all" in Christ;
it does not come to "coincide" existentially with what takes place in
faith. The "rise and continuation" of faith are in no sense to be identified
with the work of salvation (IV/1, 615). The work of salvation and the
occurrence of faith are not to be conceived as constitutively interdependent. Jesus Christ is not to be conceived as "the author and initiator of
what has to be fulfilled in and through us on the same level" (IV/1, 229).
On the contrary, salvation "is not a redemptive happening which embraces both him and us, but the redemptive happening which embraces
us in his existence, which takes us up into itself" (IV/1, 229). The existential moment of the individual's salvation "is utterly dependent upon
and can be known and determined only by the objective" (IV/1, 87). It
is "already included in the true objective, and will be found in it and not
elsewhere" (IV/1, 87). The moment of proclamation is not identical with
the objective moment of salvation, or is identical with it only indirectly,
only insofar as it represents the truly objective moment, namely, the decisive history that occurred in Christ. Faith is thus not the actualization
of salvation as a possibility created by Christ, but the acknowledgment
of salvation as an actuality accomplished by him and in him for our sakes
(IV/1, 285). Salvation and faith are thus conceived as standing in a certain constitutive relationship. The work of salvation is not correctly accounted for in terms of the occurrence of faith. Salvation is therefore
conceptually independent of faith. The occurrence of faith, on the other
hand, is correctly accounted for in terms of the work of salvation. Salvation is therefore conceptually prior to and independent of faith, and
faith is conceptually subsequent to and dependent on salvation.

Spirituality and virtue are likewise rejected as versions of the individualistic type of existential soteriology. They are rejected, that is, insofar
as spirituality refers to an assumed need to prepare oneself for the recep-

tion of grace by means of devotional exercises, and insofar as virtue refers to an interior state of being or an interior capacity supposedly acquired on the basis of habit. Against spirituality in this sense Barth writes:

> But if by devotion we mean an exercise in the cultivation of the soul or spirit, i.e., the attempt to intensify and deepen ourselves, to purify and cleanse ourselves inwardly, to attain clarity and self-control, and finally to set ourselves on a good footing and in agreement with the deity by this preparation, then it is high time we realized that not merely have we not even begun to pray or prepared ourselves for prayer, but that we have actually turned away from what is commanded us as prayer. (III/4, 97)

Against virtue a similar polemical line is to be found. We have our being, Barth characteristically insists, only in act, only in the event of God's relationship to us and of our relationship to God. "No abstract being comes into question" (III/4, 663). No being comes into question, that is, that would be a real being within us on the basis of some innate capacity and therefore at least partially independent of our encounter with God. "Nor does any habitual having come into question, i.e., no such having as would be a possession outside the divine giving and our receiving at God's hand, no such having as would be real having apart from the event of this giving and receiving" (III/4, 663; cf. I/2, 374–75). What spirituality and virtue both seem to have in common, in other words, is that they both in one way or another understand salvation to have a constitutive, innate, and therefore independent basis within us (whether it be reflected by way of spiritual preparation or spiritual acquisition), apart from the miracle of grace which, both ontically and noetically, takes us beyond our innate capacities and thereby overcomes our preoccupation with ourselves—ontically, because our being is concrete only as our being in Christ; and noetically, because our true being as our being in Christ can be known only as we acquire (and continue to acquire anew) this knowledge from Christ (in the event of the correlation of Word and Spirit as they are present to us in faith). Again, therefore, salvation is not to be accounted for in terms of spirituality or virtue, but is conceptually prior to and independent of them.

Against Existential Soteriology: The Social Type

Against the social type of existential soteriology, Barth argues in a similar pattern that the decisive locus of salvation is not to be shifted from Christ to society. The principal exponent of such a shift, as perceived by

Barth in his own milieu, was "religious socialism," a movement that, in its understanding of the decisive locus of salvation, was perhaps not entirely dissimilar to the "liberation theology" movement of our own day. The removing of social evils under which we and others suffer, however important it might be, is not to be understood, Barth urged, as the actualization of a salvation that would otherwise remain merely potential. The removing or ameliorating of social evils is not to be understood as though everything finally or decisively depended on human resolution and struggle here and now. Nor is it to be understood as though God were no more than some sort of religious resource who added a "pious blessing" by enabling us to motivate, legitimate, and evaluate our own all-important political programs, convictions, and activities (III/3, 146).

We fallen human creatures are not the final or decisive actors in the drama of salvation; society or culture is not the decisive locus of the drama's occurrence; and God is not a useful (though perhaps ultimately dispensable and certainly optional) source of support and assistance in the social struggle. "On the contrary, in drawing humanity to himself in Jesus Christ, God inaugurates a new world and causes it to break through. This work of reconciliation, in the consummation to which Jesus Christ pointed and which he is to fulfill, is the divine removing of the things under which we now see both ourselves and others suffer" (I/2, 428 rev.). God is the decisive actor against evil in all its forms; Jesus Christ is the decisive locus in which evil has been overcome; and our role in the drama is not that of cooperators or eliminators, but that of forgiven sinners who at best can become witnesses to what God has done.

Barth's argument is not to be misunderstood as a brief for social or political indifference. Capitalism could be described as "almost unequivocally demonic" (III/4, 531). The oppressed and needy are said to have a "sacramental character," because the reality to which their suffering stands as the sign is the suffering of Jesus Christ, who has made their suffering his own (I/2, 429). Faith is said to involve "a political attitude, decisively determined by the fact that we are made responsible to all who are poor and wretched in our eyes, that we are summoned on our part to espouse the cause of those who suffer wrong" (II/1, 387 rev.). The point of Barth's polemic is rather that the status of social and political witness not be misconceived.

Social and political witness, as Barth understood it, has nothing to do with the false and futile promise of an activity in which God is merely the resource and we are the real achievers. "The Christian community does not exist for itself; it exists for the Gospel" (III/4, 506). At the same time, it exists among those who have not yet perceived the futility that lies "at the heart of their great attempt to live without God." The community sees "their countless small attempts to help, justify, sanctify and glorify themselves." It sees "the evils they thereby inflict on themselves," "the misery they bring upon themselves," and "the resultant excitement, anxiety and care in which they must exist." Knowing that "all this is unnecessary," the community will take care not to reinforce them in their various attempts to live as though Jesus Christ were not, in life and in death, their only help, justification, sanctification, and glorification. It will not collaborate with them in their attempts, which are "outmoded from the very outset," to live as though Jesus Christ did not exist (III/4, 506).

Therefore the community will take care not to confront them "with a program, plan or law in the performance of which they must abandon that great attempt to live without God, counterbalancing it by the opposite attempt to return to God and with his help to make everything different and better" (III/4, 506 rev.). The community, which exists for the sake of the gospel, has no right to make proposals to the people of the world "as though they could now help, justify, sanctify and glorify themselves more thoroughly and successfully than hitherto" (III/4, 507). On the contrary, in word and in deed, and therefore also in the form of social and political witness, the community will continually point to "the one truth that God has already begun to do something for them and that he will also complete it in spite of their opposition, outbidding all the attempts which spring from this opposition, overlooking and bypassing all their perversity and futility" (III/4, 507). The community will therefore take care that its social witness exists for the sake of the gospel, not the gospel for the sake of its social witness. It will point away from all our human efforts to save ourselves to the only true salvation—that which was procured by and is to be found in Jesus Christ alone.

The logic of Barth's argument, therefore, is once again the same. It is not salvation which is to be accounted for in terms of social action, but social action which is to be accounted for in terms of salvation. Salvation is conceptually prior to and independent of social action, and social action is conceptually subsequent to and dependent on salvation. Salvation is related to social action as its ground, orientation, and limit; social action is at best related to salvation as its witness, parable, and analogy. Social action is not prior to and independent of salvation, and salvation is not subsequent to and dependent on social action.

Against Existential Soteriology: The Sacramental Type

Against the sacramental type of existential soteriology, finally, Barth again argues in a similar pattern that the decisive locus of salvation is not to be shifted from Christ to the church, and especially not to the so-called sacraments. Baptism and, by implication, the Lord's Supper (although Barth did not live long enough to arrive at the point in the *Church Dogmatics* where the logic of his antisacramentalism would have been worked out for the latter) are not to be understood as sacraments in the sense that they are not "a means of salvation." Neither the divine work nor the divine revelation of salvation occurs by means of them. They are "neither a causative nor a cognitive *medium salutis*" (IV/4, 156). Our participation in these liturgical events brings about neither the reality nor the knowledge of our salvation. Our participation in them does not take place without our participation in the person and work of Jesus Christ, but our participation in Christ does not take place by means of these activities. These liturgical activities are not conditions that have to be met for our salvation, but are rather activities undertaken freely and in gratitude for our salvation. These activities take place because of our participation in Christ, but our participation in Christ does not take place because of these activities. A church which tries to transform these activities from a free response to grace into a necessary and effective means of grace is a church which is illicitly trying to displace Christ by making itself into the decisive locus of salvation (I/2, 128; II/1, 160; IV/1, 625; IV/4, 71, 79, 88, 101–2, 143, 156, 212). Formally speaking, therefore, the status of liturgical action in Barth's theology is exactly the same as that ascribed to social action. To avoid the tedium of unnecessary repetition, let it simply be noted that if the term "liturgical action" is substituted for "social action" in the previous paragraph, the exact relation between salvation and liturgical action, as Barth conceives it, will be made manifest.

Against Existential Soteriology: The Problem of Instrumentalism

Concealed within each type of existential soteriology—whether individualistic, social, or sacramental—there is, Barth suggests, a kind of instrumentalism. Instrumentalism, as the term will be used here, refers to one of two ideas: either that there is some independent end to which salvation in Christ is the means, or else that there is some independent means to which salvation in Christ is the end. In the first case salvation in Christ depends for its *significance* on some factor outside itself. In the second case this salvation depends for its *occurrence* on some such external factor. Either way, salvation in Christ depends on some factor other than itself for its essential meaning and truth.

First, consider the way in which existential soteriology establishes some independent end to which salvation in Christ is the means. This soteriology shifts the decisive locus of salvation from what is actual in Christ to what is or needs to become actual in us. Insofar as what needs to become actual in (or among) us is conceived as some independent good or gift (e.g., a virtuous disposition, social justice, eternal blessedness), then salvation itself becomes externalized as "something different from him, some general gift mediated by him," rather than being identical with himself. Thus "at the last moment, we ignore him as though he were only a means or instrument or channel" (IV/1, 116). If Christ himself were actually to be so detached from salvation, then our faith, hope, and love as those who are called by him "would not really be directed to him as the Giver, but to the goods and gifts appointed for our own consumption, and to himself only to the extent that what is truly desired and valued, i.e., grace and salvation in all these forms, would be received and enjoyed, not without him, yet nonetheless only through him" (IV/3, 595–96 rev.). Whether the appointed "goods and gifts" are understood individualistically, socially, or sacramentally, there is the danger that Jesus Christ "might well become for the Christian no more than the instrument which is serviceable for the attainment of this high and important purpose but subordinate to it" (IV/3, 596).

Although the issue at hand includes a moral or practical aspect, it is important to see that Barth is making an essentially logical point. Insofar as existential soteriology posits salvation in Christ as subsequent to and dependent on the attainment of some external good or gift, it incorporates the logic of instrumentalism. For when this soteriology accounts for the significance of Jesus Christ in terms of attaining some kind of good or gift, such that that good or gift is conceptually independent of him and of salvation as actualized in him, then that good or gift is set up as an external end to which he stands related as the means. This logic would obtain even if the relationship in question were conceived as one of interdependence. Each term of the relation might be conceived as in some sense prior to and yet dependent on the other. Such interdependence would complicate, yet still generate, an account in which salvation in Christ was at some point conceptually subsequent and instrumentally related to attaining some independently constitutive good or gift. Goods or gifts like a virtuous disposition, social justice, and eternal blessedness, insofar as they are conceived as independent constituents of salvation, make salvation in Christ conceptually subsequent to and dependent on their attainment. Christ himself is thereby conceived as the means to some end not included in himself and his finished work. But as Barth reads the New Testament, this conception is impossible. Jesus Christ and his salvation cannot possibly be conceived as subordinate to the attainment of some other good or gift.

Correlative to this fatal subordination (as Barth regards it) embedded in the basic structure of existential soteriology is the moral or practical aspect of the problem. The logic of instrumentalism is not far from the logic of egoism. Correlative to the instrumentalism of this soteriology, there lurks the danger of "a deeply suspect pious egocentricity" (IV/3, 568). When Jesus Christ is regarded "only as a motive or exponent or cipher" of some good other than himself (IV/3, 198), he is no longer the object of one's highest devotion and can thereby be esteemed as merely the means to the end of one's self-gratification. Note that this analysis does not commit Barth to the idea that the moral or practical aspect of the problem will automatically be solved by dispelling the logical confusion of existential soteriology. It simply commits him to the idea that the moral or practical aspect ought not to be compounded, exacerbated, and reinforced by an apparent conceptual legitimation which is already confused in itself. In any case, the seriousness of the whole situation may be gathered from Barth's conclusion, after a detailed consideration of the New Testament stories about Judas, that finally and fundamentally, for Judas, discipleship to Jesus was "not an end in itself, but a means to some other end" (II/2, 463).

Just as there is no independent end to which salvation in Christ is the means, so also, Barth contends, there is no independent means to which salvation in Christ is the end. Although important aspects of this contention must await the discussion of divine and human agency in chapter 7, the issues here can perhaps be initially clarified by developing a brief contrast between Aquinas and Barth on nature and grace. The pattern which governs the relationship between divine grace and human freedom in Aquinas's theology is, arguably, one of conceptual interdependence. That is, just as divine grace seems to precede, facilitate, and perfect human freedom, so human freedom seems to follow, cooperate with, and supplement divine grace. Insofar as human freedom is in some sense independent of divine grace (as it seems it must be at some point for

Aquinas), divine grace is dependent on human freedom for the attainment of the individual's salvation. Although human freedom is certainly in some sense conceptually subsequent to and dependent on divine grace, in another (if perhaps secondary) sense divine grace is nonetheless conceptually subsequent to and dependent on human freedom.[6] By contrast, as previously suggested, Barth's position on such matters is always one which repudiates a scheme of conceptual interdependence in favor of a scheme in which divine grace cannot be understood except as conceptually prior to and entirely independent of human freedom.

By reviewing Aquinas's discussion of the justification of the unrighteous, the contrast between the two theologians can be sharpened. In what sense, Aquinas asks, might this justification be considered to be a miracle? Three possible senses of miracle are distinguished. First, insofar as a miracle is something which can be done only by divine power, justification can be considered a miracle. Second, insofar as a miracle is something which actualizes a possibility not inherent in nature, justification cannot be considered a miracle. Finally, insofar as a miracle is something which operates outside the usual order of cause and effect, justification may or may not be considered a miracle, depending on the circumstances. (In cases where an instantaneous conversion actualizes perfect righteousness in an individual all at once, as occurred with St. Paul, justification can be considered a miracle; otherwise, righteousness is perfected within the individual by grace as it operates inside the usual order of cause and effect.)[7]

It is the second of these points which provides the best contrast with Barth. Barth agrees with Aquinas that the justification of the unrighteous person is something which can occur only by divine power, but disagrees that in justification (and thus in salvation) grace actualizes a possibility inherent in human nature. Barth considers justification to be a miracle in the very sense that Aquinas rules out. Indeed, Barth must do so, precisely because he disallows a key premise articulated by Aquinas in this context, namely, that "the soul is by nature capable of or open to grace."[8] If this premise is granted as used by Aquinas, divine grace and human freedom must necessarily be conceived as interdependent in the work of salvation. But one could not grant this premise without denying (or at least seriously modifying) the axiom that God's grace is not conditioned by anything other than itself, and Barth believes he has overriding reasons not to deny or modify this axiom. (Mainly, he believes, grace would not be grace—it would not be sovereign, free, and gratuitous—if human freedom were not conceptually subsequent to and entirely dependent on it.) Largely by force of this axiom, he thus conceives of the relationship between divine grace and human freedom as in no sense one of interdependence. In no sense is divine grace conceptually subsequent to and dependent on human freedom, and human freedom conceptually prior to and independent of divine grace.

In this light it becomes clear why matters like faith, social action, and liturgical action (as forms of human freedom in relation to grace) cannot be regarded, within the logic of Barth's theology, as independent means to the end of salvation in Christ. In no sense can they be regarded as contributing to the actualization of salvation, and certainly not by exercising a capability inherent in human nature. Barth's denial that any such capability exists (whether conceived Thomistically or not) goes hand in hand with three basic theological affirmations: that divine grace is absolutely unconditioned by anything other than itself, that in Christ the salvation of the human race is fully and objectively actual, and that all forms of human freedom with respect to salvation are miraculous (not natural) in basis, even as they are testimonial and ostensive (not contributory and instrumental) in status. In short, rather than positing nature as capable, Barth posits grace as unconditioned. In the work of salvation, nature thereby depends on grace for a capability not inherent in itself, whereas grace is in no sense subsequent to and dependent on nature.

Barth's critique of existential soteriology can therefore be interpreted in terms of the problem of instrumentalism. Insofar as this soteriology, in whatever form, sets up some independent end to which salvation in Christ is the means, it makes that salvation depend for its significance on some factor outside itself. And insofar as this soteriology sets us some independent means to which salvation in Christ is the end, it makes that salvation depend for its occurrence on some such external factor. Either way, these instrumentalist conceptions result in what Barth regards as untenable theoretical and practical outcomes. Theoretically, they result in an untenable conceptual relationship between divine grace and human freedom (interdependence). And practically, they result, as least apparently, in an untenable conceptual reinforcement or legitimation of ''a deeply suspect pious egocentricity'' (IV/3, 568). Barth's objectivist soteriology is designed, in large measure, to make both of these untenable outcomes conceptually impossible.

Excursus: What Barth's Objectivist Conception Needs to Show, How it Might be Threatened, and How It Might Respond

If Barth is successfully to uphold his conception of divine grace and human freedom, he must show that the reality of human freedom is in-

ternal rather than external to the operation of grace in the work of salvation as actualized in history by Jesus Christ. At least two obvious threats
to the reality of human freedom would seem to arise for this conception.
The first threat may be formulated as follows. The very historicity of the
work of salvation would seem so to encapsulate it that human freedom
has no access to it and therefore cannot participate in it. The reality of
human freedom would therefore be external to the operation of grace (and
the door might thereby be opened to conceiving them as interdependent).
Barth's solution to this problem is very complex, and a full-length study
would be required to elucidate it in its own right. Only the sketchiest of
expositions can be ventured here.

In its full historicity and its full actuality—in other words, in its objectivism—the work of salvation is accessible to human freedom, Barth believes, because the very Christ who actualized and embodied it is contemporaneous to every human being. Seen from below, so to speak, this
contemporaneity is based on the resurrection of Jesus from the dead; seen
from above, it is based on the eternal (though dynamic and significantly
differentiated) presence of Jesus to history by virtue of his having been
assumed (without violation of his historicity) into personal union with the
eternal Son of God. Seen from below, the contemporaneity of the work
of salvation is accessible to human freedom, in a way that the work can
be explicitly known for what it is, only by virtue of church proclamation
in accord with scripture (and therefore only by faith). Seen from above,
human freedom (whose reality in relation to God is not so readily to be
taken for granted) is made accessible to the work of salvation, in ways
currently beyond all human knowing, by virtue of the dynamic and differentiated yet ubiquitous and hidden presence of the eternal unity of this
work in Jesus Christ.

The unity of this work calls for special notice. The work of salvation,
as Barth conceives it, is such that (for example) pretemporal election, the
cross of Christ, the outpouring of the Holy Spirit, and the return of Christ
at the Last Judgment are regarded as four different events, and yet also
as four different forms of one and the same event. Seen from below, this
unified and complex work appears as a differentiated series of events, all
of which are centered on the cross of Christ. (In an attempt to capture
the dynamism of this complex and differentiated work, the study at hand
sometimes speaks, with regard to the motif of actualism, of the work of
salvation in the history of Jesus as a "self-transcending event" and as
not being "encapsulated in his history in an unqualified way.") Seen
from above, this differentiated series of events appears as a unified and

complex work, yet still always centered on the cross of Christ. Whether seen from below or above, the primary affirmation which needs to be made within the logic of this conception is that human freedom is made accessible, in ways known and as yet unknown, to this unified, differentiated, and living event because of the human race's incorporation into the humanity of Christ by means of the miracle of grace.

Although this sketch may have raised more questions than it answers, it will have to end here. Enough has been said to indicate the kind of account Barth would be able to give in response to the objection that his conception fatally externalizes human freedom from the work of salvation. If that work were simply historical (in some ordinary sense of "historical") and nothing more, then human freedom would indeed be external to it, and some different operation of grace would be required in order to internalize that work (so to speak) in human beings. But since that work exhibits a complex, differentiated and dynamic eternal unity which becomes present in Christ to each and every human being, the miraculous elicitation and sustenance of human freedom with respect to that work can be conceived as internal to the work itself.

There is, however, a second threat which Barth's objectivist conception would need to meet, this time from the opposite direction. This second threat may be formulated as follows. The very sovereignty by which salvation is accomplished—namely, by Jesus Christ alone—threatens to include the reality of human freedom only by completely overwhelming it and thereby rendering it meaningless. Human freedom might well be internalized into the saving work of grace, yet only at the price of its effective nullification. If human freedom is in no sense independent of divine grace, then that freedom would seem to forfeit all reality in its own right, being totally overridden by grace as a sovereign and irresistible power.

This threat raises the larger question of just how the existential moment of salvation is to be described within the framework of Barth's objectivist soteriology. If the existential moment, however conceived, does not contribute to the actualization of salvation, if it is not conceivable as constituting salvation in any sense, if it in no sense functions as the decisive locus of salvation, then just what status is that moment thought to have? Is there really any role for it at all? Doesn't Barth's conception finally result in a kind of monism (some have called it "christomonism") whereby the existential moment is so absorbed into the objective moment that it finally disappears? Doesn't whatever needs to take place in human existence finally reduce to a mere epiphenomenon of what has already occurred so impressively and conclusively in Christ? Or, even if human existence does not completely disappear into the reality of Christ, doesn't Barth finally construct an unenviable determinism (perhaps a ''christo-determinism'')? Isn't Jesus Christ so decisively and sovereignly the acting subject of salvation that human agency is simply overpowered? Aren't human beings finally little more than passive objects in an overdetermined drama of salvation which takes place entirely above their heads, only to be dropped down on them like a stone from heaven? Barth has sometimes been read this way. Monism and determinism are common objections to his objectivist soteriology. Once again his rejoinder is complex, but this time will be discussed at greater length. Although the discussion of objectivism must be drawn to a close, Barth's rejoinder to this objection will, in effect, be the subject of the next two chapters.

Conclusion: The Two Types of Soteriology and the Two Forms of Objectivism Each Compared

In conclusion, it may be noted that the two types of soteriology seem to differ regarding three main points: the means, the locus, and the definition of salvation. For existential soteriology, in whichever form, the means of salvation includes some kind of fundamental human preparation, reception, or enactment which contributes to the actualization of salvation. For Barth's objectivist soteriology, by contrast, all such contributions are systematically excluded. For existential soteriology, the locus of salvation is decisively existential in the sense that without actualization in the individual, the society, or the sacrament (or some combination thereof), salvation remains a mere possibility or an unattained ideal. For Barth's objectivist soteriology, by contrast, this locus is entirely objective in the sense that salvation's actualization in Jesus Christ has already embraced the entire human race and taken it up into himself, whether human beings know this yet or not. Finally, for existential soteriology, salvation is often so defined that it becomes a general good or gift detachable from Jesus Christ himself (such as a virtuous disposition, social justice, or eternal blessedness). For Barth's objectivist soteriology, by contrast, the definition of salvation is entirely christocentric in form and content; all lesser goods and gifts are not only included in Christ and constituted by him, but are also in principle relinquishable here and now for the sake of serving him in faithful witness as the cost of discipleship.

It remains to draw a brief comparison between the two basic forms of objectivism—revelational and soteriological. Hiddenness is a central category in both conceptions. The reality of God and our true reality as human beings are both conceived as hidden in Jesus Christ. The hiddenness of the divine reality pertains to an ontological divide, whereas the hiddenness of our human reality pertains to an ontological connection. What is divided by nature is, in both cases, connected by grace. God's ontological difference from humankind is overcome by the freedom of grace in Jesus Christ. Likewise, sinful humankind's soteriological distance from God is overcome by the same freedom in Jesus Christ. Jesus Christ is thus the true Mediator in whom these realities are both hidden. Their hiddenness cannot be penetrated except by faith. Faith is the act of apprehending and acknowledging that the human nature of Jesus Christ mediates the truth of God's reality to humankind (revelation) and the truth of humankind's reality to God (salvation). The hiddenness of the mediation will, in both cases, not persist indefinitely, for one day the truth of these realities will be manifest openly to the sight of all. Even in the final situation of open disclosure, however, Jesus Christ will still be the Mediator by whom human beings will know and love God as they are already known and loved. The transition from faith to sight will disclose the once hidden glory of the Mediator which was actual, in revelation and salvation, all along.

CHAPTER 6

Truth as Encounter

Personalism, the sixth and last motif, signifies that in Barth's theology truth is ultimately a matter of encounter. Truth is not something neutral but something self-involving, and so is apprehended not by a solitary intellect, but by the whole person in fellowship with God. The mediation of truth in Jesus Christ—the truth of God's identity and also of humankind's identity in him—does not remain merely objective (though it never ceases to be objective). It encounters men and women at the core of their beings, Barth argues, liberating them from being closed in upon themselves. They thereby come to recognize the truth of their being in Jesus Christ, to participate actively in that truth, and to serve it as witnesses here and now. This active service involves the mystery of personal fellowship established in Christ between divine freedom as truly divine, and human freedom as truly human. The occurrence of fellowship in freedom extends not only to men and women's vocation of witness, but also to their destiny of eternal life. Truth as encounter thus pertains to their status, their task, and their destiny in Christ before God.

Soteriological objectivism, as examined in the previous chapter, left us with the question of the status of the existential moment of salvation. Jesus Christ, it will be recalled, is described as the decisive means, locus, and content of human salvation. Salvation occurs by him alone, is to be found in him alone, and is finally simply identical with him alone. Corresponding to these affirmations is a series of negations. Salvation does not occur by means of human action, it is not directly discernible in human existence, and it is not detachable from Jesus Christ himself as though he were merely the means to some sort of ensuing transformation here and now, whether individualistically, socially, or sacramentally conceived. Perhaps most striking is Barth's rejection of the idea that salvation is somehow constituted as an inward and immanent transformation of human existence by means of one's coming to faith.[1] Does this rejection imply that Barth thinks faith can occur without such a transformation? If not, what is the content of the existential transformation, and what status does it have, if not that of a decisive actualization of salvation?

The problem of how to relate the existential to the objective moment of salvation is one to which Barth finds himself returning again and again. Especially because he lays such great stress on the unconditional priority of the objective moment, he realizes that the integrity of the corresponding existential moment is in danger of being underplayed or even undercut. "Reality which does not become truth for us," he writes, "obviously cannot affect us, however supreme may be its ontological dignity" (IV/2, 297). A salvation, an ontological connection of Christ to us, that remained merely objective with no existential counterpart would be a salvation that remained inaccessible and hollow. Yet a salvation whose truth and reality somehow depended on our preparation, reception, or enactment would be a salvation in which the existential moment was at some point (whether overtly or covertly) grounded in us rather than in Jesus Christ. When the reality of salvation becomes true for us, Barth argues, then at the same time we recognize that it was already true apart from us (and even against us). Whatever preparation, reception, or enactment may have been involved (and continues to be involved), our recognition is not to be conceived as in any sense constituting the truth or actuality of salvation. Our recognition is simply our awakening to the fact that, in Jesus Christ, salvation's truth and actuality really pertain and apply to us as well, that we are included in them, that they are real for us, precisely by having been established apart from us. Our awakening does not do anything to make salvation as such true or actual. It merely means that we have come to see that we are not outside but inside this saving truth and actuality. But precisely because we are inside and not outside, it is necessary that salvation *also* take place in our own life. When salvation does take place in our life, however, it is not the existential occurrence that brings about the actuality and truth of salvation, but rather the actuality and truth of salvation that bring about the existential occurrence. The existential occurrence is a manifesting, not a constituting, of salvation's actuality and truth.

Everything depends on noticing that Barth is attempting to think this matter through concretely rather than abstractly in his special (actualist) sense of the terms. Everything depends, therefore, on seeing that he does not think in terms of the real and the ideal, but rather in terms of the real and the unreal (or of the possible and the impossible). What is real, possible, and concrete is what God has established in Jesus Christ. In Jesus Christ we see that God does not exist without humanity and that humanity does not exist without God. God without humanity and humanity without God are conceived as abstractions that do not really exist in the sense that they have no ultimate reality. God does not exist without humanity, because God has decided in Jesus Christ not to be God without us. Likewise, humanity does not exist without God, because Jesus Christ has decided in our place and for our sakes not to be human without God. Everything else about us, as noted more than once before, is regarded as an abstraction that is destined to disappear. By virtue of an existential encounter with God, our old situation (abstract, unreal, and impossible as it is) can and should be left behind even now. The salvation which as such was already true and actual for us in Christ thereby becomes true and actual in our own lives as well. What was already effective and significant de jure becomes effective and significant de facto (however provisionally) here and now.

The existential moment of salvation (as established through the event of encounter) is, it is important to see, understood primarily in terms of vocation rather than justification or sanctification. Justification and sanctification are primarily conceived, in Barth's theology, as the objective aspects of salvation to which vocation is the corresponding existential aspect. Thus as Barth moves into part 3 of volume 4 of *Church Dogmatics,* where vocation is discussed, a much more recurrent and prominent use of "in us" can be found than in parts 1 and 2, where justification and sanctification as they occur "in Christ" are the respective topics of discussion. Much earlier it was suggested that objectivism is understood as the external basis of personalism, and personalism as the internal basis or telos of objectivism. To this it may now be added that justification and sanctification, as Barth presents them, can be interpreted as the external basis of vocation, and vocation as the internal basis or telos of justification and sanctification.[2] As the internal basis of the objective moment of salvation, vocation is thus understood as follows. The event of vocation takes place through an encounter established and effected by God. In this event the integrity of both the divine and the human partners is so carried through that the encounter is self-involving for each. The goal of vocation is conceived as fellowship (IV/3, 520–54), and its essence is conceived as witness (IV/3, 575). As the existential moment of salvation, vocation is thus a matter of encounter, integrity, mutual self-involvement, fellowship, and witness.

Vocation as a Matter of Encounter

Vocation is a matter of encounter. "The object and theme of theology," writes Barth, "and the content of the Christian message is neither a subjective nor an objective element in isolation. That is to say, it is neither an isolated humanity nor an isolated God, but God and humanity in their divinely established and effective encounter, the dealings of God with the Christian and of the Christian with God" (IV/3, 498 rev.). As the primary form of the divine–human encounter, "vocation should not," Barth takes pains to emphasize, "be divested of its concrete historicity nor transcendentalized" (IV/3, 498 rev.). Note that these are precisely the charges (divestment of historicity or transcendentalization) commonly leveled against Barth's understanding of salvation's existential moment. Perhaps one (but certainly not the only) reason for this standard objection is simply that it has not always been noticed that vocation rather than justification or sanctification is the primary rubric under which Barth chooses to address this question in a sustained way. In any case, regarding vocation Barth continues: "We do not speak of it correctly, nor of God as its acting Subject, if we speak of it docetically, as though it became and were real, true and certain only beyond the historical existence of humanity in time, as the work of God which is not also his work on us, and which merely touches our existence as it were from without" (IV/3, 498 rev.). From this remark it may be gathered that vocation is understood to touch our existence from within (not merely from without), that it is God's work on us (in correspondence to God's work apart from us), and that it is real, true, and certain within the historical existence of humanity in time (not merely beyond it). By intention Barth clearly means to present vocation as an event in our existence that is real, historical, and concrete.

At the same time, however, two further points are especially striking. First, the pattern of thought clearly proceeds from "without" to "within," from "apart from us" to "on us," from "beyond historical existence" to "within" it. The decidedly christocentric rather than anthropocentric orientation of Barth's theology is reflected in this ordering (a matter to which we shall return). Second, the argument clearly takes it for granted that God can be conceived as the acting Subject of vocation without lapsing into docetism (or, to invoke a corresponding category, monism). Yet how can vocation be spoken of correctly if its acting Subject is conceived as God? Doesn't this conception necessarily eliminate the possibility of one's being an acting subject in the existential moment of one's own salvation? Doesn't this conception (which is certainly typical of Barth) inevitably land in just the docetism or monism that Barth would like to avoid? The answer given by Barth to this and related questions will form the climax to our consideration of personalism. No more can be indicated here than the direction of his answer. Not only does he deny that his conception of divine agency commits him to anything like docetism or monism. He goes on to ask whether the premise hidden behind this recurring criticism would not in itself actually commit the critic in one way or another, if not to docetism, then perhaps to some equally unfortunate theological outcome.

Vocation as a Matter of Integrity

Vocation, as Barth understands it, is not only a matter of encounter, but also a matter of integrity. As an event that occurs concretely, it actually serves to establish (rather than to undermine) the integrity of human personhood before God. We are encountered in person by Jesus Christ (IV/3, 508). His history "emerges from the apparent distance in which it is played out for us" (IV/3, 181). That is to say, his history acquires voice. "It is a declaration. And as it comes to us, it is an address, promise and demand, a question and answer. . . . It encounters us, speaks with us, addresses us in terms of I and Thou" (IV/3, 83). Jesus Christ bears witness to himself by this history, coming immediately and directly before us through his Word. When he encounters us in this way, his Word comes upon us "like lightning striking and splitting a tree, or more gently like a seed falling into the earth and there relentlessly perishing" (IV/3, 505). Yet it is not only the identity of Jesus Christ that is manifested, but at the same time our human identity as well. We are addressed and acknowledged as persons, the persons God has made us to be in him. The integrity of our humanity is claimed and confirmed. We are called (and called again) to be and become who we are (IV/3, 555). We come to see that we are (and are to be) in him and for him and with him, just as he is (and is to be) with us and for us and in us. The integrity of his person is understood to establish and include within itself the integrity of ours as well (IV/3, 594–95).

The same point is often made with God as the subject of the personal address. "As God addresses us," writes Barth, "he acknowledges and reveals us as someone, a particular individual, this human being" (III/4, 328 rev.). Just because it is personal, the divine address cannot be understood as applying itself to a faceless mass of generalized humanity. "The Word of God not only presupposes a reality different from itself, a life-process, but many specific life-acts. It relates to them all, yet not to a mere totality, but to individual and unique rational creatures" (III/4, 328). The God revealed to us by name is the God who addresses us by name, acknowledging us in our distinctive particularity. "God knows who and what we may be. God calls us by our name" (III/4, 329 rev.). Neither God nor we can remain unnamed, for this Word is spoken "by the divine I to the human Thou." It is a Word by which each person is both claimed and confirmed. It claims "the supremely particular hearing of this specific person." It thereby confirms and reveals "the individuality of the person's being and life" (III/4, 329 rev.). Truth as encounter is thus understood as a concrete and personal truth. "It is the truth as it is God's speaking person, *Dei loquentis persona*. . . . God's Word means the speaking God. . . . God always speaks *concretissimum*" (I/1, 136–37). But this means that we ourselves are always addressed and called in our concrete reality as persons, having individual particularity, identity, and integrity.

Vocation as a Matter of Mutual Self-Involvement

Vocation, as Barth understands it, is not only a matter of encounter and integrity, but also a matter of mutual self-involvement. Men and women receive their vocation from God in the course of an ongoing, personal encounter that involves them to the full. "The real truth of God and humanity," writes Barth, "is valid when God and we are engaged in eye-to-eye and mouth-to-ear encounter. It is valid as the truth of the event of a common history" (IV/3, 485 rev.). The common history in which we are mutually involved with God may be described as a history that engages each participant from the heart. The heart, as Barth explains the biblical meaning of the term, signifies at once the personal center and yet also the very essence of the whole person (III/2, 435–36). The encounter in which we are seen to be engaged with God, eye-to-eye and mouth-to-ear, is an encounter involving each participant from the heart, in the sense that the center and essence of each is at stake. The real truth of God and humanity may thus be described as a common history in which each is engaged to an extent than which no greater can be conceived.

With respect to the personal essence and center of God, "heart" is a term that Barth characteristically reserves for signifying the depth of divine mercy, especially as manifest in the event of the cross. The concept of God's mercy, as Barth explains its biblical meaning, presupposes that we as God's creatures are in evident distress. Mercy is God's free inclination to take up our cause and come to our assistance. "God's very being," writes Barth, "is mercy. The mercy of God lies in his readiness to share the distress of another, a readiness which springs from his inmost nature and stamps all his being and doing" (II/1, 369). God wills that our distress should cease, and therefore wills to do what is necessary to remove it. Only God is in a position to relieve us from the distress we have brought on ourselves through sin. In an act of inconceivable mercy God therefore enters fully into this distress that it might once and for all be removed. God does this by suffering and dying in our place in and through Jesus on the cross.

The divine mercy, Barth urges, is capable of sharing and removing our distress in this inconceivable way. If God were merely "an impersonal absolute," God would of course be incapable of such a "movement of the heart" (II/1, 370). "But the personal God has a heart. He can feel, and be affected. He is not impassible. He cannot be moved from outside by an extraneous power. But this does not mean that he is not capable of moving himself. No, God is moved and stirred . . . in his own free power . . . to relieve this distress" (II/1, 370). The divine decision to enter into our extremity is thus not contrary to God's being as God, but is "rooted in his heart, in his very being and life as God" (II/1, 370).

The cross of Christ—the means by which God participates in and relieves humankind's distress—therefore expresses God's "innermost being, his heart, his divine person, his divine essence, himself as the One he is" (IV/3, 412). The cross signifies the incomprehensible lengths to which God was ready to go in order to remove the ultimate condition of all that troubles and destroys us: "Only God himself could bear the wrath of God. Only God's mercy was capable of bearing the pain to which the creature in opposition to him is subject. Only God's mercy could so feel this pain as to take it into the very heart of his being. And only God's mercy was strong enough not to be annihilated by this pain" (II/1, 400). The divine self-involvement with us is therefore such that no greater can be conceived. The divine mercy consists in God having taken to heart the full distress of our estrangement from God. Indeed, writes Barth, "he bore it in his heart. . . . For in him who took our place God's own heart beat on our side, in our flesh and blood, in complete solidarity with our nature and constitution, at the very point where we ourselves confront him, guilty before God'' (II/1, 402). The God who encounters us in the Word of the cross is therefore involved from the heart. The divine self-involvement in our common history is unqualified. The inmost being of God is given over to suffering and death on the cross that we ourselves might be spared (IV/1, 347; IV/2, 225; IV/3, 413–16).

No less complete than the divine self-involvement on our behalf, Barth believes, is the corresponding self-involvement from the human side. No less than the full engagement of our inmost being is presupposed, revealed, and claimed by the Word of the cross. When this Word encounters us in the existential moment of our salvation, no neutrality is possible. We are engaged in our hearts as wholly as God has engaged us from the heart. As we come to know that Jesus Christ's history is our history as well, we also come to recognize that sin, repentance, and new life determine our existence as a whole, and therefore at the very heart.

No neutrality is possible when we are confronted by the Word of the cross. The "basic form" of revelation occurs when our distance from the cross is overcome and destroyed. Through the Word, the cross itself approaches us, "encroaching and impinging upon us, disclosing itself to us and making itself the subject and content of our knowledge'' (IV/3, 183 rev.). We therefore come to have "a specific knowledge.'' It is at once the knowledge of a specific history and the knowledge of a specific person. No knowledge of the person is possible without the history, and no knowledge of the history is possible without the person, in the moment when our distance from the cross dissolves. The person without the history would be a mere anonymous presence, and the history without the person, mere neutral information; but in the moment of encounter a "new and strange Counterpart''—the person of Jesus Christ, who died for us on the cross—confronts us as One with whom we "cannot avoid wrestling'' (IV/3, 183). As we come to know him and grapple with him, we come to know his history as the history of our salvation. In the Word of the cross that confronts and claims us, the person and the history are one. The person and the history are disclosed by the Word of the cross, the history of the cross identifies the One who confronts and claims us, and we ourselves are caught up in an encounter that transforms us to the core of our being (IV/3, 183).

This unity of personal, informational, and transformative knowledge is itself described as a history in which we become aware of another history which touches us profoundly, at first from without but then also from within. It is this kind of knowledge which is said to be characteristic of the Bible. Neither "neutral information" nor "passive contemplation" are what is meant by this special kind of knowledge (IV/3, 183). Knowledge is rather a process or history that engages us, requiring us to observe and think, to use our "senses, intelligence and imagination" as well as our "will, action and 'heart.' " It thus engages us as whole persons. In this knowledge we become aware of another history that at first encounters us as "an alien history from without." Yet we become aware of it "in such a compelling way" that we can no longer remain neutral toward it. Instead, we find ourselves "summoned to disclose and give ourselves to it in return." We are to "direct ourselves according to the law which we encounter in it, to be taken up into its movement." In short, we are "to demonstrate the acquaintance which we have been given with this other history in a corresponding alteration of our own being, action and conduct." Knowledge in the biblical sense is thus a knowledge in which the personal, informational, and transformative elements all cohere and mutually condition one another. "We can and should say even more emphatically that knowledge in the biblical sense is the process in which the distant 'object' dissolves as it were, overcoming both its distance and its objectivity. It thereby comes to us as acting Subject, entering into us who know, and subjecting us to this transformation" (IV/3, 183–84 rev.).

When encountered by the Word of the cross, we cannot avoid recognizing that our existence is determined by sin. A specific knowledge of sin is enclosed in our knowledge of the crucified Christ. As we come to know him through the Word of the cross, we come to know what sin is, what it means for humanity in general, and what it means that we personally are sinners. No other source of this knowledge is finally either necessary or possible. Sin is not finally known except on the basis of an encounter with Christ through the Word of the cross. It is not to be conceived apart from the centrality of the cross, whether from "biblical or extra-biblical materials" or from "our own self-communing" (IV/1, 389). Conceptions of sin which exclude the cross can only finally be regarded as deficient. For it is the crucified One who "is present, living and speaking and attesting and convincing" us of the magnitude of our sin (IV/1, 389–90).

What sin is, what it means in general, and what it means in particular are all spoken clearly and inescapably when we are confronted by him through the Word of the cross: "Thou art the one! This is what thou doest! This is what thou art! This is the result!" (VI/1, 390 rev.). The knowledge of sin is regarded as personal knowledge acquired from an encounter with the crucified Christ. "We hear him and we hear this verdict. We see him, and in this mirror we see ourselves, ourselves as those who commit sin and are sinners'' (IV/1, 390). No room exists for ''fine distinctions'' such as that between sin and sinner. We can only acknowledge that we are ''wholly unrighteous'' (IV/1, 390). Our being is implicated as a whole. ''We are arrested, marched away and locked up. There can be no pardon attained by our own devices, no explanation and interpretation of sin and the sinner, when we are confronted by Jesus Christ and hear the Word spoken in his existence. We are simply there as this one'' (IV/1, 390 rev.).

All thought that we might somehow be able to rectify matters by a better or more resolute use of our own capacities is excluded on principle. ''There can be no question of any thought of redemption which we can manipulate, any capacity for redemption which we can put into effect'' (IV/1, 390). No final reserve of freedom exists for us to draw upon, no remnant of an effective capacity in which our lives might be reinterpreted and transformed. Knowledge of sin in the existential moment of salvation is conceived as cutting to the heart. It ''consists in the knowledge: I am this one. To this extent it is the knowledge of real sin'' (IV/1, 390 rev.). In short, an I–Thou encounter with Christ through the Word of the cross involves one in direct personal knowledge of sin. Sin is known in this encounter as an existential determination that is wholly self-involving.

Yet when encountered by the Word of the cross, one's existence is also being caught up in a process of conversion. This occurs not so much through one's giving of oneself to Christ as through the self-giving of Christ to oneself. ''When he calls, he . . . calls with power. For . . . he calls with liberating and creative force, summoning non-being into being, giving himself unreservedly to the one whom he calls, delivering himself up to this one, really calling this one to himself'' (IV/3, 530 rev.). Through the self-giving of Jesus Christ, the one called is empowered to hear and obey, to move from one form of existence to another, ''self-evidently and without argument . . . on no other basis than the obviously all-sufficient basis of his call'' (IV/3, 530). The one called through this encounter thus embarks upon a new way of life—a life centered in Jesus Christ, based on his power, and oriented in service to the Word of the cross.

The process of repentance or conversion is, like the sinful existence it leaves behind, wholly self-involving. Human beings are grasped as whole persons with all their ''possibilities and experiences and attitudes,'' when Jesus Christ becomes the object of their knowledge in this relentless and compelling way. They are grasped as whole persons when he ''takes and retains the initiative'' by reorienting their existence, turning them right about to face him so that they come to be "wholly oriented" upon him (IV/3, 220). No doubt is left about the totality of this reorientation. "It takes place to and in us. It involves the total and most intensive conscription and co-operation of all our inner and outer forces, of our whole heart and soul and mind, which in the biblical sense in which these terms are used includes our whole physical being" (IV/2, 556 rev.). Everything that we are and have is to be brought under the influence of this event. Not only our relationship to God but also our relationship to others, not only our inward disposition but also our outward action, not only our private affairs but also our public responsibilities—all these are at sake in the movement from the old form of life to the new (IV/2, 563–66). That God exists for us, and we for God, is "a total reality" which asserts itself in our life "in the power of total truth," setting us "wholly and not merely partially" in the movement of repentance or conversion (IV/2, 563).

The totality of this movement is especially evident from the way it extends through the course of one's life. Repentance or conversion is not to be regarded as an instant that can be left behind after it has occurred. Although a decisive turning point may (or may not) have been experienced (depending on the individual), repentance or conversion is conceived as something that is never past except in such a way that it is also always future as well. The movement (as the motif of actualism would lead us to expect) is regarded as an ongoing event that recurs throughout one's life. "It is neither exhausted in a once-for-all event, nor is it accomplished in a series of such acts. Otherwise how could it be an affair of the whole person?" (IV/2, 566 rev.). (Note that, in accord with the actualist motif, "wholeness" is conceived here as essentially temporal.) It is not a matter of "individual moments" but of "the totality of the whole life-movement" of the particular person concerned (IV/2, 566). Conversion to Christ through the Word of the cross means "to be raised and driven with increasing definiteness from the center of this revealed truth, and therefore to live in conversion with growing sincerity, depth and precision" (IV/2, 566). (Note that the possibility of progress in the Christian life is here taken into account and not, as is sometimes thought of Barth, ruled out by virtue of the conspicuous actualism.)

The essential point is that the work of conversion always stands before us afresh, because the living Word of God is never done with us but always moves on before us. "For the One who has called us, Jesus Christ, is and will be the same as he was. He is Omega as well as Alpha. He is the living One who calls again those whom he has called" (IV/3, 518 rev.). No one whose life comes to center on him does not need to become centered anew. "And none of those whom he has called does not need and is not totally directed to be called, illuminated and awakened by him again. None is not directed to the mercy of God which is new every morning" (IV/3, 518). No one who has turned to Christ initially does not need to keep on turning to him continuously. "It would not be his vocation if it were only *vocatio unica,* only initial and once-for-all illumination and awakening, and not also *vocatio continua*" (IV/3, 518). As *vocatio continua* the call to conversion is an ongoing event, recurring through one's existence in time.

Although from one point of view the Christian's conversion to new life can never be described too modestly, from another point of view "the radical nature of what commences" can never be signified too strongly (IV/3, 674). Those called by Christ are not met outwardly only to be left inwardly unchanged. The Word which impinges from without proceeds to transform from within. In calling men and women to himself, Jesus Christ approaches from without "in all his strangeness and novelty." But through the power of what he says, they are transformed from within, "existentially and totally." They become another person than they were before, "called instead of uncalled" (IV/3, 516). The external Word thus meets them "with inwardly victorious power" (IV/3, 520).

Not only, therefore, is the human subject affirmed in the integrity of its individual particularity, and not only is it negated in the corruption of its sin; it is also "newly created and grounded as such, from above" (IV/2, 89). Through the call to conversion by the Word of the cross, human subjectivity is opened up, reestablished, and redetermined (II/1, 14). Nothing less than "a new human subject" is introduced to replace the old human subject as determined by sin. This subject, furthermore, is really "the true human being," for beside and outside this new subject "God does not know any other" (IV/1, 89 rev.). But just how does this new human subject come to be what it is as "a temporal and historical reality" (IV/3, 519)?

It is a peculiarity of Barth's theology that conversion, for all its concomitant existential and ethical implications, is presented primarily in noetic terms. The new human subject comes into being precisely as it is illuminated by the "event of revelation and knowledge." It is in the event of "illumination" that the human subject is "not only affected, but seized and refashioned." The subject thereby comes to be a "new being" in correspondence to its reality as established "in Christ" (IV/3, 519).

By virtue of a spiritual "awakening," the subject befriends the real being that it is "in Christ and therefore in truth" (IV/3, 544). This befriending of Christ and the truth of one's reality in Christ is the work of the Holy Spirit in the subject's heart. For the Holy Spirit is "the *doctor veritatis*. He is the finger of God which opens blind eyes and deaf ears for the truth, which quickens dead hearts by and for the truth, which causes human reason, so concerned about its limitations and so proud within those limitations, to receive the truth notwithstanding its limitations" (IV/2, 126 rev.). Blindness is transformed into sight, deafness into hearing, dead hearts into quickened hearts receptive of the truth. When it is thus no longer concealed that God in Jesus Christ has befriended us, and that therefore we may befriend God, what takes place in us "is not a question of improvement but alteration. It is not a question of a reformed or eno-bled life, but a new one" (IV/2, 560). God's revelation shines on us not only from without, but now also wholly from within. What is addressed to us in the Word of the cross is now heard, received, and appropriated.

This inward illumination of the human subject is itself conceived as the great transformation. It occurs "not with new and special organs, but with the same organs of apperception with which we know other things, yet not in virtue of our own capacity to use them, but in virtue of the missing capacity which we are now given by God's revelation" (IV/3, 509 rev.). It is this bestowal of "the missing capacity" that makes God's grace "subjectively strong and effective" (IV/1, 88). It is this that is the miraculous work of the Holy Spirit in the human heart. It is thus this bestowal that makes us not "a corrected and revised edition" of the old human being, but a new human being and a new creation altogether. A new subjectivity is bestowed at the core which affects one's being as a whole. "As the work of God becomes clear to us, its reflection lights up our own heart and self and whole existence through the One whom we may know on the basis of his own self-declaration. Illumination and therefore vocation is the total alteration of the one whom it befalls" (IV/3, 510 rev.). This new subjectivity in grace, like the old and superseded subjectivity in sin, is again an existential determination that is wholly self-involving.

To sum up: in the event of vocation through which human beings are confronted by the cross, both God and human beings are regarded as engaged from the heart. Total self-involvement on the divine side is seen in the way God's mercy so fully enters into human distress that it leads God in Jesus Christ to die in our place on the cross. In the passion of Christ, God's inmost being, essence, and heart are at stake. God holds back nothing in order that human beings might be spared. When the Word spoken in the event of the cross touches our hearts from within, we too come to see that we are just as involved from the heart as God is involved with us. Total self-involvement on the human side is seen in the way we are affirmed, negated, and reconstituted on a higher plane. In our concrete particularity, identity, and integrity as human beings, we are wholly affirmed. In our concrete and personal sinfulness as disclosed in the event of the cross, we are wholly negated. In our concrete reception of a new being converted to and centered on Jesus Christ by the ongoing miracle of grace in our lives, we are wholly reconstituted on a higher plane. Affirmation, negation, and reconstitution are all understood to take place not for their own sakes, but for the sake of vocation in service to the Word of the cross.

Excursus: How Are the Cognitive and Performative Aspects of Truth Related?

A point of clarification would now be appropriate. The point concerns the relationship between the conceptions of self-involvement and truth. Truth, it has been stressed, is understood by Barth to be wholly self-involving. When human beings are addressed by the Word of the cross so that its distance from them dissolves and its presence transforms their hearts from within, then a significant transition has occurred both in their relation to the truth and in the relation of the truth to them. They come to be personally related to the truth by a new and transforming awareness, and the truth comes to be personally engaged with them here and now in a way that they begin to reciprocate concretely. Their personal relation to the truth involves them from the heart, and the truth's personal relation to them from the very heart of God becomes manifest to them in their lives. Their self-involvement with the truth comes to correspond existentially to the prior self-involvement of the truth with them.

To say that the truth of the gospel is self-involving, however, can be taken to imply—and here is the point to be clarified—that the truth of the gospel in some sense depends on the quality of a person's self-involvement. Consider, for example, the following proposal as recently advanced by George Lindbeck. When the crusader in the pitch of battle cries *"Christus est Dominus,"* and when this cry is used by the crusader to authorize his cleaving the skull of an infidel, then in such circumstances, Lindbeck argues, the utterance *"Christus est Dominus"* is false. The usage of the utterance would so contradict its correlative form of life as to falsify the utterance itself. The cognitive truth of a religious utterance, according to this proposal, depends on how the utterance is used. Religious utterances acquire cognitive truth only insofar as they are rightly used within a correlative form of life molded by such religious activities as prayer, worship, proclamation, and service. Right use—or, to pick up the terms of the previous discussion, the proper kind of self-involvement—is thus proposed as a condition for the possibility that the sentence *"Christus est Dominus"* be true. Such sentences correspond to reality and are therefore cognitively true only insofar as they are used properly within a correlative form of life. Conversely, insofar as the use of such a sentence stands in contradiction with the correlative form of life, the sentence is false. Valid performance (the proper kind of self-involvement) is thus a condition for the possibility of cognitive truth. Cognitive truth in the sense of correspondence to reality is not an attribute religious utterances can have when considered in and of themselves.[3]

Three preliminary points may be made about this proposal. First, it has been associated with a larger theological formation. "As his frequent references to Barth and his colleagues at Yale . . . make clear, Lindbeck's substantive position is a methodologically sophisticated version of Barthian confessionalism. The hands may be the hands of Wittgenstein and Geertz but the voice is the voice of Karl Barth."[4] Surely no question could stand closer to the core of any theological position than that of how truth is conceived. And surely no such conception would be complete without stating how the cognitive and performative aspects of truth are related. Can it fairly be said, however, that Lindbeck and Barth are so closely in agreement on this matter that the words of the one convey the voice of the other?

Second, this latter question can be answered, it would seem, without delving deeply into Lindbeck's own technical vocabulary. The issue at stake has to do with the semantic features of a sentence such as *"Christus est Dominus."* To what extent, if any, do the semantic features of such a sentence vary with the context in which it is used? Is truth in any sense a property of such sentences, or is it purely a relation of such sentences and their contexts of usage? And if truth is in some sense a relation between sentences and contexts, what would be the total relevant context to be taken into account for an utterance such as *"Christus est Dominus"?* The Lindbeck proposal would seem to involve the idea that truth is not a property which pertains to sentences so much as to the forms of life in which sentences are used. It is not sentences in themselves but religious forms of life as a whole which may properly be said to correspond (or fail to correspond) to reality (i.e., ultimate reality). Insofar as this kind of correspondence actually obtained, the religious form of life would be true. Religious sentences would therefore be true only insofar as they were used in conformity with the truth of a religious form of life. Even if truth were defined as the conformance of the mind with reality *(adaequatio mentis ad rem),* the same basic relations would hold. The mind would not be conformed to reality apart from the mediation of the form of life. Because truth describes that relationship whereby the form of life corresponds to reality, neither the mind nor the sentence can correspond to reality in some independent or nonmediated way. If the mind and the sentence do correspond to reality, it can only be as they partake of that prior correspondence to reality which is an attribute of the form of life. The truth of the form of life thus mediates any possible correspondence of the mind or the sentence to reality. A mind not shaped by the form of life and a sentence not used in accord with it would lack a necessary condition for the possibility of truth. Namely, it would lack that correspondence to reality which by definition can only be an attribute of a religious form of life which possesses categories adequate to enable such correspondence to occur in practice.[5]

Third, the issues at stake in this proposal can perhaps be elucidated by introducing a distinction between validity claims and reality domains. Four types of validity claim can be distinguished, and each type may be held to represent a different domain of reality. (1) Claims of *intelligibility,* it might be said, relate to the domain of language; they would thus pertain to formal matters of logic, internal consistency, and sense. (2) Claims of *truth* relate to the domain of external reality; they would pertain to matters of cognitive content, predication, and reference. (3) Claims of *rightness* relate to the domain of social reality; they would pertain to performative content, patterns of behavior, and communal norms and values. (4) Claims of *truthfulness* relate to the domain of internal reality; they would pertain to matters of intention, sincerity, and aptness of emotive expression. Intelligibility, truth, rightness, and truthfulness may thus be regarded as distinct validity claims which pertain to the domains of linguistic, external, social, and internal reality respectively.[6]

If these distinctions are adopted, the Lindbeck proposal might be interpreted as follows. In religious matters at least, claims of *rightness* (and perhaps also of truthfulness) are logically prior to claims of *truth* (and perhaps also of intelligibility), because the domain of *social reality* (and perhaps also of internal reality) necessarily mediates all relations of correspondence to the domain of *external reality* (and perhaps also all construals of the formal domain of language). More precisely, *rightness* becomes a necessary condition for the possibility of *truth,* just because what corresponds to ultimate reality is the religious form of life as such, not minds or sentences independent of that form of life or in conflict with it. A kind of social coherentism seems to be the result. The coherence of linguistic usage with behavior in accord with communal norms *(rightness)* in a condition for the possibility of using a sentence to refer accurately to the external domain of ultimate reality *(truth)*. No religious utterance can be true which is not rightly socially embodied, and any religious utterance is false which arises from within the community and yet is so used that it contradicts that rightness by which the community in its form of life corresponds to reality. The sentence *"Christus est Dominus"* as uttered by the crusader when cleaving the skull of the infidel is thus false, because the sentence is being used to authorize behavior which contradicts communal norms and values. Its falseness is its contradiction from within the community of what the community's form of life as a whole affirms about ultimate reality.

The question now to be considered is not the possible adequacy or inadequacy of the Lindbeck proposal, but rather the extent to which it may or may not converge with what Barth says about truth as personally self-involving. In what ways might Barth's personalist conception of the truth in Christian theology be thought to concur with Lindbeck's proposal, and in what ways to conflict with it? Points of convergence are not entirely lacking in Barth's theology. The idea that the truth of the gospel is necessarily self-involving entails for Barth the idea that "the existential determination of the Christian" has a significant impact on the validity of the Christian's witness (IV/3, 655). Anyone who is called to attest the living God has necessarily been touched and apprehended by God's love. The person's "whole being" has been engaged. The love of God must therefore be reflected in that person's life. Without this reflection of divine love in the person's life and testimony, even the purest orthodoxy "becomes an idle pursuit." "Even the trinitarian God of Nicene dogma, or the Christ of the Chalcedonian definition, if seen and proclaimed in exclusive objectivity"—that is, with no regard for the love that must accompany all such seeing and proclaiming—"necessarily becomes an idol like all others, with whom one cannot live and whom one cannot therefore attest. And there is something menacing and dangerous in an orthodoxy of this kind" (IV/3, 655). Here, it would seem, is the idea that the attitude and behavior of the Christian can falsify the most orthodox teachings of the church. Even the venerable dogmas of the Trinity and the Incarnation can be turned into their very opposites—idols that render both life and testimony impossible.

Even stronger, if possible, are certain statements Barth makes about "the act of love" as a necessary accompaniment to "the act of witness." As it takes place between one person and another within the Christian community, the act of witness can be fulfilled "only as we love one another" (IV/2, 812). The act of witness pertains to the love of God as attested in scripture and confirmed in our lives. It thus involves imparting information "which would otherwise be inaccessible" and confirming claims "which have no other means of confirmation." One human being witnesses to another when the truth of the gospel is imparted and confirmed in this personal way. "The truth and reality" of the divine love "stand or fall" with the love of the person who attests it. The more important and indispensable the testimony to God's love, "the more important and indispensable is the existence and activity of the one who gives it, the witness" (IV/2, 812). Here, it would seem, is a convergence with the more grammatical remark that right performance is a condition for the possibility of using a sentence in a way that is cognitively true. The form of the human action—the extent to which it is grounded in love—is said to answer for the truth and reality of God's love, just as the truth and reality of God's love are said to stand or fall with the form of the human action. The backing for these statements is found in the nature of God's love itself. For God's love is real, says Barth, "not as a general truth about God," but only "in God's constant activity." God's love is such as to actualize itself continually in and through loving human action (IV/2, 812). The motifs of actualism and personalism, when taken in combination, would seem to point toward accepting the proposition that proper self-involvement is a necessary condition for uttering true theological statements.

On closer inspection, however, there are also signs of divergence. Even in the examples just cited, the convergence is not complete. On careful examination even they seem to have more to do with rightness and truthfulness than with truth and intelligibility per se. The possibility that an otherwise true theological claim can be seriously abused never seems to imply for Barth as unequivocally as for Lindbeck that in some particular instance the abused claim could be falsified without qualification. The basic reason for this difference is that truth and intelligibility never seem to depend as fully for Barth as for Lindbeck on the rightness and truthfulness with which a theological claim is made. Thus in the same passage where Barth speaks of neutralizing orthodox teachings to the point of falsification, he also speaks of "the objective superiority" of the teachings over their human reception (IV/3, 655). Presumably, this superiority would imply that even in an abusive situation the truth of the claim could not be completely nullified by the abuse. Or again, in the same passage where he speaks of human love as necessary for attesting divine love, Barth also speaks of the truth and reality of God's love as occurring "primarily and intrinsically" on another and different plane (IV/2, 813). Presumably, the difference between these two planes of love implies that the validity of utterances about the divine plane can neither be totally established nor totally undermined by the human plane on which they are uttered. In both passages, it would seem, certain theological circumstances are perceived which mitigate against a more complete convergence with Lindbeck. Barth seems clearly to presuppose that the truth and intelligibility of theological claims are in some sense *logically* independent of the rightness and truthfulness with which they may either be advanced or contradicted on the human plane. This line of interpretation is borne out by what Barth says elsewhere about questions of intelligibility and truth.

Intelligibility is viewed as independent of social and personal conditions, as for example when Barth states that the content of the gospel is "intrinsically clear" in itself (IV/3, 848). The gospel may not be generally knowable, "but it is generally intelligible and explicable." In principle no special assistance is needed to understand what the gospel is claiming, for its content is marked by "inner clarity, rationality and perspicuity" (IV/3, 848). Similarly, the truth of the gospel seems to be viewed as something independent of social and personal conditions, when Barth writes that the content of the gospel is "intrinsically true" (IV/3, 657). "The love of God does not await my response to love to be eternal and omnipotently saving love. Nor is it the case that the truth is conditioned by the fact or manner of its expression in your or my existence" (IV/3, 656). Its being the truth cannot be conceived as resting on anthropological considerations. "It would be the truth even if it had no witnesses." It also remains the truth despite how its witnesses may perform. "It is the truth even though its human witnesses fail. It does not live by Christians, but Christians by it" (IV/3, 656).

On the skull-cleaving crusader's cry that *"Christus est Dominus,"* therefore, Barth would certainly be able to say that it is meaningless. A situation of absurdity is created by the contradiction between the utterance in its normative usage and the deed it is used to authorize. Barth would also be able to say that what the crusader means by *Dominus* is manifestly false. For according to the communally normative definition of scripture, Christ's lordship is exercised as suffering servanthood. Up to this point Barth would be in covergence with Lindbeck. He would agree that in these ways the word is falsified by the deed. Yet he would diverge from Lindbeck on the extent of this falsification and on its grounds. For he would also insist that the deed is falsified by the word. Why, he might ask, should the meaning of what the crusader says (and thus its possible truth) be determined simply by the use to which the crusader puts it? Why should meaning and truth be treated so atomistically? Are there not standard and paradigmatic uses which create a background against which any particular use operates?[7] And why should meaning and truth be treated so anthropocentrically? What exactly establishes the total relevant context? Is it not finally determined by God in such a way that cultural–linguistic considerations (or any other anthropological considerations), however valid they may be on their own plane, cannot be either decisive or exhaustive?

Jesus Christ is viewed by Barth as the truth of the gospel. This truth takes secondary form in the written testimony of the scripture, and tertiary form, so to speak, in the verbal testimony of the church. Neither form of testimony occurs in such a way that the truth of Jesus Christ is simply a semantic feature of those sentences by which this testimony is expressed. Yet the verbal form of this testimony is thought to be so indirectly identical with Jesus Christ that he continually discloses himself through it (I/1, 88–120). Neither this indirect identity in itself (realism), nor the event by which Jesus Christ discloses himself through it (actualism), is thought to depend in any logically tight or predetermined way on the rightness or truthfulness of the witnessing community. Rightness and truthfulness in themselves cannot guarantee that even the community's most orthodox statements about Jesus Christ will be divinely attested. Yet neither can the community's wrongness and bad faith in using such statements simply undermine the verbal form by which they are indirectly identical with Christ (even though they can create serious and humanly insurmountable obstacles for divine attestation). Even in a situation of abuse as illustrated by the skull-cleaving crusader, the total relevant context would be so established by the pattern of divine activity as mediated by scripture and proclaimed by the church that *"Christus est Dominus"* would retain a margin of truth over the abuse to which it was put, standing in real though implicit condemnation over the act of abuse itself (cf. I/1, 110–11, 154).

What is finally decisive for Barth in any consideration of the performative aspect of theological truth is not the human but the divine mode of involvement. Does not God's use of the community's theological utterances, Barth might ask, so overrule its use of them that even its most right, truthful, and orthodox usage does not guarantee that an utterance will actually be divinely attested and thus made to correspond to reality in any given situation, whether for the one who utters it or for the one to whom it may be addressed? Conversely, does not God's normative though indirect self-attestation in the written form of scripture mean that even the community's most flagrant abuse of scriptural assertions cannot in itself serve totally to nullify the objective superiority of the assertion over the abuse? The first question pertains to Barth's actualism; the second, to his realism. The first points to the freedom and sovereignty of God's grace and to the incapacity of either the witness or the addressee to make the utterance (or the mind) correspond to reality apart from the miracle of grace which attests it. In this sense it is the miracle of grace, not use in accordance with a correlative form of life, which is decisive for the correspondence of a theological utterance with reality. What is decisive for the event of correspondence is the divine, not the human, activity.

The second question, in turn, points to the scriptural mediation of God's Word. As God's Word assumes secondary form in the written word of scripture, scripture is made into a normative and verbally stabilized witness to the events of divine self-revelation and therefore to the living God. In this normative and verbally stabilized form, scripture becomes the semantic vehicle by which human utterances are brought into correspondence with the reality of God. Although this vehicle remains inert apart from the miracle of grace, its semantic features were established to play an integral part in the ongoing history of God's self-revelation. The truth of these features needs to be actualized for the addressee in a self-involving way by the miracle of grace in an encounter with the living God, but it is just these features whose truth is actualized. These semantic features, established by God, retain their objective superiority even in situations where they may be falsified as much as is humanly possible by an act of abuse. In this sense it is scripture itself, not the correlative form of life it shapes, which serves as the vehicle of correspondence between theological utterances and the reality of God. What is decisive for establishing the cognitive truth of such utterances are the semantic features of scripture, whose validity rests once again, Barth believes, on divine, not human, action.

What would finally seem to characterize Barth's overall position on the relationship between self-involvement and truth, therefore, is not the dependence of truth on self-involvement, but the dependence of self-involvement on truth. The cognitive truth of a theological assertion does not finally depend on the rightness of the community's (or the individual's) performance in a correlative form of life. Rightness and truthfulness are by no means irrelevant to the valid assertion of the truth, but neither are they the final and overriding conditions for its possibility. They always have an important and powerful role to play, but never so important that they can condition and determine the truth of assertions embedded in the gospel itself. Even in situations where such assertions are badly abused by adherents, their truth retains objective superiority over the abuse.

Vocation as a Matter of Fellowship

Vocation, to resume where we left off, is conceived not only as a matter of encounter, integrity, and mutual self-involvement. It is also and supremely a matter of fellowship. Fellowship, as "the goal of vocation," is the heart of the personalist motif (IV/3, 520–54). As such it is not surprising that the previous three themes of vocation are reiterated with respect to fellowship. That of mutual self-involvement is reiterated in terms of *intimacy,* that of *integrity* is reiterated directly, and that of encounter is reiterated in terms of *asymmetry.*

From the very first, God created humanity for the sake of an encounter that would be "strikingly intimate and personal" (III/1, 247). That an encounter so conceived should be the divine purpose for the creation is rooted in God's very being. For the divine being itself exists only in the act of love, and love in action is the full expression of this being. Who God is in relation to us may thus be described as follows: "God is he who in his revelation seeks and creates fellowship with us" (II/1, 274). Seeking and creating fellowship are definitive of God's reality. As in eternity so also in time God is essentially a God of sociality, the triune deity who loves in freedom. The divine majesty, holiness and ontological otherness of the eternal Trinity, moreover, are regarded as the presupposition, not the barrier, to the relationship of intimacy, the I–Thou encounter, which God seeks to establish with us. For in the freedom of God's triune love, "the antithesis between the Creator and his creatures" is at once fully posited yet also embraced and overcome (II/1, 274). Fellowship is thus the ultimate meaning and purpose of creation, for it is in fellowship that God wills to be our God and wills us to be God's people. "He wills to be ours, and he wills that we should be his. He wills to belong to us and he wills that we should belong to him. He does not will to be without us, and he does not will that we should be without him" (II/1, 274). Fellowship is the highest blessing that can be given. "There is no greater blessing—no greater, because God has nothing higher than this to give, namely himself; because in giving us himself, he has given us every blessing" (II/1, 275).

The fellowship that God wills with us is not "external and casual," but "internal and essential" (IV/2, 757). It involves the most "inward and central and decisive" act of our heart (IV/1, 757), in which "our existence cannot continue to be alien to his but may become and be analogous" (IV/2, 757). In this fellowship God in Jesus Christ "gives and imparts himself" to us, "entering into" us, binding us to Jesus Christ with "intimacy and intensity" (IV/3, 538, 539). By the power of the Holy Spirit, it thereby comes to pass not only that we are "in Christ," but that Christ is also "in us" (IV/3, 555). Christ makes those into whom he enters companions in fellowship. "This is what he makes them as he calls them to himself, as he does this really and totally, as he does not leave them to themselves, as he does not remain outside them, as he gives himself to them, as in the divine power of his Spirit he unites himself with them" (IV/3, 542). Christ enters into their lives, setting his power and truth in them, that they should exist for him just as he exists for them. "That they may become and be those with whom he unites himself by his Word; that they may be those who are born again from above by his presence and action in their own lives; that they may be continually nourished by him—this is, from their standpoint, the *ratio* of Christian existence" (IV/3, 542).

Intimacy is a theme that is impressively developed in terms of "the mutual union of Christ and the Christian" (IV/3, 651). This union is described as true, total, and indissoluble: "true and not ideal; total and not merely psychical and intellectual; indissoluble and not just transitory" (IV/3, 540). Union with Christ in "perfect fellowship" is the definition of Christian existence. This fellowship so conceived "takes place and consists in a self-giving which . . . is total on both sides. In this self-giving Christ and the Christian become and are a single totality, a fluid and differentiated but genuine and solid unity" (IV/3, 540). Christ lives so fully in the Christian, and the Christian so fully in Christ, that both may be said to exist "eccentrically"—centered, that is, on one another respectively (IV/3, 548). The Christian places herself or himself at Christ's disposal just as Christ has placed himself at the disposal of the Christian. The Christian comes to live from "the center of [Christ's] intention and action," and Christ takes up his abode in the Christian's "innermost being or heart" (IV/3, 594). "The self-giving of Christ to the Christian and the Christian to Christ" is thus described as at once "the goal of vocation" and yet also "the true being of the Christian" (IV/3, 594).

This theme of fellowship as a union of mutual coinherence is ulti-mately signified by "the unprecedented fact of a kinship of being" (IV/ 1, 599). The idea that in Jesus Christ human beings are brought into an "ontological kinship" with God is an idea that comes within a hair of the traditional Eastern Orthodox understanding of salvation as "divini-zation" *(theosis)*. Human beings are finally drawn beyond being merely God's "covenant-partners" to the point of being God's "children," where to be a child is understood as the event of "an ontological relationship" by which salvation is "crowned" and "anchored" (IV/1, 599). The idea of "divinization," which in itself might well imply a kind of ultimate monism, is avoided, however, by grounding this kinship of being in an ongoing distinctiveness of particulars maintained by the mystery of grace. Our ontological kinship with God, Barth states explicitly, is not to be conceived as our divinity (IV/1, 600). This kinship is only ascribed, im-parted, and given to us, and we are only adopted and received by God as God's children. We are "only instituted as such." Yet God is so intimately bound to us by grace, and we to God, that we finally have not only the gift but "the right to a being with him, the right to immediate access to him, the right to call upon him, the right to rely upon him, the right to expect and ask of him everything" that we need (IV/1, 600). Interestingly, in this right of our divine kinship is seen "the essence of every human right" (IV/1, 600 rev.). In any case, fellowship as union, mutual self-giving, and finally ontological kinship are all indications of intimacy as it is seen to have been established in the event of Christian vocation (cf. IV/3, 651).

Integrity signifies the unimpaired wholeness and distinctiveness of each partner in the relationship. In light of the great lengths to which Barth is prepared to go in his depiction of fellowship as intimacy, it becomes all the more important to reaffirm this theme. Intimacy, as we have seen, is represented as a matter of mutual self-giving and coinherence to the point of ontological kinship. Although Barth has never quite been able to shake off the reputation acquired from his earlier writings that he leaves us with a God who is so radically transcendent that no real relationship with humanity is finally possible, his depiction of fellowship as intimacy ac-tually raises the opposite sort of question. Coinherence and ontological kinship are conceptions that might well cast doubt on whether Christ and the Christian are not finally seen to be so thoroughly and mutually intermingled as to lose their respective identities. It is thus important to note that in the midst of describing the intimacy of their fellowship, Barth also takes pains to reaffirm the unimpaired wholeness and distinctiveness of each.

"In the language of the New Testament," writes Barth, *"koinonia* or *communicatio* is a relationship between two persons in which these are brought into perfect mutual coordination within the framework of a definite order, yet with no destruction of their two-sided identity and particularity, but rather in its confirmation and expression" (IV/3, 535). Fellowship does not destroy but confirms and expresses the identity and particularity of the two persons. In the special relationship with Christ established in one's life by vocation, writes Barth, this fellowship occurs "in unique perfection" (IV/3, 535). However, despite the "uniquely close and direct" self-giving which takes place "in the perfection of the mutual address of the two partners," the intimacy of the encounter does not lead (and should not be thought to lead) either to an identification of Christ with the Christian or to an identification of the Christian with Christ. "It belongs to the perfection of this fellowship," writes Barth, ". . . that in it Christ does not merge into the Christian nor the Christian into Christ. There is no disappearance of the one in favor of the other" (IV/3, 539). On the contrary, both partners are validated and sustained in their distinctiveness. "In their fellowship both become and are genuinely what they are, not confounding or exchanging their functions and roles nor losing their totally dissimilar persons" (IV/3, 539). In short, in the fellowship between Christ and the Christian, intimacy and integrity, so far from canceling each other out, are so related that intimacy presupposes integrity, and integrity expresses itself in intimacy.

Asymmetry, the final point to be considered regarding fellowship, is meant to indicate that each partner in the encounter has a different conceptual status. In the course of depicting integrity, Barth was seen to speak in passing of "the framework of a definite order" and of "totally dissimilar persons"—remarks in which the question of asymmetry has already been anticipated. The problem that now arises is at once the direct opposite yet also the reassertion of that which emerged regarding intimacy. Intimacy between Christ and the Christian was at times so strongly depicted as to raise doubts that their respective identities could be maintained in the midst of their mutual coinherence. Ontological kinship, in particular, suggested that the human identity of the Christian could not consistently be maintained because of what appeared to be its virtual absorption into the being of Jesus Christ.

Asymmetry, on the other hand, with its emphasis on Christ's complete priority to and independence of the Christian and the Christian's complete subsequence to and dependence on Christ, now threatens Barth's conception of fellowship, it would seem, from the opposite direction. Perhaps Barth's reputation as a theologian of unmitigated transcendence deserved to persist after all. For how can there conceivably be a fellowship of mutual self-giving between two partners (Christ and the Christian) who are said to be "totally dissimilar"? Moreover, when the question of agency is taken into account, the problem is compounded. For once again, as noted earlier when the theme of encounter was being considered, Christ as the acting Subject typically appears to be presented in such domineering terms that no conceivable place would seem to remain in the relationship for genuine human agency. Human agency would seem to be so subordinated to the superior divine–human agency of Christ that the former in effect becomes null and void. Asymmetry, therefore, would seem to be a theme which generates an unenviable dilemma. It seems to generate at one and the same time two diametrically opposite problems. For it seems to posit not only an irreconcilable dualism ("totally dissimilar persons"), but also an inescapable monism (the dissolution of the Christian's human agency into the divine–human agency of Jesus Christ).

Just as the discussion of integrity led to the assertion that there could be no identity between the Christian and Christ, so the discussion of asymmetry leads to the assertion that there can be no parity between them (IV/3, 729). The structure of the fellowship between Christ and the Christian is said to occur in a "definite and irreversible order" (IV/3, 598). The order is one of "super- and sub-ordination" (IV/3, 537). "Christ is always superior and the Christian subordinate" (IV/3, 598). The different conceptual status of Christ from the Christian is not to be overlooked. "Vocation does not imply the obliteration of the distinction between the Lord and his servant or their respective functions" (IV/3, 651). An "irreversible order" and an "indissoluble differentiation" thus always mark the relationship (IV/3, 594). "We have in view the divine–human action in divine–human sovereignty when we speak of the being and life of Christ, and human action in human freedom when we speak of the being and life of the Christian" (IV/3, 598). The problem, of course, is how Christ's sovereignty and the Christian's freedom can be coherently maintained at one and the same time, given everything else Barth says about both the otherness and the omnipotence of Christ.

The problem can be delineated either "from above" or "from below." From above the problem appears as the domineering sovereignty of Jesus

Christ. Fellowship, we are told, does not mean "the surrender but the exercise" of Christ's "supreme sovereignty" over the Christian (IV/3, 594). The supremacy of this sovereignty is, as already suggested, marked by both otherness and omnipotence. Of Christ's otherness or total dissimilarity from the Christian, Barth writes: "There can be no question of any neutralizing of the distinction between Creator and creature or of the antithesis between the Holy One and sinners, nor of any establishment of the kind of equilibrium which may exist between things but can never obtain between persons, and especially between the divine Jesus Christ and the human person" (IV/3, 539). The divine Jesus Christ is conceived as ontologically other than the finite and sinful human being. No equilibrium or parity is therefore possible in the relationship between the two.

Of Christ's sovereignty over the Christian, a similarly forceful line is taken. This sovereignty is "unrestricted" (IV/3, 547). It means that Christ's responsibility for the relationship is "sole and total" (IV/3, 537). It means that Christ claims "the right of lordship" over Christians, a right Barth does not hesitate to develop in terms of "the right of the owner to his property" (IV/3, 536). Christ is so related to Christians that "he is their owner and they his possession" (IV/3, 537). Christ's majesty in relation to the Christian is an "alien majesty," his divine power is fully "effective," his "control" over his possession (the Christian) is unchallenged and complete (IV/3, 538). Jesus Christ is therefore the Subject who not only "initiates" his union with the Christian, but who also "acts decisively" within it (IV/3, 541).

Of course, a great deal of abstracting from the context has to occur in order to extract this sort of material and to present it in isolation. Taken in context, Christ's "unrestricted sovereignty" is immediately connected with validating and honoring the Christian's freedom (IV/3, 547). Christ's "sole and total responsibility" is immediately connected with "guidance and care" for the Christian (IV/3, 537). The "right of lordship" as a kind of property right is immediately connected with "free and liberating power" in contrast to "any power of compulsion" (IV/3, 536). Christ's "alien majesty" is immediately connected with total self-giving, his "effective power" with the initiating of fellowship, his sovereign "control" with the Christian's "spontaneous being" (IV/3, 538). The problem that arises from these juxtapositions and connections is not one of the author's intentions, but rather of the argument's internal coherence. How can these apparently contrary terms be coherently paired together? The answer, if there is one, is by no means self-evident from the immediate context.

The view "from below" can be seen to involve a similar set of problems. If Christ is the "decisive Subject" and the "sovereign owner" who has property rights over the apparently hapless Christian, then it follows that the Christian must be regarded as "a pure recipient" in relation to this decisive Subject and as one who has "no right or claim" in relation to the sovereign owner (IV/3, 668). Although it is held to be true that in fellowship with Christ the Christian "acts as well as receives," it is also held to be true that neither the acting nor the receiving originates from the person of the Christian, "but both can be understood only as the creation of the call of Christ" (IV/3, 539). How can the Christian be said to act, if this acting is actually created by Christ, in contrast to arising from the Christian's own acting person? A similar problem emerges when we are told that the Christian's spontaneity is "both caused and liberated" (IV/3, 520). How can this be said coherently? More comprehensively, how can the structured fellowship between Christ and the Christian coherently be advanced as "ordered yet free," when the proposed concept of order, attended as it is by such strong domineering conceptions, seems to stand in direct conflict with the proposed concept of freedom (IV/3, 537)? Problems such as these not only seem to plague Barth's discussion of fellowship, but are arguably characteristic of how the relation between divine and human agency is treated throughout the *Church Dogmatics*. At all points, divine and human freedom would seem to be condemned to unresolved conflict despite the author's best intentions.

Mixed results would therefore seem to attend our consideration of the theme of fellowship. On the one hand, intimacy and integrity would seem to represent what Barth primarily wants to affirm. Fellowship is presented as a matter of intimate personal union between Christ and the Christian. The two enter into a history of such perfect self-giving that each lives solely centered on the other in a relationship of mutual coinherence. At the same time the unimpaired integrity of the two partners in fellowship is fully affirmed. Neither is to be identified with or disappear into the other, but each is understood to come to a full expression of itself in intimacy. Integrity is the precondition of intimacy, and intimacy the fulfillment of integrity. On the other hand, asymmetry as a further determination and clarification of integrity is a conception by which intimacy and integrity would both seem to be jeopardized. Intimacy is apparently jeopardized by the otherness, and integrity by the omnipotence, of Christ. Christ's otherness seems to be incompatible with the reciprocity ascribed to the fellowship, and his omnipotence seems to be incompatible with the freedom and spontaneity ascribed to the human subject. Otherness as "total dissimilarity'' seems logically to require a disrelation, and omnipotence as "unrestricted sovereignty" seems logically to require manipulation. Dualism and monism thus seem to plague Barth's conception of fellowship, despite his best intentions, at one and the same time.

Although regularly overlooked by critics and defenders alike, Barth has a distinctive rejoinder to the problem of apparent incoherence as just outlined. Regardless of whether the rejoinder is finally judged to be satisfactory or not, it at least deserves to be taken into account. Before we do so, however, another matter requires a brief discussion. It has to do with the relationship by which Barth sees fellowship connected to the themes of witness and eternal life. This relationship is of significance for the light it casts on vocation as the existential moment of salvation.

Vocation as a Matter of Witness
and Its Relation to Eternal Life

Noetic terms have been seen to dominate Barth's presentation of the existential moment of salvation. Vocation is explained primarily by categories like revelation, knowledge, and illumination. The Word of the cross comes from without and reveals itself from within. Knowledge determines the context in which we are engaged to the full. It sets the stage on which all our personal capacities are exercised, not just the cognitive but the affective, volitional, conative, and intuitive as well. Illumination awakens us to the vocation which finds its goal in personal fellowship. Terms like encounter, conversion, and fellowship—which might be thought to have a certain predominant or unambiguous experiential content in the affective or volitional sense—are all interpreted within this cognitive context, and are thus given a decidedly noetic cast. They are all known by faith despite their hiddenness and ambiguity in the present. If the relation of the objective to the existential moment of salvation can be summed up as a manifesting of the truth, the relation of the existential to the objective moment would seem in turn to be primarily a matter of acknowledging the truth. The reality and truth of Jesus Christ as divinely manifest and humanly acknowledged seems to be the controlling idea in Barth's doctrine of salvation. At the same time it must be remembered, however, that the truth which is being manifested and acknowledged is precisely the truth of one's personal participation in the salvation wrought by Christ. The truth being acknowledged (by faith and not by sight) is thus the truth of being called to encounter with Christ, and thus to mutual self-involvement and fellowship with him here and now. In this sense, acknowledgment and participation go hand in hand.

It is important to underscore, therefore, that the noetic dimension, while predominant, is not exclusionary. It does not eliminate the more experiential aspects of salvation. It merely situates them in the perspective of a larger context. Barth's move at this point is both deliberate and carefully considered. Everything, as he understands it, depends on this move. For it is by granting primacy to the noetic that the present ambiguity of our experience is rightly assessed, and also and even more, that the exclusive uniqueness of Jesus Christ is rightly conceived. Jesus Christ is exclusively unique, Barth believes, not only as the sole agent of salvation, but also as its decisive locus. Our salvation as human beings occurs by virtue of our inclusion in him, and our inclusion in him is his work, not ours, having taken place once and for all in the event of the cross. It therefore follows, Barth argues, that our salvation must be so conceived that it does not in any sense *consist* of its experiential aspects, even though it will not be lacking in such aspects (II/1, 158). The experiential aspects are not constitutive but reflective of salvation, just because the central moment is, objectively, the cross of Christ, and, existentially, our awakening to the significance of his cross. The noetic moment is thus existentially central, just because the cross of Christ is objectively central. The experiential aspects of salvation must therefore be placed in a noetic context which, though it does not ignore them, does emphatically relativize them.

Witness and eternal life as facets of the theme of fellowship can help to shed light on how the noetic and experiential aspects of salvation are seen to be existentially related. Witness is seen as the penultimate, and eternal life as the ultimate, form of fellowship. Witness is seen as a matter of declaring, and eternal life as one of enjoying, the salvation accomplished in and by Jesus Christ. Witness consists of fellowship with Jesus Christ in his prophetic work; eternal life, of fellowship with him in his royal work. Witness participates with Christ in his resurrection; eternal life participates with Christ in his glory. Witness shares in the prophetic task of the risen Christ to declare the salvation accomplished in and by the cross; eternal life shares in the royal splendor of the glorified Christ as the crown of that salvation so accomplished. Witness occurs in the penultimate setting where the noetic moment necessarily takes precedence; eternal life occurs in the ultimate setting where the experiential moment of salvation, in and with the noetic, is fully realized. In short, the priestly work of Jesus Christ on the cross is accomplished by him alone; the prophetic work of the risen Christ is shared with the Christian in a fellowship of witness; and the royal work of the glorified Christ is shared with the Christian in a fellowship of eternal life. The priestly work of Christ is finished and complete in such a way that it needs acknowledgment but not repetition. The prophetic is so related to the priestly work of Christ that, in this life, the noetic necessarily takes primacy over the experiential aspect of salvation. The royal is so related to the priestly work of Christ that, in the life to come, the experiential is fully and finally realized in and with the noetic aspect of salvation. The primacy of the noetic in this life is thus related to the eschatological situation of declaration; the removal of this primacy in the life to come, to the final revelation of all things as glorified in and by Jesus Christ.

Eternal life is by no means regarded as absent from the present, but it is present primarily in the mode of promise—of faith and not sight. Where, asks Barth, do we find the "new situation" of eternal life unambiguously in our present experience? "Where and when do we find it as an assured state in our present? If we ever could or can find it, then it is surely only as the promise which is given us by God and which we had and have to recognize and take as such" (IV/1, 587). As an assured state, eternal life is present, but only as the presence of the future. Eternal life is present "only as the future to which we could go forward and have in fact gone forward with more or less certain steps, only to be instructed again and again that it would be newly disclosed to us as our future, that it will be disclosed to us as such even in our present" (IV/1, 587). As "enclosed in the promise of God," eternal life is something that "can only be hoped and awaited and prayed for," but this mode of its presence "does not in any way limit it or lessen its power" (IV/1, 587). As the future in which our sins are forgiven (justification), our lives made holy (sanctification), and our faith replaced by sight (glorification), eternal life is present and takes place even now. We "can and should receive it and have it in the same present" in which we know that we are "always utterly in need of it." In and with the promise, its "whole content" enters existentially into our present (IV/1, 587). Where the promise is trusted, accepted as true, and applied to oneself even now, there eternal life already takes place, there one receives a "new freedom" and "the only true capacity," there one can and should dare to live as someone destined for fellowship in eternal life with God (IV/1, 599 rev.).

To make the *beneficia Christi* as received here and now the center of the Christian life, however, would be, Barth argues, to succumb to an eschatological miscalculation. The essence of the Christian life does not consist in the reception of benefits, but rather in the reception of a task. Just as here and now the noetic takes precedence over the experiential aspect of salvation, so also does the reception of the task take precedence over the reception of benefits. The precedence of the task over the benefits, and the subordination of the benefits to the task, is precisely the force of urging vocation as the controlling principle of the Christian life. Vocation means that Christians are called primarily to the task of witness (IV/3, 554–614).

Witness is thus the true context of fellowship with Christ in this life. It is the context into which the Christian has been called in order to accompany Christ in the prophetic task of declaring the salvation of the cross. The special vocation of the Christian is to share in the living self-witness of the Crucified. This sharing results in a fellowship of action and a fellowship of suffering. The act of witness will lead to suffering, and the suffering will function as an act of witness to the cross (IV/3, 598, 608, 637–42). It is especially in this context that intimacy becomes the expression of integrity and that integrity is sustained by intimacy. It is especially in this context that the Christian becomes the free slave of Christ and that Christ exercises liberating sovereignty over the Christian. And it is especially in this context that mutual coinherence and mutual self-giving occur. The task, not the benefits, becomes the center of the Christian life. Anything else would mean a distorted schedule of priorities (IV/3, 563–68, 593–97). The "true being of the Christian"—and therefore of the existential moment of salvation—is found essentially in the vocation of witness, that is, in bearing witness in the world to God's love for the world as shown forth in the event of the cross (IV/3, 599). In any case, the centrality of the cross—as noetically apprehended, experientially reflected, and vocationally proclaimed—is what explains the penultimate relativization of the more positive experiential and beneficial aspects of salvation in Barth's soteriology (cf. IV/3, 408–21).[8]

To sum up: truth in Barth's theology is ultimately a matter of an encounter with the living Christ, who bears witness to himself through the Word of the cross. The distance between Christ's cross and the present dissolves for the person so encountered and personally addressed. The person is affirmed as God's creature. At the same time the person recognizes his or her condemnation as a sinner, but only as one put to death forever with Christ on the cross. The person also discovers that his or her true reality is not to be found directly in what the self knows of itself by experience. One's true reality, regardless of everything that might seem to speak against it, is discovered to reside in who and what one has been made to be, apart from oneself in Jesus Christ. This recognition becomes the center of one's life, as one is drawn into fellowship with Christ. In response to his act of self-giving, the Christian learns to enact self-giving in return.

For the time being, this fellowship occurs not so much as an end in itself as in the context of a particular vocation. The vocation to which the Christian is called (along with the whole community of faith) is a vocation of witness to Jesus Christ as disclosed by the Word of the cross. The *beneficia Christi* are to be received essentially in this context. The Christian receives the high calling of sharing with Christ in his prophetic work. It is therefore a sharing in the work by which the significance of his priestly work is made known as something completed and unrepeatable in itself. At the same time it declares, awaits, and reflects the future of his royal fulfillment as the one true Mediator in the glory of eternal life to come. For now, however, the noetic and vocational take precedence over the experiential and glorious aspects of salvation. The status of the existential moment of salvation is therefore primarily if not exclusively noetic, for it looks to Christ by faith in memory and hope as the One in whom the salvation of the world is accomplished. The task of the Christian is to bear witness with Christ to this salvation by word and by deed. The destiny awaited by the Christian in hope is the full and final manifestation of the universality of this salvation in and through the particular One in whom and by whom alone it has been brought to pass. The Christian is engaged with the truth of this soteriological status, task, and destiny in a way that is wholly self-involving. For this truth is finally none other than the living Christ himself, who was and is and is to be wholly self-involved with each one for the sake of all.

CHAPTER 7

Double Agency
as a Test Case

The deferred question may now be taken up of Barth's possible rejoinder to the charge of incoherence in his presentation of divine sovereignty and human freedom. What could Barth possibly say that might rescue his conceptuality from logical collapse? How can he avoid the consequences of disrelation, and therefore finally of dualism, that seem to be so obviously entailed by his conception of the divine otherness? Moreover, how can he avoid the consequences of determinism, and therefore finally of monism, that seem to be so obviously entailed by his conception of the divine omnipotence? Don't the conceptions of otherness and omnipotence entailed by his notion of asymmetry render impossible the intimacy and integrity he posits in his account of fellowship as the goal of vocation? Conversely, don't the notions of intimacy and integrity require him to abandon his notion of asymmetry, if the viability of fellowship as he conceives it is to be sustained? Three points above all are to be developed in reply to such questions.

Divine and Human Agency: The Chalcedonian Pattern

First, Barth's account of fellowship in particular and of divine and human agency in general cannot possibly be understood unless it is seen that his conception falls within the terms of the Chalcedonian pattern. From the very beginning of the *Church Dogmatics,* where the question is first given a detailed consideration under the heading "The Word of God and Experience" (I/1, 198–227), to the very end, where it receives detailed exposition in the material we have been considering on fellowship as the

185

goal of vocation (IV/3, 520–614), and repeatedly in between, the Chalcedonian pattern governs the discussion at every point virtually without exception.

At times "the great pattern" of the Incarnation is invoked so explicitly that Barth's deliberate use of its terms cannot be missed (III/3, 247). At other times the use of the pattern is wholly implicit, but still discernible if one knows to watch for it. At still other times the terms of the pattern are employed without explicit attention being drawn to their Chalcedonian provenance. An instance of the terms being used without mention of their provenance would be the following:

> It is God who absolutely precedes and humanity which can only follow. Even as sovereign acts and words of God, as his free acts of rule, judgment, salvation and revelation, these events are also human actions and passions, works and experiences, and *vice versa*. If in their Old Testament presentation and attestation [on which Barth is commenting] now one side and now the other is given prominence, there is a general acceptance of their coexistence and coinherence, of their basic unity, though without any confusion or mixture of the two elements, or transformation of the one into the other. And if this history in its totality and interconnection speaks as prophetic history it does so in attestation of this living divine–human unity. Its word is prophecy which combines rather than divides, which unites rather than separates, because it comes from the center and proclaims the center where what is above and what is below, transcendent God and lowly humanity, are together. (IV/3, 63 rev.)

This passage is a nearly classical expression of Barth's approach to the problem of divine and human agency. The three formal aspects of the Chalcedonian pattern—asymmetry, intimacy, and integrity (i.e., the very themes which emerged in the discussion of "fellowship as the goal of vocation")—are all present here along with certain important material features as well. Asymmetry is in evidence when Barth speaks of God as absolutely preceding and of humanity as only following, of God as ruling and of humanity as ruled, of what is above and of what is below, of God as transcendent and humanity as lowly. Intimacy is in evidence when we hear of divine actions coinciding with human actions (and vice versa), of their coexistence and coinherence, of their basic unity, of their historical interconnection, of their combination and unity rather than their separation and division ("without separation or division" being a direct Chalcedonian allusion), of their togetherness in the word of prophecy, and most interestingly, of their "living divine–human unity." Integrity, finally, is in evidence when we hear of the two coexisting and coinhering without any confusion or mixture (another direct allusion) and without the transformation of the one into the other (also a standard Chalcedonian remark). Of material interest is the point that the divine–human unity is said to be a "living" unity, that this unity comes "from the center," and that all these ideas are developed as an exposition of scripture (matters to which we shall return). For now, however, the basic point is simply that there is virtually no discussion of divine and human agency in the *Church Dogmatics* which does not conform to this scheme.

A more explicit set of Chalcedonian allusions occurs, interestingly enough, throughout the discussion of fellowship as the goal of vocation. At precisely the point where Barth was seen to insist not only that an "antithesis" exists between Christ and the Christian, but also that the acting and receiving of the Christian are the "creation" and "product" of Christ, the Chalcedonian analogy is invoked: "Even as a child of God, and therefore in the analogy of the Christian's existence to that of the eternal Son in the flesh, the Christian is not what the latter is, and alone can be" (IV/3, 539 rev.). Despite this asymmetrical relation, the very same analogy is also invoked to stress the intimacy of Christ with the Christian. The discussion turns on refreshment as offered to Christians through the self-giving of Christ. "But as he calls them to himself in the divine power of his Spirit, he refreshes them by offering and giving himself to them and making them his own." Then comes the crucial analogy: "That he wills and does this is—in analogy to the mystery and miracle of Christmas—the true *ratio* of Christian existence as this is celebrated, adored and proclaimed within the community of Christians in the common administration of the Lord's Supper, instituted to represent the perfect fellowship between him and them which he has established—an implication which we cannot do more than indicate in the present context" (IV/3, 542). The Lord's Supper, a topic implicitly being deferred here to an unwritten section of the fourth volume of the *Dogmatics,* was obviously going to be developed as a fellowship of intimacy as understood along Chalcedonian lines.

The most important invocation of the pattern, however, is one that appears at the very outset of the discussion and that is therefore meant to bracket everything else Barth goes on to say about fellowship as the goal of vocation. As in the passage just cited, the salient terms in what follows—on which a great will be seen to turn—are those of "miracle" and "mystery."

The mystery of vocation, of the fact that there takes place this calling of human beings within human time and history, is very great. In its own manner and place it is no less than the Christmas mystery of the birth of the eternal Word of God in the flesh in which it has its primary basis. And the miracle which denotes this mystery, i.e., the miracle of calling, of its possibility, of the way which God takes with human beings when he causes their calling to take place, is also great. In its own manner and place it is no less than the Christmas miracle of the birth of Jesus Christ of the Virgin Mary in which it has its pattern. Those to whom Jesus Christ in calling them gives the freedom *(exousia)* to become the children of God, so that his call does not return empty but reaches its goal, are not those who are born of blood, nor of the will of the flesh, nor of the will of any human being, but of God (John 1:12–13). When we put our question, we do not violate either the mystery or the miracle of vocation. Good care is taken that we shall always be astonished afresh as we contemplate it. Yet this does not alter the fact that God knows what he wills in the vocation of the human person, and that this cannot be hidden for a moment from the person who is called. We are concerned with a lofty event, yet not with one that is without meaning or purpose, but one which is controlled by an intrinsically clear *ratio,* like the primary event of Christmas. (IV/3, 520 rev.)

From this statement, whose significance for understanding "fellowship as the goal of vocation" can scarcely be overestimated, the following preliminary points may be gleaned. There is, Barth presumes, a primary mystery and a primary miracle. It is the mystery of the Incarnation and the miracle of the Virgin Birth, the miracle and mystery of Christmas. The mystery is said to be denoted by the miracle. The miracle is said to signify both the possibility and the manner of God's dealings with humanity in Jesus Christ. There is also a secondary mystery and a secondary miracle. Although secondary, it is said to be very great. It is the miracle and mystery of calling. The secondary is said to find both its basis and its pattern in the primary miracle and mystery. Calling is thus in its own way thought to be as miraculous and mysterious as the Incarnation in which it is based and to which it is essentially analogous. Calling is never thought to be anything other than a matter of freedom. It is always, however, a matter for fresh astonishment. Care must be taken that its mystery and miracle are not violated in the course of conceptual description. Although the event of calling is lofty, it is not without an intrinsically clear meaning and purpose, as will certainly be evident to the person who is actually called. In its clarity of purpose vocation is again analogous to the event of Christmas which supplies its basis and pattern.

Divine and Human Agency: The Miracle
and the Mystery as Absolute

These considerations lead directly into the second point concerning Barth's rejoinder to the charge of incoherence. Although regularly overlooked by Barth's critics and defenders alike, his conception of divine and human agency cannot be understood unless the following is seen and appreciated. Barth's conception is not to be interpreted as *also* miraculous and mysterious, but as *essentially* and *wholly* miraculous and mysterious. Miracle and mystery are central, not peripheral, to his understanding of the phenomenon. They are as central to his understanding of "double agency" (the coincidence and distinction of divine and human agency in a single event) as they are to his understanding of the Incarnation. They are so central as to be definitive. Like the Incarnation which grounds and patterns it, the event of double agency, as Barth understands it, presents not a quandary to be solved, but a miracle to be respected and a mystery to be revered. The theologian's job, accordingly, is not to explain away the miracle or to resolve the mystery, but rather to describe an event that ultimately defies description. Description of the indescribable, not reductive explanation or conceptual resolution, is regarded as the essence of the theological task.

"Miracle" is a category at the heart of the actualistic motif. It describes the basic pattern of grace as Barth conceives it. Insofar as the I–Thou encounter with God, the event of fellowship, is predicated on the miracle of grace, the motif of personalism may be regarded as structured by that of actualism. Since the pattern of grace is the same, however, across a wide range of topics Barth discusses, material will be cited from several different contexts in order to elucidate the background by which the actualization of miracle is thought to be central in the event of double agency.

"In the Bible," writes Barth, "miracle is not some event that is hard to conceive, nor yet one that is simply inconceivable, but one that is highly conceivable, but conceivable only as the exponent of the special new direct act of God in time and in history" (I/2, 63). God's free crossing of the ontological divide in the event of self-revelation is always essentially a miraculous event. "In the form in which it acquires temporal historical actuality, biblically attested revelation is always a miracle, and therefore the witness to it, whether direct or indirect in its course, is a narrative of miracles that happened" (I/2, 63–64). Miracle is thus conceivable as a reality "grounded only in itself" (I/2, 244), which is the same as saying that it is conceivable only as "a possibility grounded in the being of God" (IV/1, 194). It is the sort of event that is made possible only as it is done (IV/1, 223). If and when it takes place, "what does it matter what may be said against the possibility of it" (IV/1, 222)?

Nonetheless, as a self-grounded event, "it is not the kind of event which . . . can be made clear or intelligible as such" (IV/1, 301). As a predicate of the event of revelation, miracle occurs with "a sacred incomprehensibility" (IV/2, 146). "By its sacred incomprehensibility we mean its necessary and essential and distinctive newness and difference and strangeness as the event of revelation" (IV/2, 146). It is an event that necessarily stands in no analogy to other kinds of events and is therefore inexplicable in terms of them. "Its occurrence involves an element which has no parallel to other events, which cannot be explained as an object of human acceptance, or repeated as an object of human thought, in the face of which human acceptance and thought and therefore knowledge can consist only in the assertion of its factuality" (IV/2, 147). The content of revelation is so strange that it demands a miraculous form. "How could this revelation take place in the world except in this most alien of forms? How could there be any knowledge of it without an acknowledgement of this alien character" (IV/2, 147)? Indeed, the knowledge of revelation is itself an extension of the miracle, so that perception of the event in its significance is no less miraculous than the event itself. "The actuality of this new being and occurrence, grounded in the divine act of majesty, creates the possibility of a special perception to meet it, a perception which is controlled and mastered by it, attaching itself to it, following and accompanying it, imitating and repeating it" (IV/2, 120).

Miracle, however, is of no interest in its own right. It is significant only as the attribute of revelation. Revelation is by no means to be deduced from miracle, and miracle can certainly be acknowledged without grasping the content of revelation. "But as miracle as such does not imply God's revelation, the acknowledgement of miracle does not imply acknowledgement and therefore the recognition of the event of revelation in its majesty—the knowledge of the Lord" (IV/2, 148). It is a characteristic of the New Testament Easter narratives, for example, "that it is not the miraculous character of the event as such which interests them and to which they draw attention. . . . Always, however, it is the Lord himself who is in the center of the picture, and not the miracle of his appearing (although this is emphasized too)" (IV/2, 148). Any viewpoint in which the miracle became central at the expense of Christ would be woefully "abstract" instead of "concrete" (IV/2, 239). "It is to him and not to the miracle that the believer gives attention and interest. . . . In all the majestic incomprehensibility of the miracle he himself is the true and decisive factor which makes it incomprehensible. . . . What is learned from the miracle is who and what he is—the Lord" (IV/2, 239).

The fact that miracles "break into the regular course of events" is actually "the least important and not the decisive element in the essence of biblical miracles" (III/3, 540). They are beyond and contrary to the ordinary course of nature "only because they are signs of the divine reality, and therefore, of course, of our own future reality." They represent "something fundamentally new in the realm of creation"—the self-revelation of God. They do not mean that God "sets aside and destroys his own order," but that "the richness and comprehensiveness of the divine ordering of things" is beyond our human imagining (III/3, 540–41). They indicate that the way of God "cannot be calculated or foreseen," that there "will constantly be surprises even for the wise," that God is "always doing something new and disclosing something new," that God is "the God of miracles" (III/3, 161). Above all, they disclose that it is God "who is the law of all occurrence" (III/3, 129).

At this point it needs to be remembered from the discussion of the realist motif that "the Gospels are testimonies not sources" (I/2, 64):

> The fact that the statement "God reveals himself" is the confession of a miracle that has happened certainly does not imply a blind credence in all the miracle stories related in the Bible. If we confess the miracle, we may very well, at least partially and by degrees, accept additional light from the miracles as necessary signs of the miracle. But even if we confess the miracle, why should we not constantly find this or that one of the miracles obscure, why should we not constantly be taken aback by them? It is really not laid upon us to take everything in the Bible as true *in globo,* but it is laid upon us to listen to its testimony when we actually hear it. A person might even credit all miracles and for that reason not confess *the* miracle. What it means is to confess revelation as a miracle that has happened; in other words, it means that . . . "God reveals himself." (III/3, 65 rev.)[1]

God is not identical with any cosmic process, and therefore God is "not identical with the laws known to us" (III/3, 161). God is identical only with God's sovereign freedom, "with the free disposing and directing of his own good-pleasure." God does not overthrow the order of creation when miraculously engaging in self-revelation. "Naturally there can be no question of his contravening or overturning any real ontic law of creaturely occurrence. This would mean that he was not at unity with himself in his will and work." We must allow, however, that our perception of these laws is creaturely and finite. "We must allow that he can ruthlessly ignore the laws known to us, that is, our own perception of the ontic laws of creaturely occurrence. . . . He is not bound by our human concepts of order, however great may be the noetic clarity and certainty we believe them to possess" (III/3, 161). Everything depends on theology's offering a conceptual redescription of the biblical narratives that remains faithful to the witness that is found there:

> The more definitely the coming of the Son of God is announced in the Old Testament, and the more directly his revelation is attested in the New, the more natural it appears to unprejudiced reason that mention has to be made of events which can be understood only as an activity *supra et contra naturam*, as an ordering and forming which is beyond the stage of development so far reached by our concepts. And the final revelation of the Son of God at the end of all times will be an event of the same kind. The creation of heaven and earth at the beginning of all times was an event of this kind. We must be quite clear in our minds that what is revealed in these events is not a *miraculous* exception but the *rule* of divine activity, the free goodwill of God himself, i.e., the law at which we are aiming with our concept of law. And we must also be quite clear in our minds that with all our concepts of law we can never do more than aim at this law. (III/3, 129–30)

With this material as background, the place assigned to miracle in the event of double agency may now be sketched. Grace is said to come upon the creature "as absolute miracle, and with absolute power and certainty. It can be received by the creature only where there is a recognition of utter weakness and unworthiness, an utter confidence in its might and dignity, and an utter renunciation of willful self-despair" (II/2, 19). No place exists in the miracle of grace for a prior claim to grace, for a self-grounded appropriation of grace, or even for a revocation of grace on the part of the creature. "Grace cannot be called forth or constrained by any claim or merit, by any existing or future condition, on the part of the creature. Nor can it be held up or rendered nugatory and ineffective on the part of the creature" (II/2, 19). Grace rules out "all creaturely self-determination" by fully overruling all "human volition and achievement" (II/2, 19). This is precisely what it means to understand "grace as grace," grace as the freedom of God. "For what kind of grace is it that is conditioned and constrained, and not free grace and freely electing grace? What kind of a God is it who in any sense of the term has to be gracious, whose grace is not his own most personal and free good pleasure?" (II/2, 19). Grace is thus an event that defies all ordinary categorization. "In the absolute sense its reality can only take place, and it can do so only as a miracle before the eyes of every person, secular and religious, Greek and Jew'' (I/1, 223 rev.).

In the absolute miracle of grace, the radical incapacity of the creature is at once relentlessly disclosed and mercifully overcome. The Word of God inexorably reveals that as human beings, finite and fallen into sin, we are ''not actually free for God'' (I/2, 257). Our incapacity for God is not partial but total. ''It is not merely that we lack something which we ought to be or to have or to be capable of in relation to God. We lack everything.'' Our condition is not merely ''dangerous and damaged,'' but ''finished and impotent.'' We are not only ''sick'' but ''dead.'' We do not possess ''the possibility of communion with God'' (I/2, 257 rev.). ''To become free for God we must be convinced that we are not already free. We must make room for the miracle of acknowledging the Word of God'' (I/2, 258).

The grace that judges is, mercifully, not a grace that destroys but a grace that renews. Grace does not mean ''the catastrophic destruction of nature. It means radical judgment upon nature. It means its radical trans-formation and renewal. But it does not mean its violent end'' (II/1, 411). The miracle of grace means the *Aufhebung* of nature—the ongoing, in-conceivable event of its affirmation, cancelation, and radical renewal. ''Human and therefore sinful action'' is refashioned by the grace of God in order to become capable, miraculously, of fulfilling the will of God (IV/2, 618). This ''divine gift'' is something which can only be ''contin-ually prayed for and received.'' It is not the actualization of a reality or a capacity inherent in human nature. It is rather ''an omnipotent act of the special divine mercy addressed to it,'' a mercy which makes use of our ''human and therefore sinful action,'' but which ''does not proceed from it and cannot be understood in terms of it'' (IV/2, 618).

Because the absolute miracle of grace is an ongoing event of radical judgment and radical renewal, those who are encountered by grace, re-ceiving the judgment in shame, and the renewal all the more deeply in gratitude, are constantly summoned to look away from themselves to the gracious God. ''Grace points them away from self, frightens them out of themselves, deprives them of any root or soil or country in themselves, summons them to hold to the promise, to trust in him, to boast in him, to take guidance and counsel of him and him alone'' (I/2, 393). In the Yes to grace ''which comes from all their heart and soul and mind and strength,'' the love of God for them ''reaches its goal.'' For then they know and live by the miracle and secret of divine love: "Grace demands of them that they trust only in grace, and live only by grace—and by grace really live" (I/2, 393).

The possibility of knowing God and doing God's will is thereby affirmed in the only way it can be, namely, in the mode of trust, expectation, and hope. "Their affirming of this possibility can only be a self-relating to the new and future event of the actualization of this possibility which is always included and taken up in its actualization" (I/1, 226). Grace which ceased to be a miracle and instead became the actualization of an inherent capacity would be grace for which faith ceased completely to look forward in new hope. It would cease to be grace which demanded the impossible—fellowship with God. It would cease to be grace which alone empowered the human creature "to achieve what is demanded" (III/4, 76). It would cease to be the grace which human creatures can never control but which always comes to them radically anew.

But, Barth continues, God's grace does not cease to be grace, and therefore it does not cease to be an absolute miracle. It does not cease to grant human beings the capacity they would otherwise completely lack to love and cooperate with God. "They have no claim on God for that. They on their side have no power to cooperate with God. It can only turn out that they do so in fact to the extent that God takes the initiative towards them, he himself cooperating with them and giving them on their side the opportunity—beyond any capacity of their own—to cooperate with him" (III/3, 110). Grace is the absolute and ongoing miracle in which God bestows the capacity, which must ever be sought anew, to so align human volition with the divine that God may be served in fellowship and loved.

"Mystery" is a category at the heart of the particularist motif. It defines the cognitive status of grace as a miraculous event. Although the terms are always used with great flexibility, Barth tends to think of miracle as the form to which mystery is the corresponding content in any particular case (as when the mystery of calling was said to be denoted by the miracle). "The miracle," Barth comments at one point on a particular biblical text, "is the form of the mystery. It cannot be separated from it. But it must be distinguished and considered apart" (III/4, 320). He then proceeds to generalize from the case: "Here as everywhere the miracle has the particular and indispensable function of indicating and at the same time characterizing the mystery, of giving it its definite and distinctive sense and interpreting it as it is to be understood. Here as everywhere the form cannot be separated from the matter, nor the matter from the form."

The faith called for by the New Testament witness is always a faith in the mystery of God as "described by the witness in the form of the account of a miracle, so that faith in it is impossible without knowledge of this miracle." The miraculous form and the mysterious content of the events attested are said to signify a process which "defies all analysis, conception or interpretation" (III/4, 320–21).

Insofar as the I–Thou encounter with God, the event of fellowship, is predicated upon the mystery of grace, the motif of personalism may be regarded as structured by that of particularism. Particularism signifies that the fellowship with God established by the event of grace is beyond human comprehension. This is a matter on which it is especially important to be clear. Not only does this fellowship have the logical status of a *particular,* as Barth conceives it, and not only does it have the logical status of a particular *event,* and not only does it have the logical status of a particular event that is *unique.* It also has the logical status of a particular event that is unique *in kind.* The procedure of thinking from the particular to the general, it will be recalled, is premised on the stipulation of just such events. The procedure of defining the terms by the subject matter rather than the subject matter by the terms is premised on the stipulation that the divine mystery is hidden and revealed in just such events. The event of fellowship itself is conceived as such an event. The idea of mysterious particularity, like that of miraculous actualization, is deeply embedded in the pattern of grace by which Barth conceives of double agency. (And, of course, it is only by virtue of miraculous actualization that events so mysterious can be spoken of at all.)

Divine self-revelation, as Barth conceives it, is peculiar, because it is so exceptional in the range of all our knowledge. "The particular reality of revelation does not correspond, as do other particularities, with a general possibility, a truth, an idea, a notion of value, even the highest value of temporal or historical life in general, on the basis of which revelation may subsequently be judged and evaluated" (I/2, 59 rev.). Revelation is not the content which perfects a general form with which we are already familiar, and therefore it is not to be assessed or perhaps even proven on the basis of how well it perfects the form. Matters based on revelation, like double agency, are considered to be "divine facts" which are either credible in themselves or not at all. They cannot be externally grounded, for they are grounded in the revelation which is "the starting point for all our demonstrations" (II/2, 777). "Divine facts" are contrasted to "creaturely facts." The latter need to be assessed from a particular standpoint of some kind before they can be accepted as valid or real or significant. "But we need not and cannot consider divine facts in this way. Factuality, significance, and force cannot be conceded to them. We misunderstand and deny them if we treat them in this way." Facts of this kind, as accepted only by faith, are known through the power of their self-demonstration; for they are based on revelation—on "*the* divine fact, which as such speaks for itself" and which is "beyond any inward or outward discoveries we may make for ourselves" (II/2, 776).

The mystery of revelation may thus be described as follows:

> It is the ground on which we stand, the horizon by which we are bounded, the atmosphere in which we breathe. It is the life of our life. It is inaccessible and concealed just because it is so real—with a divine reality over which we have no control, but which controls us with a force with which none of the known and accessible elements of our life can even remotely compete. It is not in the sphere of our knowledge because it is wisdom itself, without whose light our knowledge would not be possible even in its limitation. We have no power over it because it is omnipotence, by which all our power is created, and without which it would be impotence. It does not exist as one of the facts which we seek and can discover because it is we who are searched and discovered in our existence by it. (II/2, 777)

The revelation of such a "fact" does not prevent it from being a mystery, and the mystery does not prevent it from being revealed. "In other words, it becomes the object of our knowledge; it thus finds a way of becoming the object of our experience and our thought; it gives itself to be apprehended by our contemplation and our categories" (I/2, 172). But as it becomes an object, it retains its essential uniqueness. The mystery of revelation remains "beyond the range of what we regard as possible for our contemplation and perception, beyond the confines of our experience and our thought." It thereby comes to us as something radically new. "It comes to us as a *Novum* which, when it becomes object for us, we cannot incorporate in the series of our other objects, cannot compare with them, cannot deduce from their context, cannot regard as analogous to them. It comes to us as a datum with no point of connection with any other previous datum." Its mode of apprehension must be as unique and mysterious as the object itself. "The act of knowing it is distinctive as one which we actually can achieve, but which we cannot understand, in the sense that we simply do not understand how we can achieve it." The possibility of knowing the mystery thus comes mysteriously from beyond ourselves. "We can understand the possibility of it solely from the side of the object, i.e., we can regard it not as ours, but as one coming to us, imparted to us, gifted to us. In this bit of knowing we are not the masters but the mastered." Mystery precludes mastery, just because it confronts the human mind with something it can never control—an event inconceivable though real and real though inconceivable. Its inconceivability does not detract from its reality, and its reality does not detract from its inconceivability. It can therefore only be acknowledged, confessed, described, and received as the utterly unique and mysterious act of God (I/2, 172–73).

The inconceivability of the divine mystery does not mean that it is absurd or that it is to be explained as an absurdity (I/2, 160). The Word of God is inconceivable, but not self-contradictory. "There is no fault in it, nor does it contradict itself. It cannot be recalled or replaced by any other Word of God. In the face of it all contradiction is ill-grounded, impotent, and untenable, and therefore condemned to be silenced and removed" (IV/3, 160). The mystery of the unsurpassable Word of God carries its criterion within itself. It is not only the "first and original," but also the "last and final truth." It is thus "the truth itself and as such. It cannot then be subjected to any criterion of truth different from itself. It is itself the criterion of all different truths. Declared by God it authenticates itself" (IV/3, 160; I/1, 222). It is the truth that relativizes, transcends, and finally eradicates all real contradictions.

The event of double agency is described entirely within this context. The event in which divine and human actions coincide, in which they coexist and coinhere, in which they are historically interconnected and exist in differentiated unity—the event of fellowship according to the mystery of the Chalcedonian pattern—is regarded as an event that is absolutely unique in kind. "We can and must actually put our hand in the fire," writes Barth, "for its character as a unique possibility" (IV/3, 160). It is an event whose possibility is not generally accessible or neutrally apprehensible. It is an event that is absolutely incomprehensible on any terms other then its own, and that can be known only in its actual occurrence. It cannot be deduced from any principle, normalized by any law, or divested of its incomprehensibility by any conceptual scheme. The mystery of double agency comes into view only "as it is actualized," and it is actualized in defiance of all known possibilities (I/1, 224). It has the logical status of a "divine fact," the condition for whose possibility can be found only in God, just as the condition for the possibility of its apprehension can be found only in the divine self-revelation as attested in scripture. The event of double agency is either accepted and described as a datum given by revelation, or it is not accepted and described at all. It simply occurs as a "fact" that "the two subjects are together and they work together, but this fact can be understood only as the gracious mystery of an encounter in which that which is quite inconceivable and unexpected and undeserved has actually come to pass" (III/3, 106).

> To the glory of God, we have at any rate to declare as open and manifest the fact that in the operation of God as a cooperation with that of the creature we have to do with the mystery of grace in the confrontation and encounter of two subjects who cannot be compared and do not fall under any one master-concept. And that means that from the standpoint of the creature what takes place in the divine operation is always inconceivable, unexpected and unmerited. It is not merely that the divine Subject is quite unlike the creaturely, but also that the divine operation is itself quite unlike the creaturely, being not simply a conditioning and determining of what already exists but a free and absolute positing and therefore a conditioning and determining in a way which is impossible for creaturely activity. Hence the divine work is not merely done after a higher and superior fashion, but within a completely different order. And the fact that there is still a connection between them, a positive and indeed an intimate and direct connection, the fact that the divine activity is fulfilled in and with and over the creaturely, and that the creaturely is itself the fulfillment of the divine will— this is the high truth and the high mystery of grace which we now have to bear in mind. (III/3, 135)

How can the divine otherness not logically lead to an ultimate disrelation or dualism in relation to the creature? How can the divine omnipotence not logically lead to an ultimate determinism or monism? "The difficulty with which we are faced appears to be an insuperable one, and it would be so, and would remain so, if we had to consider whether we could give an answer, and if so what, merely within the framework of a general philosophy of God and the world" (III/3, 139). But we cannot move in this case from the general to the particular, and therefore from philosophy to theology. For there is no "master-concept," no "common denominator," no "genus," no "synthesis"—no conceptual scheme based on general considerations—"in which God and the creature can be brought together" (III/3, 106). That the divine otherness establishes a "fellowship of intimacy" with the creature in which the integrity of each partner is maintained, that the divine omnipotence establishes a "fellowship of freedom" with the creature in which the unconditional sovereignty of the divine partner is fully expressed without crushing and indeed by liberating the creature's full spontaneity—these assertions are descriptions of the indescribable, conceptions of the inconceivable, and apprehensions of the inapprehensible.

The answer to the question of the *modus* of the divine activity in establishing fellowship on just these terms—the answer to the problem of the How?—turns out to be "given in the event of the divine operation itself" (III/3, 142). For the answer to the problem is that it is not a problem, that it cannot be solved, that it is not supposed to be solved, that it is a category mistake to conceive of the How? as anything other than a miracle and a mystery to be respected and revered. The answer to the problem is that the event of fellowship "actually takes place, continually becoming an event, and demanding to be known and recognized" for what it is—an event "for whose peculiar nature there is no parallel in the creaturely sphere" and therefore whose miracle is on principle irreducible and whose mystery is equally irresolvable (III/3, 140, 136). The answer to the problem is that the event of double agency "does not rest upon conjecture but upon knowledge," that this knowledge "is not an assertion but a confession," and that no other mode of knowledge will ever be possible or necessary for the mystery of God as confessed by faith (III/3, 142).[2]

No resolution or removal can be envisaged for "the difference in order between the working of God in, with and over the creature, and the working of the creature under God's lordship." The "difference in order" remains in force even when God mercifully condescends to the creature and the creature is wondrously exalted into "close proximity" with God (III/3, 136).

> It is the secret of grace that God does this, and the creature experiences it. But it is also the secret of grace that even when he does it he alone is God, that he alone has and retains the divine essence, that the essence of the creature is not affected or altered. By his unconditioned and irresistible lordship he does not subtract anything from the creature or add anything to it, but he allows it to be just what it is in its creaturely essence. Even in the union of the divine activity and creaturely occurrence there remains a genuine antithesis which is not obscured or resolved either by admixture or transference, either by divine influence or infusion. There is still a genuine encounter, and therefore a genuine meeting, of two beings which are quite different in type and order. (III/3, 136–37)

It is this unparalleled difference in order, not only between the two partners, but also in the asymmetrical mode of the relationship itself, that necessitates the very different and peculiar usage of terms characteristic of the particularist motif. Terms have to be wrested from their ordinary contexts and subjected to extraordinary demands, if they are even to approximate the mysterious and miraculous events to which they are intended to point. It is understood that the terms will always be inadequate in themselves and that they will ultimately be able to work referringly only by being drawn themselves into the miracle and mystery of grace. Nonetheless, three strategies may reasonably be undertaken: a reformist use, a dialectical use, and a diversified use of terms. (It is to be understood, therefore, that at this point the personalism is not only structured by the particularist motif, but that the particularism involved intersects with and presupposes the realist motif insofar as the analogical reference of inherently inadequate terms is at stake, and that the realism in turn intersects with and presupposes the actualistic motif insofar as the inherent linguistic inadequacy is understood to be overcome by the miracle of grace.)

No terms are more inevitable and at the same time more problematic in describing the event of double agency than "cause," "operation," and "effect." They are inevitable, because without them it is virtually impossible to do justice to the unconditional nature of the divine sovereignty; but at the same time they are exceedingly problematic, because with them it is virtually impossible to avoid the implications of determinism, mechanism, and monism—implications excluded on principle by the actual nature of the event. It is at this point that a reformist strategy is explicitly adopted. Barth writes: "What is needed is a radical rethinking of the whole matter. First we have to drop the ordinary but harmful conception of cause, operation and effect. Then, when we know who God is and what he wills and how he works, we have to take it up again, but giving to it a new force and application in which we do not look back to what are at root godless notions of causality" (III/3, 118). "Cause," "operation," and "effect," in other words, are to be subjected to a kind of *Aufhebung*. They cannot be assimilated directly but only critically and innovatively. If, as Barth urges, God is known to be the One who loves in freedom, then it is not "the One who loves in freedom" who is to be defined by the term "causality," but the term "causality" which is to be defined by "the One who loves in freedom." The ordinary meaning of the term is understood to be at once included, canceled, and transcended, when used of God. The divine mode of causation is understood to be of a different and higher order than any causation otherwise known to us, for it is a causation not contrary to, but defined and therefore pervaded by, the divine love and freedom without which God is never God (III/3, 94–119). Barth's discussion of divine causality thus represents the reformist strategy of *Aufhebung*.

The strategy of dialectical usage—a strategy already implicit in the

Chalcedonian pattern itself—is so closely related to that of diversified usage that the two may be presented in one exposition. These strategies run (as does the reformist strategy) through the *Church Dogmatics* from beginning to end, as the following representative (and in some ways random) sampling will suggest. The coexistence of God and humanity is "not a coexistence on the same level" as that on which ordinary events occur (I/1, 200). Therefore "it is impossible to see it from a higher vantage point and to view it in its possibility." It is a coexistence in which our human "self-determination" is subjected to an "absolutely superior determination" by the Word of God. In this determination, human self-determination is "not in the least affected or destroyed," but is instead given a "direction," placed under a "judgment," and impressed with a new "character" (I/1, 200, 201 rev.). Here the conception of a "different level" of occurrence, or of a "completely different order" (the essence of particularism), is used in connection with a dialectical interplay between the "self-determination" and the "absolutely superior determination" of human freedom in which no higher or comprehensible synthesis is regarded as possible (though their transcendent unity is regarded as actual).

At other times dialectical interplay without higher synthesis is suggested by using a more classically Reformation scheme of "wholly/wholly" (in contrast to "partly/partly," as in "wholly justified and wholly sinful at the same time"). The church, for example, is said to build itself up as it is built up by Christ, and to be built up by Christ as it builds up itself. "As his community (his body), this cannot be merely a passive object or spectator of its upbuilding. It builds itself up. And we are forced to say that as its upbuilding is wholly and utterly the work of God or Christ, so it is wholly and utterly its own work" (I/2, 634). An entirely parallel point can be made about the reality of faith. The reality of faith is said to "transcend" the "antitheses" of above/below, without/within, objective/subjective. "Faith is altogether the work of God, and it is altogether a human work. It is a complete enslavement, and it is a complete liberation. And it is in this way, in this totality, that it is raised up and lives as it is awakened by the Word of God" (III/3, 247 rev.). Or again, the antithesis of active/passive is seen as transcended in divine love as the basis for human love: "And to understand the difference and the connection between divine love and human we have to take into account the fact that the second can take place only as it is absolutely conditioned by the first, by the fact that the first takes place, so that in the first love we have to do in fact with the creative basis of the second" (IV/2, 780).

Essentially the same underlying formal pattern is also characteristic of more nearly noetic (than volitional) contexts:

> In the act of the knowledge of God, as in any other cognitive act, we are definitely active as the receivers of images and creators of counter-images. Yet while this is true, it must definitely be contested that our receiving and creating owes its truth to any capacity of our own to be truly recipients and creators in relation to God. It is indeed our own viewing and conceiving. But we ourselves have no capacity for fellowship with God. . . . He is far from us and foreign to us except as he has of himself ordained and created fellowship between himself and us—and this does not happen in the actualizing of our capacity, but in the miracle of his good-pleasure. (II/1, 182)

Note that the idea of fellowship (the essence of the personalist motif) is here presupposed as the context within which knowledge of God takes place, and that it is said to take place through a miracle (the essence of the actualist motif) in which the antitheses of active/passive and creative/receptive are transcended and overcome. The strategy of diversity is also at work when human action is said to be "stimulated and moved and determined and ordered," or again to be "called and empowered and ordered and directed," by Christ (IV/2, 189, 190). All these different modalities and terms and conceptions can be used, just because the subject matter is captured by none but potentially illumined by all. Freedom and flexibility of usage is demanded by a subject matter in which ordinary antitheses are included, superseded, and surpassed. That is what Barth was characteristically trying to convey when, in discussing fellowship as the goal of vocation, he was seen to remark at the very outset that, when a person is met by the call of Christ, that person is "both caused and liberated and therefore spontaneously moved to hear it" (IV/3, 520).

Divine and Human Agency:
What Really Counts as Incoherence?

The third point concerning Barth's possible rejoinder to the charge that his conception of double agency is incoherent is implicit in the previous two. By shaping his conception according to the Chalcedonian pattern, and by stipulating miracle and mystery as definitive predicates of revelation in general and double agency in particular, he has committed himself to the position that coherence and incoherence are not context-neutral but context-dependent terms. Barth's theology is regularly taken to task by critics who presume that there is one neutral and apparently field-encompassing notion of incoherence which can be duly applied to his work. No notice is taken that, from Barth's standpoint, the very application of this notion would be regarded as an essentially contestable point. Within the scheme of Barth's theology, what counts for significant incoherence is essentially different from the neutral conception used to assess his work.

Use of the neutral conception begs some important questions. Roughly speaking, it would seem to imply either one of two things: either the external critique that Barth's claim to be describing a mysterious and miraculous subject matter is unjustifiable on principle, or else the more internal critique that his claim is unjustifiable because the legitimate place for mystery and miracle in Christian theology has in this case been misconceived. An argument might be made, of course, for either sort of implication. The point, however, is that without such an argument the significance and validity of using the neutral conception of incoherence are (to say the least) difficult to assess, and that they are by no means self-evident.[3] Consideration of the possible directions that might be taken by the external critique, that the claim is unjustifiable on principle, would lead us too far afield. The internal critique, however, can be given limited consideration. Barth can be read as arguing that his view of mystery and miracle is not unjustifiable within the context of his beliefs, and that certain counterpositions must themselves be ruled out as incoherent. He would wonder whether these counterpositions can equally well be avoided by his internal critic.

Coherence in the framework of Barth's theology is subject to two basic kinds of testing. Both kinds are dependent on his construal of the subject matter of theology. The one is coherence with the witness of scripture, and the other is coherence with the cluster of doctrines derived from theological reflection on scripture. From a consideration of personalism in relation to soteriological objectivism, we have come a long way around to the motifs of actualism and particularism as they structure the motif of personalism (through the conceptions of miracle and mystery as they bear on double agency), and now to the motifs of realism and rationalism. Barth's rejoinder to the charge of incoherence would lead him back to the question of scriptural interpretation (an important aspect of realism) and to the question of coherentist doctrinal testing (an important aspect of rationalism).

The question of scriptural interpretation need not detain us, for again it would lead too far afield. Note need only be taken that Barth's appeal to scripture on these matters has already emerged in passing. Not only has the Chalcedonian pattern been glimpsed as an interpretive device for describing the patterns of double agency in biblical narratives. The realistic reading of scripture, as centered on Jesus Christ, with its reliance on conceptions of intratextual and extratextual analogical reference, has also been in force as the means by which the conceptions of miracle and mystery are initially derived and ultimately justified. In this sense realism is bound up with justifying miracle and mystery as coherent with the central testimony of scripture. The reading of scripture generates conceptions of miracle and mystery, and the conceptions are then justified as coherent with the subject matter of scripture as so read. Realism is thus significant in establishing the terms of the "discrimen" or "hermeneutical circle" in Barth's theology.[4]

Testing for Incoherence Within the Framework of the Chalcedonian Pattern

The coherentist mode of testing, as it emerged in the survey of rationalism, also plays a decisive role in Barth's justification of his position on double agency. Directly and indirectly, therefore, it serves to justify his reliance on the conceptions of miracle and mystery in that position. On the exegetical or hermeneutical premise that the terms of the Chalcedonian pattern are rooted in the biblical testimony regarding how divine and human agency are related, the mode of doctrinal testing proceeds as follows. The Chalcedonian pattern is used to specify counterpositions that would be doctrinally incoherent (and also incoherent with scripture). "Without separation or division" means that no independent human autonomy can be posited in relation to God. "Without confusion or change" means that no divine determinism or monism can be posited in relation to humanity. Finally, "complete in deity and complete in humanity" means that no symmetrical relationship can be posited between divine and human actions (or better, none that is not asymmetrical). It also means that the two cannot be posited as ultimately identical. Taken together, these considerations mean that, if the foregoing conditions are to be met, no nonmiraculous and nonmysterious conception is possible. The charge of incoherence (as previously defined) thereby reveals itself to be abstract, in the sense that it does not adequately take all the necessary factors into account. It does not work inductively from the subject matter (as attested by scripture)—as the motif of particularism would prescribe. Instead, it starts from general considerations such as formal logic and applies them to certain isolated aspects of the more "concrete" position.

At the same time, the charge may well have implicated itself, wittingly or unwittingly, in one of the rejected counterpositions.

Without Separation or Division:
Against Independent Human Autonomy

No *independent* human autonomy, Barth argues, may be posited in relation to God. The idea of an independent human autonomy posits the kind of illicit "indeterminism" that Barth finds to be characteristic of Pelagian and semi-Pelagian positions counter to his own. The actuality of human autonomy or freedom or self-determination (and so on) is, it is important to see, not in question. What is in question is the condition for the possibility of human autonomy, freedom, and self-determination. The Pelagian position finds this condition to be entirely inherent in human nature as created by divine grace, whereas the semi-Pelagian position finds it to be only partially inherent in human nature. The Pelagian sees no need, whereas the semi-Pelagian sees some need, for the special operation of divine grace, if the human creature is to act freely in fellowship with God (I/1, 199–200; II/1, 562–63). Neither position survives Barth's coherentist form of testing, for neither is seen to do justice either to the radicality of sin or to the finitude of the creature. The same basic inadequacy can be restated with reference to other doctrinal beliefs, and these are actually thought to be the more fundamental. Christologically, the counterpositions fail to do justice to the cross of Christ (as it discloses the radicality of sin) and to the necessity of the mediation of Christ (as it overcomes not only sin, but the finitude of the creature, by exalting the creature to eternal life). Theologically, moreover, the counterpositions fail to do justice to the divine righteousness (as it discloses the radicality of sin) and to the divine majesty (as it discloses the essence of creaturely finitude).

In discussing the question of double agency, it is most often the radicality of sin and the majesty of God to which coherentist appeal adverts (although the other beliefs do not cease to be presupposed, of course, and are sometimes invoked). The radicality of sin, as already documented on more than one occasion, is regarded as meaning that we have "completely lost the capacity for God" (I/1, 238). The majesty of God, on the other hand, is characteristically conceived in terms of the "conditioned" and the "unconditioned." "The creature which conditions God is no longer God's creature, and the God who is conditioned by the creature is no longer God" (II/1, 580). Or again: "Grace would not be grace if it were not free, but were conditioned by a reciprocal achievement on the part of the one to whom it is addressed" (I/1, 45). Or again: "Grace cannot be called forth or constrained by any claim or merit, by any existing or future condition, on the part of the creature. . . . Both in its being and in its operation its necessity is in itself" (II/2, 19). That God's grace is absolutely free in relation to the creature, and that the creature can in no way condition God, is as axiomatic in Barth's theology as he believes it to be axiomatic in scripture. Pelagianism and semi-Pelagianism both fail, because they posit a creature who *by nature* conditions God, and a God who *by nature* can be and is conditioned by the creature. What is worse, these counterpositions do so even in the face of the radicality of sin. They are therefore judged to be incoherent from the standpoint of doctrinal testing. "What takes place in the covenant of grace takes place wholly *for* the human creature and not—even in part—*through* the human creature. A *creatura mediatrix gratiarum* or even *corredemptrix* is a self-contradiction" (I/1, 45).

Barth's position over against these counterpositions may be briefly restated. The actuality of human freedom is affirmed (and by no means denied). But the condition for its possibility in relation to God is found not at all in human nature itself, but entirely in divine grace. In the event of fellowship human autonomy is not at all independent. It is entirely subsequent to and dependent on grace. The missing capacity for freedom in fellowship with God is given and received as a gift—"not as a supernatural quality, but as a capacity which is actual only as it is used, which is not in any sense magical, but absolutely free and natural in its exercise" (III/3, 244). The capacity for this freedom "is not independent but mediated" through Jesus Christ (II/1, 128). In and through him it is called by grace "out of nothingness into being, out of death into life." The event of grace on which the capacity for freedom completely depends is thereby a miracle and a mystery. But in and with this complete dependence, it is "real in the way in which creation generally can be in its relationship to the Creator." Human freedom in all its reality is thus "encompassed," "established," "delimited," and "determined" by divine grace (II/1, 128). The "mystery of human autonomy" is clearly not "an autonomous mystery" (II/2, 194). It is rather included within "the one divine mystery." It is, that is to say, included within "the mystery of grace," within "the mystery of God's triumphant affirmation and love." Only in this sense (but certainly in this sense) is it included within "the mystery of God's omnipotence." The reality of human freedom takes place, therefore, not as "the second point in an ellipse" (the Pelagian and semi-Pelagian counterpositions), but as "the circumference around one central point of which it is the repetition and confirmation'' (II/2, 194). Divine grace and human freedom stand, in other words, in a conceptually asymmetrical relationship rather than in one of conceptual interdependence.

The features of this argument may also be stated in terms of the various motifs. The reality of fellowship is in question by way of the problem of double agency (personalism). The mode of testing for incoherence takes place in terms of the remaining web of doctrinal beliefs (rationalism). The bestowal, by grace, of freedom for fellowship with God is described as a miraculous event (actualism). This event also takes place in such a way that divine omnipotence and human freedom coexist in mutual love and freedom as the mystery of God with humanity and of humanity with God (particularism). Furthermore, the miracle and the mystery of the event are said to be dependent upon and mediated through the saving person and work of Jesus Christ (objectivism). The counterpositions (Pelagianism and semi-Pelagianism) are shown to be incoherent at essential points with the presupposed web of doctrinal beliefs (especially "the radicality of sin" and "the majesty of God"), whereas the position in question is shown in fact to be coherent with it in the mode of miracle and mystery (rationalism, actualism, particularism). Since the web of presupposed beliefs is taken to be in accord with scripture, it follows (granted this assumption) that the challenged position is also in accord with scripture, and that the proposed counterpositions are not (although this could and would need to be argued also on independent exegetical grounds) (realism). Thus all six motifs are in force in one way or another in the mode of testing for the possible coherence or incoherence of the challenged belief.

Without Confusion or Change: Against Determinism or Monism

No divine determinism or monism, the second point to be considered, may be posited in relation to humanity. The idea of a divine determinism or monism posits a kind of "mechanism" and "fatalism" that Barth finds to be characteristic of "metaphysical dogmas" (IV/2, 494). Metaphysical dogmas attempt to "systematize" divine and human actions. They attempt to conceive these actions within a rationally comprehensible explanatory scheme. Within the scheme they attempt *to explain how* these actions are related. They appeal to a supposedly higher principle or a supposedly higher order which stands above the actions and normalizes them. Above all, they assume that God is accessible to ordinary schemes of explanation. The ontological difference in order between divine and human actions (which for Barth is ineradicable) is conceived as one that can be resolved and removed. Metaphysical dogmas, in other words, derive explanatory schemes from general observations which are then applied to the case of divine and human actions—as if the case of their relatedness were the instance of a class. These dogmas represent the opposite of everything signified by particularism.

In Barth's theology mechanism and monism are denied, because the possibility of explanatory systematization is denied, and the possibility of this systematization is denied, because it can achieve only a formal or technical coherence at the expense of a truly material coherence. No system can contain all the affirmations found within the cluster of basic doctrinal beliefs. At some point adherence to the system will require a material or doctrinal sacrifice. The charge of determinism or monism accurately perceives that a merely formal concept of the unconditional sovereignty of divine grace would necessarily result in the loss of human freedom. But just what conception of human freedom does the charge suppose is being lost? Is there a neutral or context-independent conception that can simply be taken for granted? Does the charge presuppose that one systematization is to be rejected (determinism or monism), because a better systematization can be found to replace it? Are Pelagianizing tendencies, for example, to be rejected with equal vigor?

The rejection of systematization has already been explored in detail. Particularism, as found in Barth's theology, excludes systematization on principle. It is because systematization is excluded that determinism and monism are also excluded. The exclusion of determinism on these grounds is exemplified by the following passage:

Let us suppose for a moment that we found it quite impossible to perceive or understand from this biblical center that which we have already said generally concerning the sovereignty of the will and work of God in relation to the creature. In that case "God" would be a purely formal conception, denoting a supreme being endowed with absolute, unconditioned and irresistible power; the "will of God" would be a purely formal concept denoting the unconditioned and incontrovertible purpose of this supreme being; and the "work of God" would denote the unconditioned and irresistible execution of this purpose over against and in and on the activity of the creature. It is obvious in what an impasse we should then find ourselves. We could think of God's rule over and with and in the creature only as that of sovereign caprice, in the hands of which the creature would appear to act, but in fact would only be acted upon, and this in pursuance of a purpose which is utterly obscure. The demand for belief in a God would then be a demand for the recognition and willing acceptance by us of the unconditioned work of the unconditioned will of this unconditionally supreme being, and our willing submission to it without any real perception of what it is that we must approve, or of the extent to which there can be any question of real willingness on our part. And what will our reaction be when we find ourselves in such a position? (III/3, 113 rev.)

Note that his "thought-experiment," conducted in the mode of testing, is predicated on prescinding from the "biblical center." The "living divine–human unity" and the "center" from which it comes are deliberately left out of account (IV/3, 63). The actual event of fellowship with God as attested by scripture and known by faith is deleted. The particular basis on which everything depends is removed from consideration. Under these circumstances the particular uniqueness of God also disappears. God as "the One who loves in freedom" can no longer be upheld as the controlling conception. "God" instead becomes a purely formal concept. "Absolute, unconditioned and irresistible power" (as a comprehensible explanatory conception) now occupies the center otherwise occupied by an event unique in kind (a conception comprehensible from an explanatory point of view, only in its incomprehensibility). Mystery and miracle are flattened out into a theological conceptuality that exhibits little more than the thin virtue of technical consistency. "God" dwindles into "a supreme being"—"a product of our own thinking, a concept and principle and therefore an instrument with the help of which we can master and solve any problem," including the "problem" of how divine and human actions are related (IV/3, 707). The order of this relation no longer appears conceptually as "an antithesis which makes insignificant all the antitheses in human thinking" (IV/2, 215). The ordering (and therefore explanatory) principle will perhaps be conceived as something very great— as "the extraordinary," "the inconceivable," or "the supernatural," or perhaps as "an epitome of formal transcendence," or as "an absolutely superior omnipotence which encounters human existence anonymously." But it will not be conceived in any case as "an absolute miracle" (which as such eludes these ordering principles), and it will therefore arouse the lingering suspicion that what has here been conceived is merely "the empty secret of human existence" (IV/2, 215 rev.).

When the biblical center is restored, on the other hand, and the living divine–human unity is taken back into account, it is the determinism that disappears. Just as determinism follows inevitably from a certain form of systematization, so the mystery of freedom follows from fellowship conceived as an event unique in kind. Of "the awakening to conversion" as the gateway to fellowship, Barth writes that all "magical or mechanical or automatic associations" must be left behind:

> When Paul speaks of a person led to conversion by the Spirit of God, it is not at all the case that the person is betrayed into the sphere and influence of an overwhelming impulse consisting in an alien movement with which the person has to cooperate. . . . It is true, of course, that it is by the omnipotence of God that one is awakened to conversion and set in movement. But the omnipotence of God is not a force which works magically or mechanically and in relation to which one can only be an object, an alien body which is either carried or impelled, like a spar of wood carried relentlessly downstream by a great river. It is a matter of God's omnipotent mercy, of his Holy Spirit, and therefore of one's liberation, and therefore of one's conversion to being and action in the freedom one is given by God. To be sure, there is a compulsion. One *must* pass from a past only too well-known to a future only just opening up, "to a land that I shall show thee;" from oneself as the old to oneself as a new human being; from one's own death to one's own true life. There is necessarily a compulsion. . . . But the compulsion is not a mere compulsion. It is not abstract. It is not blind or deaf. We have to realize that a mere compulsion is basically evil and demonic. The compulsion obeyed in conversion is not of this type. It is the compulsion of a permission and ability which have been granted. It is that of the free person who as such can only exercise freedom. The omnipotence of God creates and effects in the person awakened to conversion a true ability. The person who previously vegetated to death under a hellish compulsion, in a true analogy to the driftwood carried downstream, may now live integrally and wholly as a human being. . . . It is for this that one is freed, and free. In this freedom there has been taken away once and for all any mere choosing or self-deciding. In the exercise of this freedom—still as the person one was, already as the person one will be—one fulfills one's conversion. (IV/2, 578–79 rev.).

In this account, language corresponds to event as conceptual antithesis corresponds to mysterious actuality.[5] Antitheses spin within antitheses, for their terms are understood to be reconciled in actuality in a way that cannot be duplicated in thought. The great reconciled antithesis between the Spirit of God and the person in conversion embraces other such reconciled antitheses within it. Not only, on the divine side, is there no mercy without omnipotence and no omnipotence without mercy. Mercy and omnipotence are also posited in a relationship ordered by freedom. Although there is no mercy not informed by omnipotence, there is no omnipotence not expressive of mercy. Mercy is the dominant term to which omnipotence is freely subordinate. Neither the mercy nor the omnipotence nor their being freely ordered could be conceptually omitted without losing correspondence to the actuality. Similarly, on the human side, there is no freedom without compulsion and no compulsion without freedom. Yet here the case is more complex, for the relationship in question is not immanent within the divine being but extends across the ontological divide. Once again, however, the relationship is conceived as one of reconciled antitheses ordered in freedom. Insofar as compulsion is conceived as the ground of freedom, the two are asymmetrically related. The compulsion of grace is conceptually prior to and independent of human freedom, and human freedom is conceptually subsequent to and dependent on the compulsion of grace. Yet insofar as freedom is conceived as the goal of compulsion, the two are conceived as reconciled in actuality and ordered in freedom. The compulsion of grace is conceptually instrumental to human freedom, and human freedom is conceptually teleological to the compulsion of grace. Thus again, neither the freedom nor the compulsion nor their being freely (though asymmetrically) ordered could be conceptually omitted without losing correspondence to the actuality. Neither mercy and omnipotence nor freedom and compulsion can be brought under the control of a higher principle. Neither relationship can be rendered comprehensible by reference to anything other than the event in which its terms coalesce in just the way described—just as the relationship between the Spirit of God and the person in conversion cannot be rendered comprehensible in any other explanatory way. Just because the uniqueness of the event is the controlling factor, the claims of formal consistency, which dominate all "false systematizations," must yield to the logic of mystery (II/1, 598).

To the mysterious actuality and the antithetical conceptuality that signifies it, there corresponds, it bears reiterating, a definite disclosure situation. Jesus Christ is not a principle, grace is not a neutral consideration, and truth is not a speculative idea. Jesus Christ is "a living person who comes and speaks and acts with the claim and authority of God" (IV/3, 706). Grace is "a free and sovereign power." Truth is "a free and self-disclosing truth." A principle, a neutral consideration, a speculative idea might logically be developed into a system that would transcend and overcome "all possible antitheses." The system could then be contemplated in detachment and its subject matter perceived with no claim to personal commitment. The truth and grace of Jesus Christ, however, are inaccessible to this kind of contemplation and perception. "The grace of

God addressed to the world in Jesus Christ is that which exists supremely, but quite uniquely.'' It exists "only as . . . it was and is and will be event.'' It is "recognizable only in gratitude for the fact that it is real and true, and in prayer for ever new recognition of its reality and truth.'' That this truth should be essentially self-involving, as indicated by the personalist motif, and also essentially mysterious, as signified by an irresolvable antithesis, is emblematic of authentic theological discourse (IV/3, 706–7). The conceptual antithesis thus corresponds not only to the mystery of the actuality it denotes, but also to the disclosure situation in which the actuality cannot be mastered by those whose perception it claims. The basic position on "double agency'' can thus be affirmed as follows: "The unconditioned and irresistible lordship of God means not only that the freedom of the creature is neither jeopardized nor suppressed, but even more that it is confirmed in all its particularity and variety'' (III/3, 146 rev.). But it can then immediately be added: "The basic condition for a perception and understanding of this proposition is not intellectual but spiritual'' (III/3, 146).

Rejection of determinism and monism in Barth's theology clearly goes hand in hand with nonsystematic exposition. Antitheses are developed which on principle are not to be resolved and which are given the logical status of descriptions of an event. The antitheses, moreover, are established (among other things) precisely to *deny* conceptual resolutions in the direction of determinism or monism, for *both* terms in any given antithesis are meant to be taken seriously. The tension between the terms is essential to the description of the mystery and is thus not to be effaced. Within the context of this position, Barth has no difficulty rejecting determinism and monism, and such rejections are a regular feature of his exposition. The giving and receiving of the Word of God, he writes, "does not take place in any mechanical way but in a spiritual communion corresponding to the individuality of the human Jesus and of all his witnesses'' (I/2, 703 rev.). In relation to God, human beings are affirmed as "active subjects'' who make "their own responsible decision'' (IV/4, 163). "Matters are not decided over their heads. They are not just objects who are discussed, moved and pushed around. Precisely in the covenant of grace . . . there can be no talk of divine omnicausality'' (IV/4, 163). God is not to be conceived as an impersonal, anonymous force. "His authority is divinely majestic just because it has nothing in common with tyranny, because its true likeness is not the power of a natural catastrophe which annihilates all human response, but rather the power of an appeal, command and blessing which not only recognizes human response but creates it" (I/2, 661).

The point is repeatedly made with reference to freedom—the fundamental term of fellowship as the essence of the personalist motif. "Because the Word of God has and exercises freedom in itself . . . there is also human freedom" (I/2, 669). Determinism would obviously transform the human being "into another and non-human being—an idea which we have exerted ourselves to repudiate from the very outset" (IV/2, 494). Everything depends on thinking "concretely." "Freedom is not an empty and formal concept. . . . It does not speak only of a capacity" (IV/2, 494). It speaks concretely of the event in which the capacity for freedom is given and actualized by God as it is received and utilized by the creature (IV/2, 494). In receiving and using this capacity the person "does not at all act creatively" (I/1, 211). But this assertion is not to be interpreted as meaning that the person does not act imaginatively (without a full engagement of aesthetic sensibilities), nor as meaning that the person does not act spontaneously. It merely means, as a way of making the standard actualistic point, that the capacity does not "originally" pertain to, but rather accrues to, the person from God (I/1, 211). Grace is the only basis of the capacity, which is not given except as it is actualized; but in the event of actualization both the divine and the human subjects are conceived as fully and spontaneously engaged. The human action is "not a kind of prolongation" of the divine. It is not the "overflowing" of the divine action into human life, as though the human subject had "to serve as a kind of channel, being merely present and not at bottom an acting subject" (IV/2, 785). That notion would merely represent the kind of monism which prefers fluid to mechanistic or manipulative analogies. Manipulative analogies, of course, are also excluded. In the event of actualization the human subject is really at work, "not as God's puppet," but fully engaged from the subject's "own heart and soul and strength, as an independent subject who encounters and replies to God and is responsible to him as his partner" (IV/2, 768). In the event of actualization, freedom and obedience coincide, but freedom is the logical precondition of obedience, even as obedience is the spontaneous expression of freedom. If the human action were not free, "but took place naturally or inevitably or automatically"—as though the human subject "had to love what God wills, under constraint and not voluntarily"— then "how could it be real obedience? A puppet does not obey. It does not move itself. It dances and gesticulates as it is moved." Whether governed by fluid or mechanistic or manipulative analogies, determinism obscures what actually takes place in the event—that "to be quickened by the Holy Spirit is to move oneself, and to do so in obedience, listening to the order and command of God" (IV/2, 800).

The salient point, then, is this: "Between the sovereignty of God and the freedom of the creature there is no contradiction. The freedom of its activity does not exclude but includes the fact that it is controlled by God. . . . Freedom apart from this limit would not be creaturely freedom, but the freedom of a second God. To claim this kind of freedom would be sin and death for the creature" (III/2, 166). "Control by God" is helpfully explained as follows: "Both in general and in particular God himself fixes for the creature its goals, that is, goals that it will actually attain. In one way or another it will ultimately realize the divine decree" (III/2, 167). The control is obviously regarded as inexorable but noncoercive. Therefore "divine freedom cannot destroy and suspend human freedom. Always and in every respect the former draws the latter to and after itself" (I/2, 710). (This is the point against determinism.) Yet on the other hand, "human freedom cannot encroach upon divine freedom. Always and in every respect the latter precedes the former" (I/2, 710). (This was the point against Pelagianism.) Everything to be said in this connection, however, carries the constant proviso that the majestic, unconditioned, and irresistible sovereignty of God as the One who loves in freedom "is always beyond our control and inscrutable to us" (I/2, 710).

It remains only to suggest where this analysis might leave Barth's internal critic. A putatively neutral conception of incoherence, it will be recalled, was thought to be employed. Upon examination, however, this very conception would seem to commit the critic implicitly or explicitly to some form of systematization. It would seem to imply the possibility of some principle that could render the How? of divine and human relatedness in mutual freedom comprehensible. It would seem to remove "the unbearable tension of the assertion that God is all in all" (III/3, 114). It would attempt to conceive of the conceptually impossible as possible. "The demand for belief in God becomes a possible one because in effect it resolves itself into the twofold invitation, to believe in the divine will and work as it is limited by the creature, and to believe in a creaturely will and work which limit the Creator." Can reducing everything to these alternatives be avoided by the internal critic? If not, then wouldn't mere formal or technical consistency have been achieved at the expense of coherence with the real subject matter of Christian theology? What kind of belief would be necessary or even possible, if God is to be subsumed within a system? What is there to believe, if the creature by nature conditions God, or if God by nature coercively determines the creature? Barth asks:

> What is there to believe? At a pinch, such a relationship could be imagined quite apart from God. But even in that form, does it really give us God when it offers us a supreme being whose will is not sovereignly executed in all the activity of the creature, whose eternal knowledge is not [God's] will and work but only the knowledge of a helpless or disinterested spectator, whose activity is "concurred" in and conditioned by that of the creature? And does it really give us the creature of God when it offers us a creature which can "concur" in the activity of God, conditioning and influencing this activity and forcing its accommodation to its own creaturely activity? And if we subject ourselves to the will of God on this presupposition, is it really the Christian obedience of faith? Is it subjection at all? Is it not another form of unbelief, and perhaps the worst form of all, seeing that it removes this serious demand? But to be fair we must admit that if the first two possibilities fall to the ground because of their manifest impiety, what is there but this third possibility with its secret impiety—always assuming, of course, that we have only that formal knowledge of God and of the will and work of God. (III/3, 114–15)

Counterquestions to the internal critic, therefore, would be epistemically coherentist in terms of Barth's scripturally based web of doctrinal beliefs. The real majesty of grace as grace, the real finitude of the creature as creature, and the real obedience of faith as faith—at least one of these basic beliefs, if not more, would seem inevitably to be jeopardized by the use of the neutral conception of coherence as a decisive criterion of doctrinal assessment.

Divine Precedence and Human Subsequence: Against Dialectical Identity

Logically speaking, there is still a way out for the internal critic.[6] The baleful consequences of Pelagianism on the one hand and determinism on the other could still be avoided without abandoning the neutral conception of incoherence and therefore without abandoning the possibility of systematization. A dialectical rather than an indeterministic or a deterministic solution could be proposed. This type of solution is associated in Barth's mind with Roman Catholicism, Lutheranism, and ultimately Augustine (II/2, 193; I/1, 199). In this solution the problem of double agency is solved by appealing to "a simultaneity, interrelation and unity in tension between divine and human determining: What is seen from one side as grace is freedom when seen from the other side and *vice versa"* (I/1, 199). In this solution, it might seem, human action is thought to coincide with the divine in much the same way that Barth suggests when describing the event of fellowship. Yet Barth rejects this proposal as vigorously as the other two.

Whereas indeterminism violates the Chalcedonian stipulation of intimacy ("without separation or division"), and determinism violates that of integrity ("without confusion or change"), the dialectical option can be interpreted as violating the stipulation of asymmetry as Barth understood it ("complete in deity and complete in humanity"). (The relationship posited by the "and" in the latter formula is to be interpreted asymmetrically.) God's (inscrutable) precedence and independence in granting the capacity actualized in fellowship is conceived as being complete, just as the human partner's (inscrutable) subsequence and dependence is also conceived as being complete. If God's conceptual precedence and the partner's conceptual subsequence were somehow less than complete, God would cease to be God, and the partner would cease to be human. God would be conditioned by a capacity in the partner, and the partner would condition God by this capacity. If divine precedence and human subsequence are complete, however, then the human partner receives a capacity that it did not bring to the event. It receives a capacity that is not given except in the event by which it is actualized. The capacity is therefore entirely a consequence of, and in no sense a condition on, grace.

The dialectical option, on the other hand, implies that the possibility of fellowship has not one but "two sources" (II/2, 193). Dialectic functions as an ordering principle by which a divine capacity for fellowship is coordinated with a human one. The two capacities are "complementary" (II/2, 193). The divine capacity to grant fellowship is, seen from another point of view, just the human capacity to receive it (and vice versa). "In this way," writes Barth, "we can, of course, coordinate above and below, receptivity and spontaneity, gift and demand, indicative and imperative, inner and outer, being and becoming (in the general neutral sense of all these conceptions)" (I/2, 791). The relationship between the two capacities has been systematized. Dialectic renders the relationship comprehensible.

The flaw seen in this conception is not primarily—as it was in the case of Pelagianism—that the human capacity conditions the divine. That flaw, of course, might also be present. If the human capacity for fellowship with God is grounded in grace alone, then it is obviously a consequence of, not a condition on, grace. If, however, the capacity is in some sense grounded in human nature (say, human nature as created), then in that sense the capacity is not entirely a consequence of the event in which fellowship is graciously actualized. In some sense it precedes the event, is presupposed by it, and to that extent conditions it. The capacity on the human side is thus in some sense the condition and not the consequence of the event. Even if (contrary to all versions of Pelagianism) the use of the capacity has been lost entirely because of sin, and even if it can only be actualized by divine grace, the capacity still does not have the logical status of an absolute miracle. It still somehow precedes, and to that extent conditions, grace in the event in which fellowship is granted. From Barth's point of view, however, even human nature as created did not in itself possess a capacity of this kind for fellowship with God but could only receive it again and again *de novo* as an absolute gift (III/2, 124–28, 157–66). Grace is thus in no way conditioned by even a "formal" capacity in the creature.

The primary flaw seen in the dialectical conception, however, is not located at this point. The primary and overriding flaw is rather that dialectic has the baleful consequence of rendering the divine and human capacities "secretly identical" (I/1, 200). The divine capability as actualized in the event of fellowship is "dialectically equated" with a capability inherent in the human creature (I/1, 199). For by definition, divine grace and human freedom have been established from the outset as virtually the same reality, seen from two different angles. "What is theologically impossible," writes Barth, "is a study of these two realities as though they are on the same plane, as though there can be between them coordination, continuity or interchange, or as though in the last resort they are somehow identical" (I/2, 790–91). Divine grace and human freedom, Barth insists, simply cannot be coordinated in this way, that is, in a relation of conceptual symmetry or interdependence. What he writes in another connection applies equally well here: "We cannot ask concerning a place where they can be seen together and understand as components, as partial forms and aspects, of one and the same reality, and therefore in the last resort as one" (IV/2, 740). "All these are ideas which are possible only on the basis of the view which ruined the old Catholic Church, that there is coordination, continuity, interchange and finally identity between 'nature' and 'supernature' " (I/2, 791). Systematic coordination is possible only for realities that are creaturely. "It may all be very true with regard to 'nature' and 'supernature.' But theology is concerned, not with the encounter between nature and supernature, but with the encounter between nature and grace, or concretely, with the encounter between the human being and the Word of God" (I/2, 791 rev.). The end result of attempting a systematic coordination based on a principle of dialectic is "a deification of the human being" (I/1, 239 rev.).

Or at least that result would be the worst conceivable. There might be another possibility. At a point, dialectic might stop short of deification by settling instead for synergism, conceived as a human cooperation with grace in some sense unconditioned by grace. It would even be "a subtle synergism—the kind which is never quite acknowledged, the reproach of which is always avoided, which is never quite clear even to those who hold it," but which results from an abstract fear of determinism that has lost "specific and concrete relation to the central point of biblical testimony" (II/2, 193–94). The central point of the testimony is, from this point of view, the essential asymmetry of the relationship between divine grace and human freedom as given in particular events unique in kind. Only when this asymmetry is duly acknowledged, can all the necessary doctrinal beliefs be maintained at one and the same time. "On this presupposition we can gladly and unhesitatingly ascribe to the divine work the honor which is due to it. It is an unconditioned and irresistible work. And the flight to synergism becomes unnecessary," for human freedom occurs entirely within, and in no sense without, its conditioning by divine grace (III/3, 144). For if the supremacy of the divine work is "the supremacy of the Word and Spirit, it does not prejudice the autonomy, the freedom, the responsibility, the individual being and life and activity of the creature, or the genuineness of its own activity, but confirms and indeed establishes them" (III/3, 144). Within the orbit of grace alone, the relationship between divine grace and human freedom "is still necessarily two-sided, and its mystery must be thought of as the mystery of the human decision as well as the divine" (II/2, 193). The mystery of an asymmetrical relationship allows what systematization prevents: coherence in a theologically meaningful sense of the term.

The Mystery of Double Agency:
Against Phenomenological Description

Two final points may be made in clarification of the theme that no nonmysterious conception of double agency is possible which would still be coherent with the full range of doctrinal beliefs as derived from scripture. First, no phenomenological description, neutral in status, can meaningfully be made (according to the logic of Barth's position) of the human contribution to the event of double agency. For no special psychological, rational, or perhaps "transcendental" condition, immanent within human nature, is necessarily presupposed in the event of fellowship by which God is known and loved. As far as knowing or loving God is concerned, any phenomenological description of the event would only bring results that are theologically uninformative. Humanity is simply presupposed in the event in the fullness of its humanity. Since the event is unique in kind, however, and therefore miraculous and mysterious, with the condition of its possibility wholly in God, no psychological, intellectual, or transcendental conditions accessible to neutral description would require special consideration, not if one is really interested in the event as it gives itself to faith and not perhaps to sight (cf. IV/1, 741). Nontheological anthropologies are not thereby consigned to "a night in which all cats are gray," for that is a separate question entirely. They may be judged, on the basis of theological anthropology, as being more or less compatible with the latter without ever being thought to become identical with it (III/2, 71–132). They might even spark insights which theology could appreciate in the mode of assimilation. Even at best, however, they cannot directly contribute to our knowledge of the relevant conditions that make possible the event in which God is known and loved.[7]

From the beginning of the *Church Dogmatics* to the end, Barth not surprisingly took this position, since it was the only one that could have been taken consistently, given the themes of particularism and actualism. There is no need, he wrote, "to claim, discover or assert any unusual or hidden anthropological centers as the basis for the possibility of human experience in God's Word"—and the same may as well have been said of human freedom (I/1, 203). The relevant conditions are just not accessible to neutral description, and what is so accessible is always ambiguous. "Is it not the case that we do not see or grasp the possibility at all in this process itself, which might as such be very different from that possibility?" (I/1, 216). Neutral description cannot illumine the reality of faith but only the uncertainty of the phenomena. "We have seen that the act of acknowledging the Word of God, so far as its immanence in the consciousness can be established from outside, historico-psychologically, by observation of ourselves or others, cannot even be characterized unequivocally as this act, let alone known in its relation to the Word of God" (I/1, 223). The miracle and the mystery of faith are themselves articles of faith and are not otherwise accessible to description. From a neutral point of view, "all that can be established are human possibilities

in immovable promixity and indissoluble similarity to other possibilities"
(I/1, 223). The possibility of faith rests not in human existence as phe-
nomenologically describable, but wholly and invisibly in God. "Real acknowledgement of the Word of God does not rest at all on a possibility
imparted to human existence and thus integral to it or immanent in it, but
in God's Word itself, which human existence and its possibilities can in
no sense precede but only follow" (I/1, 223 rev.).

This theme at the very beginning of the nearly ten thousand pages
that constitute the extended argument of the *Church Dogmatics* reappears
toward the very end (and does not disappear in between). In discussing
"the event of vocation," the question of phenomenological description
again needs to be asked. Is there an *ordo salutis*—"a logical and tem-
porally differentiated series of acts in the history of salvation enacted in
and on a person, or a way of salvation to be taken in ever deeper and
broader and more powerful experiences" (IV/3, 505 rev.)? (A succes-
sor to the old Protestant-scholastic idea of an *ordo salutis* is sometimes
called "faith development" today. From the standpoint of Barth's theology, "faith development" would have nothing to do with what the Bible
calls faith, but merely with the psychological development of the faithful.
It might thereby prove useful and interesting, in certain settings, but would
have no direct bearing on the subject matter of Holy Scripture as the
central preoccupation of the church.) Does the event of vocation fall into
"an order of salvation"? Can it be described in neutral terms as a temporal and historical process? Is there a human standpoint from which "it
might be divided into a series of successive events in which each is sup-
plemented and transcended by the next"? Is there "a kind of ladder, a
psychological genetics of the Christian state" in which "vocation as the
first and lowest rung would bring us to the initial point of its genesis"
(IV/3, 505)?

"We are well advised," remarks Barth, "not to embark on this venture" (IV/3, 506). A neutral, phenomenological description of the process of salvation—"a psychological and biographical description of the
evolution of the Christian"—would fail to respect "its truly spiritual
character." Any attempt to reinterpret salvation so as "to make it more
readily perceptible and manageable in practice" could take place only
"at the expense of its truly spiritual character." "The Bible does not
offer any such schema," "the biblical witnesses were not interested in
the process as a psychological and biographical evolution," and "in this
respect, important though it no doubt was, they had nothing to say." The
concepts used by the biblical witnesses have to be pressed and extended

"intolerably . . . to work them up into such a scheme. For the concepts are inevitably weakened and devalued when they are wrested as is done in attempts of this nature" (IV/3, 506).

The essence of vocation—its radical newness, its unparalleled task of witness, its incomparable goal of fellowship with God, its miracle and mystery—can by way of neutral phenomenological description never come into view. "The very question answered by this whole attempt implies an attack on the substance of a genuine understanding of the process of vocation. For it directs our attention away from that which in this process is done on and in the person by God, by Jesus Christ and by the Holy Spirit" (IV/3, 507 rev.). It does not think concretely on the basis of the actual event as known and confessed by faith in conformity to the witness of scripture. "It turns abstractly to the reflection of this act of God and Christ in the person, to the person's Christian experiences and states." Salvation in the unity and totality of its concrete integrity as centered on Christ has been overlooked. "When we are guilty of this abstraction, and project the concepts on this level, we have already turned away from the Lord and his salvation in its unity and totality. . . . The relevant and important thing is no longer God's active dealing with the person, but in isolation and independence the active dealing of the person with God" (IV/3, 507 rev.). The truly spiritual character of the event eludes the method of neutral description, and necessarily so. "What place is left in this picture for the truly spiritual nature of the process of salvation? We can find no answer to this question, and therefore we must tread a very different path in our understanding of this process" (IV/3, 507). The path then trodden was centered, as shown earlier, noetically on the objective moment of salvation (as accomplished in and by Jesus Christ), and practically on the task of witness (in fellowship with the risen Christ engaged in his prophetic work), not on the "experiental" benefits of salvation. Vocation was thus described in essentially spiritual rather than neutral terms.

The Mystery of Double Agency:
Its Fulfillment in Prayer

If the idea of an *ordo salutis* represents a nonmysterious description of salvation that overlooks the true dynamics of the event of double agency as Barth conceives it, the idea of prayer represents the mysterious conception at its very epitome and height. Prayer in all the richness and complexity in which Barth understands it cannot be explored here. It can be mentioned only as it bears on the question of double agency, and even then only at the high point rather than in the ascending argument of the exposition. Prayer in Barth's theology is conceived as the deepest moment in the intimacy of fellowship between the human being and God. Prayer is not conceived as a means to the end of achieving ecstatic experiences. Nor is it conceived as being merely an exercise by which a dispositional or even a truly spiritual change is wrought in the believer. Prayer is not regarded as significant essentially for the transformation it may bring subjectively on the human side.

After all the repeated and perhaps unsurpassable emphasis on the theme that God by nature is not and cannot be conditioned by the creature, it would be well to note an important and characteristic counteremphasis. It pertains to what is actual and possible, not by nature but by grace. "On the basis of the freedom of God himself," writes Barth, "God is conditioned by the prayer of faith" (II/1, 510–11). Prayer thus has not merely a subjective but primarily an "objective bearing" (III/3, 284). God is and wills to be known as the One who comes to the aid of the creature, as a helper in time of trouble and a friend in the midst of need. "God is and wills to be known as the One who will and does listen to the prayers of faith" (II/1, 510).

All this is understood as taking place not against but within the framework established by the conception of double agency. "There is no creaturely freedom which can limit or compete with the sole sovereignty and efficacy of God. But permitted by God, and indeed willed and created by him, there is the freedom of the friends of God concerning whom he has determined that without abandoning the helm for one moment he will still allow himself to be determined by them" (III/3, 285). God is "not the prisoner of his own resolve and will and action." God is rather "free and immutable as the living God, as the God who wills to converse with the creature, and to allow himself to be determined by it in this relationship." God is thus "moved and affected" by the faithful creature at prayer, conversing with it and listening to what it says. In an act of "incomprehensible hearing," God does not exercise sovereignty without sharing it and so displays "incomprehensible grace" (III/3, 285).

> Again it is quite inconceivable that this new and special characteristic should be the distinctive mark of the order of grace, that God's hearing prayer and granting this activity to the creature should belong to his dealings with the sinful world, and that it should be sinful human beings whom God should raise to such an unheard of dignity and function as they are awakened to faith and enabled to be vigilant in faith. But its inconceivability is no reason

why we should deny prayer is heard or even forget it or treat it as something which is dispensable or inessential to faith. For what is inconceivable is God's grace. But faith cannot try to live by anything but by God's inconceivable grace in its fullness and totality. It can will only to be obedient to grace, fully obedient, however inconceivable this may seem to it. It is therefore essential for faith to be faith in the God who listens to prayer. (II/1, 512 rev.)

Summary: Double Agency and the Question of Coherence

To sum up: Barth's conception of double agency is dominated by the Chalcedonian pattern. This pattern establishes not only the conception itself, but also, by implication, the counterpositions to be ruled out. The conception itself posits a relationship of asymmetry, intimacy, and integrity between God and the human being. It posits a fellowship of mutual coinherence and mutual self-giving, mediated in and by Jesus Christ. This fellowship occurs as an absolute miracle, because it subjects the human being to a kind of *Aufhebung*. The human being is affirmed in wholeness, canceled in sin and mere finitude, and taken up into an inconceivable fellowship of participation in the eternal life of God. The fellowship therefore also occurs as an absolute mystery, because it draws the human being into an event that is unique in kind and that thus surpasses all understanding. The majesty of the God whose grace is sovereign, unconditioned, and irresistible; the radical sinfulness of the human being whose sinfulness provides no ultimate barrier to the fellowship established by grace; the finitude of the human being who can in no way condition God or enter into fellowship with God on the basis of an immanent or neutrally describable capacity; the true freedom of the human being in prayer and fellowship and witness through faith by grace alone— these are some of the basic and relevant doctrinal beliefs understood to be required by scripture and to be organized along Chalcedonian lines. The miracle and mystery of double agency is thus understood to be patterned after the great miracle and mystery of the Incarnation, in which the former finds its basis, limit, and final hope.

The charge of incoherence, based on a neutral conception of formal logic, was suggested to be more problematic than might be apparent at first glance. Making the neutral conception a decisive criterion of doctrinal assessment would seem to commit an internal critic to some baleful form of systematization. Indeterminism, determinism, and dialectical identity would seem to exhaust the logical types within which a systematized account of the event of double agency would have to fall. None of these three logical types, however, can be made fully coherent with the body of basic and relevant doctrinal beliefs which constitute the subject matter of theology as derived from scripture. Indeterminism exalts the creature at the expense of God; determinism exalts God at the expense of the creature; and dialectical identity exalts the two at the expense of each other (insofar as the creature is divinized or God is humanized as the cost of systematic coordination). Coherence is thus shown to be a context-dependent rather than a context-neutral term for which the basic choice in theological construction is either to adopt the logic of an explanatory system or to describe the logic of a specifiable mystery—or so all these matters would appear from within the framework of Karl Barth's theology.

Christ the Center

Realism and rationalism have emerged from this study as the foundational motifs of Barth's theology. As the motifs which govern truth as correspondence and truth as coherence, they provide faith with various methods by which to derive, test, and explicate its basic doctrinal beliefs. Realism provides a method of reading scripture which allows for analogical reference, both intratextually and extratextually. It allows faith to derive its basic beliefs from scripture while avoiding the pitfalls of nonanalogical (literalist and expressivist) interpretations. Scripture as read realistically by faith is the ultimate court of appeal for all doctrinal disputes. Rationalism presupposes realism in the sense that its meditation on the internal coherence of doctrinal beliefs presupposes the reality and truth of those beliefs in their extratextual analogical reference. Internal coherence as a method of testing the validity of doctrinal beliefs is therefore understood primarily in a material rather than in a merely formal or technical sense.

Doctrinal beliefs must first cohere with the events attested in scripture (as realistically read). They are therefore primarily hermeneutical in force, and are primarily accorded the logical status of descriptions of events. Only in a secondary sense, however prominent it may be, are these beliefs considered to be inferences which display the conceptual presuppositions and implications of these events. Hermeneutical adequacy is conceptually more important for the doctrinal beliefs than complete technical consistency among themselves. The peculiar nature of the events that doctrinal beliefs must conceptually redescribe is such as to require conceptions which assume an irresolvably antithetical form. If the antithetical form were to be resolved for the sake of achieving mere formal consistency among the beliefs themselves, the result would be a set of abstractions which no longer corresponded to the events. Coherence thus presupposes correspondence in a strong sense. Correspondence takes precedence over coherence whenever coherence in itself would strive for a maximal satisfaction at the expense of correspondence. For it is the correspondence which makes the coherence theologically meaningful. The same thing can be said more aphoristically (and with apologies to Emerson): technical consistency is the hobgoblin of theological minds. Or so it appears Barth would have us believe. And of course, not entirely implausibly, he thinks that is what the New Testament would require of us when read in realistic terms.

Actualism and particularism, furthermore, have emerged from this study as structural motifs in Barth's theology. As the motifs which govern truth as event and truth as unique in kind, they do not stand on their own so much as they pervade and structure the other motifs. Actualism, for its part, would seem especially to structure the motifs of realism, objectivism, and personalism. Truth as correspondence, truth as objectively mediated in revelation and salvation, and truth as encounter are all described as events in the special actualistic sense. They are all essentially (not just secondarily) miracles, and they are all not just miracles but absolute miracles. They are miracles in a way that cannot finally be denoted by any concept of miracle. Truth as correspondence is an actualistic event, because no human language in itself is adequate to cross the ontological divide and to function referringly in relation to God. The possibility of reference lies entirely with God, and God grants the condition which our language lacks in order that it may assume this function. The granting of the condition may perhaps be thought of as both de jure and de facto. On this assumption Barth would be saying that the language of the church as based on scripture has received a de jure referential function that still needs to be actualized de facto from one situation to the next, and that it is the de facto actualization which is decisive. Without the assumption of de jure reference, however, it would be difficult to see how the language of scripture could be regarded as the *norma normans non normata*.

Truth as objectively mediated in revelation and salvation is also an actualistic event. The objective means of revelation and the objective means of salvation are to all appearances merely creaturely, yet in both cases they secretly enclose the divine self-enactment in our midst. The divine work of revelation and salvation is enacted objectively, not only with respect to the means, but also with respect to the status of the enactment. The work of revelation and salvation is regarded as valid and effective in status regardless of whether it is acknowledged or received. Again, perhaps a distinction between de jure and de facto would clarify how matters are to be interpreted. Validity and effectiveness would then be conceived as already decisively in force de jure, and as manifesting themselves, penultimately and ultimately, de facto in a variety of different forms. Such a distinction is regularly used in Barth's discussion of salvation and may be regarded as implicit in his conception of revelation.

Whereas the conception of *Aufhebung* would seem to be implicit in the event of truth as correspondence, the conception of dialectical inclusion would seem to be implicit in that of truth as mediated. In the event of correspondence, human language is affirmed, canceled, and reconstituted on a higher plane. It effectively transcends itself by the miracle of grace. In the event of mediation, a complex temporality is assumed in which the whole is somehow (that is, in various forms) included in each part without making any part superfluous. The whole is already valid, effective, and complete in such a way that it is yet to be valid, effective, and complete ever anew; as such it becomes present in various forms even now. Barth's much lamented fascination with primal beginnings needs to be reconsidered in light of a close reading of how the pattern of dialectical inclusion coalesces with the actualist motif. The conception of divine and human temporality, it may be suggested, is much more complicated, much more interesting, and much more profound in Barth's theology than has usually been recognized. The eschatology is more robust, furthermore, because the overall pattern by which it is governed is much more deeply trinitarian, in a dynamic and *perichoretic* sense, than has yet been appreciated. The event of truth as mediated, so that it is already valid and effective in itself, could be fully explicated only within the context of the conception of temporality—a discussion beyond the scope of this study.

Truth as encounter is again conceived as an actualistic event. The complex temporality by which truth is mediated leads to an encounter with the truth in the present that is wholly self-involving. The self-involvement itself, however, takes place differently in penultimate than in ultimate form. In penultimate form the self-involvement is dominated by the task of witness as it occurs in a fellowship of action and suffering. In an ultimate form prefigured by the first, it is seen as a fellowship of eternal life and an eternal life of fellowship—a relationship of mutual self-giving in patterns of love and freedom. In ultimate perhaps as well as penultimate form, it is conceived as a fellowship that is never past except in such a way that it is also always future. In penultimate form, at least, it is conceived as needing to be sought and received (in connection with disciplines and practices of the spiritual life) ever anew. It is conceived, that is, according to the pattern of the actualist motif.

Particularism, for its part, would seem especially to structure the motifs of rationalism, objectivism, and personalism. Truth as coherence, truth as mediated, and truth as encounter are all structured by truth as unique in kind. Truth as coherence must allow itself to be limited at the decisive point by truth as unique in kind and therefore by concepts irresolvably antithetical in form. Truth as mediated and encountered, moreover, is essentially (not just secondarily) mysterious, and not just mysterious but absolutely so. It is mysterious in a way that cannot finally be denoted by any concept of mystery. Truth as coherence is decisively limited by truth as unique in kind, because coherence presupposes correspondence with events that are comprehensible only in their incomprehensibility. Truth as mediated and encountered, moreover, is essentially mysterious in content even as it is also essentially miraculous in form. The mystery of truth as mediated is the mystery of the Incarnation, and the mystery of truth as encountered is the mystery of fellowship. The Incarnation is the great mystery which grounds and patterns the mystery of fellowship in which the great mystery finds secondary reiteration. The great mystery is that of the objective enactment of divine self-revelation and human salvation. Its secondary reiteration is the mystery of the acknowledgment and personal reception of that which has been objectively enacted, and the mystery of fellowship with the absolute sovereign who enacted it. These mysteries are themselves structured by the Chalcedonian pattern, as shown at some length in the case of fellowship, as an instance of double agency; when seen as a whole, their temporal relationship is structured, in a way that could be barely suggested, by the trinitarian pattern of dialectical inclusion. In all cases the divine crossing of the ontological divide in order to establish an ontological connection with us is understood as an absolutely miraculous event whose truth is absolutely mysterious in content and therefore can only be conceived as unique in kind.

Objectivism and personalism, finally—as grounded in the foundational motifs of realism and rationalism, and as informed by the structural motifs of actualism and particularism—might be thought of as the freestanding motifs in Barth's theology. They are the bearers of its essential content. The objective takes place for the sake of the personal, and the personal takes place on the presupposition of the objective. The metaphor by which their relationship is illuminated is primarily that of the center and the periphery. The objective is the center. It is the decisive locus of revelation and salvation. Its truth so avails and prevails that its periphery cannot fail, in one way or another, to be established. The personal is the periphery. Its truth is that of the center. It is not the decisive locus of revelation and salvation. Yet in the revelation and salvation of the center, the personal is not excluded but included. It is included miraculously and mysteriously, for the center is miraculous and mysterious. The truth of the center thus becomes the truth of the periphery in a way for which the metaphor breaks down. For the truth of the center so implicates itself in the periphery, and the periphery is so implicated in the truth of the center, that the center in the periphery does not cease to be the center, while the periphery in the center is enhanced inconceivably beyond itself without ceasing to be, precisely, the periphery of this center.

It remains only to indicate briefly that Jesus Christ is the center of the motifs. They are all descriptive of him. With him in mind they are meant to be instructive and thought-provoking. Without him they are meant to be nothing. They are of no interest in and of themselves, but only as they point to him. Only as they point to him are they meant to be used; but if they do point to him, and thereby enlarge the understanding and devotion of faith, it is thought to be enough. "To look to him is to see him at the very center, to see him and the history which, accomplished in him, heals everything and all things, as the mystery, reality, origin and goal of the whole world, all human beings, all life" (IV/4, 150 rev.).

Jesus Christ is the center of the foundational motifs. Realism and rationalism indicate no truth as correspondence or as coherence which does not originally and finally center in him. He is the center of the realist motif, because he is regarded as the center of scripture. He is the center which illuminates the whole, and the whole finds its meaning and unity only as it refers to him. "He is the One who is visible, who makes himself visible, in the documents of this whole historical nexus" (IV/3, 44). No analogical reference to him can be true which abstracts from the content of his scriptural picture, but the picture can be true only by reference in analogical form. "It is he who lives, not the picture. But he himself lives only in the form which he has in the picture. For it is not a picture arbitrarily invented and constructed by others. It is the picture which he himself has created and impressed upon his witnesses" (IV/3, 44). The language of scripture as realistically read is therefore the indispensable vehicle of reference to the risen Christ.

Jesus Christ is the center of the rationalist motif, because he is regarded as the Word and therefore the rationality of God. "God alone is truly rational" (II/1, 328), and since he himself is the Logos of God, the divine rationality is made manifest in him. It is because he is the rationality of God that the divine revelation "has the character of knowledge," that it "has a rational character" (IV/2, 412). It is because he is the rationality of God that faith must seek understanding, attending "to what is denoted" by the biblical witness, pressing on "to the point of exhausting its knowability and therefore our own possibility of knowing what we say when we are not silent concerning it, . . . but try to say something about it" (III/3, 373). It is because he is the rationality of God that doctrines may legitimately be derived and tested. "Believing in Jesus Christ, the Christian enters into a given presupposition, and now draws out the deductions implicit in that presupposition, but implicit only as deductions" (III/3, 248 rev.). It is because God addresses us as rational creatures in him that we may confidently use our powers of reason in theological hearing and obedience (III/4, 328).

Jesus Christ is also the center of the structural motifs. Actualism and particularism indicate that there is no truth as event or as unique in kind which does not originally and finally center in him. He is the center of the actualist motif, because his history is the miracle of God. His history is a "self-multiplying history" (IV/3, 212). It has happened once and for all, but it has not therefore ceased to happen. It is "not enclosed or confined" to the past (IV/2, 107). "This history is present. . . . And it has also a forward reference. It is still future and will still happen—'even unto the end of the world' " (IV/2, 107). Jesus Christ lives as the Crucified who was raised from the dead. "That Jesus Christ lives also tells us, however, that his existence is act; that it is being in spontaneous actualization" (IV/3, 40). He lives in spontaneous divine actualization. "Primarily and supremely we have again to say *actus purus,* the actualization of being in an absolutely sovereign spontaneity, after the manner in which the Creator, God, actualizes himself, so that his life-action is identical with that of God himself, his history with the divine history" (IV/3, 40). His being in act is at the same time the prototype for all creaturely being as manifested in him. "Again, however, we must add that the actualization is also after the manner in which it is given to the creature to actualize itself, to exist historically in its conditioned and limited spontaneity. This is its existence as life in particular; actual existence; existence in fulfillment." The two life acts united in him, that of God and that of the creature, are held together by the Chalcedonian pattern. "As Jesus lives, there takes place in him both creative actualization of being, yet also in and with it creaturely actualization; creative and creaturely life together, without the transformation of the one into the other, the admixture of the one with the other, or separation or division between them. This is how Jesus Christ is seen and attested in Scripture" (IV/3, 40). The actualization of creaturely being as such at the periphery derives from and in its own way reiterates the actualization of creaturely being in union with the divine at the center in the person of Jesus Christ.

Jesus Christ is the center of the particularist motif, moreover, because he is the mystery of God. That he is truly and really the Word become flesh is "absolutely the sole point in which the New Testament witness originates" (I/2, 124). No "higher vantage point" is to be sought, because none is to be found. It is the only place from which one can start; it is strictly originative and in no sense derivative. "Whatever we think or say about it can only be with the aim of describing it again and again as a mystery. . . . At all costs we must make it clear that an ultimate mystery is involved here. It can be contemplated, acknowledged, worshiped and confessed as such, but it cannot be solved, or transformed into a non-mystery" (I/2, 124–25). The language of theology must therefore "be determined entirely by the unique object in question" (I/2, 125). It is the uniqueness of the object which requires the procedure of moving from the particular to the general. "We must realize that the Christian message does not at its heart express a concept or an idea, nor does it recount an anonymous history to be taken as truth and reality only in concepts and ideas" (IV/1, 16). On the contrary, it "declares a name," binds everything "strictly and indissolubly to this name," and presents its message "as the story of the bearer of this name." "This means that all the concepts and ideas used in this report (God, humanity, world, eternity, time, even salvation, grace, transgression, atonement and any others) can derive their significance only from the bearer of this name and not the reverse" (IV/1, 16 rev.). No independent meaning of any such ideas can be allowed to control the discussion. "They cannot say what has to be said with some meaning of their own or in some context of their own abstracted from this name. They can serve only to describe this name—the name of Jesus Christ" (IV/1, 16–17). The uniqueness of the object thus requires a particularist use of terms—reformist, antithetical, diversified.

Jesus Christ, finally, is the center of the freestanding motifs. Objectivism and personalism indicate that there is no truth as mediated or as encountered which does not originally and finally center in him. He is the center of the objectivist motif, because he is the Mediator of the truth of God with us and of us with God. That he is indeed the Word become flesh means, from the standpoint of revelational objectivism, that he is "the first, original and controlling sign of all signs" (II/1, 199). He is "the great possibility, created by God himself," by which God may be known and conceived and articulated. For as we creatures "view and conceive" Jesus Christ, so we can speak of God. We cannot do so "without the veil, and therefore without the reservation of his hiddenness," but with that veil and reservation we can indeed do so. "In his revelation, in Jesus Christ, the hidden God has indeed made himself apprehensible. Not directly but indirectly. Not to sight but to faith. Not in his being, but in sign. Not, then, by the dissolution of his hiddenness—but apprehensibly" (II/1, 199). But indirectly, by sign and to faith, the objectivity of God is objectively mediated and revealed in Jesus Christ.

That he is indeed the Word become flesh means, moreover, from the standpoint of soteriological objectivism, that in and by him "the new reality of world history" has already come into being (IV/3, 712). Faith "does not see in Jesus only what might be, or ought to be, or one day will be; it sees what is, what has come into being in him and by him" (IV/3, 713). It sees that in him "the absolutely new thing," the divine work of salvation, has come to pass. He is the objective center of the salvation which is real, hidden, yet to come, and universal in scope. The community "can and must keep to the fact that what has happened in him has the dignity, power and validity of the first and last thing in world-occurrence. Hidden though it may be from the world and even the community, it will come to light as the reality of all history" (IV/3, 713). What will emerge is he himself as the center of all things rather than any of the other matters which may partially claim the attention of the community and which wholly claim the attention of the world (IV/3, 713). The complex and self-transcending event of salvation (an event which in its unity has three distinct tenses) has already occurred in him.

That Jesus Christ is indeed the Word become flesh means, finally, from the standpoint of personalism, that "this happening has as such a voice. It is a declaration" (IV/3, 83). It is a Word with the contours of a cross, and it encounters us as a personal address. "And as it comes to us, it is an address, promise and demand, a question and answer. . . . It encounters us, speaks with us, addresses us in terms of I and Thou" (IV/3, 83). He himself, his history as it centers in the cross, is at the heart of the encounter in which all human self-sufficiency is shattered and God's "contradiction of our contradiction" is known to be "effective" (II/2, 752). From the standpoint of personal self-involvement, this recognition takes place finally in prayer. "In actual fact, it can be achieved only in prayer. . . . The point is neither remote nor unattainable so long as we pray, and believe as we pray, and in faith participate in the death of Jesus Christ, and in this participation abandon every other life" but that of the fellowship in action and suffering to which we are called by him (II/2, 752).

In short, as the living reality to whom his scriptural depiction analogically points, and as the divine rationality by whom the understanding sought by faith is warranted, Jesus Christ is the center of the foundational motifs. As the event of the absolute miracle of grace and as the absolute mystery of its content, Jesus Christ is the center of the structural motifs. And as the objective Mediator of revelation and salvation, in whom the truth of God may be known and the reality of humanity found, and as the Word of personal address encountered in fellowship, attested in witness and appropriated by prayer, he is the center of the freestanding motifs. Realism, rationalism, actualism, particularism, objectivism, and personalism, as they shape Karl Barth's theology, are directed toward Christ the center.

EPILOGUE

Secular Parables
of the Truth

"Whenever . . . we meet with heathen writers," wrote John Calvin, "let us learn from the light of truth which is admirably displayed in their works, that the human mind, fallen as it is, and corrupted from its integrity, is yet invested and adorned by God with excellent talents. If we believe that the Spirit of God is the only fountain of truth, we shall neither reject nor despise the truth itself, wherever it shall appear, unless we wish to insult the Spirit of God."[1] Karl Barth's inquiry into "secular parables of the truth," as found in volume 4, part 3, of *Church Dogmatics,* might well be regarded as an extensive commentary on this passage from Calvin's *Institutes.*[2] Salient differences between the two are of course immediately apparent. Where Calvin speaks of "the Spirit of God," Barth prefers to speak of "the prophetic work of Jesus Christ;" where Calvin speaks of the human *mind* being invested and adorned with "excellent talents," Barth prefers to speak instead of human *words* being invested and adorned, miraculously, with a capacity they do not intrinsically possess. Yet Barth shares a number of emphases with Calvin. He too believes that, despite the human mind's being fallen and corrupted from its integrity, truth is still to be found and admired in writers ignorant of or hostile toward the Gospel. And he too affirms that suppositions to the contrary would fail to honor God properly, since there is and can be only one fountain of truth. To be sure, Barth addresses a different set of questions insofar as he defines christologically a problem that Calvin had defined anthropologically. Barth's problem is not (as it had been for Calvin) how to explain the occurrence of truth in heathen writers, given the magnitude of the fall, so much as it is to explain that phenomenon, given the

234

sheer exclusivity of truth in Jesus Christ. Barth's reasoning shows that it would be a mistake to conclude, as is too often done by superficial readers of his theology, that his exclusivist christology is incompatible with recognizing truth (i.e., theological truth) in non-Christian sources and writers.

This chapter will attempt to do two things. First, a close reading will be offered of the section where Barth presents his idea of "secular parables of the truth." Second, the material will be interpreted here and there by using the various motifs and patterns that have been explicated elsewhere in this work. In this way, it is hoped, the analytical apparatus as previously developed will continue to show its usefulness, while at the same time Barth's conception of truth will be rounded out by paying attention to one of its features which, while undeniably basic, has not yet been discussed in these pages.

The caption or programmatic summary which Barth customarily places over the major divisions of his *Church Dogmatics* is this time taken from the first article of the "Barmen Declaration": "Jesus Christ as attested to us in Holy Scripture is the one Word of God whom we must hear and whom we must trust and obey in life and in death."[3] What precisely does it mean to say that Jesus Christ is "the one Word of God"? This far-reaching question (which dominates the entire division, not just the small portion to be studied here) is answered within the framework of a deceptively simple distinction. What it comes to Jesus Christ as the one Word of God, event is distinguished from word, history from attestation, and life from light. The aspects of event, history, and life are accorded a subtle priority over those of word, attestation, and light, even though both are said to exist together in indissoluble unity. The larger distinction between reconciliation and revelation is informed by this differentiated unity. The occurrence of *reconciliation* is a matter of the event, history, and life of Jesus Christ, while the occurrence of *revelation* is a matter of his word, attestation, and light. The two occurrences are really one in him, and he himself is the agent of each. "As the reconciliation is his work, so is its revelation, in its past and present and future occurrence. As the reconciliation takes place in him, its revelation takes place through him" (pp. 38–39). Reconciliation does not occur in its own right without its at the same time having the character of revelation. As Barth succinctly sums it up: "The occurrence itself is also speech" (p. 38).

This conception of reconciliation as *also* revelation finds not only its background but also the condition for its possibility in Barth's understanding of the person of Christ in conjunction with his conception of eternity. For the sake of clarity, it will be helpful to sketch this background in. Although the idea of secular parables does not emerge in this particular material, this material is everywhere in the background when the discussion turns to secular parables. That is, Barth's discussion of secular parables presupposes his conception of reconciliation as revelation, which in turn presupposes certain larger and more difficult ideas about the person of Christ in conjunction with eternity. It will therefore behoove us to proceed somewhat circuitously as follows. First, the mystery of Christ's person in conjunction with the mystery of eternity will be sketched in as background, insofar as these bear upon the question of reconciliation as also revelation. Then the question of secular parables will be taken up as the foreground by which this background is presupposed. In choosing this roundabout route from background to foreground, we will be not only retracing the steps taken by Barth's own presentation, but also following a path that will eventually (if perhaps not immediately) make sense in and of itself.

The first step, then, is to ask about the mystery of Christ's person in conjunction with the mystery of eternity. The logic of Barth's position, in an initial approximation, may be said to go something like this: Jesus Christ lives as a person with a particular history. There is a twofold emphasis to be seen here. Jesus Christ lives as a person *with a particular history*. Without this particular history, he would not and could not be the Reconciler. Jesus Christ *lives* as a person with a particular history. Without his being alive in the way that he is, he would not and could not be the Revealer. His history, conceived as the occurrence of reconciliation, can also be revelation, precisely because he is uniquely the one who lives. As the one who uniquely lives, he discloses himself as the one in whose history reconciliation has occurred. His history is thus doubly important. He lives as the one who identifies himself *by means of* this history, and this history is the *content* of his self-identification. The miracle of revelation is precisely the miracle of the word which attests and illumines this history as the history of reconciliation that it is.

The miracle of revelation, as it attests and illumines the history of reconciliation, thus depends for its intelligibility on what it means to say that *Jesus Christ lives*. Again we may notice a twofold emphasis. It is *Jesus Christ* who lives. Jesus Christ is the person who at once exists in the manner of God and yet also in the manner of a human being. Existing in the manner of God, he exists with a kind of transcendental priority. That is, he exists "prior to all else that exists, not grounded upon any other, referred to no other existence or support, in unconditional freedom and power" (p. 39). Yet in the manner of a human being, he also exists with a kind of immanent contingency. That is, he exists "like all other created beings, in the freedom and power of such a being as divinely determined and limited, in the relative dependence of a single member in the natural and historical nexus of the created world" (p. 39). The co-existence of these two sets of predicates (divine and human) in a single subject is, as Barth understands it, the supreme mystery of the Christian faith. Its terms can be described, but its occurrence defies, inevitably, explanation by means of some larger conceptual pattern or scheme.

Indeed, it is the mystery of the person of Jesus Christ which sets the terms within which all else is to be explained or understood. Nothing is to be conceived—and this is a basic rule governing all of Barth's later theology—as existing except as together with him. "The Creator, God himself, exists only as he does so together with this One who also exists as human being, and each and everything in the created world exists only together with this One who also exists as human being" (p. 39 rev.). Jesus Christ is, in other words, the grand Mediator *in whom,* as it were, all "externalities" are to be conceived as existing in a complex web of "internal relations." Jesus Christ—in all his concrete and unique partic-ularity—assumes in Barth's theology a role that might otherwise be taken over by a universal or metaphysical scheme: "As God exists only to-gether with this One, and so too the world, *his* [Jesus Christ's] *existence as such is the fact* in which God and the world, however they may oppose or contradict one another, are not of course one and the same, but do exist together in an inviolable and indissoluble co-existence and conjunc-tion" (pp. 39–40, emphasis added). Insofar as metaphysics sets out to interpret the relationship between God and the world, this conception of the Mediator might be regarded as a "metaphysics of the particular." Yet insofar as metaphysics is thought to rest on the speculations of un-aided reason, the conception might better be regarded as the abolition of metaphysics altogether. In any case, neither God's reality nor the world's is to be conceived as existing apart from its mediation by the concrete particularity of Jesus Christ.

It will be evident, drawing from the earlier exposition, that among other things both the Chalcedonian and trinitarian *formal* patterns are at work in this conception of Jesus Christ as the Mediator. In him (the Mediator) all relations between God and the world are thought to subsist along lines which parallel and recapitulate the Chalcedonian mystery. As subsisting in the Mediator, there can be between God and the world no identity or sameness ("without confusion or change"), and yet their coexistence is indissoluble ("without separation or division"), while at the same time God properly retains his transcendental priority and the world its immanent contingency ("distinctive ordering"). The familiar pattern which describes the person of Jesus Christ in particular is, by correspondence and extension, the very pattern which describes all relations more generally between God and the world, for *all* such relations are inviolably and indissolubly centered in and mediated by him.

Inscribed within this "Chalcedonian" mystery is yet another *formal* pattern—the one previously designated as "trinitarian," namely, the (mysterious) pattern of "dialectical inclusion." For not only are God and the world thought of as being dialectically included in the Mediator, but in and through the Mediator they are thought of as being dialectically included in one another as well. In Jesus Christ the Mediator, a great catena of relations is thought to subsist in which the whole is always (dialectically) in the part and the part in the whole, without either losing its distinctivenesss. All relations between God and the world in Jesus Christ are ultimately conceived, in one way or another, as relations of "coinherence" or of mutual, inner participation.

Indeed, Jesus Christ is himself conceived as the "center" coinherent (always in a differentiated, appropriate way) in every "part" (or, perhaps better, in every "term" of relation), and each and every "part" (or relational "term") is likewise conceived as coinherent in him in an appropriate (and thus dialectical) way. To refine the "rule" formulated earlier: nothing is to be conceived in which Jesus Christ is not somehow coinherent and which in turn is not somehow coinherent in him. Whereas the earlier formulation of this "rule" concerned the sheer *fact* of coexistence, its refinement has to do with coinherence as the *mode* by which all things coexist in and with Jesus Christ. These patterns of mutual coexistence and coinherence (as governed by the Chalcedonian mystery), this intricate network of internal relations, is (in part) what Barth means by "The Glory of the Mediator" (the title of this entire major division of IV/3).

In light of this depiction of Jesus Christ's *person* as the glorious Mediator, we may return to ask in a new way what it means to say that he *lives*. Barth's leading idea might now be stated like this: the life which Jesus Christ enacts is always an eternal life lived in indissoluble connection with a particular history. The complex temporality implicit in this statement could be (and, over the course of the *Church Dogmatics,* actually is) developed with reference to the pretemporal, posttemporal, supratemporal, and temporal aspects of the life of the Mediator. For our purposes, however, the statement may usefully be glossed in two directions. First, it means that Jesus Christ always lives as one whose life is in act. The active character of his life needs to be stressed, especially in an exposition like this one which works with formal patterns so extensively. In and of themselves patterns like the Chalcedonian and the trinitarian could easily become misleading, if the relations they sought to describe were to be regarded not only as formal but also as static. In Barth's theology, however, the formal, dialectical relations described by these patterns are always regarded as active rather than static. The active character of these relations is brought out with regard to both the patterns mentioned.

The relations described by the Chalcedonian pattern are explicitly conceived as active relations. The being of Jesus Christ is said to be a "being in spontaneous actualization" (p. 40). As the concrete individual who exists at once in a divine and yet also a human manner, the spontaneity with which he actualizes his being is at once "absolutely sovereign" and yet also "conditioned and limited." His life action is "identical with that of God himself" yet also with that of a human "life in particular." "As Jesus Christ lives, there takes place in him both creative [divine] actualization of being, yet also in and with it creaturely actualization; creative and creaturely life together, without the transformation of the one into the other, the admixture of the one with the other, or separation or division between them" (p. 40). No doubt can exist that the person of Christ, as described formally by the Chalcedonian pattern, is not conceived statically, but as living in spontaneous self-actualization.

What is true of Jesus Christ in his own right finds its parallel and extension in his special capacity as the Mediator. Neither God nor any living creature is thought to exist except in and with the life act of the Mediator. "It is as he lives that the living God lives and all that is by him [God] and outside him, so that, in spite of all possible and actual problems in their relationship, they live together (though not in identity) in the indestructible conjunction of *the differentiated act* in which both Creator and creature exist" (p. 40, emphasis added). Whether it is a matter of the relations by which the person of Christ is constituted, or of the relations between the Creator and the creature which he mediates so exclusively and universally, their unity, differentiation, and order are not conceived as existing in any other way than in modes of spontaneous actualization.

Moreover, what is true of the one pattern regarding Jesus Christ as the Mediator is also true of the other. The relations described by the pattern of dialectical inclusion are also conceived as active. The personal act in which Jesus Christ lives is viewed as universal in its relatedness: "But we must add at once that *with his own life-act,* which is directly that of God himself fulfilled as being human, there takes place *all the life-acts* of those who as free subjects (within their determined limits) are creatures of God. In other words, there takes place all human life" (p. 41 rev., emphasis added). The universal relatedness of Jesus Christ, as described here, is clearly a matter of living activity. To live as a human being means to live in the sphere established by the life and activity of the Mediator, "so that, whether we realize it or not, the decision is made that God will accomplish his life-act only together with us, and we can accomplish ours only together with God." Here the active relatedness of Christ's person is described more nearly in terms of coexistence than of coinherence. "This co-existence may take different forms. But the fact that Jesus Christ lives as attested in the biblical testimony means that there is this *union* between God and each of us human beings, and that it is indestructible" (p. 41 rev., emphasis added). Elsewhere the *mode* of this personal union and coexistence is specified in terms of active coinherence, as occurs expressly in the discussion of "secular parables."

The life of Jesus Christ is a life lived *in act.* This has been the first point in reflecting upon the indissoluble connection between his eternal life and his particular history. This connection, we have observed, is described as one of spontaneous actualization. As divine yet also human, as eternal yet also historical, he is constituted by (or perhaps better, he himself constitutes) a complex set of relations. The complexity is one of differentiated unity and dialectical inclusion. This unity and this inclusion are always free, living, and active. Both the differentiated unity of Jesus Christ's person and, in and with him, of all that he so exclusively and universally mediates, are conceived as subsisting in active and spontaneous modes of coexistence and coinherence.

With regard to Jesus Christ's *life* as eternal yet also historical, a second point may now be developed. As noted, to say that Jesus Christ lives means that his life is always an *eternal* life lived in indissoluble connection with a particular history. Just what is the specific force, it may now be asked, of saying that his life is an eternal life? Because the life which Jesus Christ lives is always an eternal life, his past and present and future must not, Barth argues, be separated from one another abstractly. Instead, they must be seen concretely in the unity that is proper to them. This unity is again understood as a complex action, and its complexity is indeed that of the trinitarian pattern in its paradigmatic form. That is, the (active) complex unity of eternity itself (and therefore of Jesus Christ's eternal life) is conceived as "perichoretic."[4]

The doctrine of the perichoresis, as explicated in the doctrine of the Trinity, is the paradigm for the pattern of dialectical inclusion or coinherence. Eternity is conceived, in Barth's theology, as perichoretic not only in itself, but also in its reception of history. Thus what Barth says in a somewhat different but related connection might well be applied to past and present and future as the threefold form of Jesus Christ's eternal life:

> It is not merely that these three forms are interconnected in the totality of the action presented in them all, or in each of them in its unity and totality, but that they are mutually related as the forms of this one action by the fact that *each of them also contains the other two* by way of anticipation or recapitulation, so that, *without losing their individuality* or destroying that of the others, they participate and are active and revealed in them. (p. 296, emphasis added)

Or as he says quite directly about Jesus Christ's life as eternal life: It "does not extinguish but integrates and to that extent overcomes the differences between what we call past, present and future. For even as human life, it shares the sovereignty of the life of the divine Subject over these distinctions" (p. 45). Temporal distinctions are not conceived as being absent from eternity, but rather as being (mysteriously) present with a simultaneity that does not efface their sequence.

Therefore, insofar as the life of Jesus Christ is eternal, the interconnection of the various *temporal* forms of this life (past, present, future) is one of mutual coinherence. These forms are the temporal forms of his one life action. In eternity the totality of this action is present in an ever-living, dynamic, and differentiated unity. Whether by way anticipation, recapitulation, or synchronicity, each temporal form in eternity contains the other two, yet the individuality of each is not destroyed but retained. Each form participates in the others and is active and revealed in them. In the eternality of his one life action, the differences we know between past, present, and future are not extinguished, but integrated and to that extent overcome. The pattern of their integration is the dynamic, perichoretic pattern of mutual coinherence.

Furthermore, insofar as his one life action *is* historical, it is indissolubly connected with the sovereign overcoming and integration of temporal forms in eternity. "His history did not take place," writes Barth, "to take place no more. It has not to take place as though it had not yet taken place. It takes place, yet not as one which is merely present at a single point, but in the power of a history which has already taken place and will do so again'' (pp. 44–45). His history takes place in the spontaneous actualization of his one life act. But this actualization is not only spontaneous. It is also differentiated. Its historical occurrence takes place in the genuine sequence of past, present, and future as real temporal forms. Therefore, just as the reality and sequence of these forms is presupposed by their simultaneous integration in eternity, so their simultaneous integration lends these forms a transcendental uniqueness and power peculiar to the one life act of this person.

Jesus Christ lives as a complex person (divine yet also human) and therefore in and with a complex temporality (eternal yet also historical). The historicity of his life is fully real, and he cannot be known without it, for he never lives without it. Yet he is not encapsulated in this historicity in an unqualified way. For his historicity is indissolubly connected with his eternality. It is therefore at once affirmed, negated, and reconstituted on a higher plane. Its mere historicity is transcended and overcome. Its distinctive particularity is at once preserved and yet overcome by being integrated into the perichoresis of eternity. It is made integral to the eternal life of Jesus Christ and therefore acquires a differentiated presence and distinctive power in relation to all other historical moments and historical beings. In all its concrete particularity and uniqueness, it becomes the Word of God that is ultimately addressed to each and every human creature. "And the upshot is the same if we say also that it is the life of grace which was and will be addressed to each and every human being as such, and which is addressed to them precisely as that which was and will be'' (p. 45 rev.).

Jesus Christ lives. He lives as a person with a particular history. He lives a uniquely eternal life with which his particular history is inextricably bound. His uniquely eternal life is one which overcomes and integrates his real historicity in dynamic patterns of mutual coinherence. These patterns of coinherence in eternity are a condition for the possibility of his self-revelation to each and every human being as such. Whether by way of anticipation or recapitulation (and in a variety of differentiations), they make it possible for him to reveal his history as the history which not only identifies who he is, but which he himself has enacted to accomplish the world's reconciliation with God. As the one who enacts and reveals this history, and who eternally embodies it, he lives as "the one Word of God." He lives, that is, a uniquely perichoretic life in indissoluble connection with a particular history such that this history is at once contemporaneous and luminous in relation to all other historical moments and creatures. In ways known and as yet unknown, he is and has been and will be present to each and every human being as such, as the luminous Word which discloses the particular history of his one life action for what it is: the reconciliation, the mediating center of all things in relation to God.[5]

Jesus Christ *lives* as the one Word of God. It has been this statement, with this emphasis, that the foregoing considerations have been meant to clarify. In what follows, the statement will remain the same, but the accent will shift. Jesus Christ lives as *the* one Word of God. What does it mean to stress the definite article in this statement? If the event, history, and life of Jesus Christ are exclusively the one Word of God, then what kind of exclusivity does Barth ascribe to it? How does he conceive the exclusive truth of this Word in relation to the occurrence of other and different words? If the truth of this Word is so exclusive and indeed exhaustive, how can any other true words be conceived as occurring at all?

"Jesus Christ is the light of life" (p. 86). This is the statement Barth formulates to address questions such as those just posed. Precisely so as not to falsify the relationship between the light of Jesus Christ and all other lights, the strongest possible accent is placed on sheer exclusivity. That Jesus Christ "is the *one and only* light of life" is said to mean two things. "Positively, it means that he is the light of life in all its fullness, in perfect adequacy; and negatively, it means that there is no other light of life outside or alongside his, outside or alongside the light which he is" (p. 86, emphasis added). Even from this initial remark, however, the salient point should already be clear. Despite (or because of) his fullness, perfection, and all-sufficiency as the light of life, Jesus Christ is not conceived as excluding other possible or actual lights. What the preeminence of the one great light excludes is not other lights as such, but rather certain impossible modes of relationship between the one and the many. Two modes in particular are excluded. No other light of life may be conceived as being *outside,* and no other as being *alongside,* the one great light. That other and different lights may somehow occur within the one great light, and in full (thought subordinate) collaboration with it, is a possibility that is distinctly left open.

The possibility is not explored, however, until several prior clarifications are firmly in place. Certainly if Jesus Christ could be regarded simply as one light among others, as merely *a* word of God, however urgent and important, then the whole difficulty of his exclusiveness would be eliminated at a stroke. In that case his proclamation as the Word of God would arouse no suspicion, generate no unpopularity, and provoke no offense "to anyone, least of all to ourselves" (p. 87). But if the truth of Jesus Christ is indeed unique in kind, as Barth believes it to be on the basis of his reading of scripture, then it cannot be comprehensively combined with other relatively independent truths. It cannot be placed in a series of truths as though it were merely one alongside many others. Any such synthesis between the one truth and the many would rob the one great truth of its "dangerousness," of "its revolutionary force," of its "foreignness in the world," to say nothing of the "shame" and "vulnerability" which accompany it (and all those who align themselves with it) (pp. 88–89). For this truth confronts us with the offense of "an absolute claim," and nothing could be more natural "than the desire to escape this" (p. 89).

Those who embrace this truth will certainly expose themselves to reproach, not only from the world but also inwardly from their own hearts. The reproach will confront them from essentially three sides. The statement that Jesus Christ is the one Word of God, besides whom there is no other, will be castigated as too restricted (the intellectual reproach), as deplorably arrogant (the moral reproach), and as dangerously authoritarian (the political reproach) (p. 89). Although a constant temptation will thus exist to suppress or dilute the offending statement, Christian freedom really "stands or falls by whether it is freedom for this confession" (p. 90). Indeed, it is this confession that gives every Christian statement its urgency, weight, and binding force. Why should the world be expected to meet this confession with anything but reproach at first? "It would not be the world, but already the community, if it were in a position to receive and interpret it differently" (p. 90).

The confession of Jesus Christ as the one Word of God, says Barth, has nothing to do with an arbitrary self-glorification of Christianity, the church, or the Christian. It is strictly "a christological statement" (p. 91). As such it does not entail any exaltation of the Christian over the non-Christian, but rather an important bond between them. For the statement confronts Christian and non-Christian alike with "the one truth superior" to them both. "Thus the criticism expressed in the exclusiveness of the statement affects, limits and relativizes the prophecy of Christians and the church no less than the many other prophecies, lights, and words relativized and replaced by it" (p. 91). In a move that will be decisive for his whole analysis, Barth thus sets the superiority of the Word over against all human words as such, whether they arise from the Bible, the church, or the world. All human words as such are relativized by the Word and thus joined in a certain solidarity. But insofar as they enter into rivalry with the Word, they are shown to be impotent and are inevitably replaced by it.

To confess the offending christological statement is therefore not to be regarded as a matter of Christian self-glorification or self-exaltation. It is rather a matter of bowing to the authority of the One who declares himself through it. "For [the church] has not found or fashioned for itself this statement which its witness declares" (p. 91). The church does not venture this statement on its own authority, but only by adhering to that of the biblical witness. "Much Christian anxiety in the face of this reproach would disappear of itself . . . if we remembered that as Christians we are not summoned or committed to thinking and speaking on our own authority and responsibility, but kept modestly yet steadfastly to the direction of Holy Scripture" (p. 92).

What, then, is the *direction* of Holy Scripture in this regard? It is not a matter of isolated teachings, says Barth, but of underlying modes of thought. It is these modes of thought which he sees as authoritative for Christians. He offers two examples pertinent to the discussion. The first pertains to the question of theological truth. On this question, Barth observes, the biblical witness always moves in a *circulus virtuosus*. It always assumes and never tries to prove the truth of its witness to God. Indeed, as Barth says elsewhere, circular argument in theological discourse is simply unavoidable. "Human beings would have to be God himself if they were to speak of God otherwise than in forms of circular arguments" (III/1, 359 rev.). The biblical mode of thought on questions of theological truth is thus exemplary.

The second example pertains to the question of revelation. When it comes to this question, Barth notes, the biblical witness always presupposes "the uniqueness and the absolute normativeness" of what it has received and attests (IV/3, 92). Certainly the Old Testament writers were not unaware of what is today called "pluralism." "But," says Barth, "to the best of my knowledge there is not a single word in any of the prophets to indicate that this fact made any impression on them" (p. 93). There is no trace that the action and speech of Yahweh in the history of Israel are considered to be valid only as one divine revelation among many. Moreover, for the evangelists and apostles of the New Testament, the situation is no different. When they speak and write, the question of pluralism is already behind them. "From the point where they start, there can be no thought of wrestling with strange and in some sense perhaps impressive and normative conceptions of God and the world. As there can be no other sons of God, so there can be no other lords nor witnesses to the truth apart from or side by side with Jesus Christ'' (p. 93).

Pluralism is thus rejected, because it posits, by definition, other sources and norms of revelation outside or alongside Jesus Christ. It thereby violates the fundamental axiom of *how* the one light is related to the many, and offends against biblical modes of thought. ''As the history of Israel speaks in the Old Testament, and that of Jesus Christ in the New, the decision is made that other divine pronouncements, no matter where they come from or however they might be grounded or intended, are not to be heard or taken seriously as independent utterances, and can have no claim to our trust or obedience'' (p. 93). From this remark we may note two things. First, whether such utterances might be taken seriously as dependent (if not independent) words, lights, or truths is again left open. Second, in all cases what is finally at stake is regarded as a matter of lordship. Revelation is not just a matter of sources and norms but of lords, and therefore of trust, humility, and obedience. It claims not only our assent but our lives. It is fully self-involving. The question of pluralism, as here understood, cannot be divorced from the question of worship and allegiance.

In short, when faced with the reproach against exclusivity, two modes of thought are commended as biblical: the impossibility of noncircular argument in theological discourse and the impossibility of revelational pluralism.[6] The truth of the biblical witness to God, according to the one mode of thought, is something that in the nature of the case can never be humanly proven. It can only be assumed, in all its exclusivity, as something whose proof lies beyond human power. The bearing of faithful witness—which Barth throughout this section refers to as ''prophecy'' or ''prophetic work''—is a work that occurs from both the human and the divine side. From the human side it is a matter of adhering to biblical modes of thought, and from the divine side a matter of using such human witness as the means through which the truth of what is asserted is ''proven,'' miraculously, by the One to whom witness is borne. Revelation, moreover, is not to be conceived as something that arises from a plurality of possible sources and with a variety of possible norms. It can have no source and no norm outside or alongside Jesus Christ. It can therefore permit trust and obedience toward no other Lord but him. For according to biblical modes of thought, its normativity is absolute, its content unique, and its claim to allegience total. No exploration of what it means to say that Jesus Christ is the one Word of God can possibly be fruitful, urges Barth, if it does not adhere to these distinctive thought forms of the Bible (pp. 94–96).

With these preliminary clarifications in place, the question can now be posed more precisely. "Jesus Christ is the one Word of God." What does this actually say, according to Barth, and what does it not say?

1. *Jesus Christ as the one Word of God is related to all other true words as their sovereign source and norm. His status is that of the truth; theirs, that of witnesses to the truth.* (pp. 96–99)

No other word than Jesus Christ is the one Word of God, for he alone "shares the uniqueness of God" (p. 96). All other words, insofar as they are true, will somehow be oriented to him as witnesses. He will therefore be related to them as their sovereign source and norm. Two spheres of witness may be distinguished: an inner sphere, consisting of the Bible and the church, and an outer sphere, consisting of the world. The Bible is his "direct witness," the church his "indirect witness," the world his unwitting witness. The inner sphere of Bible and church is thus "luminous" in a way that the outer sphere of the world is not (p. 96). Yet it does not follow that all words from the outer sphere are words "of false prophecy." It does not follow that they can only be "misleading" or that they are "necessarily untrue" (p. 97). On the contrary, it follows only that all human words, from the inner as well as the outer sphere, are *delimited* by what is declared "in and with the existence of Jesus Christ" (p. 97).

"Words of great seriousness, profound comfort, and supreme wisdom" are to be found not only in the Bible and the church but also in the world. How can it be otherwise, if Jesus Christ is really sovereign over the whole world of creation and history? How can he help but exercise authority in the outer as well as in the inner sphere? "In both cases there are human words which are good because they are spoken with the commission and in the service of God. In both spheres there are words which are illuminating and helpful to the degree that God himself gives it to them to be illuminating and helpful as such words." Good words of this kind may be heard "continually," says Barth, in the Bible, the church, and the world (p. 97).

Yet none of these good words in itself and as such is the Word of God. None of them can be set beside Jesus Christ as the Word spoken by God himself. None can be regarded as a supplement to him, to say nothing of replacing or crowding him out. For this Word, being spoken directly by

God, is not only good, serious, comforting, and wise, but is all these things "incomparably and absolutely" (p. 98). It is not just valid but "absolutely valid," not just good but unsurpassably good, not just instructive but redemptive. It is not really we who decide about it so much as it which decides about us, blessing even as it judges. By it we are freed yet unconditionally bound. "It is the Word of God which we must trust and obey in life and in death" (p. 98). No human word can speak in this way and accomplish these things. For this, "God's direct presence is needed." Jesus Christ is not the only word, nor is he the only true word, but he is indeed the only Word in itself and as such spoken with divine authority and power. "He is the only Word which all human words, even the best, can only directly or indirectly attest but not replace or rival, so that their own goodness and authority are to be measured by whether or not, and with what fidelity, they are witnesses of this one Word" (p. 98). It is especially to be noted (as indicated in the opening of this chapter) that this Word is consistently defined by means of the (biblically attested) history of a particular person. This Word distinguishes itself from all others as the Word "spoken in the existence of Jesus Christ" (p. 99). This existence as such is the occurrence which is also speech.

2. *Jesus Christ as the one Word of God is the truth in all fullness and perfection. His truth is original and sovereign; that of all other words, derivative and fiduciary. Their truth cannot complete, compete with, combine itself with, or transcend him. Yet his truth can do any of these things, as appropriate, with them: complete them, defeat them, combine itself with them, or transcend them.* (pp. 99–103)

Jesus Christ—his life, his history, his existence—is God's "total and complete" declaration (p. 99). In the history of this person, God speaks definitively about himself and also about the human beings addressed by him. "What (God) is for us and wills of us, but also what we are for him . . . is exhaustively, unreservedly and totally revealed to us in Jesus Christ as the one Word of God" (p. 99). Therefore this Word stands in no need of completion by any others. Any addition from some other source could only, in this case, be a subtraction; any supposed enhancement, a diminution; any improvement, "a perversion of our knowledge of the truth" (p. 100).

If there is any place for speaking of "completion," it can only be with regard to the liveliness of the Word in relation to the poverty of our knowledge. The living Word may thus be said to be engaged "in a continual completion of himself, not in the sense that the Word spoken by (God) is incomplete or inadequate, but in the sense that our hearing of it is profoundly incomplete. For he himself is in himself rich and strong enough to display and offer himself to our poverty with perennial fullness'' (p. 99). The Word continually completes itself by adding to, enhancing, and improving our self-impaired or otherwise limited grasp of the truth.

Just as the one Word of God cannot in itself be completed, so also it cannot be exposed to any serious challenge, competition, or threat. From what side could such a challenge or threat be mounted? It could really come only from another Word of God, spoken perhaps by a hidden God who was not identical with God as revealed, or who was ''identical only in irreconcilable contradiction'' (p. 100). But what cause could we have to reckon with such a self-contradiction on God's part? ''We have every cause to keep to the fact that [God] is faithful, and that in Jesus Christ, we have his total and unique and therefore authentic revelation, the Word in which he does full justice both to himself and to us'' (p. 100).

Certainly the Word is not without opposition in the world, ''also and supremely, as we must not forget, in the church'' (p. 100). Certainly in the world there are ''many sinister powers,'' many forms of darkness, all somehow connected with human sin, by which they are empowered and unleashed. These forms of opposition must certainly be taken seriously. ''Jesus Christ can certainly be unrecognized, despised and rejected in the world and among his own people'' (p. 100). But God is faithful and does not contradict himself. His one Word addressed to us in the existence of Jesus Christ is worthy of our trust and obedience in life and in death. No one who believes in him will finally be put to shame. ''For, although he has enemies, he has none who can put him to shame, or who will not be put to shame by him'' (p. 101).

Moreover, just as the truth of Jesus Christ can tolerate no external completion and no competition, so also can it tolerate no combination with other words, prophecies or truths. ''That he is the one Word of God means . . . that his truth and prophecy cannot be combined with any other, nor can he be enclosed with other words in a system prior to both him and them'' (p. 101). There can be no question of his being ''systematically coordinated'' with ''truths'' derived from other sources and governed by other norms. ''As the one Word of God he wholly escapes every conceivable synthesis envisaged in them'' (p. 101). Indeed, systematic coordination is regarded as prohibited by the First Commandment: ''You shall have no other gods before me'' (Ex. 20:3). The commandment itself

suggests that direct apostasy as such may be less of a problem than syn-
cretism. By it Yahweh "radically and automatically refuses to allow his
Godhead to be equated with other divinities, or his Word to be heard
with other words" (p. 102). Yet throughout the entire history of the church,
"revealed already in the *gnosis* attacked in the New Testament," such
attempted combinations have repeatedly been "the weak point." Insofar
as these attempts succeed, Jesus Christ simply departs, leaving nothing
but "suspiciously loud but empty utterances" of his name. "No one can
serve both the one Word of God and other divine words" (p. 102 rev.).

However, the converse also bears consideration; for while the truth of
Jesus Christ cannot be subjected to human control by means of a superior
conceptual scheme, he himself remains free to bring his truth "into the
closest conjunction" with other words. "He can make use of certain
human beings, making them his witnesses in such a way that to hear them
is to hear him" (p. 101). Both inside and outside the sphere of Bible and
church, he has actually done so. Whether in the one sphere or the other,
however, "this type of union can be legitimate and fruitful only through
his act, as his work, as a form of his free revelation of grace" (p. 101).
This kind of union—free, living, ad hoc—is very different from any
syntheses arbitrarily devised by Christians or non-Christians between the
one Word of God and other words.

Finally, the truth of Jesus Christ cannot be transcended by any other.
Neither in content, nor in depth, nor in urgency can the truth of his Word
be surpassed. For he himself is the crown of "all that is really worth
knowing," "the source and norm of all truth," and "the one thing"
really necessary to be known (pp. 102–3). All other words of "goodness,
seriousness, comfort and wisdom" pale by comparison, and in all these
respects they can only be "abased and exalted, disqualified and qualified" by his truth (p. 103). The only sense in which his truth can be
transcended is through "self-transcendence." Some day the glory of his
truth will no longer be hidden, but revealed with a clarity that is universal, direct, and definitive. "In this *eschaton* of creation and reconciliation, there will not be another Word of God. Jesus Christ will be the one
Word of God and we shall then see the final and unequivocal form of his
own glory which even now shines forth from his resurrection into time
and history, all times and all histories" (p. 103).

In short, the truth whose perfection cannot be completed completes
itself, whose sovereignty cannot be defeated vindicates itself, whose freedom cannot be controlled imparts itself, and whose glory is yet to come

transcends itself. It can thus be completed, deposed, systematized, or transcended by no other truth.

3. *Jesus Christ as the one Word of God is the truth which is incomparably unique. His truth speaks for itself in a way that no other word can match, and the singularity of what it says can be conveyed by no other word in its stead.* (pp. 103–10)

Why should anyone feel free or compelled to say that Jesus Christ is the one Word of God? On what basis can this statement be made? This question, which was discussed more generally at the opening of this chapter, may now be answered more specifically. The general form of the answer, notes Barth, still holds: "The revelation of God vouches for its uniqueness as it does for itself as such. If Jesus Christ is the one Word of God, he alone, standing out from the ranks of all other supposed and pretended divine words, can make himself known as this one Word" (p. 104). The question now to be addressed in more detail is: What is the "concrete content" of this Word (p. 105)?

The concrete content of this Word is, *in nuce,* the life of Jesus Christ. This life, it will be recalled, is viewed as the life of a complex person, at once divine and human. As such it is a particular existence, a narratable history, in which God subjects himself to abasement so that humanity might be delivered and exalted. "It is the life in which God gives himself up to death, and humanity is made the conqueror of death. . . . It is the life of reconciliation. It is the life of Jesus Christ" (p. 106 rev.). Yet this life as such is also light. "In itself and as such this life is Word, revelation, *kerygma.*" This life speaks for itself, and "in the form of this life," it is God who speaks (p. 106 rev.). This life speaks of what took place in it for our sake—our justification and sanctification, our reconciliation with God, our deliverance, conversion and even glorification (pp. 106–7). As such this life is the light of our lives as well as of his. But why should it be thought of as the *one* Word of God?

Because, Barth urges, no other word says the same thing. "For can we think of any word actually spoken, or any conceivable word which might be spoken, that says what the life of Jesus Christ says?" (p. 107). Words from elsewhere may certainly say things which are good, illuminating, and helpful. "But none of them says what the life of Jesus Christ says." Such words may even remind us of his life. "But even so they say something different." Even the closest of parallels will "say these things rigidly and abstractly," so that they can really be no substitute.

"Being set in a different context, they cannot fail to be somewhat distorted, or at least different from what is said to us in Jesus Christ" (p. 107).

Note that Barth is thinking here of the relations between the whole and the part. In circumstances where Jesus Christ himself does not set the context, but where the context is set instead by some other word, his life cannot and does not speak for itself. No denigration of other words in themselves is implied by this observation. "We may quietly listen to others. We may hear what is said by the whole story of religion, poetry, mythology and philosophy. We shall certainly meet there many things which might be claimed as elements of the Word spoken by Jesus Christ" (p. 108). Yet if divorced and abstracted from the contextual whole established by the concrete life of Jesus Christ, these elements cannot help but say something else. "But what a mass of rudiments and fragments they are, saying in their isolation and absoluteness something very different from the Word!" (p. 108 rev.). Set in other contexts, these elements inevitably lack Jesus Christ himself as their proper and unifying center.

Consider, then, the concrete content which sets this Word uniquely apart from all others:

> What other word speaks of the covenant between God and the human race? What other of its character as the work of God, and indeed of the effective and omnipotent grace of God on the basis of eternal love and election? What other of the fulfillment of this covenant in the humiliation of God and the exaltation of the human race? What other of a comprehensive justification of the human race by God and sanctification for it? What other of the fact that this reconciliation of God with the human race and the human race with God is no mere idea but a once-for-all event? What other pronounces that unconditional *Deus pro et cum nobis,* thus indicating that a new situation has already been created for all humanity, setting each human being at this new beginning and pushing each one on from this point? . . . What other is directed so concretely to each and every human being? (pp. 107–8 rev.)

The concrete content of this Word occurs nowhere else precisely because, as such, it is a singular and unrepeatable history.

The statement that Jesus Christ is the one Word of God, says Barth, is axiomatic for dogmatic theology. It has and can have no other basis than the one it provides for itself. "It is its own basis" (p. 109). As it speaks for itself, it shows that the "only conclusive argument" on which it relies is "the Holy Spirit" (p. 109). As the statement is affirmed to be singular in content, so its basis is affirmed to be unique.

4. *Jesus Christ as the one Word of God is the truth which miraculously calls forth parables of itself, not only in the inner sphere of Bible and church, but also in the outer sphere of the world.* (pp. 110–18)

The three main points just considered—on the normativity, the superiority, and the singularity of the Word—may now be reviewed and applied more extensively. Human words that are good and true, it may now be assumed, are found not only in the Bible and in church proclamation, but also *extra muros ecclesiae*. What exactly is the status of these words, and on what basis do they arise?

(1) The truth of human words, from whatever sphere, depends on "the faithfulness, genuineness and reliability of what they impart" (p. 110). These are qualities which can be assessed only with reference to the *normativity* of the Word and the larger contextual whole it establishes. No human words can be true if they do not stand "in the closest material and substantial conformity and agreement with the Word of God itself" (p. 111). Note that it is here not a question of whether the Word agrees with these words in whatever context they may establish of themselves, but whether these words stand in material agreement with the Word in its own self-established context. If human words are to be true in such a context, then the truth of the Word "must dwell within them." They will therefore be true in their own distinctive way, because "they say the same thing" (p. 111).

(2) However, although human words may come to stand in material agreement with the Word, such agreement does not imply that the *superiority* of the Word is somehow forfeit in relation to them. "They can hardly have, or arrogantly claim, equal truth for themselves. Even as true words of God, they must still distinguish themselves from this one Word, keeping their distance and conceding and accepting the fact that it alone is truth" (p. 111). Only insofar as they are prepared to declare the one Word of God "without subtraction, addition or alteration" are they in a position to "stand alongside" it, to "correspond" to it, and thus to "confirm" it. "Only in this relationship can they be called true words" (p. 111).

(3) Because the one Word of God, in all its *singularity*, finds its basis only in itself, no true human words will find their basis in themselves, but only in the Word as it encounters them from without. True human words will be true "quite beyond any capacity of their own" (p. 111). Their truth will not be based on some innate capacity, but on the good pleasure of the Word of God "to allow itself to be in some sense reflected

and reproduced in the words of these human beings" (p. 111 rev.). Precisely because the Word provides no other basis than itself, the truth of human words will always be extrinsically based.

Words which conform and agree materially with the Word, not as equals but as servants, and not by any capacity of their own but by grace, are words ascribed, in Barth's discourse, with the status of *parables*. Parables are defined as "secondary forms" of the one Word of God, and their function is to "accompany and attest" it (pp. 112–13). The parables told by Jesus, as Barth interprets them, were not really like new wine poured into old wineskins so much as they were like new wine that transformed old wineskins into new. That is, whereas their content was "something new to all human beings, and newly to be apprehended by them," their form was that of everyday events transformed into something beyond themselves (p. 113). "Under his hand, recounted by Jesus, these everyday happenings become what they were not before, and what they cannot be in and of themselves." They become real testimonies to the real presence of the kingdom in and with Jesus himself. They are taken up and transformed into something they otherwise are not. This transformation and elevation of form by content, and of the everyday by the new, is taken as the prototype for the transformation and elevation of human words by the Word. "In sum, the New Testament parables are as it were the prototype of the order in which there can be other true words alongside the one Word of God, created and determined by it, exactly corresponding to it, fully serving it and therefore enjoying its power and authority" (p. 113).

The status of parables—of the Word's secondary forms—can readily be ascribed, it would seem, to the words of the Bible and of the church. For one thing, it can be ascribed to the prophets and apostles (i.e., to their testimony as a unified and differentiated whole), because "as they themselves participated in the history of Israel and that of Jesus Christ, [their word] was directly formed and guided by the one Word of God" (pp. 113–14). Similarly, it can be ascribed to the word of church proclamation insofar as it is "continually tested, awakened, directed and corrected" by the biblical word (p. 114). These words, of the Bible and the church, can thus be called "the two secondary forms" of the one Word of God (p. 113). As they are informed and sustained again and again by the Word, they are elevated to the status of "true parables" (p. 113). "To the biblical witnesses, and to all the witnesses of the Christian community, it is promised and given to be parables of the kingdom of heaven" (p. 114).

Can something similar be said about true words spoken outside the sphere of the Bible and the church? Although this question is more complicated (and preoccupies Barth for the remainder of the discussion), the community must reckon, he says, with the possibility and the actuality of secular parables of the truth. It must allow that secular words as such may be secondary forms of the one Word of God. Secular parables will be recognized by the fact that they drive the community "more truly and profoundly than ever before to Scripture" (p. 115). They will not contradict but illumine, will not denigrate but accentuate, the biblical word, opening it up for the community in a new way and for a particular situation. They will always encourage the community in the execution of its sometimes dispiriting task. For they will indicate that, despite appearances, the Word itself is at work in the world incognito, not leaving it destitute but raising up "witnesses to the truth from the darkness of the nations" outside the community's own sphere, as the Bible itself well knows. These secular parables will therefore demand a real hearing from the community, not deflecting it from "its own mission to preach the one Word of God," but assisting, comforting, and strengthening it on the way (p. 115).

"But are there really such true words spoken in the secular world and addressed to the community from it? How can we count on this?" (p. 116). The community can expect to encounter secular parables in the full sense of the term for reasons that are strictly christological. Did not Jesus Christ suffer and die for the sake of all? Is not the reconciliation he accomplished universal in its scope? Was he not raised from the dead and seated at the right hand of God? Is not the realm of his dominion greater than the little sphere of the community, extending even to the ends of the earth? If the community recognizes Jesus Christ for who he truly is, then it will also recognize that not only the community itself, "but *de jure* all human beings and all creation derive from his cross, from the reconciliation accomplished in him, and are ordained to be the theater of his glory and therefore the recipients and bearers of his Word" (p. 117 rev.). Therefore the community can and must expect to hear his voice arising from the secular sphere, prompting the community itself to become a "better, more attentive and convincing" servant of this Word (p. 117).

The occurrence of secular parables, Barth hastens to add, is not to be explained by recourse to "the sorry hypothesis" of natural theology. The familiar Barthian objections are reviewed and applied to the matter at hand. Natural theology, he argues, puts forward three unfortunate things: falsifying abstractions, neutral generalizations, and nonexistent capaci-

ties. For one thing, natural theology does not speak concretely about the
triune God, but abstractly and therefore falsely about "the Supreme Being"
or "Providence" and some supposed human responsibility toward it. For
another thing, it is not interested in specific and self-involving forms of
theological truth, but merely in provisional and nonbinding views of God
and humanity in general. Finally, it is not based on the self-disclosing
Word, but on a knowledge of God supposedly "given in and with the
natural force of reason or to be attained in its exercise" (p. 117).

Therefore the idea of secular parables has nothing to do with natural
theology. Above all, "nothing could be further from our minds than to
attribute to the human creature as such a capacity to know God and the
one true Word of God, or to reproduce true words corresponding to this
knowledge" (p. 118). Even in the special sphere of the Bible and the
church, no such capacity is at stake, let alone in the sphere of the world.
What holds for the one holds all the more for the other: "If there are true
words of God, it is all miraculous." It is not a matter of some innate
human capacity. It is a matter of "the capacity of Jesus Christ to raise
up of stones children to Abraham." Human creatures, who are quite without
any capacity of their own, are taken up into the service of the Word,
being empowered for it and caused to speak in it. From such creatures
Jesus Christ has the capacity to create witnesses for himself, "quite apart
from and even in the face of their own knowledge or volition." Not only
can he do so within the sphere of the Bible and the church, but also
outside it in the sphere of the world. "Our thesis is simply that the capacity of Jesus Christ to create these human witnesses is not restricted to
his working on and in prophets and apostles and what is thus made possible and actual in his community. His capacity transcends the limits of
this sphere" (p. 118). His own self-witness generates and operates through
a variety of secondary forms, not excluding secular parables.

The "wider sphere" from which Jesus Christ raises up his "extraordinary witnesses" is a sphere that divides into two distinct configurations,
one whose secularism approaches being "pure and absolute," and one
whose secularism is merely "mixed and relative" (p. 118). What differ-
entiates the two, Barth says, is their proximity to the sphere of the Bible
and the church, the one type of secularism standing in a more distant and
the other in a closer "periphery." To what extent do extraordinary witnesses to the truth arise in the midst of these distinct secular settings?

In pursuing the answer given to this question, it will be important to
note the implicit but somewhat extended use that is made of the metaphor
of the "spheres." The image, characteristic of Barth, is one of three

concentric spheres, an inner sphere (that of Bible and church) surrounded by two distinct outer spheres (those of mixed and, farther out, of pure secularism). All three are envisioned as having Jesus Christ as their center (at least insofar as true words arise from within them). This imagery conveys an important point about context. It indicates that the context to be considered is the one set by Christ himself, so that it is now the words which are being compared to the Word, not the other way around. The familiar Barthian point about irreversible relationships—that there is no way from us to God, but only from God to us—is thus being applied to the case at hand. There is no way, Barth wants to say, from the words to the Word, but only from the Word to the words. In this application, however, neither the one nor the other is considered apart from certain respective and accompanying contexts. Thus the full point goes something like this: there is no way from secular words in their larger, self-established contexts to the Word, but only from the Word in its larger, self-established context to secular words. As Barth reflects on the characteristics peculiar to the two distinct spheres of secularism, this point about irreversibility is carefully made about each.

The more distant sphere of secularism is taken up first. The people in this sphere have never, or never adequately, been reached by the gospel "in its biblical and churchly form," and when it does reach them, their reaction is likely to be hostile. Not only will such people be found in territories never penetrated by the gospel or in nations whose state religion is officially atheism, but indeed "in the greatest proximity to the Christian churches, a proximity which may contain within itself the greatest inward distance" (p. 119). Regardless of their proximity or geographical location, these people will show, by word and deed, that they are closed to the message of the gospel. "There is a whole world," writes Barth, "which for various reasons is not yet or no longer attached to any religion, and certainly not to the Word of God, but obstinately boasts of its own sovereignty" (p. 119).

Can it be said, therefore, that no true or theologically valid words are to be expected from this sphere, or at the very least that such words are not at all likely to occur? It would be a mistake, Barth contends, to draw this conclusion. The very message of the gospel points in the opposite direction. It must not be forgotten, says Barth, that while human beings may deny God, God does not deny them. No matter how hostile or closed they may be to the gospel, the gospel remains open, not hostile, to them. "But this means that in the world reconciled by God in Jesus Christ there is no secular sphere abandoned by him or withdrawn from his control, even where . . . it seems to approximate dangerously to the pure and absolute form of utter godlessness.'' Because any other conclusion would underestimate the resurrection of Jesus Christ, we must ''be prepared at any time for true words even from what seem to be the darkest places'' (p. 119). Pure secularism is not necessarily an obstacle to the emergence of theologically valid words.

What, then, may be said about the other, less distant sphere of secularism? Does it perhaps possess some advantage not enjoyed by the purer and more remote sphere? The inhabitants of this sphere are, by definition, those who have been reached and to some extent affected by the gospel in its biblical and churchly form. In this sphere the gospel, being more or less accepted (or at least not openly denied), exerts some degree of influence. Yet what is missing on the whole is a real and vital connection to its substance. Instead, what is found at bottom, despite all ambiguities, is not the kingdom proclaimed by the gospel, but ''a very different world resting upon and impelled by its own laws and tendencies'' (p. 120). It is finally a sphere in which allegiance to the gospel is nominal, apparent, and external.

Yet because of its contact with the gospel, might it be that within this sphere true words that attest the one Word of God are ''much more likely, more easily possible and therefore more readily to be expected'' (p. 120)? After all, where the gospel has been concretely attested, how could echoes of the gospel fail to arise? Barth's answer to such questions is interesting for the way in which it coverges with and diverges from a more Kierkegaardian attack upon Christendom. What he offers is less of an onslaught than a nuanced set of remarks. On the one hand, the cultural influence of the gospel, its partial displacement of the prevailing secularism, is something to be taken seriously. ''Why should we not expect to hear true words from this world which only to a limited extent rests upon and is impelled by itself?'' (p. 120). The supposition that true words might actually be more probable in the nearer than in the more distant sphere is not to be summarily dismissed.

On the other hand, countervailing insights are given their due. ''The power and cunning of a worldliness affected, colored and embellished by Christianity may be as dreadful as we may fear them to be, and as Kierkegaard and others have presupposed'' (p. 121). The heightened sense of possibility is offset by a sober sense of the machinations of human sin. ''How can there be true words where it is sincerely or insincerely thought that due honor and even reverence should be paid to the Gospel but the art has long since been learned of accepting it without allowing it to intrude upon what are still at bottom secular thoughts and desires?'' (p. 120). The point can be made forcefully and at length:

> We must continually ask ourselves whether this mixed and relative secularism might not be characterized by perhaps an even greater resistance to the Gospel for the very reason that it is used to being confronted by and having to come to terms with it, and is thus able the more strongly to consolidate itself against it, making certain concessions and accommodations no doubt, parading in large measure as a world of Christian culture, but closing its ears the more firmly against it, and under the sign of a horrified rejection of theoretical atheism cherishing the more radically and shamelessly a true atheism of practice. (p. 120)

However, neither of these considerations—neither the heightened sense of possibility nor the stronger, countervailing sobriety—is given the final word. Ultimately what is at stake are not cultural or anthropological but christological considerations, and therefore the sovereignty and miracle of divine grace. From this vantage point the situation is essentially no different in the one secular sphere than in the other. ''If true words are to be uttered and heard from such a world of mixed and relative secularism, no less a miracle is needed than where we seem to have the express and unequivocal secularism of militant godlessness'' (pp. 120–21). Humanly speaking, the partial displacement of secularism by the gospel may indeed seem to be canceled out by the crosscurrents of a Christendom consisting of little more than secularization in Christian dress. ''Yet all these obvious fears must not result in a basic lack of confidence in the power of the message, however well or badly delivered'' (p. 121).

In other words, no matter how seriously the secular deformation of theology and church is taken—and in some situations it can scarcely be taken seriously enough—the power of the gospel and the miracle of grace are not to be written off. Everything depends on whether or not the promises of God are true, and on whether or not we ourselves believe them.

> But if they are true, and we believe them, why do we not also believe in the miracle—as it will always be—that the Word of Jesus Christ as well or badly attested by Christian proclamation, if not the proclamation itself, is stronger than the power and hardihood of the mixed and relative secularism of a ''Christian'' culture and society which confronts the community and continually penetrates and determines even the community itself? (p. 121)

In these words may be seen Barth's measured acceptance and implicit critique of a more Kierkegaardian attack upon a ''Christianized'' culture and a ''secularized'' church. In Barth's alternative the accent is deci-

sively and unmistakably shifted from sin to grace, from despair to hope
in the midst of despair, from the failings of Christendom to the vitality
of Christ. It is Jesus Christ, not secular deformation, who determines the
whole and who has the last word. "For him neither the militant godlessness of the outer periphery . . . nor the intricate heathenism of the inner,
is an insurmountable barrier" (p. 121). No room is left for excessive
skepticism. "We are summoned to believe in him, and in his victorious
power, not in the invincibility of any non-Christian, anti-Christian or
pseudo-Christian worldliness which confronts him. The more seriously
and joyfully we believe in him, the more we shall be able to receive true
words from it" (p. 122). In short, Kierkegaardian invective is relativized
and displaced by exactly that same basic confidence which allows the
community to remain expectant about finding true parables in the secular
realm.

    In order to clarify the status of true secular words, Barth at this point
introduces a set of eschatological considerations. At the same time he
offers an extended reflection on the relationship between "the center"
and "the periphery," although (apparently for the sake of simplicity) the
imagery shifts from "sphere" to "circle." The eschatological point is
relatively straightforward. True words from the secular realm have, as
Barth has said before, no status other than that of signs, attestations, or
parables. Like any true or theologically valid words in this life, they are
to be regarded as "signs of [Jesus Christ's] lordship," as "attestations
of his prophecy," as "real parables of the kingdom of heaven" (p. 122).
What is new is the more developed eschatological setting in which Barth
now places this familiar terminology. The terms "sign," "attestation,"
and "parable" indicate a provisional status. This status will obtain only
until the glory of Jesus Christ receives its "direct, universal and definitive
revelation." This revelation will be in the primary form of "his direct
Word," not in the secondary form of sign, parable, or witness. Prior to
that final occurrence, when the great "song of praise . . . will ring out
on a new earth under a new heaven," no merely human word can express
or articulate in any direct, universal, or definitive way "the truth of the
one Word of God" (p. 122). Nonetheless, a certain continuity in status
is thought to obtain between the current, more provisional state of affairs
and the one that will be final and definitive. This continuity is brought
out by means of the image of the center and the periphery.

    The relationship Barth sets forth between center and periphery, being
anything but straightforward, is highly dialectical and complex. On the
basis of the previous discussion, it might be expected that Jesus Christ as

the one Word of God would be identified with the center, and that human words would be assigned to the periphery. However, although this expectation is not entirely contradicted, neither is it entirely borne out. Instead, everything is subjected to a dialectical intensification and deepening. The truth of the one Word of God is not only identified with "the center of a circle," but also with "the whole periphery constituted by it" (p. 122). One single truth is seen as manifesting itself at the center and yet also at the periphery. Center and periphery, it might be said, are regarded as two forms of single truth. Of these two forms, the center is the primary, and the periphery the secondary. Implicitly, however, the secondary form has now been distinguished eschatologically into two different aspects—the one provisional, veiled, and parabolic; the other ultimate, manifest, and transparent. Yet in either aspect, the truth of the Word at the center and the truth of the words at the periphery are regarded as a single truth. More precisely, the truth of the Word at the center assumes secondary form in the truth of the words at the periphery.

Moreover, the unity of the whole is regarded as indissoluble. The center cannot be had without the periphery (nor the periphery without the center). Nor can the part be had without the whole (nor the whole without the part). Nor can any "segment" of the periphery be had without the periphery in its entirety (and therefore without the center, and therefore without the whole). Everything is mutually entailed by everything else (p. 122).

It is evident that two familiar formal patterns are in the background of this conception of the circle with its center and periphery. The differentiated unity of center and periphery suggests the Chalcedonian pattern. The connection between the two is indissoluble ("without separation or division"), yet each retains its distinctive identity ("without confusion or change"), and the one is primary and formative while the other is secondary and derivative ("distinctive ordering"). Moreover, the dialectical inclusion of the truth of the center in the forms at the periphery further suggests the trinitarian pattern of coinherence (as suggested in the opening of this chapter). It has already been seen that, for human words to be true, the truth of the Word "must dwell within them," and that therefore in their own way these words will "say the same thing" (p. 111). The idea of indwelling by the one in the other already suggests the pattern of coinherence.

This idea is carried forward when Barth goes on to say that the words at the periphery "do not express partial truths" (p. 123). As something that may be qualified but not quantified, "the one truth of Jesus Christ is indivisible.'' Human words at the periphery cannot and do not fragment this truth. "They express the one and total truth from a particular angle, and to that extent only implicitly and not explicitly in its unity and totality.'' In other words, the truth of the center in its unity and totality is always implicitly present in any of its manifestations at the periphery. The whole as a differentiated unity is always implicitly present as such in the part without either of them losing its identity or becoming superfluous. True human words—whether from the Bible, the church, or the world—are all in essentially the same situation. Insofar as they are true, they are holistic manifestations of "the one light of the one truth.'' From a particular standpoint they are a holistic refraction of "the one light.'' Each in its own "particular and individual way'' reflects and reproduces the truth of Jesus Christ in its totality. As each word is "enlightened by the truth of the Word itself,'' it both draws upon and manifests this light in "its fullness'' (p. 123). The mode of relatedness which emerges might therefore be stated like this: whereas the truth of the periphery imparts itself to the center by participating in and manifesting the totality which the center has established, the truth of the center imparts itself to the periphery by filling it and endowing it, at each and every point, with the fullness of uncreated light. Center and periphery are thus related by a mutuality of self-impartation. They are mutually (though differently) implicated in each other through a pattern of reciprocal coinherence.[7]

With this conception, Barth's discussion has reached its climax. The problem of secular parables, and more generally the problem of how the one great light is related to the many, is solved by recourse to the pattern of dialectical inclusion. If one may borrow certain Tillichian categories only to fill them with Barthian content, then Barth's position can be elucidated in terms of autonomy, heteronomy, and theonomy. The problem has been to conceive the mode of relatedness between the one great light and the many, with special reference to secular parables. It will be recalled that Barth rejected the possibility that other lights might be conceived as being *alongside* the one great light. Other lights, it might be said, are not to be conceived as enjoying a simple autonomy in relation to the one great light. They are not to be conceived as self-contained, self-sufficient, and self-grounded but rather as the reverse: incomplete, dependent, and contingent. Apart from the one great light, these other lights would neither arise nor endure. They are not an inner law unto themselves.

Also rejected was the possibility that these other lights might be conceived as *outside* the one great light. Simple heteronomy, it might also be said, is therefore ruled out as well. Other lights are not to be conceived as external or alien to the one great light and its self-established sphere. They do not represent some essentially different content or truth which would then need to be reconciled or synthesized with the one great light by means of some organizing principle larger than itself. Other lights do not pose an exterior law with which the one great light would need somehow to come to terms. Neither simple autonomy nor simple heteronomy represents the mode of relatedness by which true human words (and especially secular parables) are conceived as coexistent with Jesus Christ as the one Word of God.

The pattern of coinherence, as a proposed mode of relatedness, might be regarded as the theonomous alternative. The dialectical inclusion of the center in the periphery and of the periphery in the center suggests a distinctive, theonomous ordering of the truth. In a theonomous situation, it might be said, a single truth is manifest in a variety of distinctive forms without either the center losing itself in the periphery or the periphery losing itself in the center. The truth of the center—the truth of the one Word of God—has its own unique form in and of itself, which is indeed self-contained, self-sufficient, and self-grounded. It does not expend itself into the periphery without remainder, nor does it need the periphery's secondary forms in order to be fully itself.

Yet the center posits a periphery other than itself in order to reflect itself and reproduce itself within it. Therefore, by the mystery of creation, the periphery does not collapse into the center, but has its own real freedom (relative autonomy) and real existence (relative heteronomy) as a gift bestowed by the center. In a theonomous situation, the periphery is fully determined and governed by the truth of the center, but not violated or overwhelmed by it. In such a situation, therefore, both simple autonomy and simple heteronomy are deepened, negated, and surpassed. The order of creation is perfected, the disorder of the fall is abrogated, and the order of redemption is established. In this theonomous situation, "there can be other true words alongside the one Word of God, created and determined by it, exactly corresponding to it, fully serving it and therefore enjoying its power and authority" (p. 113). That is to say, the truth of the one great light at once contains and transcends, establishes and retrieves, the truth of all little lights at the periphery. Conversely, the truth of all little lights at the periphery, and each in its own distinctive way, at once reflects and contains, however indirectly, the primordial truth of the one great light in its unity, centrality, and totality. In short, in and with Jesus Christ all truth is essentially theonomous, being varie-

gated throughout the whole and the part by means of center and periphery
in patterns of reciprocal coinherence (cf. II/2, 177–81).

Although this theonomous pattern of relatedness would apply to all true
human words, it is of course secular words which here occupy Barth's
attention. As distinct from true human words which arise from the sphere
of the Bible and the church, true words from the secular sphere pose a
special problem of contextual ambiguity (or at least they do so more
acutely than do true words from the other sphere). Simply by virtue of
their arising from a secular setting in a fallen world, true secular words
will seem to carry with them a larger contextual whole which exists in
abstraction from and opposition to the contextual whole established by
and centered in the one true Word of God. To some extent they will
inevitably seem to be "segments of circles with other centers" (with false
words being really nothing but segments of such circles with other centers) (p. 122). Yet insofar as any secular word is true, it will not be
reducible to its immediate, secular context in an unqualified way. It will
only apparently be at home in this alienated context. In reality it will
actually be a segment in the periphery of the luminous circle established
by and centered in the truth of the one Word of God. Therefore, insofar
as human words arise from and participate in a secular context alien to
the one Word of God, they are not and cannot be true. "Spoken and
received abstractly, none of them can be a true word of itself" (p. 123).
Yet insofar as this alien origin and participation are only apparent rather
than real, these words actually originate in the one Word and are therefore true because Jesus Christ declares himself in them. "They are true
words in their presupposed and implied, if not always immediately apparent, connection with the totality of Jesus Christ and his prophecy, and
therefore as they indirectly point to this, or as this indirectly declares
itself in them" (p. 123).

This point about the contextual ambiguity of secular parables—their
immediate context being merely apparent, their true context being veiled
though real—suggests the extent to which Barth tends to think in terms
of differing contextual wholes that are at once inwardly integral and mutually incompatible. The contextual whole established by the one Word
of God is incompatible with any other, since, by definition, any other
would be established by an alien, competing, and ultimately illusory controlling center. The inward unity and mutual incompatibility of differing
contextual wholes explains why there is no way from secular words in
their larger, self-established contexts to the Word. On the other hand, the
larger, self-established context of the Word itself is, as Barth has repeat-

edly stressed, wider than the relatively narrow sphere of the Bible and the church. The sovereign freedom of the Word is such that it can and does declare itself through unwitting witnesses in the secular sphere (whether its secularism be pure or mixed). Insofar as the one Word of God declares itself in this way, in the form of secular parables, it becomes clear that, despite all ambiguity, the real contextual whole in which these words participate is only apparently secular; in reality it is actually christocentric. The sovereign freedom of the Word explains why there is indeed a way from the Word in its own self-established context to secular words. Thus the distinctively Barthian points about irreversibility, coinherence, and contextuality are all closely related. Essentially secular contexts, with their own intricate and dialectical interconnections of center and periphery (coinherence), effectively obviate the possibility of a progression from secular words to the Word. Yet the sovereign freedom of the Word, with its ability to posit a periphery whose scope extends beyond the sphere of the Bible and the church, effectively opens up the possibility, nonetheless, of a progression from the Word to secular words. It is on the actualization of this possibility that the occurrence of secular parables depends.

Given the possibility and actuality of theological validity in secular words, what might their content include? The list of examples which Barth provides extends throughout the entire sweep of Christian doctrine. No possible area is excluded. Creation, fall, reconciliation, and redemption are all explicitly mentioned. Various themes of theology proper such as God's majesty, mercy, or munificence, as well as themes of theological anthropology such as human finitude, sociality, dignity, corruption, forgiveness, and joy, are all indicated as possibilities. In each case the secular word will only apparently arise in isolation or abstraction from the context established by and centered in Jesus Christ, but on closer examination will be found in reality to point to him as "the One whom no single human word will declare, but to whom each may well point, so that he for his part may well declare himself in such words, making them his instruments, signs and attestations of his self-revelation and therefore of his truth" (p. 123).

In considering any secular word as a possible expression of truth, the Christian community will need to strike a delicate balance between faithfulness and perplexity, suspicion and openness, and self-affirmation and self-criticism. It will need to remain faithful above all to its own special task of speaking true theological words in the freedom and power promised to it. Since it knows of no such task and promise given outside its own bounds, it will not be able to see or understand how true words can be spoken from within the secular sphere (apart from seeing that a miracle is implied in the speaking of *any* true word, even from within the sphere of the Bible and the church). The community will thus do well to maintain a healthy skepticism toward such candidates from the secular sphere, wary of the dangers that can lurk in abstractions and distortions. Yet it will do even better if it does not allow this skepticism to outweigh its basic confidence, not in the secular sphere, but in the potentialities of Jesus Christ as the world's Lord and Savior. Finally, although the community will do well to preserve and affirm the integrity of its proclamation where that exists, it will do even better to allow itself to be corrected and chastened by a secularism which has often attested aspects of the truth entrusted to the community "far better, more quickly and more consistently" than the community itself seems to have done (p. 124).

Extended consideration is given to this latter point. An extraordinarily rich and suggestive inventory of topics is offered on which Barth thinks the community might well have something weighty to learn from the secular sphere. Only a small sampling can be reproduced here:

> We may think of the mystery of God, which we Christians so easily talk away in a proper concern for our own cause. . . . We may think of the radicalness of the need of redemption or the fullness of what is meant by redemption if it is to meet this need. . . . Especially we may think of a humanity which does not ask or weigh too long with whom we are dealing in others, but in which we find a simple solidarity with them and unreservedly take up their cause. (p. 125 rev.)

All these phenomena and more, Barth suggests, may be found "with striking frequency" outside the bounds of the church. Is there not something, he asks, to be learned from them? "Is not their language, however alien their forms, that of true words? Are they not 'parables of the kingdom of heaven' " (p. 125 rev.)?

From the actuality of secular words with such salutary and remedial content, Barth moves on to ask about the criteria for testing them. A process of discernment will be necessary in assessing the truth of any theological word. In the case of secular words, their subjective presuppositions will need to be distinguished from the objective relationship in which they really stand to the lordship of Jesus Christ. True secular words will always be more than what they seem to be in and of themselves, and they may even speak "against themselves." Yet in these respects secular words are not so different from words arising from within the sphere of the church. "Even in Christian circles is it not grace and miracle, and the continual transcending of a whole mass of subjective ineptitude and distortion, if true words are spoken and heard?" (p. 125). Criteria will always be needed "to distinguish the truth of true words themselves from the untruth which will also cling to them" (p. 126). Four primary criteria are therefore proposed: formal, material, practical, and ecclesiastical.

The formal criterion acquires "its critical force" by virtue of its being also "the decisive material norm," namely, the biblical witness. Both formally and materially, Holy Scripture—taken as a differentiated and unified whole centered in Jesus Christ—is the decisive norm against which secular words are to be tested for possible expressions of theological truth. Thus the task is not to show (as in more apologetic theologies) that scripture is anticipated and confirmed by secular words, but rather that secular words are anticipated and confirmed by scripture. Positively, the decisive test is that the secular word "will harmonize at some point with the whole context of the biblical message as centrally determined and characterized by Jesus Christ" (p. 125). The negative reverse of this test is thus that at no point will "the general line" of the biblical message be contradicted, disrupted, suppressed, or usurped. Insofar as such tendencies are present, we are not dealing with a true word. No secular word may be allowed to prevent the Bible from being "perceived and understood in light of its center." Note that the issue is simply one of compatibility or logical consistency. Secular words are not expected flatly to repeat what is already known of the content of scripture, but rather to cast light on scripture by virtue of being compatible with it.[8] Secular words will thus be true by virtue of their being "a good commentary sounding out of the word of the Bible." To the extent that scripture stands "in evident and easily displayed agreement" with secular words, "we may confidently believe that the latter are true words, and thus be ready for obedience, in the direction indicated, not to the words as such, but to the word of scripture illuminated and made more pressing by them" (p. 125).

In applying the scriptural criterion the community will need to be sensitive to the double imperative of conservation for the sake of the past and innovation for the sake of the future. The imperative of conservation will be fulfilled by respecting the historic dogmas and confessions of the church. Although their authority is decidedly secondary in relation to scripture, secular words "must certainly be tested by this norm" (p. 125). Respect for these dogmas and confessions of the past occurs "in due fulfillment of the Fifth Commandment" (p. 127). If secular words "lead

to a breach with them, they will show themselves to be false words.''
Yet the imperative of conservation must be balanced against that of innovation. It will be necessary for the community to learn new things for
the future which go beyond the past and which could not have been
taught when the dogmas and confessions were formulated. These new
things will not arise directly from the dogmas and confessions, not even
"from their own inner movements," but will be given to the community
by its Lord "afresh from without." Nonetheless, these new things "will
somehow be an extension of the line visible in the dogmas and confessions." Therefore, in the midst of innovation, continuity with the past
will not be broken, but will be taken up and continued "with new responsibility on the basis of better instruction" (p. 127). Conservation and
innovation, it might be said, will need to be held together in a kind of
reflective equilibrium, always governed by Jesus Christ as the living center of each.

Along with scripture as the formal and material criterion, two other
criteria are proposed. The first of these might be called "practical." To
some extent the truth of secular words can be assessed by looking at the
fruits they have borne in the outside world where they arise. When it
comes to the practical effects of these words, not all cats will prove to
be gray. Although it will not always be possible to distinguish the good
from the bad, it should at least be possible to distinguish the better from
the worse. What effect do these words appear to have in the secular
sphere? "What spirits do they seem to evoke? In what direction do they
impel people? . . . To what enterprises and actions have they summoned
them? Have they led to their greater freedom or their greater bondage?
. . . Have they built up or thrown down, gathered or scattered, quickened or slain?" (p. 128 rev.). These distinctions, Barth stresses, will
always be relative. Yet if on the whole the fruits seem less good, "we
may readily suspect that there is little or no truth in the words which
produce them. But if we may cautiously discern better fruits, this may
well be a sign that there is a positive relationship between the words
which have produced them and the one Word of truth, so that in them
we have to do with true words." This criterion, which must not be thought
of as standing on its own, will have to be used with great care; but it will
sometimes prove to be quite powerful. "We have thus to keep our eyes
open in this direction" (p. 128).

Finally, there is what might be called the "ecclesiastical" criterion.
Throughout the entire discussion Barth's stance has obviously not been
that of a detached or disembodied observer, but has always been self-

consciously located in the tradition of a particular community with a particular history. It would not seem too much to surmise that Barth (in contrast to certain modernist theories) supposes no other sort of standpoint actually to exist.[9] In any case, the question which he now poses is, what will secular words signify, if true, for the Christian community? The answer which he offers, in brief, is that such words will show themselves to be true by virtue of their offering the community no criticism without affirmation and no affirmation without criticism. True secular words will always confront the community at once with a summons to faith and yet also with a call to repentance. They will always manifest that "indissoluble unity" of affirmative and critical features which Barth takes to be an ineffaceable feature of the relationship between gospel and law. Secular words, he says, "will show themselves to be genuine parables of the kingdom in this unity" (p. 128).

Any true call to repentance, Barth holds, whether from within the community or without, may be known by the fact that its criticism, challenge, and confrontation will always be those of the gospel. They will always occur in a larger context that is affirmative, supportive, and accepting. In any true call to repentance, therefore, "the community is always raised up as well as cast down, not being plunged into a sterile melancholy, remorse or abasement, but stirred with new resolution and clarity to represent its good cause" (p. 129). No critical word is true, if it is not also one with the word by which the church is comforted in the biblical sense. "A word which merely pacified and confirmed, or unsettled and shattered, would by its very nature reveal that it had nothing whatever to do with the one truth of Jesus Christ, that it was not then a true word, and that it should not therefore be heard" (p. 130). Secular words, insofar as they are true, will never engage the community one-sidedly but always in this twofold sense.

From a consideration of criteria Barth moves on to one last question. If secular words show themselves to be true, what is the right use to be made of them by the Christian community? Both a "general" and a "specific" answer are offered to this question. Barth's general answer is that neither pride nor sloth should be allowed to prevent the community from hearing the truth of secular words when they occur. The community's attitude is to be one of receptiveness. What it stands to gain is a better understanding of scripture and a needed correction and reformation of its tradition. For secular parables will impress themselves upon the community not merely as true, but as "free communications of the will of its Lord which it must not stiffly refuse but accept" (p. 130).

Barth's more specific answer develops a contrast between two modes of address. If secular parables address the community as free communications from its Lord, then how are these communications related to scripture, which, in the power of the Holy Spirit, is also a mode of address to the community from its Lord? The basic line developed in answer to this question is that, whereas secular parables are occasional, context-specific, and irregular modes by which the community is addressed, scripture in this regard is constant, universal, and regular.

Scripture, says Barth, is not only to be conceived as a "source and norm," but also as an "abiding whole" by which Jesus Christ accompanies the community throughout its history. "Holy Scripture may be compared to the fiery cloud and pillar which in every age precedes the community and all its members as an invariably authentic direction to the knowledge of its Lord, to the gift which he gives and the accompanying task which he sets" (p. 130). The community, which receives guidance from scripture by day and by night, is always and everywhere to gather around its word, "to regard its claim, . . . to pursue its investigation, exposition and application" (p. 131). In it true words are always to be sought and found. It is always the way of Jesus Christ. "As I see it," says Barth, "it is the regular way to which we are directed" (p. 131).

The same cannot be said of secular parables, even though they too are to be regarded as modes of address from the Lord. "Indeed, we must not say this concerning them if we are to estimate them aright" (p. 131). Secular parables are distinctive as free communications of Jesus Christ. They are specific to particular times and particular places and are therefore not to be canonized as a binding authority for all times and all places. They will need to be tested as the church's history proceeds, and not without the utterance and reception of new and perhaps countervailing secular parables. Their status will always be extraordinary. Therefore they cannot be regarded, like scripture, as a normative source of revelation. Nor can they be laid alongside scripture as a second norm. They can only be received in confirmation and illumination of scripture. Only within these limits can they be respected, but within these limits they must be respected. They "can and should be made fruitful for the community" (p. 134). The process by which they are made fruitful—enhancing and reforming the tradition—may be long and arduous. Yet those in the vanguard, who first see a secular parable for what it is, need not despair that its free communication will finally be thwarted. "If it is a true word, the time will inevitably come sooner or later when it can make its way and do its work in and to the whole community" (p. 135).

As a concluding note, Barth acknowledges that he has offered no specific examples of a secular parable. To have done so, he says, would have detracted from his real purpose. He has intended only to address certain fundamental questions of principle. What is the condition for the possibility of true words from the secular sphere? In what mode can such words be thought to coexist with the one true Word of God? By what criteria can the possible truth of such words be tested? What use of true secular words is appropriate to the Christian community? These questions can be addressed without trying to come to a decision about any particular case. All such cases will be doubtful and contestable in and of themselves. But "what is not doubtful and contestable," says Barth, "is the prophecy of Jesus Christ and its almighty power to bring forth such true words *extra muros ecclesiae* and to attest itself through them" (p. 135). That alone was the matter to be discussed.

Up to this point the several motifs which have been the special object of this study—actualism, particularism, objectivism, personalism, realism, and rationalism—have been conspicuous by their absence. This omission has been deliberate. It has been meant to drive home the point that the motifs are of no interest in themselves. They are not useful except insofar as they illuminate the Barthian text as categories of discernment. They are as formal as can possibly be, possessing no content which can be stated apart from their specific instantiations and applications to matters of substance. Barth's employment of these motifs is various, creative, and often unpredictable. Yet to the attentive reader their presence in our discussion of secular parables will have been discernible, in one way or another, at almost every point. In conclusion, they may now be drawn in explicitly in order to summarize and sharpen the analysis.

(1) *Actualism.* This motif has been present primarily at three points. First, the condition for the possibility of secular parables was explained without recourse to positing any innate human capacities and therefore without recourse to natural theology. Secular parables, like any true human words (including those of the Bible and the church) find the condition for their possibility strictly in the miracle of grace. They are free actualizations of a possibility which belongs to (and remains with) Jesus Christ alone. "If there are true words of God, it is all miraculous" (p. 118).

A second point where the actualist motif has been present is in the discussion of revelation. The reproach which will inevitably arise against the claim to exclusivity is not seen as something that can be overcome by apologetic or philosophical argumentation (or indeed by any autonomous form of human endeavor). That there is only one theological truth, that it is exclusively the truth of Jesus Christ, and that all other truths must be conceived dialectically as distinctive forms, reflections, and reproductions of the one great truth—all this is regarded as something for which the "only conclusive argument" is "the Holy Spirit" (p. 109), regardless of its internal plausibility and consistency within the network of certain Christian beliefs.

Finally, actualism informs the doctrine that all theological truth is coinherent. In a theonomous situation the giving and receiving of truth is conceived as a miracle of free reciprocity. The freedom of the periphery is not overpowered by that of the center, nor is the freedom of the center diminished by that of the periphery. The truth of the center freely gives itself to the periphery, and the truth of the periphery freely receives it, reflecting it distinctively back to the center. The idea of free reciprocity is characteristic of Barth's theology, as for example when he says that in and with the one life act of Jesus Christ, "there takes place all the life-acts of those who as free subjects (within their determined limits) are creatures of God" (p. 41). Free reciprocity between the Word and the words is an instance of the miracle of grace.

(2) *Particularism*. This motif—which has to do with respecting the concrete particularity of Jesus Christ and therefore with the mystery which surrounds his incomparable uniqueness—has been present primarily with the question of how the one great light is related to the many. This question can be distinguished into at least two aspects. First, the primary term of this relatedness needs to be properly conceived (viz., Jesus Christ as the one great light). Second, the peculiar mode needs to be properly conceived in which the two basic terms coexist (viz., how the one great light and the many other lights are related). In neither case, it is thought, can the problem be solved by recourse to conceptual schemes or systems, drawn from general or ordinary experience, that are susceptible to complete rational closure. Rather, in each case antithetical lines of thought are allowed to stand unresolved in deference to the peculiarity of the subject matter and in humility vis-à-vis the perceived limits of human understanding. In each case, that is to say, the relations at stake are not only conceived as active (as brought out by the previous motif), but also as mysterious, even though the mysteries arrange themselves into patterns.

The Chalcedonian pattern, which describes the mystery of the person of Christ, is applied in solution to the first aspect of the problem. As has been repeatedly noted, Barth believes that Jesus Christ as the one Word of God is not properly conceived unless it is seen that he exists not only in the manner of a human being, but also at the same time in the manner of God. Because Jesus Christ alone has this status, whereby he "shares the uniqueness of God" (p. 96), he alone confronts us with the "absolute claim" that he is himself "the source and norm of all truth" (pp. 89, 102). When conceived along Chalcedonian lines, the mystery of his person thus implies the further mystery that he himself is the source on which all other truth is dependent, the norm by which all other truth is judged, and the center to which all other truth testifies and points. The unique particularity of Christ's person is thereby carried over into Barth's proposal for how to conceive of Jesus Christ as the primary term of relatedness in questions of truth.

Similarly, the trinitarian pattern, which describes the mystery of the inner being of God, is applied in solution to the second aspect of the problem. That is to say, the mystery of dialectical inclusion, which finds its supreme instance in the perichoresis of the divine triunity, is applied by way of analogy (no more than that!) to the problem of the mode by which the one great light is related to the many. That mode, as has been explained in detail, is taken to be one of coinherence. The one Word dwells in and with the many, and the many words dwell in and with the one. There is no truth which is not finally the one truth. The one truth manifests itself in all truths without making any of them redundant, and all truths reproduce the one truth without in any way fragmenting or exhausting it. The unique particularity of the divine triunity, in conjunction with the mysteries of creation and redemption, is thus carried over, by way of certain analogies, into Barth's proposal for how to conceive the mode of relatedness between the Word and the words in the question of truth. The idea of reciprocal indwelling is meant to signify a mode of relatedness whose actualization is not only spontaneous but also mysterious.

In short, with regard to both aspects of the question, recourse to specifiable patterns of mystery is thought to be necessary in order to respect the uniqueness and particularity of the subject matter.

(3) *Objectivism and personalism.* The motif of *revelational* objectivism does not appear in Barth's discussion of secular parables, except tacitly as a background belief that is everywhere presupposed. That is, Barth presupposes but does not discuss the idea that the church's knowledge of God is decisively mediated through the secondary objectivity of Jesus Christ's humanity. Much more in the foreground, however, is the motif of *soteriological* objectivism. What is especially interesting is the

conceptual unity which Barth achieves between this motif and that of personalism. This unity is above all evident in the discussion of three topics: (a) the conception of reconciliation as also revelation, (b) the rejection of natural and apologetic theologies, and (c) coinherence as a mode of relatedness.

First, the unity of the two motifs is evident in Barth's conception of reconciliation as also revelation. Whereas reconciliation is conceived (as one would expect) along the lines of soteriological objectivism, revelation is conceived, rather dramatically, in terms of personal address. Their unity may be stated as follows. Reconciliation—the finished and objective work accomplished in the history of Jesus Christ—does not remain merely objective. Rather, it actually confronts each and every human being, by a miracle of grace, as revelation. It confronts them, that is, as the Word of God in the mode of personal address. It addresses them personally with the costly and reconciling work that took place for them objectively. Furthermore, since the work and the person who did the work are inseparable, it may be said that the person who did the work addresses each human being personally with the reconciling work which took place objectively for all and therefore also for the person addressed. The one Word of God, presenting this content in the mode of personal address, claims each person who is addressed totally. The only response appropriate to this Word is completely self-involving.

The condition for the possibility of this event, insofar as it involves complex questions of temporality, was discussed at the opening of this chapter. This discussion is relevant as background to the unity posited between personalism and objectivism. Revelation is conceived precisely as the miracle whereby the divine eternity mediates a particular history to each and every human being as a Word of personal address. The finished and objective work of reconciliation is taken up as the one Word of God. This work is itself the Word "which was and will be addressed to each and every human being as such, and which is addressed to them precisely as that which was and will be" (p. 45 rev.). Reconciliation and revelation thus exist together in indissoluble unity, and therein the unity between objectivism and personalism is also displayed.

A major reason why Barth rejects both natural and apologetic theologies is that he seems to see them as severing this unity. That is, he seems to see each of them as offering some version of objectivism without personalism. His objection to natural theology, as it emerged in the discussion, was not only that it put forward falsifying abstractions and nonexistent capacities, but also that it put forward neutral generalizations. Natural theology, we might say, offended not only against the motifs of particularism and actualism, but also against the motif of personalism. It obscured not only the mode of God's concrete particularity and the mode by which God is made known, but also the mode by which God is truly apprehended as God. God is not truly apprehended as God, Barth seems to be saying, without our personal conversion, renewal, and commitment. From this point of view what natural theology seems to offer is at once the absence of personalism in conjunction with a spurious objectivism (spurious, because it makes no reference to the mediation of Jesus Christ).

Apologetic theology, as may be noted more briefly, seems to offer the same kind of neutral generalizations. When Barth insists that the offense of truth's exclusivity in Christ cannot be overcome on apologetic grounds, he seems to be saying that it cannot be overcome apart from a personal encounter with and apprehension of God's Word. This apprehension does not occur unless our trust, humility, and obedience are fully engaged. Apologetic theology, like natural theology, seems to defer the moment of personalist apprehension while offering an objectivist generalization which strangely deletes reference to Jesus Christ. By contrast, what Barth seems to be saying is this: insofar as Jesus Christ himself is inalienable to an authentic objectivism, personal encounter and commitment are inalienable to our apprehension of God. The two are so indissolubly united that neither can be had without the other.

Finally, the unity of objectivism and personalism can be seen in Barth's conception of truth as coinherent. At first glance perhaps the personalist aspect of this conception is more evident than the objectivist. The coinherent mode by which the Word and the words are related is conceived not only as spontaneous and mysterious, but also as interpersonal. Although a distinction between words and the persons who utter them can be analytically useful, in Barth's discussion of secular parables this distinction is not allowed to harden into anything like a separation or even an opposition. The truth of the word is finally inseparable from the person who utters it. The concept by which words and persons are held together is the concept of witness. A careful reading shows that the discussion moves fluidly back and forth between regarding words and persons as witnesses. At another level, of course, the same sort of interrelation occurs, for the Word of God and the person of Christ are also regarded as identical. In one way or another Barth seems tacitly to presuppose that the word is finally always in the person, and the person in the word.

Therefore, even in the question of truth, the distinctive features of coinherence—reciprocal indwelling and mutual self-impartation—are ultimately to be regarded not merely as verbal but as fully interpersonal.

The objectivist aspect of this coinherence can be explained by returning to the image of the circle with its center and periphery. To say that Jesus Christ occupies the center of this circle as the one Word of God is to say that the event of coinherence cannot be understood except as mediated by him. What is said in another connection can be applied directly to coinherence: "It does not take place, and therefore cannot be seen or understood, apart from him or in any way in itself" (p. 39). He is "its Mediator and Accomplisher in his own person" (p. 38). Apart from his objective mediation of God's Word to us and our words to God, the event of coinherence does not take place. The coinherence in question is to be regarded not only as spontaneous, mysterious, and interpersonal, but also as objectively mediated. Therefore the unity of the two motifs is also apparent. For in the conception of coinherence (as always for Barth), there is no personalism without objectivism and no objectivism without personalism.

(4) *Realism and rationalism.* These motifs, which pertain to the proximate criteria by which any theological assertion is to be tested, may be considered together. Realism has to do with the question of whether any such assertion is in accord with scripture and, if it is, the mode by which that assertion may be thought to refer to its subject matter. Rationalism, on the other hand, has to do with demonstrating the internal and external modes of consistency appropriate to those Christian theological assertions which are taken to be authentic (i.e., in accord with scripture). In Barth's discussion of secular parables, each of these motifs is present in a way that casts light on its larger place and function within his theology.

The truth of secular words could not be explained without taking into account the truth of biblical and ecclesiastical words, nor could the truth of any of these be explained without taking into account their various relationships to the one Word of God. The truth of the one Word of God, as indicated at length, establishes itself as the center of a differentiated and unified whole. In this whole, the truth of all human words is included via the dialectical pattern of coinherence. Neither true secular words nor true ecclesiastical words occur, however, as the primary instance of this pattern. Its primary instance is rather to be found in scripture.

Scripture, that is to say, is regarded as a centered, differentiated, and unified whole. Its assertions, when properly ordered and conceived, have a privileged status with respect to truth. The general coinherence between the Word and the words is not only objectively mediated (by Christ) but also textually mediated (by scripture). The textual mediation of this coinherence is regarded as real though secondary and secondary though real. To put it somewhat differently, scripture at once uniquely exemplifies and, in so exemplifying, mediates the coinherence of the Word and the words. It exemplifies this coinherence in the following way.

First, the subject matter to which scripture points cannot be investigated independently of its scriptural mediation (particularism). Second, the subject matter to which scripture points remains the Lord of its scriptural mediation (actualism). Third, the subject matter to which scripture points speaks through its scriptural mediation in the mode of personal address (personalism). Fourth, the subject matter to which scripture points centers its scriptural mediation in the work, history, and accomplishment of the Mediator (objectivism). Fifth, the subject matter to which scripture points unifies its scriptural mediation as a whole by serving as its controlling center (rationalism). In short, the subject matter presents itself through its scriptural mediation uniquely, spontaneously, sovereignly, objectively, and coherently.

For the sake of its own mediation, the Word itself "directly formed and guided" the historical development of Holy Scripture (p. 113). The resulting scriptural word (characteristically stated in the singular rather than the plural) is taken to be so unified, differentiated, and centered as a whole that all its various parts can be read as referring, directly or indirectly, to Jesus Christ. "The word of the Bible" is to be "perceived and understood in light of its center" (p. 126). Because "the whole context of the biblical message" is "centrally determined and characterized by Jesus Christ" (p. 126), "in Holy Scripture true words are always to be found" (p. 131). Therefore, despite its attendant flaws, limitations, extraneous elements, and other inadequacies as an all-too-human word, this text mediates the Word in a way that exemplifies the larger dialectic of coinherence. The Word does not cease to be divine, nor does the scriptural word cease to be human. Yet the Word dwells in and with the scriptural word, and the scriptural word in and with the Word.

Although not especially prominent within the discussion of secular parables, the motif of rationalism clearly emerges at some crucial points. The problem of rationalism within the bounds of dogmatic theology is the problem of identifying, elaborating, and applying appropriate modes of consistency and coherence within the web of those doctrines and beliefs regarded as authentic to the Christian community. As indicated repeatedly in the analysis of particularism, there will be some doctrinal statements at the center of the Christian faith which, Barth argues, must be allowed to stand in apparent inconsistency for the sake of their scriptural authenticity and the uniqueness of the subject matter which they attest. The primacy accorded to authenticity in such cases, however, does not eliminate, but simply delimits, the use of principles of internal and external consistency in the course of theological reflection.[10]

In the discussion of secular parables, Barth uses these principles at important points. Internal consistency, for example, becomes the decisive criterion on a number of occasions, only one of which will be mentioned here. In considering the reproach against exclusivity, the whole question is finally resolved by arguing that Christian freedom "stands or falls" by whether it confesses Jesus Christ as the one Word of God (p. 90). This conceptual resolution may be regarded, in part, as an assertion that the Christian community cannot abandon the doctrine in question without lapsing into serious doctrinal self-contradiction. External consistency, on the other hand, as already indicated at length, is the decisive criterion not only by which other doctrinal schemes must be rejected as wholes, but also by which true words can nonetheless be discovered within them. As these examples suggest, the motif of rationalism operates within the bounds established especially by the motifs of realism and particularism.

In conclusion, Barth's overall position on secular parables of the truth might be characterized as *exclusivism without triumphalism* or, alternatively, *inclusivism without compromise*.[11] Barth's position is *exclusivist* in the following sense. It holds that one scheme of theological doctrines (Christianity), taken as a whole, is true in a way that no other such scheme, taken as a whole, can be. Indeed, when taken as a whole, any other such scheme, regardless of its form—whether secular or religious, theoretical or practical, implicit or explicit—can only be regarded as false. Any such scheme when taken as a whole can only be false, because (by definition) it organizes itself around some central doctrines other than those concerning Jesus Christ as he is attested for us in Holy Scripture.[12] Any unified and differentiated theological scheme or whole, organized around a different controlling center, can only stand in contradiction to (and in competition with) Christianity as an alternative scheme of truth. Simply by virtue of an extended principle of consistency, such alternative schemes can (logically can) only be regarded as mutually exclusive. Taken as wholes they confront one another with an either/or. From within the Christian scheme, therefore, any other theological scheme *as such* must be regarded as false.[13]

In the following senses, however, Barth's position is *not triumphalist*.

It does not hold that all other schemes are mistaken on all points of theological significance. It does not hold that salvation is necessarily limited to those who espouse Christianity. And it does not hold that the Christian community has nothing of theological significance to learn from others. On the contrary, it is expected that other theological schemes (in whatever form) will be by no means be mistaken on all points of significance. To suppose otherwise would be inconsistent with belief in the resurrection and universal lordship of Jesus Christ. Moreover, because Barth holds that Jesus Christ actually (and not just potentially) died for all, and that all are elect in him, it is to be expected that salvation will not necessarily be limited to those who have espoused Christianity as an interrelated set of beliefs and practices. However, neither the extent of such cases of salvation nor the manner by which they may be effected is thought to be a matter upon which the gospel gives Christians license to speculate, let alone to depart from their divinely given mission of proclamation. What it does give license to is humility, openness, and hope. Finally, as indicated in our exposition at some length, the community may have a great deal of significance to learn from others. Indeed, it must actually regard true secular words as nothing less than free communications from its Lord for the enrichment, correction, or reformation of its doctrine and common life.

Barth's position is therefore *inclusivist* in the following sense: it holds that truth is where one finds it. It does not foreclose in advance just where *extra muros ecclesiae* any truth might actually be found. Nor does it foreclose in advance just what doctrinal topic a true secular word might address. On the contrary, it holds that true words may by found outside the church which need to be heard within the church, and that such words might pertain to any aspect of the church's belief or practice. Given that Jesus Christ (and not the church) is the source, norm, and center of all truth, there is no truth of theological significance not included within the sphere that he establishes. Furthermore, given both the finitude and the fallenness of all words (whether from within the church or without), all true human words will be included on the same basis. They will all be abased, elevated, and transformed from outside themselves by the miracle of grace. Their truth will never be grounded in themselves, and none of them will be true except in the same sense as one can also speak of a "justified sinner." [14]

Finally, in the following senses Barth's position is *uncompromising*. Subjectivism, pluralism, and relativism (three compromises associated with inclusivity) are all ruled out. Insofar as *subjectivism* means that the doctrines of any theological scheme are valid by virtue of meeting the spiritual needs of those who adhere to them, Barth's position is antisubjectivist. Insofar as *pluralism* means that any theological scheme is valid to the extent that it expresses a healing and authentic form of religious experience, his position is antipluralist. And insofar as *relativism* means that the truth of a theological scheme is so conditioned by the cultural context of its adherents that more than one such scheme can be valid, his position is antirelativist.

Barth's position rules out *subjectivism*, largely by disallowing the subjectivist premise that spiritual needs can ostensibly be defined and met as though Jesus Christ were irrelevant to them. His position rules out *pluralism*, largely by disallowing the pluralist premise that some sort of generic religious experience or piety is the criterion of theological truth. And his position rules out *relativism*, largely by disallowing the relativist premise that the reality of cultural conditioning decisively determines the truth of theological schemes. More broadly, his position rules out all three counterpositions by disallowing a premise sometimes found in any of them. According to this premise, the relevant criteria are to be derived by lining up various theological schemes alongside one another and then privileging whatever it is that they are thought to have in common. In Barth's view, as noted, it is precisely what theological schemes *as such* have in common that renders them mutually exclusive (at least relative to the Christian scheme).

One last note: *exclusivism without triumphalism* or *inclusivism without compromise* can be interpreted as Barth's attempt to encourage what is best (and discourage what is worst) in certain ecclesiastical formations. The logic of his position would seem to sponsor what he once somewhere described as a "confessing-ecumenical, liberal-conservative church." Perhaps the promise of Barth's theology might be seen in the way that it at once transcends, yet also overlaps and comprehends, the standard terms of ecclesiastical conflict and debate in the modern world.

Notes

Preface

1. The term "coherentist," as used in this study, requires some explanation. In contemporary epistemology "coherentism" is distinguished from "foundationalism," and within coherentism a distinction is made between "the coherence theory of justification" and "the coherence theory of truth." Barth's theology does not share any of these views at the theoretical level. In actual practice, however, his procedure for testing or justifying a proposed doctrinal belief converges closely with the procedure recommended by the coherence theory of justification, and it is this convergence which justifies the use of the term "coherentist" in this study. The term is meant to signify no more than such convergence in practice, but does seem illuminating in that sense.

Insofar as Barth's theology incorporates aspects of the *correspondence* theory of truth, on the other hand, it also converges with certain aspects of foundationalism. Of course this theology makes no attempt to argue that theological assertions can be justified by appealing to (or claiming the status of) assertions that are neutral, self-evident, and universally accessible. In this sense the divergence from foundationalism could not be wider. At the same time, however, doctrinal beliefs are not thought to be justified merely because they are members of a coherent set (the view of pure coherentism). They are rather thought to be justified also and primarily because they are suitably grounded in revelation as normatively attested in scripture. (Thus perhpas to some extent, "revelation" might be thought to occupy the logical space filled by "sensory experience" in foundationalist epistemologies.) For Barth, like foundationalism and unlike coherentism, some beliefs are basic such that other beliefs may be reliably derived from them. By combining aspects of the coherence theory of justification with aspects of the correspondence theory of truth, Barth seems to approach, at the theoretical level, the position that is called "weak" (as opposed to "pure") coherentism.

Barth's views on these matters are discussed more fully below in ch. 2. An excellent discussion of the philosophical questions may be found in Jonathan Dancy, *Introduction to Contemporary Epistemology* (Oxford: Basil Blackwell, 1985).

It might be added that Barth seems explicitly to repudiate the view of pure coherentism. This view succeeds as little in theology, he seems to say, as in any other field of academic discourse. The witness of the biblical authors, Barth writes, "is not a kind of logically developed human doctrine and theory which, like every human doctrine and theory, for all its logic can and necessarily will reveal at some point an hiatus and contain and tolerate its own contradiction within itself" (II/1, 105; cf. II/1, 580). The possibility of rejecting pure coherentism in this way seems currently to have more philosophical standing than perhaps it once did: "There is, I have been suggesting, a kind of Gödel's Theorem in human affairs: Every attempt to systematize life or to govern it by a set of axioms rich enough to encompass the totality of experience leads to a contradiction" (Stanley Rosen, *The Ancients and the Moderns: Rethinking Modernity* [New Haven: Yale University Press, 1989], p. 17). In any case, Barth makes his own argument against something like pure coherentism strictly on theological grounds: "The biblical witness is not at all a doctrine and theory of this kind. It is the witness to God's revelation. In other words, it does not spin out a human idea, alongside which other and contradictory ideas can and must have a place, as is the case with all human systems of thought; but even in the form of human thoughts it points above all human thoughts to the event of the encounter of God with humankind in Jesus Christ" (II/1, 105 rev.). In other words, even given the impossibility of pure coherentism, theology ought not to strive for complete conceptual systematization, not even the dialectical kind that seeks to incorporate its contradiction within itself.

2. The cartographic metaphor suggests something of the limits as well as the possibilities of this study. Learning to recognize what the motifs signify (with or without the help of the motifs themselves) is necessary for any adequate reading of the *Church Dogmatics,* but of course is by no means sufficient. No claim is made that other important questions are somehow circumvented by the scope of this study. It is possible, however, that questions of how Barth's thought developed internally as well as how it is related to various external contexts (historical, sociological, cultural–intellectual, ecclesiastical, etc.) might be illuminated by attending to the sort of pattern recognition which this study offers.

Prologue

1. Hans Urs von Balthasar, *Karl Barth: Darstellung und Deutung seiner Theologie* (Cologne: Jakob Hegner, 1951). English translation: *The Theology of Karl Barth* (Garden City, N.Y.: Doubleday-Anchor, 1972). The English translation will be followed wherever possible. All page references will appear in the

text, with the first referring to the German and the second to the English edition. Where only one reference appears, the passage was not included in the English edition.

2. Although Barth once wrote that "I regard the *analogia entis* as the invention of the Antichrist" (I/1, xiii), and although he went on to polemicize against it repeatedly, nowhere in the *Church Dogmatics* does he pause directly to define what he means by it. Indirectly, however, what he means becomes sufficiently clear. The *analogia entis* is conceived as embracing two matters at once: a constitutive state of affairs and an epistemic procedure based on it. (Where I have said "constitutive" and "epistemic," Barth would tend to say "ontic" and "noetic.") The state of affairs is one in which human beings are in some sense inherently open to and capable of knowing God. The procedure is then one in which this inherent openness and capacity are exercised such that God becomes known, regardless of how provisionally. As the premise behind natural theology, the *analogia entis* seems to underwrite almost everything Barth takes to be theologically impossible by virtue of the personalist, objectivist, actualist, and particularist motifs. (See pp. 96–99, 255–56.)

Barth's epistemic alternative to the *analogia entis* is the *analogia fidei*. The *analogia entis,* as Barth understands it, posits an analogy between the human being and the divine being by virtue of their sharing a commonality in "being" (even though the two may not be conceived as related to this commonality in the same way). (This commonality is the condition for the possibility of the human being's inherent openness to and capability of knowing God.) The *analogia fidei,* on the other hand, posits an analogy between a human action (faith) and a divine action (grace) in just a situation where no ontological commonality is conceived to exist. Grace elicits faith, and faith corresponds analogically to grace, but no ontological commonality of any kind mediates between them. Since no inherent human openness or capability exists to be exercised, grace is the sole condition for the possibility of faith. Faith is conceived as grounded in grace alone, and the mediating term with respect to the analogy is conceived not as "being" but as "miracle."

3. Colin E. Gunton, *Becoming and Being: The Doctrine of God in Charles Hartshorne and Karl Barth* (Oxford: Oxford University Press, 1978), pp. 174–75.

4. Thomas F. Torrance, *Karl Barth: An Introduction to His Early Theology, 1910–1931* (London: SCM Press, 1962).

5. G. C. Berkouwer, *The Triumph of Grace in the Theology of Karl Barth* (Grand Rapids, Mich.: Eerdmans, 1956).

6. Karl Barth, *Church Dogmatics,* vol. IV, part 3, first half (Edinburgh: T. & T. Clark, 1961). Hereafter all references to the *Church Dogmatics* will appear with abbreviations in the text as indicated in the "Abbreviations."

7. Quoted by Eberhard Busch, *Karl Barth: His Life from Letters and Autobiographical Texts* (Philadelphia: Fortress Press, 1976), p. 380.

8. For further discussion, see esp. pp. 148–49, 240–43, and Epilogue, n. 5.

9. Robert W. Jenson, *God after God: The God of the Past and the Future as Seen in the Work of Karl Barth* (Indianapolis, Ind.: Bobbs-Merrill, 1969).

10. Strong support for such a demurral has now emerged in the brilliant and groundbreaking study by Bruce McCormack, ''A Scholastic of a Higher Order: The Development of Karl Barth's Theology, 1921–31'' (unpublished diss., Princeton Theological Seminary, 1989). McCormack argues that, although Barth's ''dialectical method'' of statement and counterstatement did not largely disappear until Barth's book on Anselm (published in 1931), and although that book represents a clarification of Barth's theological method, the real methodological change actually took place much earlier than has previously been thought. It took place not in 1931, as alleged by the widely influential thesis of von Balthasar, but rather in 1924, when Barth first began to lecture on dogmatics at the University of Göttingen. McCormack's case is thus significantly different from Jenson's. Jenson urges that dialectic and analogy are simply two sides of the same coin and that Barth's view of them did not essentially change after the second commentary on Romans in 1922. McCormack distinguishes among several sorts of dialectic in the early Barth, sees them as prevailing only from 1922 to 1924, and argues that the method Barth used in the *Church Dogmatics,* allowing for positive analogical statements in a way Barth thought previously to be impossible, emerged for the first time in the 1924 dogmatics lectures. These lectures, heretofore unavailable, have now been published posthumously: Karl Barth, *Unterricht in der christlichen Religion,* vol. 1, ed. Hannelotte Reiffen (Zurich: Theologischer Verlag, 1985). McCormack's study seems to give new point to the following remark of Barth's from 1955: ''Perspicuous readers will surely notice that there is no break with the basic view which I have adopted since my parting with liberalism, but only a more consistent turn in its development'' (IV/2, x).

11. Herbert Hartwell, *The Theology of Karl Barth: An Introduction* (Philadelphia: Westminster Press, 1964).

12. See Epilogue, n. 5.

Chapter 1

1. See Theodore A. Gill, ''Barth and Mozart,'' *Theology Today* 43 (1986), pp. 403–11.

2. It follows from this point that in Barth's theology the distinction between general and specific does not necessarily coincide with that between abstract and concrete. A specific statement might well be abstract, and a general statement might well be concrete. A specific but abstract statement might be one about the ''historical Jesus'' made on strictly historiographical grounds yet used directly for dogmatic purposes. (It would have abstracted from the active, concrete unity of the two natures of Christ by virtue of the hypostatic union, which, as exegetically grounded in its epistemic status, is definitive for preaching and dogmatics.) A general but concrete statement would be that ''God's being is in act'' as devel-

oped in II/1, 257–72. For further discussion, see George Hunsinger, "Karl Barth and Radical Politics: Some Further Considerations," *Studies in Religion/Sciences Religieuses* 7 (1978), pp. 170–75.

3. See George Hunsinger, "The World Observed and the World Announced: Response to William Werpehowski," *Theology Today* 43 (1986), pp. 354–60.

4. See John Glasse, "Barth on Feuerbach," *Harvard Theological Review* 57 (1964), pp. 69–96; Joseph C. Weber "Feuerbach, Barth, and Theological Methodology," *The Journal of Religion* 46 (1966), pp. 24–36; Manfred H. Vogel, "The Barth–Feuerbach Confrontation," *Harvard Theological Review* 59 (1966), pp. 27–52; Hans W. Frei, "Feuerbach and Theology," *Journal of the American Academy of Religion* 35 (1967), pp. 250–56.

5. For a discussion of how the term "coherentist" is being used here, see note 1 to the Preface.

6. See especially Reinhold Niebuhr, *An Interpretation of Christian Ethics* (New York: Harper & Brothers, 1935). Cf. Joseph Bettis, "Theology and Politics: Karl Barth and Reinhold Niebuhr on Social Ethics after Liberalism," *Religion and Life* 48 (1979), pp. 53–62. I am indebted to this article for the point about contrasting uses of the term "impossible possibility."

Chapter 2

1. See Paul C. McGlasson, "Karl Barth and the Scriptures: A Study of the Biblical Exegesis in *Church Dogmatics* I and II" (unpublished diss., Yale University, 1986); David Ford, *Barth and God's Story* (New York: Peter Lang, 1981); David Ford, "Barth's Interpretation of Scripture," in *Karl Barth, Studies of His Theological Methods,* ed. S. W. Sykes (Oxford: Clarendon Press, 1979), pp. 55–87; George Hunsinger, "Beyond Literalism and Expressivism: Karl Barth's Hermeneutical Realism," *Modern Theology* 3 (1987), pp. 209–23.

2. Cf. David A. Kelsey, *The Uses of Scripture in Recent Theology* (Philadelphia: Fortress Press, 1975), pp. 39–50.

3. A great deal can depend in Barth interpretation on whether emphasis is placed on the *history* as personal address or on the history as *personal address.* I think Barth's ordering of objectivism as conceptually prior to personalism involves the former. "His history is the Word of God addressed to us and to the whole world" (IV/2, 103). Some theologians, especially under the influence of Eberhard Jüngel, adopt the category of "Word-event," which involves the latter emphasis. See Jüngel, *The Doctrine of the Trinity: God's Being Is in Becoming* (Grand Rapids, Mich.: Eerdmans, 1976), pp. 2, 11–16, 39–41.

4. For a helpful discussion of how Barth's theological exegesis differs from the standard exegesis of academically trained biblical scholars, see Mary Kathleen Cunningham, "Karl Barth's Interpretation and Use of Ephesians 1:4 in His Doctrine of Election: An Essay in the Relation of Scripture and Theology" (unpublished diss., Yale University, 1988).

5. The "transcendentalism" of this procedure is obviously meant to be logi-

cal, not ontological. What is at stake is strictly a matter of conceptual analysis, not some sort of synthetic or metaphysical deduction. The procedure is meant to be epistemically grounded by actual events of revelation as attested by scripture.

6. For further discussion, see pp. 240–43 and 263–64.

7. For a different view see George Lindbeck, "Barth and Textuality," *Theology Today* 43 (1986), pp. 367–68.

8. Cf. Alan R. White, "Coherence Theory of Truth," in *The Encyclopedia of Philosophy,* vol. 2, ed. Paul Edwards (New York: The Macmillan Company & and The Free Press, 1967), pp. 130–33. For a general statement of how one can believe that all forms of justification are context-dependent, while still holding a nonrelativist idea of truth, see Jeffrey Stout, *Ethics after Babel* (Boston: Beacon Press, 1988), pp. 21–31.

Chapter 3

1. On Barth's transition from dialectical to dogmatic theology, see Hans W. Frei, "The Doctrine of Revelation in the Thought of Karl Barth, 1909–1922: The Nature of Barth's Break with Liberalism" (unpublished diss., Yale University, 1956). Despite its now being superseded by McCormack's study (see note 10 to the Prologue) on the question of just when the break with liberalism occurred, Frei's work, in my opinion, is still the best study of Barth's theology available in English at the level of conceptual analysis and richness of cultural–historical detail.

2. For an explanation of the term *Aufhebung,* see pp. 85–86.

Chapter 4

1. The allusion here is to the famous Chalcedonian definition of the faith, drafted by the Council of Chalcedon in 451. The definition can be found in *The Oecumenical Documents of the Faith,* eds. T. H. Bindley and F. W. Green (London: Methuen & Co., 1950), and in *The Creeds of Christendom,* vol. 2, ed. Philip Schaff (New York: Harper and Row, 1931). Standard accounts are R. V. Sellers, *The Council of Chalcedon: A Historical and Doctrinal Survey* (London: SPCK, 1953), and Aloys Grillmeier, *Christ in the Christian Tradition,* vol. 1 (Atlanta: John Knox Press, 1965), pp. 543–57.

Of the three terms used here to characterize the gist of the definition—unity, differentiation, asymmetry—the latter perhaps requires special comment. The significance of the term "asymmetry" can be explained by contrasting it with the term "hierarchy." In Barth's use of the Chalcedonian pattern (as perhaps implicitly in the original definition itself), the relationship between the divine and human natures of Jesus Christ is conceived in more nearly asymmetrical than hierarchical terms. The relationship is not hierarchical, because the two natures are not conceived as ordered according to a scale whereby they would differ only in degree (cf. III/3, 104). The two natures are rather conceived as asymmetrically related, for they share no common measure or standard of measurement (cf. III/

3, 133). Although there is a divine priority and a human subsequence, their asymmetry allows a conception which avoids hierarchical domination in favor of *a mutual ordering in freedom*. The formal logic of this conception can be stated as follows: "A conceptual account of X is an account of what we mean, understand, and intend ourselves to be talking about, when we talk or think about X. If X is not correctly thus accounted for in terms of Y, then X is conceptually independent of Y; if Y is accounted for in terms of X, where X is not in turn accounted for in terms of Y, then X is both conceptually prior to and independent of Y" (S. L. Hurley, *Natural Reasons: Personality and Polity* [New York: Oxford University Press, 1989], p. 10). This relation may properly be designated as asymmetrical. If we let X stand for the divine nature and Y for the human nature of Jesus Christ, then we have precisely the kind of conceptual priority and subsequence ascribed to them by Barth. (The formal logic so applied pertains to their constitutive relations, as in the doctrines of the *anhypostasis* and *enhypostasis* posited by Barth in I/2, 150 and 163, not to their epistemic relations with respect to us, where by virtue of the hypostatic union X and Y would be more nearly interdependent, i.e., X could not be known without Y, nor Y without X.) This formal logic will be drawn upon later with respect to Barth's conception of the relationship between divine grace and human freedom. (See esp. pp. 137–51, 210–11, and 215–18.)

2. In this conceptuality Barth has interestingly combined classical themes from Luther ("hiddenness") and Calvin ("mediation"). See Walther von Loewenich, *Luther's Theology of the Cross* (Minneapolis: Augsburg, 1976); Edward A. Dowey, Jr., *The Knowledge of God in Calvin's Theology* (New York: Columbia University Press, 1952).

3. A common puzzlement pertains to how Barth can conceive of Jesus Christ as the central and determinative, indeed as the exclusive, Mediator without isolating him from the history of Israel and the history of the church. Barth's conception avoids this kind of christological isolation largely by virtue of the pattern of dialectical inclusion. Consider the following instance of the pattern: "God is he who in his Son Jesus Christ loves all his children, in his children all human beings, and in human beings his whole creation" (II/1, 351 rev.). Here Jesus Christ is conceived as the inclusive center who incorporates in himself a series of graded relations. In particular, he cannot be conceived as existing without his community in its twofold form of Israel and the church (II/2, 195). His humanity itself can thus be described as "the foundation of everything that God instituted and used in his revelation as a secondary objectivity *both before and after* the epiphany of Jesus Christ" (II/1, 54; emphasis added). How his humanity in its full historicity can be thought to play this foundational role is suggested by the logic of actualism as presented on pp. 148–49 and 240–43.

Chapter 5

1. Adolf Harnack, *History of Dogma*, vol. 5 (New York: Dover Publications, 1961), p. 205n.

2. It is because these events are conceived as unique in kind that they defy explanation in terms of a general theory. ''Theory makes possible the explanation of an occurrence,'' writes Louis Mink, ''only by describing it in in such a way that the description is logically related to a systematic set of generalizations or laws. One understands the power of a spring-powered watch, for example, only insofar as one understands the principles of mechanics, and this requires describing the mechanism of the watch in terms, and *only* in terms, appropriate to those principles. . . . An ideally theoretical understanding of those occurrences . . . would treat each as nothing other than a replicable instance of a systematically interconnected set of generalizations.'' (Mink, ''Narrative Form as a Cognitive Instrument,'' in *The Writing of History,* ed. R. H. Canary and H. Kozicki [Madison: University of Wisconsin Press, 1978], pp. 131–32. Quoted by Michael Root, ''Dying He Lives: Biblical Image, Biblical Narrative and the Redemptive Jesus,'' *Semeia* 30 [1985], p. 165.) Barth's conception of certain events as unique in kind thus goes hand in hand with his rejection of certain modes of systematization and explanation in dogmatic theology, and this rejection is illuminated by Mink's remarks. Mink goes on to propose a kind of ''configurational understanding,'' which is described by Root as follows: ''Configurational understanding does not abstract events from their particular context so that they can be understood as examples of a general law'' (ibid.). This mode of understanding stands in interesting convergence with Barth's approach to the interpretation of biblical narrative.

3. For these formulations I am indebted to Thomas F. Torrance, *God and Rationality* (London: Oxford University Press, 1971), p. 58.

4. Cf. pp. 38–39.

5. Compare what follows to ch. 4, n. 1.

6. Cf. Robert P. Scharlemann, *Thomas Aquinas and John Gerhard* (New Haven: Yale University Press, 1964), esp. pp. 150–53 and 230–31; Bernard Lonergan, *Grace and Freedom: Operative Grace in the Thought of St. Thomas Aquinas,* ed. J. Patout Burns (New York: Herder and Herder, 1971).

7. Thomas Aquinas, *Summa Theologiae,* vol. 30, ed. Cornelius Ernst (New York: McGraw-Hill, 1972), pp. 197–99. (The conventional way of referring to this passage would be: *ST,* 1a2ae. 113, 10.) Cf. Arvin Vos, *Aquinas, Calvin and Contemporary Protestant Thought* (Grand Rapids, Mich.: Eerdmans, 1985), p. 159.

8. *ST,* 1a2ae. 113, 10.

Chapter 6

1. For this reason (among others) it is rather misleading to characterize Barth as belonging to ''the inwardness tradition,'' as does Stephen Sykes in *The Identity of Christianity* (Philadelphia: Fortress Press, 1984), pp. 192–96.

2. Barth's express wording on this matter varies, depending on the context. Calling can be described as the telos of justification and sanctification (IV/1,

113). Justification and sanctification can be presented as the presupposition of vocation, where vocation itself is given "objectivist" connotations (IV/3, 506–7), and even stronger such connotations can emerge in a discussion of vocation in relation to election (IV/3, 483–87). The constant element, however, is the conception of vocation as Barth's primary way of characterizing the existential moment of salvation. Faith, hope, and love are understood in this context.

3. George A. Lindbeck, *The Nature of Doctrine: Religion and Theology in a Postliberal Age* (Philadelphia: Westminister Press, 1984), pp. 63–69.

4. David Tracy, "Lindbeck's New Program for Theology: A Reflection," *The Thomist* 49 (1985), p. 465.

5. For further discussion of these themes as they pertain to the Lindbeck proposal, see Bruce Marshall, "Aquinas as Postliberal Theologian," *The Thomist* 53 (1989), pp. 353–402. For Lindbeck's own strong endorsement of Marshall's interpretation of the proposal, see Lindbeck, "Response to Bruce Marshall," ibid., pp. 403–6. For an attempt to place the Lindbeck proposal in relation to both a Thomistic and a Barthian scheme of nature and grace (an attempt indebted to Marshall's work), see George Hunsinger, "Truth as Self-involving: Barth and Lindbeck on the Cognitive and Performative Aspects of Truth in Theological Discourse," forthcoming.

6. Francis Schüssler Fiorenza, *Foundational Theology, Jesus and the Church* (New York: Crossroad, 1984), p. 294.

7. For the suggestion of these formlations, I am indebted to personal correspondence from my friend Michael Root. See his essay, "Truth, Relativism, and Postliberal Theology," *dialog* 25 (1986), pp. 175–80, esp. p. 179.

8. Barth is seriously misread on these matters, in my opinion, by Gustaf Wingren, *Theology in Conflict: Nygren, Barth, Bultmann* (Philadelphia: Muhlenberg Press, 1958), and more recently by Philip J. Rosato, *The Spirit as Lord: The Pneumatology of Karl Barth* (Edinburgh: T. & T. Clark, 1981).

Chapter 7

1. Barth's position on the question of miracles, as this passage suggests, would seem to be more nearly one of reverent agnosticism than either mere skepticism or simple credence. Take, for example, the New Testament story of Jesus turning the water into wine (John 2:1–11). Barth's brief references to this miracle, when taken in context with other things he says about Jesus' miracles, would seem to imply a position something like this. Did Jesus really turn the water into wine? He very well may have. We can't know for sure on historical–critical grounds, and we don't need to know for sure for purposes of faith and doctrine. The central miracle to which this and all other New Testament stories of Jesus performing miracles point is the miracle of Jesus Christ himself—his life, death, and resurrection for our sake, his story as God's story, etc. Faith in this central miracle does not depend on whether the stories of subsidiary miracles are merely literary witnesses or are also reflective of actual miraculous occurrences. The latter need

not be ruled out, but the former are all that are necessary from the standpoint of faith. Thus Barth can write: "And one might well ask whether the miracles of Jesus are not all to be regarded as, so to speak, backward-striking rays of the glory of the risen Lord, whether ultimately the entire life of Jesus is not meant to be considered in this retrospective light" (I/1, 452). See the lengthy discussion of Jesus' miracles from this point of view in IV/2, 209–47. For a more nearly philosophical account of miracles which is parallel to and compatible with Barth's theological interpretation, see William P. Alston, *Divine Nature and Human Language: Essays in Philosophical Theology* (Ithaca, N.Y.: Cornell University Press, 1989), pp. 208–17.

2. For the distinction between a "mystery" and a "problem," see Michael B. Foster, *Mystery and Philosophy* (London: SCM Press, 1957). (Foster's way of making the distinction is more helpful with respect to Barth than is the more famous version of the same distinction in the work of Gabriel Marcel, because Foster's is less encumbered by a kind of metaphysics and is conducted more in the mode of conceptual analysis.) In some respects Barth's conception of mystery does not differ from standard Roman Catholic accounts, as for instance Thomas Gornall, "Introduction" to Aquinas, *Summa Theologiae,* vol. 4 (1a. 14–18) (New York: McGraw-Hill, 1964), pp. xxiv–xxvi. The differences between the Barthian and Catholic accounts focus, typically, on two points. First, Barth always posits the particularity of mystery (i.e., the specifiability of its terms) as a predicate of divine revelation; he has no use for the idea of an encounter with "mystery in general" or for related ideas like Rudolf Otto's "the holy" (II/1, 360). Second, in Barth's theology the particularist usage of "mystery" has a much broader scope of application because of his rejection of natural theology and its premises. Nonetheless, at least two interesting convergences between the Barthian and Catholic accounts might be noted in passing. Both accounts are at least implicitly committed to the idea that rationality and intelligibility are not identical; rationality is normative in a way that intelligibility is not. (The acceptance of revealed mysteries is thus conceived as rational rather than irrational; if limits to intelligibility actually emerge, it would be irrational not to acknowledge them.) Both are also committed to the idea that "natural truths" are to be distinguished from the "truths of faith" in such a way that natural truths might be "reduced eventually to perfect coherence, but the truths of faith have the apex of their intelligibility hidden in the transcendence of God" (Lonergan, *Grace and Freedom* [New York: Herder and Herder, 1971], p. 8).

3. I find this problem to be endemic to the criticisms of incoherence in, for example, Sheila Greeve Davaney, *Divine Power: A Study of Karl Barth and Charles Hartshorne* (Philadelphia: Fortress Press, 1986); Ronald F. Thiemann, *Revelation and Theology* (Notre Dame: University of Notre Dame Press, 1985); David Kelsey, "Aquinas and Barth on the Human Body," *The Thomist* 50 (1986), p. 686.

4. For the concept of "discrimen," see Robert C. Johnson, *Authority in*

Protestant Theology (Philadelphia: Westminster Press, 1959); David A. Kelsey, *The Uses of Scripture in Recent Theology* (Philadelphia: Fortress Press, 1975).

5. Compare what follows to ch. 4, n. 1.

6. Compare what follows to pp. 145–46 and to ch. 4, n. 1.

7. The supposed need for such a neutral description within the framework of a Barthian theology has, oddly, been embraced by Thomas F. Torrance, "Natural Theology in the Thought of Karl Barth," in *Transformation and Convergence in the Frame of Knowledge* (Grand Rapids, Mich.: Eerdmans, 1984), pp. 299–301. For an excellent discussion of related matters, see Joan E. O'Donovan, "Man in the Image of God: The Disagreement between Barth and Brunner Reconsidered," *Scottish Journal of Theology* 39 (1986), pp. 433–59.

Epilogue

1. John Calvin, *Institutes of the Christian Religion,* tr. John Allen (Philadelphia: Presbyterian Board of Publication, 1902), II, ii, xv.

2. All citations in the text, unless otherwise noted, will be from *CD* IV/3.

3. For an introduction to the Barmen Declaration, see Arthur C. Cochrane, *The Church's Confession under Hitler* (Philadelphia: The Westminster Press, 1962). A translation of the Declaration may be found in an appendix to that volume.

4. The doctrine of perichoresis, it will be recalled, pertains to the way in which the Father, the Son, and the Holy Spirit, as modes intrinsic to the divine being in eternity, are interconnected in patterns of coinherence or dialectical inclusion. Each of these modes of being in the triunity of God is conceived as definitely and completely participating in the other two. The doctrine states, Barth explains, "that the divine modes of being mutually condition and permeate one another so completely that one is always in the other two and the other two in the one." None of these modes of being "would be what it is (not even the Father) without its co-existence with the others, and . . . none exists as a special individual, but all three 'coinhere' or exist only in concert as modes of being of the one God and Lord who posits himself from eternity to eternity" (I/1, 370 rev.). The idea of eternity is always understood by Barth in the *Church Dogmatics,* whether implicitly or explicitly, along perichoretic lines. For an explicit reference, see II/1, 396.

5. Although here Barth's conception of eternity has been no more than sketched, enough has been indicated of its perichoretic multidimensionality, I think, to suggest that the standard criticisms (such as those of Moltmann, Jenson, and Roberts) are ill-formulated at best and unfounded at worst. A full exposition would need to show that Barth holds, christocentrically, a thoroughly perichoretic view of eternity, a thoroughly eschatological view of history, and a thoroughly Chalcedonian view of the relation between them, such that within the Chalcedonian framework all aspects of historicity are ultimately *aufgehoben* by eternity. The standard criticisms do not begin to take this patterned complexity adequately into

account. See Jurgen Moltmann, *Theology of Hope* (New York: Harper & Row, 1967), pp. 50–58; Robert Jenson, *God after God* (Indianapolis: Bobbs-Merril, 1969), pp. 70, 139–56, 171–72; R. H. Roberts, "Barth's Doctrine of Time: Its Nature and Implications" in *Karl Barth: Studies of His Theological Method,* ed. S. W. Sykes (Oxford: Clarendon Press, 1979), pp. 88–146.

6. The point about "lordship" could perhaps be interpreted as implying yet a third mode of thought: the impossibility of nonexclusivity, regardless of viewpoint. The idea that nonexclusive viewpoints might ultimately be impossible in theological discourse is not developed as an independent line of inquiry. Could it be, for example, that even pluralism is perhaps "exclusivist" in some relevant and inevitable sense? In any case, it should be emphasized that the "impossibilities" in question here are not regarded as merely logical or technical in some ostensibly context-neutral sense, but as internal to the logic of Christian theological discourse (as grounded in biblical modes of thought).

7. For an intriguing, if finally limited, parallel to Barth's conception here, see the discussion of holograms in *The Holographic Paradigm and Other Paradoxes: Exploring the Leading Edge of Science,* ed. Ken Wilbur (Boulder, Colo.: Shambhala Publications, 1982). Insofar as the holographic paradigm has pantheistic or penentheistic implications, the parallels with Barth's conception obviously cease. In line with the Christian doctrines of creation and redemption, Barth always takes special care not to posit unities between the Creator and the creature at the expense of their distinctiveness. The characteristically Barthian ideas that the circle has a center *and* a periphery, that coinherence is a matter of *dialectical* inclusion, and that the relevant unities are *differentiated* unities, are all meant to signal a conception which posits the ongoing and ineffaceable integrity and distinctiveness of particulars. In the midst of all unities the ontological divide between the Creator and the creature is always presupposed. The parallels between Barth's conception and the holographic paradigm pertain to similarities regarding how to view the interpenetrations between the whole and the part. But in Barth's conception language about the whole and the part is always balanced, complemented, and governed by language about the center and the periphery, so that no unities are established at the expense of the essential differences. The unities which occur on these terms, of course, are taken to be events that are unceasingly mysterious and miraculous as expressions of grace.

8. See the meticulous and illuminating discussion of "extended principles of consistency," by which religious communities may acknowledge that "alien claims" (i.e., claims of other religious communities) are consistent with their own essential doctrines (and therefore right or true), in William A. Christian, Sr., *Doctrines of Religious Communities: A Philosophical Study* (New Haven: Yale University Press, 1987), pp. 161–68. Christian rightly finds such an "extended principle of consistency" to be at work in Barth's theology (pp. 212–15).

9. Cf. Alasdair MacIntyre, *Whose Justice? Which Rationality?* (Notre Dame: University of Notre Dame Press, 1988).

10. For a sensitive conceptual analysis of the issues at stake in such cases, see Christian, *Doctrines of Religious Communities,* pp. 49–50.

11. In formulating the following paragraphs, I have been especially helped by the following two works: David Lochhead, *The Dialogical Imperative: A Christian Reflection on Interfaith Encounter* (Maryknoll, N.Y.: Orbis Books, 1988), and Joseph Runzo, "God, Commitment, and Other Faiths" in *Faith and Philosophy* 5 (1988), pp. 343–64. Although Lochhead provides a very judicious account of Barth's position, he underestimates the manner and the extent to which that position remains exclusivist. Although Runzo completely fails to see the manner and extent to which Barth's position is inclusivist, and makes the unfortunate (but commonplace) mistake of describing that position as though it were triumphalist, he offers a very useful typology of possible positions. In what follows I go on to recast this typology in terms of the question of truth (rather than in terms of the question of religion per se, which was what interested Runzo).

12. In the *Church Dogmatics* one characteristic way of referring to such doctrinal schemes, taken as a whole, is to call them "world-views." A world view need not be explicitly theological in order to hold de facto theological status. It need only present itself (implicitly or explicitly) as providing a necessary, sufficient, and comprehensive account of what is supremely significant or ultimately real.

13. As the ensuing discussion of inclusivism indicates, this interpretation of Barth's exclusivism is not meant to imply that he regards doctrinal schemes, taken as a whole, as so totally incommensurable that no genuine dialogue can take place between disputants who adhere to differing doctrinal schemes. This interpretation does imply, however, that all relevant standards of evaluation will be relative to such schemes, and that these standards will themselves be incommensurable (at least in practice for the most part). The Christian doctrinal scheme or network of beliefs is taken to be comprehensive within its sphere of interest. There are therefore no external standards of evaluation by which the truth or falsity of the Christian scheme as a whole could be conclusively assessed. Yet, by definition, any other such scheme, insofar as it presented itself as being comprehensive, would have to be regarded as false by virtue of its having organized itself doctrinally as though Jesus Christ were not the exclusive source, norm, and center of all theological truth. For a careful and sophisticated elaboration of what seems to be something like Barth's basic intuition here, see Christian, *Doctrines of Religious Communities,* pp. 125–44. See also Christian, *Oppositions of Religious Doctrines: A Study in the Logic of Dialogue among Religious* (London: Macmillan; New York: Seabury, 1972).

14. I am indebted to Lochhead (*The Dialogical Imperative,* p. 35) for this fortunate way of formulating Barth's position. Cf. I/2, 325.

Index

Dialectical inclusion (*Continued*)
227–28, 238–41, 261–63, 273,
287n., 292n.7. *See also* Coinherence
defined, 85–86
Doubt, 127–28
Dualism, 177, 180, 185, 198. *See also*
Ontological divide

Eternal life, 181–84, 227
Eternity, 14–18, 22, 56, 58, 86, 149, 236,
238, 240–42, 274, 291n.5
Expressivism, 43–49. *See also* Liberalism

"Faith development," 220
Fellowship, 98, 152, 154, 173–84, 202,
207, 213, 216–17, 223, 227. *See also*
Coinherence
Feuerbach, Ludwig, 35–36, 62
Fichte, Johann, 7
Frei, Hans, 286n.1

Geertz, Clifford, 166
Grace, 205–6, 211, 213, 223. See also
Aufhebung
as absolute miracle, 192–94
as absolute mystery, 198, 206
in Aquinas and Barth, 145–47
and faith, 106–14, 121, 130
and nature, 97–100, 193, 215–18

Harnack, Adolf von, 104
Hartwell, Herbert, 6, 19–20, 22
Hegelian pattern. See *Aufhebung*
Heidegger, Martin, 62
Herrmann, Wilhelm, 7
Historical-critical method, 46–47, 289n.1
Holographic paradigm, 292n.7

Incarnation, 34, 37, 168–69, 186–88, 223,
228, 236–37. *See also* Chalcedonian
pattern
anhypostasis and *enhypostasis* in, 287n.1
Instrumentalism, 143–47

Jenson, Robert W., 6, 15–19, 21–22
Justification by faith, 10, 70, 115, 118–19,
123, 130, 142, 154, 182, 251–52
and eschatological existence, 126–27

Kant, Immanuel, 7
Kierkegaard, Søren, 258–60

Lessing, Gotthold Ephraim, 72
Liberalism, 9–11, 35, 54, 122
Liberation theology, 141
Literalism, 43–49. *See also* Rational
orthodoxy
Lindbeck, George, 165–73
Lochhead, David, 292n.11
Luther, Martin, 139
Lutheran theology, 18, 139, 215

McCormack, Bruce, 284n.10
Metaphysics, 61–62, 207, 237. *See also*
Philosophy
in Jenson, 15, 19, 22
Mink, Louis, 288n.2
Miracle, 34, 72, 74, 75, 97–98, 121, 140,
172, 187–88, 230, 271, 289n.1
as absolute, 189–94, 223, 226
in Aquinas and Barth, 146–47
Monism, 8, 13–16, 98, 149–50, 156, 177,
180, 185, 198, 200, 204, 207–15
and determinism, 198, 215–18, 223–24
Motifs, 28–30
limitations of, vii–viii, 271, 282n.2
Mozart, Wolfgang Amadeus, 28
Mystery, ix, 19, 34, 37, 71, 107, 114,
187–88, 231
as absolute, 194–99, 223, 228
and antithetical conceptuality, 210–12,
225, 228, 272
described but not explained, 110–12,
212, 288n.2
and "problem," 199, 290n.2

Natural theology, 96–99, 255–56, 271,
274–75, 283n.2
Niebuhr, Reinhold, 38–39

Objectivism, viii, 4, 35–39, 148, 228–29,
231–32, 285n.3. *See also*
Revelational objectivism;
Soteriological objectivism
and truth as mediated in revelation, 76–
102